FOCUS:
MIDDLE SCHOOL WORLD HISTORY

COUNCIL FOR
**Economic
Education**

Teaching Opportunity

AUTHORS

Tawni Hunt Ferrarini
Sam M. Cohodas Professor
Director of Center for Economic Education and
Entrepreneurship
Northern Michigan University

Douglas A. Haskell
Field Service Associate Professor of Economics
Economics Center
University of Cincinnati

Andrew T. Hill
Economic Education Advisor
Federal Reserve Bank of Philadelphia*

Jane S. Lopus
Professor of Economics
Director, Center for Economic Education
California State University, East Bay

Bonnie T. Meszaros
Assistant Professor of Economics
Associate Director, Center for Economic Education
and Entrepreneurship
University of Delaware

Edward M. Scahill
Associate Professor
Director, Honesdale National Bank Center for
Economic Education
The University of Scranton

Phillip J. VanFossen
*James F. Ackerman Professor and Head, Department
of Curriculum and Instruction*
Associate Director, Purdue Center for Economic
Education
Purdue University

Scott Wolla
Economic Education Specialist
Federal Reserve Bank of St. Louis*

PROJECT DIRECTOR

William D. Bosshardt Jr.
Associate Professor of Economics
Director, Center for Economic Education
Florida Atlantic University

ECONOMIC HISTORIAN

Robert Whaples
Professor of Economics
Department of Economics
Wake Forest University

PROJECT COORDINATOR

Kevin Gotchet
*Director, Excellence in Economic Education (EEE)
Program*
Council for Economic Education

EDITOR

Dian Coleman
Special projects
Salem, OR

FUNDING

The Council for Economic Education gratefully acknowledges the funding of this publication by the U.S. Department of Education, Office of Innovation and Improvement, Excellence in Economic Education: Advancing K-12 Economic & Financial Education Nationwide grant award U215B050005-09. The contents of this book developed under the grant from the Department of Education do not necessarily represent the policy of the Department of Education, and you should not assume endorsement by the Federal Government.

ISBN: 978-1-56183-758-8

* Views expressed in this volume are those of the authors and do not necessarily represent those of the Federal Reserve Bank of Philadelphia, the Federal Reserve Bank of St. Louis or the Federal Reserve System.

CONTENTS

CONTENTS

ACKNOWLEDGEMENTS

The writing team thanks Kevin Gotchet and the Council for Economic Education staff for their help in bringing this project to fruition. Without them, projects such as this would not be done, and the opportunities for students to learn economic concepts would suffer.

Robert Whaples served as the economic historian for this project and wrote the introductory essay. His comments and insight provided valuable assistance, ensuring that the lessons reflect current thinking in economic history. We are extremely grateful for his help on this project.

The authors also want to express their appreciation for the field testers—teachers who took considerable time and effort to test assigned lessons and provide valuable input.

FIELD-TEST TEACHERS

Michelle Beguiristain
Lantana Community Middle School
Lantana, FL

Paul Bernis
W.C. Young Middle School
Pembroke Pines, FL

Debbie Bruister
Kossuth Middle School
Corinth, MS

Lillian Dooies
Bak Middle School of the Arts
West Palm Beach, FL

Barbara Estes
Bagley Junior High
Dora, AL

Susan Guy
Hill Intermediate School
Houston, TX

Jarred Haas
J.Henry Higgins Middle School
Peabody, MA

April Higgins
Skyline Middle School
Wilmington, DE

Jeffrey D. Huntington
Calvary Lutheran School
Indianapolis, IN

Sharonnade Jones
Cincinnati Public School – A2E
Cincinnati, OH

David Lumsden
Kingsbury Country Day School
Oxford, MI

Shawna Morgan
Nova High School
Davie, FL

Shanda Ramsey
Seymour Middle School
Seymour, TX

Karen Ray
Eastbrook Academy
Milwaukee, WI

Susan Smith
Eisenhower Middle School
Lawton, OK

Cheri Stegall
Cocopah Middle School
Scottsdale, AZ

Susan Vass
Our Lady of Calvary
Philadelphia, PA

ABOUT THIS VOLUME

This volume of lesson plans covers a large spectrum of world history. Our goal is to provide middle school history teachers with lessons that incorporate economics into a variety of world history topics. We began the project by surveying the coverage of world history in middle schools across the country. Naturally, we found wide variance in what was covered and when. However, most middle school courses focus on the earlier parts of world history—generally from the beginning of human history through the Roman Empire and sometimes quite a bit further. The rest of world history is then saved for high school. We decided to do lessons from the beginning of human history to 1776, which is the latest any middle school seemed to go. We also think that Adam Smith is an appropriate endpoint for the volume.

While the lessons are geared for the middle school, many can be easily used at a high school level. The lessons generally include an activity that engages the students. We also use original documents in a couple of lessons to give the student a feel for history as it was originally written. Finally, each lesson includes a "Connections" section. The intent of the section is to connect the lesson to other concepts or to other points in time. How the connection is accomplished varies by lesson—some include ideas of how concepts apply to other times, some include small lessons or references to websites. The Connections section should help teachers relate the economic concepts in the lesson to other historic ideas.

The process for writing this book used a team approach. As a group, the authors decided on the topics and economic concepts to be covered in each lesson. Each author was given a set of lessons to write. After each lesson was written, other members of the team reviewed it—including our economic historian and the project director. The lesson was revised and sent for field testing by teachers in the classroom. Based on the teachers' comments, the lessons were revised and finalized. For the record, we would like to identify the lead authors of each lesson (in order of appearance): Jane Lopus, lessons 1, 2 and 16; Douglas Haskell, lessons 3, 6, and 7; Tawni Hunt Ferrarini, lessons 4, 10, 23; Andrew T. Hill, lessons 5, 13, and 21; Scott Wolla, lessons 8, 9, and 17; Bonnie T. Meszaros, lessons 11, 12, and 14; Edward M. Scahill, lessons 15, 20, and 22; and Phillip VanFossen, lessons 18 and 19. Robert Whaples wrote the introductory essay.

STANDARDS

Each lesson is correlated to two sets of standards:

- Voluntary National Content Standards in Economics, 2nd edition, by the Council for Economic Education. The standards are found at: http://www.councilforeconed.org/ea/standards/standards.pdf.

- World History Content Standards, Contents of National Standards in World History for Grades 5-12. The development of the History Standards was administered by the National Center for History in the Schools at the University of California, Los Angeles under the guidance of the National Council for History Standards. The standards are found at: http://nchs.ucla.edu/Standards/world-history-standards.

Voluntary National Content Standards in Economics, 2nd edition: Council for Economic Education

Standards \ Lessons	1	2	3	4	5	6	7	8	9	10	11	12	13	14	15	16	17	18	19	20	21	22	23
1. Scarcity		✗						✗								✗							
2. Decision Making	✗																						
3. Allocation					✗		✗			✗				✗						✗			
4. Incentives	✗													✗			✗						
5. Trade						✗	✗												✗	✗		✗	
6. Specialization				✗				✗								✗							✗
7. Markets and Prices																		✗					✗
8. Role of Prices							✗								✗								
9. Competition and Market Structure															✗								
10. Institutions																					✗		
11. Money and Inflation												✗	✗										
12. Interest Rates																					✗		
13. Income															✗								
14. Entrepreneurship					✗													✗					
15. Economic Growth		✗	✗																				
16. Role of Government and Market Failure											✗											✗	
17. Government Failure											✗												
18. Economic Fluctuations																							
19. Unemployment and Inflation													✗										
20. Fiscal and Monetary Policy																							

World History Content Standards: National Center for History in the Schools at UCLA

Lessons / Standards	1	2	3	4	5	6	7	8	9	10	11	12	13	14	15	16	17	18	19	20	21	22	23
Era 1: Beginnings of Human Society																							
Standard 1	✗																						
Standard 2		✗	✗																				
Era 2: 4000 – 1000 B.C.E.																							
Standard 1				✗	✗																		
Standard 2			✗																				
Standard 3				✗																			
Standard 4			✗																				
Era 3: 1000 B.C.E. – 300 C.E.																							
Standard 1					✗																		
Standard 2								✗	✗														
Standard 3						✗	✗																
Standard 4																							
Standard 5			✗			✗	✗																
Era 4: 300 – 1000 C.E.																							
Standard 1										✗													
Standard 2																							
Standard 3																							
Standard 4																							
Standard 5																							
Standard 6																							
Standard 7							✗			✗													
Era 5: 1000 – 1500 C.E.																							
Standard 1													✗				✗		✗				
Standard 2														✗		✗					✗		
Standard 3													✗										
Standard 4												✗											
Standard 5															✗								
Standard 6											✗							✗		✗			
Standard 7															✗				✗		✗		
Era 6: 1450 – 1770 C.E.																							
Standard 1																							
Standard 2																		✗				✗	
Standard 3																							
Standard 4																							
Standard 5																			✗				
Standard 6																							
Era 7: 1750 – 1914 [1776] C.E.																							
Standard 1																							
Standard 2																							✗
Standard 3																							✗
End of this volume's coverage of standards																							

UNDERSTANDING ECONOMIC HISTORY

Robert Whaples, Wake Forest University

Studying history can be both fascinating and startling to the modern reader—young or old. Why *did* pre-modern people living hundreds or thousands of years ago do things so differently than we do? Students of history almost immediately begin to put themselves into the shoes of their ancient ancestors. Why did they do such peculiar things? Why were they so "backward"?

One knee-jerk reaction is to assume that their behaviors reflect a lack of intelligence. Economic historians are very hesitant to take this approach. We often conclude that the key difference between us and them is that we (individually and collectively) simply know a lot more than they did. Of course, mankind's knowledge base has expanded dramatically over time (especially since the scientific revolution), and these improvements in technology have been our key advantage, allowing us standards of living unimaginable to our distant ancestors. Being knowledgeable, of course, doesn't necessarily make you clever and having less knowledge needn't make you dull.

Another key advantage people in modern democracies have is the checks and balances constraining those few with political/economic/military power; those with power are much less likely to seize the wealth and output of the vast majority. In undemocratic "closed societies" the incentive to put economic resources into their most productive use is dampened by the ever-present risk of expropriation by those in power, suffocating the innovations and actions that might lead to sustained economic growth.[1]

Thus, poor technology and concentrated power help explain why pre-modern people often seem to do things in what we would consider to be a backward way. The blessings of advancing technology and supportive institutions have allowed modern populations' standards of livings to reach heights unimaginable to our distant ancestors. In 1900, the average income per person in the U.S. was a little under $7,000, one of the highest levels in the world at the time. This level of income was well above those in India ($1,050), China ($1,100), Brazil ($1,200), Japan ($1,900), Mexico ($1,950), Russia ($2,050), Italy ($2,850), France ($4,800), or Germany ($5,200). It's hard to imagine someone living on $7,000 a year, let alone a meager $3 to $4 per day—as did the typical person in India, China or Brazil about a century ago, and as do over 2 billion people today. The twentieth century brought unprecedented growth in all these places with real incomes rising over 200% in India and Russia, nearly 400% in Mexico, over 500% in Germany, almost 600% in the U.S., about 600% in France, nearly 700% in Brazil, over 850% in China, about 970% in Italy, and (hard to believe but true) over 1,700% in Japan.[2]

Modern societies take high standards of living for granted and rarely realize how extraordinary they are in the history of humankind. Our growth has come as new technologies have been devised and people (usually profit-seeking businessmen) are given encouragement to incorporate them in productive ways. Why didn't the same thing happen in the "~~good~~ bad old days"? The leading explanation is that new technologies came along so infrequently before the Industrial Revolution, that most societies were caught in or on the edge of a Malthusian trap. This argument says that most societies throughout history have had incomes only a little above the subsistence rate. Above the subsistence rate, incomes are high enough for women to become

---

[1]On "closed" societies versus "open" societies, see Douglas North, John J. Wallis and Barry Weingast, *Violence and Social Order: A Conceptual Framework for Interpreting Recorded Human History,* Cambridge University Press (2009).

[2]These figures are from Angus Maddison, *Monitoring the World Economy 1820–1992* (Paris: OECD, 1995) and IMF staff estimates in the *World Economic Outlook*, May 2000; and have been converted into year 2010 dollars.

more fecund and death rates tend to drop, so that population expands. Below the subsistence rate, incomes are so low that death rates exceed birth rates and the population contracts. The Malthusian argument suggests that technological improvements and the discovery of new resources temporarily increased the material standard of living as people became more productive, but as their incomes rose so did population which pushed incomes back down to where they began—near the subsistence rate. This theory helps explain why income levels stayed at a very low level for most people for millennia before our modern technological explosion allowed incomes to rise to unprecedented heights.

The lesson plans in *Focus: Middle School History* illustrate some of the hard tradeoffs that people have faced. Unlike most of us, they had little room for error. If they made big economic mistakes the results could be cataclysmic. In today's world declaring bankruptcy may mean losing your house and having to live in an apartment with indoor plumbing, air conditioning and adequate heat, eating brown bag lunches and losing cable TV. Poor economic decisions in the past resulted in sickness, starvation, and death (or sometimes even worse).

In the face of harsh constraints, ancient people found a range of economic solutions – sometimes simple, sometimes complex—that can often be illuminated with fairly simple economic analysis.

In the pages that follow, you'll see how just a little bit of economic theory goes a long way. Perhaps the most fundamental lesson is that trade isn't about winners and losers: there are gains to both parties from trade, and it has substantially increased the value of people's economic activities. Ancient Greece traded its valuable olive oil to acquire what it needed to build its society, as seen in one lesson.

Other intriguing lessons await you: Did the fleas and rats that spread the bubonic plague *improve* the lives of those who survived? Economic theory and empirical evidence suggest that they did. Did entrepreneurship start with John Rockefeller, Henry Ford, Bill Gates, and Oprah Winfrey? Hardly. Its roots are ancient, as reflected in the lesson on Mesopotamia. Encouragement of entrepreneurship helps explain why Christopher Columbus and the Spanish discovered and colonized the New World and not Zheng He and the Chinese. What happens when incentives stifle innovation, hard work, and the wise use of resources? The outcome for society is poor. What happens when the money supply grows rapidly? From ancient Rome, to China, to Mansa Musa and his hajj to Mecca, to Weimar Germany and modern Zimbabwe, inflation reared its ugly head. Finally, never forget the lessons of concentrated power. Concentrated power helps explain pre-modern economic arrangements that most modern observers consider dysfunctional—arrangements that are examined in chapters on India's caste system, ancient Sparta, feudalism, medieval guilds, pre-Columbian America and mercantilism.

History is complicated because people are complicated. The chapters that follow distill important lessons from the complicated record of human economic history. They invite you to impart these important lessons to the most important audience possible—our next generation of economic decision-makers.

On the Web

To download the visuals and activities for each lesson, find online lessons to extend the student activities, and find related material for each lesson, visit:

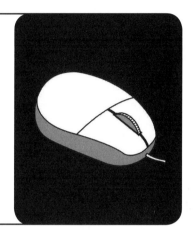

http://www.councilforeconed.org/ middle-school-history

LESSON TIME LINE

Note: The lesson time line is based on the history standards covered in the lesson.

LESSON 1

OUT OF AFRICA: WHY EARLY HUMANS SETTLED AROUND THE WORLD

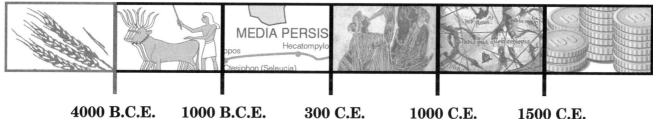

4000 B.C.E.   1000 B.C.E.   300 C.E.   1000 C.E.   1500 C.E.

LESSON 1
OUT OF AFRICA: WHY EARLY HUMANS SETTLED AROUND THE WORLD

LESSON DESCRIPTION

Students view a map showing early human migration patterns and brainstorm reasons why people may have migrated. After reviewing definitions of terms relating to migration, they participate in an activity where they identify push and pull factors for early human migrations. They are presented with an overview of reasons for human migration. The lesson concludes with a discussion of costs and benefits of migrating.

INTRODUCTION

Throughout history, many of the reasons for migration have been economic in nature. Humans have always been confronted with scarcity. Early humans had to obtain ample food, water, and shelter for survival. Humans have sought to improve their lives by migrating to areas with better climates, more space, and less-hostile neighbors. After the development of wage-labor systems, economic reasons for migrating included the desire for better jobs, more stable employment, and higher wages. Political, cultural, and environmental factors can also encourage or discourage migration. In many cases, political, cultural and environmental factors may also be viewed as economic factors because they can improve or worsen an economic situation. If the benefits of migrating are greater than the costs, migration will likely occur; if the costs exceed the benefits, migration will likely not occur.

CONCEPTS

Migration

Push factors

Pull factors

Costs

Benefits

OBJECTIVES

Students will be able to:

* Define migration, forced migration, voluntary migration, immigration, emigration, push factors, pull factors, benefits and costs.

* Analyze likely scenarios leading to early human migration.

* Identify push or pull factors.

CONTENT STANDARDS

Voluntary Content Standards in Economics, 2nd edition

* **Standard 2:** Effective decision-making requires comparing the additional costs of alternatives with the additional benefits. Many choices involve doing a little more or a little less of something: few choices are "all or nothing" decisions.

* **Standard 4:** People respond predictably to positive and negative incentives.

World History Content Standards

World History Era 1. The Beginnings of Human Society

* **Standard 1:** The biological and cultural processes that gave rise to the earliest human communities.

TIME REQUIRED

60 minutes

MATERIALS

* Slides 1.1–1.7

* One copy of Activity 1.1 for each student.

* One copy of Activity 1.2 (pages 1, 2, and 3) with each page cut into eight cards. (You may wish to make the cards on pages 2 and 3 on card stock or laminate

them for reuse. It is helpful to make the cards on pages 2 and 3 different colors.)

PROCEDURE

1. Show Slide 1.1 without showing the title. Ask students what they think the green-colored flows on the map indicate.

   (Answers will vary. Students may think the flows indicate weather patterns, for example.)

2. Reveal the map title. Explain that the map shows early human migration patterns, beginning in Africa.

3. Explain that **migration** occurs when people move from one place to another. The map shows when early humans left Africa and began migrating to other places in the world.

4. Ask students to brainstorm reasons why people may want to migrate from one place to another. Write their suggestions on the board.

   (Answers will vary. Students may know that many people migrated to the U.S. for better jobs or higher wages, for religious and political freedom, to escape from wars, or to be near their families who migrated earlier. If they think about early humans, they may mention finding food or safer places to live.)

5. Show Slides 1.2 and 1.3. Review the definitions of migration, forced migration and voluntary migration with the students.

6. Ask the students if they know of any examples of forced migration.

   (Examples in U.S. history include bringing Africans to the U.S. as slaves and the forced relocation of Native Americans from their homelands.)

7. Show Slide 1.4. Review the definitions of immigration and emigration with students. Explain that an immigrant is a person who enters one area *from* another area, and an emigrant is a person who leaves one area to settle *in* another area.

8. Show Slide 1.5. Review the definitions of push and pull factors.

9. Explain that whenever people have to make a decision, they should consider the benefits and costs of the decision. Explain that you will discuss more about costs and benefits later in the lesson.

10. Tell the students that they will take part in an activity about why early humans may have decided to migrate. Explain that early humans were hunter-gatherers. Hunter-gatherers were people who live by hunting animals and gathering edible plants for food. Hunter-gatherers were often nomads, people who did not have permanent homes but moved from place to place. When they used up the resources, such as food, in one area, they would move in search of resources in another area. A great deal of uncertainly was involved, because they usually did not know what they would find where they were going.

11. Distribute a copy of Activity 1.1 to each student. Give the students time to read the material, or read it together as a class.

12. Ask the following questions to check for understanding:

    a. What is the earliest known example of an intricate carving done by a human? Where was it found?

       (A small reddish stone carved with a geometric design, found in Blombos Cave in South Africa)

    b. What evidence do scientists have that indicates that early humans originated in Africa and then migrated around the world?

       (DNA, fossils, ancient artifacts)

    c. Do we know exactly why early humans decided to migrate out of Africa?

       (No, we do not know exact reasons; but we have clues.)

13. Divide the students into eight groups. Give each group three cards from Activity 1.2, one from each page (i.e., one Push or Pull Migration Factor card, one Push card, and one Pull card). You may wish to tell the students that a clan is a group of people or families who are usually related to one another, and that a springbok (page 1, Card 2) is a type of antelope found in Southern Africa.

14. Instruct students to read the scenario on their Push or Pull Migration Factor card and answer the two questions on the card with their group. The group should agree on the answers.

15. Call on a representative from each group to come to the front of the room, one by one. The representative should read the information on the card, but not the answers.

16. After the card is read, ask the groups to decide if the information described is a push or a pull factor. Give everyone a minute to decide. When you give a signal, groups should simultaneously raise either the Push card or the Pull card. Check for understanding by examining the responses.

17. The student in front should read the group's reason for migration. Briefly discuss the answer. Write the reasons for migration on the board, in an area separate from the reasons created in the brainstorming activity.

    Suggested answers:

    1. Climate, drought; push

    2. Food, follow the herd; push

    3. Climate, food; pull

    4. Climate, food; push

    5. Stone for tools; pull

    6. Conflict with other humans, space; push

    7. Knowledge of food supply; pull

    8. Food shortages; push

18. Show Slides 1.6 and 1.7. Review the categories shown for reasons for migrating. Point out that even though early humans did not have jobs that paid wages, there were economic reasons for migrating. When people migrated to overcome food shortages or to search for a better life in general, these are economic reasons. Economic reasons have always played a part in migration.

19. Compare the reasons written on the board during the brainstorming activity with those from the card activity. Discuss how the reasons suggested earlier compare with the reasons for early human migrations.

20. Explain to the students that human migration has occurred throughout history and is still occurring. When migration is voluntary, people evaluate the costs and the benefits of migrating in making their decision. Define the following terms.

    • Cost: A cost is what you give up when you decide to do something. A cost is not always an amount of money paid. For example, if a family today decides to immigrate to the U.S. from China, they may give up extended family, friends, and a familiar culture, which are costs.

    • Benefit: A benefit is what you receive when you decide to do something. A benefit may be monetary or non-monetary.

21. Explain to students that if the perceived benefits of an activity (such as migrating) are greater than the perceived costs, people are likely to do the activity.

22. Ask students to explain why humans moved out of Africa to all over the world, using the concepts of costs and benefits.

    (Benefits might include better climate, food, tools or avoiding hostile neighbors. Costs might include moving away from areas you know well and enduring the uncertainties of travel.)

CLOSURE

23. Remind students that if the perceived benefits of an activity (such as migrating) are greater than the perceived costs, people have incentive to do the activity. Assessing costs and benefits is part of the economic way of thinking.

24. Refer students again to the board and the suggested reasons for migrating. Ask students to decide if the factors listed are environmental, political, cultural or economic.

25. Conclude the lesson by asking students to summarize the push and pull factors affecting early human migration out of Africa.

(Answers should include those listed on the board.)

ASSESSMENT

Multiple Choice

1. Assume that a clan of early humans is living in a grassy inland area. Which of the following would be a *pull* factor encouraging them to migrate?

    a. Shortages of food in the area where they now live

    b. Climate changes making the area where they now live very cold

    c. *Knowledge that there is more food and a better climate on the coast*

    d. Hostile human groups moving close to the area where they now live

2. Which of the following best describes an example of emigration?

    a. *A family leaves China to settle elsewhere.*

    b. A family arrives in the U.S. to settle.

    c. A family gives up a vacation to save money for college.

    d. A family decides that the benefits of taking a trip are greater than the costs.

Constructed Response

1. Imagine that you are an early human living near Blombos Cave in South Africa. Write a paragraph describing why you may decide to migrate to a new area. Mention at least four reasons.

(Reasons include climate, availability of food, competition from other clans, availability of materials to make tools, among other reasons.)

CONNECTIONS: TO UNITED STATES HISTORY

Migration to the United States in the Late 19th and Early 20th Centuries

The U.S. is a country of immigrants. Tell students that a large migration of people occurred in the late nineteenth and early twentieth centuries when people left Europe to settle in the United States. Ask students to identify some of the costs that the immigrants incurred. *(Students may respond that the immigrants had to pay for transportation from Europe to the U.S., for food along the way, and for housing once they arrived. Encourage them to think about other costs [things that immigrants gave up]. Examples of costs are friends and family left behind, the comfort of living where they knew the language and culture, and possibly having to learn a new language and culture in the U.S.)*

Guide students through a discussion to identify some of the benefits of migrating from Europe to the U.S. in the late nineteenth century. *(Benefits would be religious and political freedom and more opportunities for education, to start businesses, to increase wealth and income. Some immigrants joined friends and families who had immigrated before, so this was also a benefit.)*

SOURCES

Gugliotta, Guy. "The Great Migration: Why humans left their African homeland 80,000 years ago to colonize the world." *Smithsonian* magazine, July 2008. Available at Smithsonian.com

National Geographic Society, 2005. "What is Human Migration?" Available online at: http://www.nationalgeographic.com/xpeditions/lessons/09/g68/migrationguidestudent.pdf

National Geographic Society. Human Migration Map. Available online at: http://ngm.nationalgeographic.com/ngm/0603/feature2/images/mp_download.2.pdf

Wells, Spencer. 2002. The Journey of Man: A Genetic Odyssey. Princeton University Press: Princeton and Oxford.

ACTIVITY 1.1

Out of Africa: Early Humans Settle Around the World[1]

It is over 70,000 years ago: Imagine that you are a craftsperson who has recently polished a reddish stone about three inches long. You have carved a simple geometric design onto the stone, using the point of another stone. You are sitting in a cave in a cliff overlooking a lovely body of water that will later be called the Indian Ocean. It is a beautiful place to live. You have a cool breeze from the sea in summer and you build a small fire for warmth in the winter. A flowering shrub grows above your cave. Later, this place will be known as Blombos Cave in South Africa because of the name of the shrub. The carving that you made on the stone will later be known as the oldest example of a complex carving made by a human. Why would your people migrate from this area?

Using DNA samples, fossils and ancient artifacts, scientists have come to believe that modern humans originated in Africa around 200,000 years ago. Humans remained in Africa (and only in Africa) for thousands of years. Sometime between 80,000 and 60,000 years ago, humans began to migrate out of Africa, first to Asia and later to Indonesia, Papua New Guinea, and Australia. The Great Human Migration had begun. By 40,000 years ago, humans migrated to Europe, probably by two different routes. Around 15,000 years ago, humans migrated to North America from Asia, and finally to South America. Most of this migration occurred slowly and gradually and occurred over long periods.

Because this happened so long ago and there are no written records, we do not know exactly *why* humans migrated out of Africa or why they kept migrating until they had settled throughout the world. However, we do have evidence that gives us some clues about these prehistoric times: We know that early human migrants were hunter-gatherers. We also know that climatic changes occurred. We know that human language and communication developed, as did technology, enabling the production of better tools. Many other reasons may also have led to early migrations.

The reasons for migrating are often described in terms of push factors (negative reasons for wanting to leave a place) and pull factors (positive reasons for wanting to go to a place.) When making any voluntary decision, people consider the benefits and costs, or the advantages and disadvantages, of doing something or not doing it. If the benefits of migrating are greater than the costs, the decision will be to migrate. If the costs of migrating are greater than the benefits, the decision will be not to migrate.

---

[1]The vision in the first paragraph and information in the second paragraph of the reading are adapted from "The Great Human Migration: Why humans left their African homeland 80,000 years ago to colonize the world" by Guy Gugliotta, *Smithsonian Magazine*, July 2008.

ACTIVITY 1.2
Push or Pull Migration Factors for Early Hunter-Gatherers[1]

1. Massive droughts occur where you are now living. The inland river that has served as the water supply for your clan is almost dry. Your clan migrates to a new area.

Reason for migration:_____

Push or pull?_____

2. Your clan hunts springbok and other animals for food. The herds have grown and can no longer find enough plants to eat; the herds have left your area. Your clan migrates to a new area.

Reason for migration:_____

Push or pull?_____

3. Hunters from your clan discovered a coastal area that would make living easier than it is inland. Shellfish are abundant there, which would supplement your hunting and gathering. The climate is also warmer. Your clan migrates to a new area.

Reason for migration:_____

Push or pull?_____

4. You live in an inland area where the climate is gradually becoming colder. This is changing the availability of plants that your clan gathers, as well as the availability of animals for hunting. Your clan migrates to a new area.

Reason for migration:_____

Push or pull?_____

5. You are living in a grassland area. Some people in your clan have figured out how to make stone tools that help in hunting. You have heard that more and better stones are available in an area not too far away.

Reason for migration:_____

Push or pull?_____

6. A neighboring clan has superior tool-making skills compared to your clan, making them better hunters. Because this clan has more food, they become stronger and grow larger. They are expanding closer to where you live. Your clan migrates to a new area.

Reason for migration:_____

Push or pull?_____

7. Language is developing among people. You have heard from hunters in another clan about a land bridge that crosses to a new area where there is an abundant supply of animals and plants. Your clan migrates to a new area.

Reason for migration:_____

Push or pull?_____

8. You are living in a valley near a small river. Your clan has increased in size. Finding enough food to feed everyone is becoming increasingly difficult. Some people are starving. Your clan migrates to a new area.

Reason for migration:_____

Push or pull?_____

[1]The source of ideas for these push or pull scenarios is *The Journey of Man: A Genetic Odyssey* (2002) by Spencer Wells, chapters 4 and 5.

ACTIVITY 1.2, CONTINUED

PUSH	PUSH
PUSH	PUSH
PUSH	PUSH
PUSH	PUSH

ACTIVITY 1.2, CONTINUED

PULL	PULL
PULL	PULL
PULL	PULL
PULL	PULL

SLIDE 1.1

LESSON 1 – OUT OF AFRICA: WHY EARLY HUMANS SETTLED AROUND THE WORLD

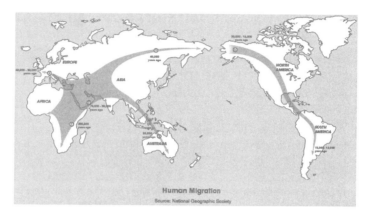

Human Migration
Source: National Geographic Society

Source: National Geographic: Available Online. Retrieved at:
http://ngm.nationalgeographic.com/ngm/0603/feature2/images/mp_download.2.pdf

SLIDE 1.2

LESSON 1 – OUT OF AFRICA: WHY EARLY HUMANS SETTLED AROUND THE WORLD

MIGRATION

- **Migration:** The act of moving from one place to another with the intent to live in another place permanently or for a longer period of time.

Source: "What is Human Migration?" 2005. National Geographic Society. Available online at:
http://www.nationalgeographic.com/xpeditions/lessons/09/g68/migrationguidestudent.pdf

SLIDE 1.3

Forced vs. Voluntary Migration

- **Forced migration**: When people have no choice and are forced to move. Forced migration is also called "involuntary migration."
- **Voluntary migration**: When people choose to move. People choose to migrate if they think the benefits (advantages) of moving will be greater than the costs (disadvantages).

Source: "What is Human Migration?" 2005. National Geographic Society. Available online at: http://www.nationalgeographic.com/xpeditions/lessons/09/g68/migrationguidestudent.pdf

SLIDE 1.4

Immigration vs. Emigration

- **Immigration**: Migration *to* a place in order to settle there
- **Emigration**: Migration *from* a place to settle in another place

Source: "What is Human Migration?" 2005. National Geographic Society. Available online at: http://www.nationalgeographic.com/xpeditions/lessons/09/g68/migrationguidestudent.pdf

SLIDE 1.5

Push vs. Pull Factors

- **Push factors**: Negative reasons for wanting to leave a place (emigrate). Examples of push factors are a lack of food or water, natural disasters, a lack of jobs, and wars.
- **Pull factors**: Positive reasons for wanting to move to a place (immigrate). Examples of pull factors are more food and water, a better climate, higher wages, and freedom.

Source: "What is Human Migration?" 2005. National Geographic Society. Available online at: http://www.nationalgeographic.com/xpeditions/lessons/09/g68/migrationguidestudent.pdf

SLIDE 1.6

Reasons for Migration: Environmental and Political

- **Environmental**
  Examples: Floods, water supply, climate, food supply for animals

- **Political**
  Examples: Political freedom, laws, wars

Source: "What is Human Migration?" 2005. National Geographic Society. Available online at: http://www.nationalgeographic.com/xpeditions/lessons/09/g68/migrationguidestudent.pdf

SLIDE 1.7

Reasons for Migration: Cultural and Economic

- **Cultural**

  Examples: Desire for religious freedom or chance for a better education

- **Economic**

  Examples: To overcome shortages of food, housing, or space; to find better employment or higher wages

Source: "What is Human Migration?" 2005. National Geographic Society. Available online at: http://www.nationalgeographic.com/xpeditions/lessons/09/g68/migrationguidestudent.pdf

FOCUS MIDDLE SCHOOL WORLD HISTORY © COUNCIL FOR ECONOMIC EDUCATION, NEW YORK, NY

LESSON 2

HOW NEOLITHIC FARMERS INCREASED THEIR STANDARD OF LIVING

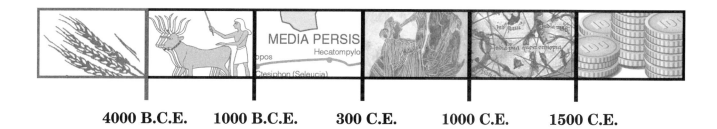

4000 B.C.E.   1000 B.C.E.   300 C.E.   1000 C.E.   1500 C.E.

Lesson 2
How Neolithic Farmers Increased Their Standard of Living[1]

LESSON DESCRIPTION

Students participate in an active simulation involving families of farmers in the Neolithic period. They make decisions about whether or not to take time to produce capital goods, with the goal of producing enough wheat to survive, better clothing, and improved shelter. They discover that investing in capital goods enables them to improve their standard of living.

INTRODUCTION

The Neolithic period was the latest part of the Stone Age, beginning about 10,700 years ago in the Middle East, and ending with the beginning of the Bronze Age in about 3500 B.C.E. During the Neolithic time, settled agriculture began as people started to plant grain, herd and breed animals, and use agricultural tools. When people were able to produce more food than needed for survival, they could take time away from producing food and raise their standard of living by producing better clothing, shelter, and other items. Students will learn that when people do not need to spend all their time producing food to survive, they can invest in capital goods that will increase production of other goods and services. They will learn that investing in capital goods and increasing production is an important key to raising living standards.

CONCEPTS

Capital goods

Consumer goods

Economic growth

Investment

Labor productivity

Scarcity

Standard of living

OBJECTIVES

Students will be able to:

- Define and understand the economic concepts of standard of living, scarcity, consumer goods, capital goods, investment, labor productivity, and economic growth.

- Analyze effects of investing in capital goods on production.

- Explain the relationship between investment in capital goods and standard of living.

CONTENT STANDARDS

Voluntary Content Standards in Economics, 2nd edition

- **Standard 1:** Productive resources are limited. Therefore, people cannot have all the goods and services they want; as a result, they must choose some things and give up others.

- **Standard 15:** Investment in factories, machinery, new technology, and the health, education, and training of people stimulates economic growth and can raise future standards of living.

World History Content Standards

World History Era 1. The Beginnings of Human Society Giving Shape to World History

- **Standard 2:** The processes that led to the emergence of agricultural societies around the world.

---

[1] This lesson is adapted from *World History: Focus on Economics* Lesson Two: Making Clothes out of Wheat. Council for Economic Education, 1996.

TIME REQUIRED

60 minutes

MATERIALS

- One copy of Activity 2.1 for each student in the class

- Game cards made from Activity 2.2 (pages 1, 2, and 3) so that for each group, there are:

  ◆ 10 1-unit pieces of wheat

  ◆ 10 5-unit pieces of wheat

  ◆ 10 10-unit pieces of wheat

  ◆ 9 hoes

  ◆ 9 sickles

  ◆ 1 irrigation canal system

  ◆ 10 woolen garments

  ◆ 1 mud-brick house

The game cards are arranged so that if you make one copy of each page of Activity 2.2 for each group, you will have sufficient game cards and some extras. (One copy of page 3 is enough for two groups. We recommend that you make a few extra cards of wheat on page 1 to make it easier to make change.) You may wish to make each page a different color (e.g., yellow for wheat, green for hoes, sickles and canals, and blue for garments and houses). You may wish to make the copies on card stock or laminate them for reuse. Cut cards apart before beginning the activity.

- Optional: Five copies of Activity 2.3 per group (enough for 10 rounds of the simulation)

- Two copies of Activity 2.4 – one for the Village Clerk, who will help conduct the simulation, and one for your reference

- Slides 2.1–2.12 (2.8 and 2.9 are optional)

PROCEDURE

1. Tell students that they are going to take part in a simulation to see how farmers in the Neolithic period were able to increase their standard of living.

2. Show Slides 2.1 and 2.2. Discuss the definitions of Neolithic period, **scarcity,** and **standard of living**. Emphasize

that although people always want to have more goods and services for themselves and for others to raise their standards of living, there are not enough resources to satisfy everyone's wants. The basic economic problem, in Neolithic times, today and at all times in between, is scarcity. Because of scarcity, individuals and societies cannot have everything they want. However, people can make choices that enable them to increase their production and consumption of goods and services and raise their standard of living.

3. Ask students how they think their standard of living today compares with that of people who lived in the U.S. 100 years ago.

   (It has increased because they have more goods and services available such as more and better cars, televisions, computers, more and better health care, better housing, and so on.)

4. Pass out a copy of Activity 2.1 to each student. Read **Part I: Background Information,** together. You may wish to comment that the simulation does not distinguish between work done by males and work done by females. In Neolithic times, men would most likely have performed the more muscle-intensive tasks such as harvesting the wheat, while women would have specialized in tasks such as making cloth.

5. Show Slides 2.3 and 2.4. Discuss the definitions of **consumer goods**, **capital goods**, and the examples of the goods in the simulation. Explain that one meaning of the term **investment** is spending on capital goods, so you often hear the expression "investing in capital goods." Show the cards representing the goods in the simulation as you mention them.

6. Show Slide 2.5. Explain to students that they can improve their standard of living in the simulation by acquiring consumer goods. Their goal is to have 20 units of wheat, 10 woolen garments, and 1 mud-brick house. Capital goods are important because investing in capital goods will enable them to produce wheat in

less time, therefore having extra time to produce woolen garments or a mud-brick house.[2]

7. Select one student to serve as Village Clerk to help you conduct the simulation. Give him or her a copy of Activity 2.4 and tell him or her to read the instructions. Have the Village Clerk stand behind a desk or table accessible to other students. Place all the cards from Activity 2.2 on the table.

8. Divide the remainder of the class into groups, each representing a family. It is recommended that you have no more than four or five groups. A small number of groups makes the simulation easier to conduct and move more quickly. Have each group sit together so they will be able to talk and make decisions.

9. Appoint one person in each group to be the Family Representative. The Family Representative will exchange wheat for other goods with you and the Village Clerk during the simulation. (Optional: If Family Record Sheets are used, you may appoint one person in each group to be the Family Scribe and to be in charge of the Family Record Sheet.)

10. Instruct students to read **Part II: Information for the Simulation** on Activity 2.1 (or read it together). Tell the Village Clerk to give each family 30 units of wheat while others are reading. Note: Giving each family three 10-unit cards is fine, as they can receive units back later.

11. When students have finished reading, show Slides 2.6 and 2.7. Review the summary of the information for the simulation, which is also given on Activity 2.1. Answer any questions about the instructions.

12. Instruct students to read the portion of Activity 2.1, **Part III: Playing the**

Simulation in Year One (or read it together). Give groups time to make decisions about what to do with their extra 10 units of wheat. Tell Family Representatives to bring 20 units of wheat to the Village Clerk to represent consumption, and to bring any extra wheat they wish to exchange for hoes, sickles, or woolen garments. The Village Clerk can give them "change" if they want to store units.

13. Announce that this is the end of Year One. Answer any questions before proceeding to Year Two.

(Students may ask if they should obtain garments or a house along the way or wait until they can purchase everything at once. The answer is that it is up to them.)

14. Remind students that the wheat they exchange for hoes, sickles, and garments represents time left over for doing other things after enough wheat is produced for survival.

15. **OPTIONAL:** If you are doing optional Activity 2.3, distribute three or four copies of the Family Record Sheets to each group, now. Be prepared to provide more if needed in later rounds. The record sheets may help the groups track their decisions and see the effects of investing in capital goods. However, the simulation can be conducted without the Family Record Sheets because the groups will have cards representing consumer and capital goods resulting from their decisions. If Family Record Sheets are used, display (optional) Slides 2.8 and 2.9. Review the parts of the Record Sheet with students.

16. Instruct students to read Activity 2.1, **Part IV: Playing the Simulation in Year Two and Following Years.** In subsequent years, follow this sequence of events:

- At the beginning of each year, announce how much wheat was produced WITHOUT the use of capital goods. In normal years, this will be 20 units of wheat; in drought years, 10 units.

---

[2] In the official U.S. national income or GDP accounts, residential housing is part of investment and not consumption. However, shelter is considered to be a consumer good in this simulation.

- Direct the Village Clerk to distribute cards for the 20 units of wheat **plus** additional wheat for each hoe, sickle, or canal system owned by each family. (See Activity 2.2 Game Cards.) Make sure Family Representatives show the cards to prove how many capital goods they own.

- Allow families time to decide what to do with their wheat.

- At the end of each year, have families turn in their wheat for consumption and purchase capital goods. Work with the Village Clerk to collect 20 units of wheat for consumption from each family and to help exchange any extra wheat for hoes, sickles, a canal system, woolen garments, or a mud-brick house.

- In Year Four, announce that it is a drought year. This year, each family only produces 10 units of wheat (not including additional amounts they produce if they own capital goods). The Village Clerk should distribute only 10 units of wheat to each family at the beginning of the year. At the end of that year, if any family does not have the required 20 units of wheat for consumption, they do not survive and must drop out of the simulation. (If you will conduct this simulation in multiple classes, you may wish to vary the drought year between Years 3, 4, and 5.)

- When a family group has 20 units of wheat, 10 woolen garments, and a mud brick house, the entire group should stand. The simulation is ended.

17. Recognize the standing group and count their cards to verify that they have succeeded in raising their standard of living in the desired manner. Declare that they have "won."

18. Ask the family group to briefly explain their strategy in achieving the goals of the simulation.

(The winning group is likely to have invested in capital goods in early years and continued to do so. They may have purchased the house and garments throughout the years or waited until they had enough wheat to purchase them all at once.)

19. Show Slide 2.10. Debrief the simulation by discussing the following questions:

   a. How could Neolithic farmers increase the overall production of consumer goods?

   (They could increase production by producing more capital goods: hoes, sickles, and an irrigation canal system.)

   b. How did producing capital goods lead to an increased standard of living?

   (Capital goods are used to produce other goods, so when families had capital goods they were able to produce enough wheat to survive and also produce better clothing and shelter.)

20. Show Slide 2.11. Continue to debrief the simulation by discussing the following questions:

   a. What is meant by **labor productivity**?

   (As shown on the slide, the amount of goods and services produced per worker in a given time period.)

   b. Did your family size did change during the simulation?

   (No, each family remained the same size.)

   c. By the end of the simulation, could your family produce more wheat in a year?

   (For most families, the answer will be yes.)

   d. Did wheat production per person increase?

(If they produced more per year with the same number of family members, then yes.)

e. Why did productivity increased in the simulation?

(Labor productivity increased because more capital goods were used.)

21. Show Slide 2.12. Continue to debrief the simulation by discussing the following questions:

a. What is meant by **economic growth**?

(As shown on the slide, an increase in the output of goods and services per person. Note: In other contexts, economic growth can refer to an increase in the total amount of goods and services produced in a country.)

b. How did using capital goods affect economic growth?

(Economic growth increased as more capital goods were used. More goods and services were produced overall.)

c. How does economic growth affect the standard of living?

(Because economic growth leads to more goods and services being produced per person, economic growth leads to increased standards of living.)

22. Explain to the students that in pre-modern times, standards of living did not tend to rise, despite the development of new technologies and investment in capital. Most economic historians conclude that this was because increased total output allowed population to rise, so that output per person stayed roughly constant over time.

CLOSURE

23. Review the major concepts from the lesson by asking the following questions:

a. What is the problem of scarcity?

(People cannot have everything they want, so they must make choices.)

b. What choices did they have to make in the simulation because of scarcity?

(They had to decide whether to store wheat or produce capital goods, which capital goods to produce, and which consumer goods to buy.)

c. What are consumer goods, and what were examples of consumer goods in the simulation?

(Consumer goods are goods that provide direct satisfaction. Wheat, clothes, and houses are examples in the simulation.)

d. What are capital goods, and what were examples of capital goods in the simulation?

(Capital goods are human-made goods used to produce other goods and services. Pointed sticks, hoes, sickles, and irrigation canals are examples in the simulation.)

e. What did you learn from participating in the simulation?

(Answers will vary, but should include a discussion about the benefits of investing in capital goods.)

ASSESSMENT

Multiple Choice

1. Capital goods are

a. goods produced in the main political city of a country.

b. **human-made goods used to produce other goods and services.**

c. goods that give you direct satisfaction and do not lead to producing other goods.

d. goods that are consumed by animals and not by humans.

2. Scarcity is

   a. a problem faced by people in Neolithic times that does not exist today.

   b. a problem that exists today, but that did not exist before the year 2000 C.E.

   c. not a problem that exists today or in the past.

   d. **a problem that has existed across time.**

Constructed Response

1. Based on your participation in the simulation, write a short paragraph answering this question: How could farmers in Neolithic times increase their standard of living?

   (Answers should include discussion of being able to devote time to the production of capital goods, if there was time left over after producing enough food for survival. The use of capital goods led to an overall increase in output and enabled farmers to produce goods such as improved clothing and houses to increase their standard of living.)

SOURCES

This lesson is adapted from *World History: Focus on Economics*, Lesson Two: Making Clothes Out of Wheat. Council for Economic Education, 1996.

CONNECTIONS: THE IMPORTANCE OF CAPITAL GOODS ACROSS TIME

- Ask students if they think that having capital goods today is important for increasing productivity and economic growth, as was true in Neolithic times.

   (Answers will vary, but students should see that capital goods such as advanced tools, machinery, and technology are important for economic growth today. When workers have quality capital goods with which to work, they can produce better goods in less time, resulting in increased labor productivity.)

- Refer students back to this question that they discussed before participating in the simulation: "How does your standard of living today compare with that of people who lived in the U.S. 100 years ago?" Ask students how capital goods developed in the past 100 years helped lead to higher standards of living today.

   (Some students will realize that there have been vast improvements in capital goods, including technology, over the past 100 years that have led to the production of more and better goods and services leading to higher standards of living.)

ACTIVITY 2.1

Simulation: Increasing Your Standard of Living in Neolithic Times

PART I: BACKGROUND INFORMATION (BEFORE THE SIMULATION BEGINS)

Imagine that you are part of a family group in the Middle East 6,000 years ago. Your family and others have settled down as farmers. You grow wheat for food. Your family cooks the wheat into a thick gruel or bakes it into unleavened loaves. Your only tools are fire-hardened wooden sticks that you use to make holes in the ground. After you make holes, you put wheat seed in them and cover the seed with dirt. If your family does not spend all of its time growing wheat, you may not survive.

You also have sheep, which you use for meat and skins for your clothing. You do not make woolen cloth from the wool, because to do so would take time away from growing wheat. However, people from your village have seen people in another village wearing woolen garments. You and your family would like to have this type of clothing. You think that it would be much better than the animal skins that you now wear.

You and your family and the other families in your village live in uncomfortable, fragile mud huts. The huts are likely to fall apart when it rains and do not provide good shelter from rain or high or low temperatures. You would like to have a mud-brick house, instead. A mud-brick house would be sturdier, more permanent and better protection against hot summers, cool winters, and rain and dust storms.

PART II: INFORMATION FOR THE SIMULATION

1. Your goal in this simulation is to raise your standard of living. Each year, your family needs to consume 20 units of wheat in order to have an adequate level of nutrition to stay alive. In order to raise your standard of living, your family would also like to have 10 woolen garments and a sturdy mud-brick house. Therefore, your goal is for your family to have:

    -   20 units of wheat

    -   10 woolen garments

    -   1 mud-brick house

    The simulation will end when one or more families have all of these goods.

2. WHEAT PRODUCED AND SURVIVAL: In a normal year, your family can produce 20 units of wheat, which is enough to feed you through the year. If in any year you and your family do not have 20 units of wheat to consume, you will all perish and drop out of the simulation. During drought years, your family can only produce 10 units of wheat. Droughts occur about every five to seven years; the last drought was two years ago.

3. WOOLEN GARMENTS: It takes time to shear sheep, make thread, weave cloth, and sew garments. To obtain the wool clothing you want, you need enough time after planting, cultivating, and harvesting wheat to make the clothing. Each woolen garment will cost your family **two units of wheat**. These two units represent the time given up from producing wheat to make the woolen garment.

Activity 2.1, continued

4. MUD-BRICK HOUSE: It takes time to form bricks from mud, lay the bricks out in the sun to bake, and build a house. In order to obtain the mud-brick house you want, you need to have enough time after planting, cultivating, and harvesting wheat to make the house. A mud-brick house will cost your family **20 units of wheat**. These 20 units represent the time given up from producing wheat to make the mud-brick house.

5. HOES, SICKLES, AND IRRIGATION CANAL SYSTEM: You must find a way to increase the amount of wheat you produce in order to have enough wheat to obtain woolen garments and a mud-brick house. In a normal year, you produce 20 units of wheat, the amount you need to survive. Your family could produce more wheat if you had capital goods such as hoes, sickles, and an irrigation canal. (**No family may own more than 9 hoes, 9 sickles, or 1 canal system.**)

    a. HOES enable you to produce more wheat because you can keep weeds out of the field more easily. To make a hoe, you must give up time that could have been spent growing wheat. Therefore, each hoe costs **3 units** of wheat. Each hoe you own increases your production of wheat by **8 units** per year.

    b. SICKLES enable you to produce more wheat because you can harvest more quickly. To make a sickle, you must give up time that could have been spent growing wheat. Therefore, each sickle costs **2 units** of wheat. Each sickle you own will increases your production of wheat by **5 units** per year.

    c. IRRIGATION CANAL: Your family lives near a river and can dig a canal to your fields to increase the amount of water for your wheat crops. Initially, digging a canal is quite time-consuming, so the cost is **20 units** of wheat. You may choose to cooperate with one other family to build a more extensive canal system. In that case, the cost will be **15 units** of wheat per family (a total of 30 units of wheat). If your family owns an irrigation canal, it increases your production of wheat by **20 units** per year.

SUMMARY OF INFORMATION FOR THE SIMULATION

- Your family must have 20 units of wheat each year to survive.

- **1 woolen garment** costs 2 units of wheat. (You want 10 woolen garments.)

- **1 mud-brick house** costs 20 units of wheat. (You want 1 mud-brick house.)

- **1 hoe** costs 3 units of wheat. Each hoe you own increases wheat production by 8 units per year.

- **1 sickle** costs 2 units of wheat. Each sickle you own increases wheat production by 5 units per year.

- **1 irrigation canal system** costs 20 units of wheat. It only costs 15 units per family if two families produce it together. A canal system increases wheat production by 20 units per year.

ACTIVITY 2.1, CONTINUED

PART III: PLAYING THE SIMULATION IN YEAR ONE

- In a normal year, your family can produce 20 units of wheat, which is enough to feed your family through the year. This year, the weather has been exceptionally good and you have 30 units of wheat. Over the coming year, your family will consume 20 units of wheat. You will have 10 units left over. You can choose to store these units in case of drought or exchange some units of wheat for hoes, sickles, or clothing. (You do not have enough for an irrigation canal or a mud-brick house at this point.)

Units of wheat produced in this year	30
Units of wheat consumed	−20
Extra units of wheat	10

- DECISION ABOUT WHAT TO DO WITH EXTRA UNITS OF WHEAT THIS YEAR
  (Write the number of units of wheat on the lines provided, if instructed by teacher.)

  - units stored in case of a drought _____

  - 2 units per woolen garment   _____

  - 3 units per hoe   _____

  - 2 units per sickle   _____

- Send your Family Representative to the Village Clerk to turn in 20 units of wheat to represent what your family consumed. At that time, the Family Representative should buy any hoes, sickles, or clothing your family has decided to purchase.

PART IV: PLAYING THE SIMULATION IN YEAR TWO AND FOLLOWING YEARS

- At the beginning of each year, your teacher will announce how much wheat your family will have produced that year (not including extra units produced by any capital goods that you own). In normal years, your Family Representative will collect 20 units of wheat **plus additional units for each sickle, hoe, and irrigation canal** your family owns. The Family Representative must show the hoe, sickle, and irrigation canal cards to the Village Clerk to collect the extra units of wheat.

- During the year, your family will decide what to do with any extra wheat over 20 units.

- At the end of each year, your Family Representative will turn in 20 units of wheat to the Village Clerk for wheat consumed. Based on your family's decisions, the Family Representative will also exchange extra units of wheat for hoes, sickles, an irrigation canal, woolen garments, or a mud-brick house.

- When a family group has 20 units of wheat, 10 woolen garments, and a mud-brick house, the entire group should stand. The simulation is ended.

IMPORTANT NOTE:

A drought may occur in any year. When it does, each family will produce only 10 units of wheat. You still need to consume 20 units to survive. Any family that does not have 20 units of wheat to turn in at the end of the year will not survive the drought and will drop out of the simulation. Your teacher will inform you if a drought occurs.

Activity 2.2

Game Cards: Wheat

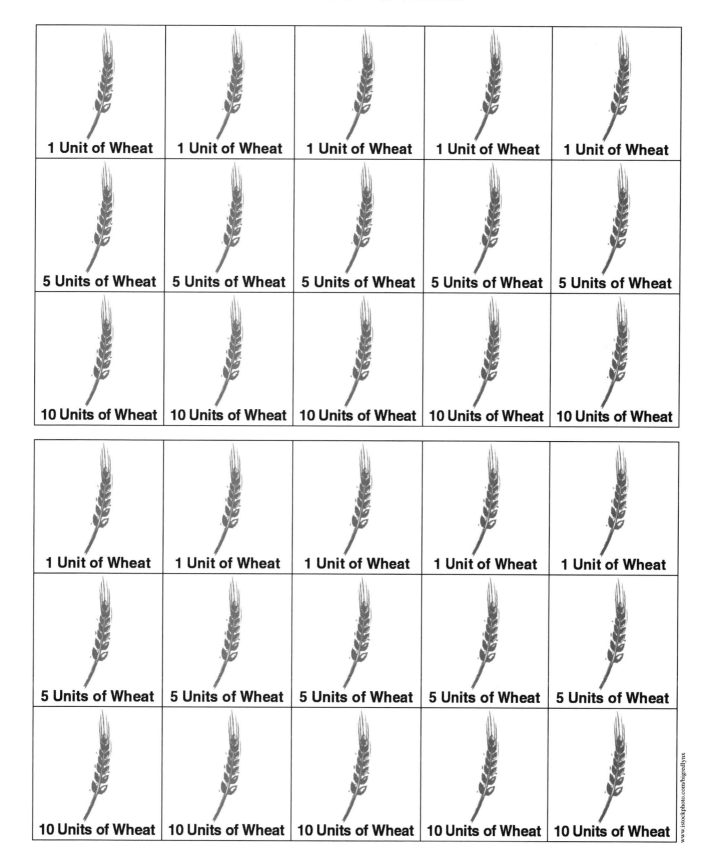

1 Unit of Wheat	1 Unit of Wheat	1 Unit of Wheat	1 Unit of Wheat	1 Unit of Wheat
5 Units of Wheat	5 Units of Wheat	5 Units of Wheat	5 Units of Wheat	5 Units of Wheat
10 Units of Wheat	10 Units of Wheat	10 Units of Wheat	10 Units of Wheat	10 Units of Wheat
1 Unit of Wheat	1 Unit of Wheat	1 Unit of Wheat	1 Unit of Wheat	1 Unit of Wheat
5 Units of Wheat	5 Units of Wheat	5 Units of Wheat	5 Units of Wheat	5 Units of Wheat
10 Units of Wheat	10 Units of Wheat	10 Units of Wheat	10 Units of Wheat	10 Units of Wheat

www.istockphoto.com/bigredlynx

ACTIVITY 2.2, CONTINUED

Game Cards: Hoes, Sickles, and Canal Systems

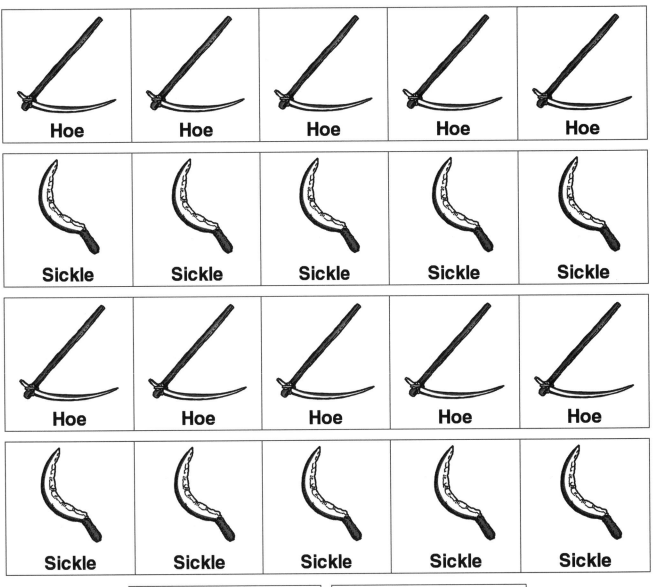

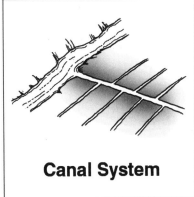

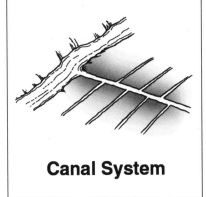

Activity 2.2, continued

Game Cards: Woolen Garments and Mud-Brick Houses

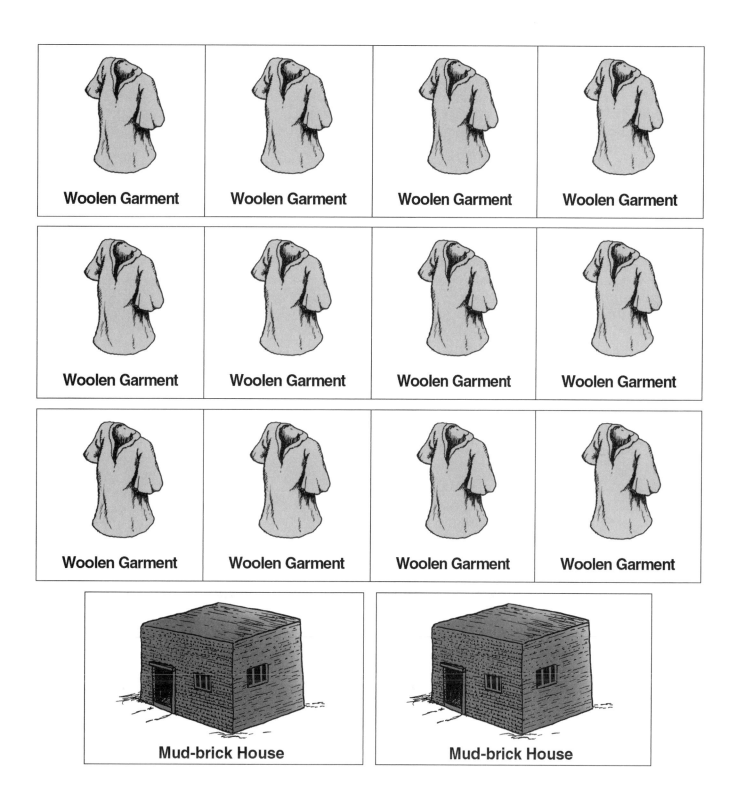

Woolen Garment	Woolen Garment	Woolen Garment	Woolen Garment
Woolen Garment	Woolen Garment	Woolen Garment	Woolen Garment
Woolen Garment	Woolen Garment	Woolen Garment	Woolen Garment

Mud-brick House   Mud-brick House

ACTIVITY 2.3

Family Record Sheet

Names _____

YEAR _____

    Units of wheat stored from prior years: _____

    Units of wheat produced this year without capital goods: _____

    (announced by teacher at beginning of year)

    Units of wheat produced this year from capital goods: _____

    (Number of hoes times 8; plus number of sickles times 5;

    plus 20 if you own an irrigation canal.)

    Total wheat you have (sum of the above):   _____

Total wheat that you have _____ minus 20 units consumed = _____ extra units this year

DECISION ABOUT EXTRA UNITS OF WHEAT THIS YEAR:

(Write the total number of units of wheat used for each purpose on the lines provided.)

- units stored in case of drought   _____
- 2 units exchanged per woolen garment   _____
- 20 units exchanged for a mud-brick house   _____
- 3 units exchanged per hoe   _____
- 2 units exchanged per sickle   _____
- units exchanged for an irrigation canal   _____
  (15 if with another family or 20 by yourself)

AT THE END OF THE YEAR, WE WILL OWN _____ WOOLEN GARMENTS AND _____ MUD-BRICK HOUSES.

— —

YEAR _____

    Units of wheat stored from prior years: _____

    Units of wheat produced this year without capital goods: _____

    (announced by teacher at beginning of year)

    Units of wheat produced this year from capital goods: _____

    (Number of hoes times 8; plus number of sickles times 5;

    plus 20 if you own an irrigation canal.)

    Total wheat you have (sum of the above):   _____

Total wheat that you have _____ minus 20 units consumed = _____ extra units this year

DECISION ABOUT EXTRA UNITS OF WHEAT THIS YEAR:

(Write the total number of units of wheat used for each purpose on the lines provided.)

- units stored in case of drought   _____
- 2 units exchanged per woolen garment   _____
- 20 units exchanged for a mud-brick house   _____
- 3 units exchanged per hoe   _____
- 2 units exchanged per sickle   _____
- units exchanged for an irrigation canal   _____
  (15 if with another family or 20 by yourself)

AT THE END OF THE YEAR, WE WILL OWN _____ WOOLEN GARMENTS AND _____ MUD-BRICK HOUSES.

FOCUS: MIDDLE SCHOOL WORLD HISTORY © COUNCIL FOR ECONOMIC EDUCATION, NEW YORK, NY

Activity 2.4

Instructions for Village Clerk

1. YEAR ONE

At the beginning of Year One, give each family 30 units of wheat.

At the end of Year One:

- Collect 20 units of wheat from each Family Representative.
- The Family Representative may exchange extra wheat for hoes, sickles, or woolen garments. If that is the case, you will give them:
  - ◆ 1 hoe in exchange for each 3 units of wheat
  - ◆ 1 sickle in exchange for each 2 units of wheat
  - ◆ 1 woolen garment in exchange for each 2 units of wheat

2. YEAR TWO AND FOLLOWING YEARS

At the beginning of each year:

- Give each Family Representative the amount of wheat announced by your teacher. This will usually be 20 units. If there is a drought, it will be 10 units.
- In addition, give each Family Representative the following:
  - ◆ For each hoe, give them 8 units of wheat
  - ◆ For each sickle, give them 5 unit of wheat
  - ◆ For a canal system, give them 20 units of wheat

At the end of each year:

- Collect 20 units of wheat from each Family Representative.
- At the request of a Family Representative, you will exchange capital or consumer goods for wheat as follows:
  - ◆ 1 hoe for each 3 units of wheat
  - ◆ 1 sickle for each 2 units of wheat
  - ◆ 1 woolen garment for each 2 units of wheat
  - ◆ 1 mud-brick house for 20 units of wheat
  - ◆ 1 irrigation canal for 15 units of wheat if with another family (30 units total), or for 20 units if by themselves

Note: No family may own more than 9 hoes, 9 sickles, and 1 irrigation canal during the simulation.

SLIDE 2.1

Neolithic Period

- The Neolithic period was the latest part of the Stone Age, beginning about 10,700 years ago and ending with the beginning of the Bronze Age in about 3500 B.C.E.
- During the Neolithic period, settled agriculture began in the Middle East as people started to plant grain, breed and herd animals, and use agricultural tools.

FOCUS MIDDLE SCHOOL WORLD HISTORY © COUNCIL FOR ECONOMIC EDUCATION, NEW YORK, NY

SLIDE 2.2

Important Terms

- **Scarcity**: The condition that exists because human wants are greater than the capacity of available resources to satisfy those wants. The problem of scarcity faces all individuals and organizations throughout time.
- **Standard of living**: How well off people are, as measured by the quantity and quality of goods and services that they have.

FOCUS MIDDLE SCHOOL WORLD HISTORY © COUNCIL FOR ECONOMIC EDUCATION, NEW YORK, NY

SLIDE 2.3

Important Terms

- **Consumer goods:** Goods that give you direct satisfaction.
  Examples from the simulation: Wheat, clothes, and houses

- **Capital goods:** Human-made goods that are used to produce other goods and services and that do not get used up in the production process.
  Examples from the simulation: Pointed sticks, hoes, sickles, and irrigation canals

SLIDE 2.4

Important Terms

- **Investment:** The purchase of capital goods that are used to produce goods and services.

SLIDE 2.5

Your Goal in the Simulation

- Your goal in the simulation is to raise your standard of living by acquiring consumer goods. You want to have:
  - ✓ 20 units of wheat
  - ✓ 10 woolen garments
  - ✓ 1 mud-brick house

Note:
You do not win the simulation by accumulating capital goods. However, capital goods can help you produce wheat in less time, which will give you the time you need to make woolen garments and build a mud-brick house.

FOCUS MIDDLE SCHOOL WORLD HISTORY © COUNCIL FOR ECONOMIC EDUCATION, NEW YORK, NY

SLIDE 2.6

Information for the Simulation

- Your family must have 20 units of wheat each year to survive.

- **1 woolen garment** costs 2 units of wheat. (You want 10 woolen garments.)

- **1 mud-brick house** costs 20 units of wheat. (You want 1 mud-brick house.)

FOCUS MIDDLE SCHOOL WORLD HISTORY © COUNCIL FOR ECONOMIC EDUCATION, NEW YORK, NY

Slide 2.7

LESSON 2 – HOW NEOLITHIC FARMERS INCREASED THEIR STANDARD OF LIVING

Information for the Simulation

- **1 hoe** costs 3 units of wheat. Each hoe you own increases wheat production by 8 units per year.
- **1 sickle** costs 2 units of wheat. Each sickle you own increases wheat production by 5 units per year.
- **1 irrigation canal** costs 20 units of wheat. It costs only 15 units per family if two families produce it together. A canal system increases wheat production by 20 units per year.

FOCUS MIDDLE SCHOOL WORLD HISTORY © COUNCIL FOR ECONOMIC EDUCATION, NEW YORK, NY

Slide 2.8

LESSON 2 – HOW NEOLITHIC FARMERS INCREASED THEIR STANDARD OF LIVING

Family Record Sheet: Part 1

YEAR _____

Units of wheat stored from prior years: _____

Units of wheat produced this year without capital goods:
(announced by teacher at beginning of year) _____

Units of wheat produced this year from capital goods:
(number of hoes times 8; plus number of sickles times 5; plus 20 if you own an irrigation canal) _____

Total wheat you have (sum of the above): _____

Total wheat that you have _____ minus 20 units consumed = _____ extra units this year

FOCUS MIDDLE SCHOOL WORLD HISTORY © COUNCIL FOR ECONOMIC EDUCATION, NEW YORK, NY

SLIDE 2.9

Family Record Sheet: Part 2

DECISION ABOUT EXTRA UNITS OF WHEAT THIS YEAR:

o   units stored in case of drought   _____
o   2 units exchanged per woolen garment   _____
o   20 units exchanged for a mud-brick house   _____
o   3 units exchanged per hoe   _____
o   2 units exchanged per sickle   _____
o   units exchanged for an irrigation canal   _____

AT THE END OF THE YEAR, WE WILL OWN
_____ WOOLEN GARMENTS AND
_____ MUD-BRICK HOUSES

FOCUS MIDDLE SCHOOL WORLD HISTORY © COUNCIL FOR ECONOMIC EDUCATION, NEW YORK, NY

SLIDE 2.10

Debriefing the Simulation

- How could Neolithic farmers increase the overall production of consumer goods?

- How did producing capital goods lead to an increased standard of living?

FOCUS MIDDLE SCHOOL WORLD HISTORY © COUNCIL FOR ECONOMIC EDUCATION, NEW YORK, NY

Slide 2.11

Debriefing the Simulation

- **Labor productivity** is the amount of goods and services produced per worker in a given time period.
  - Did your family size change during the simulation?
  - By the end of the simulation, could your family produce more wheat in a year?
  - Did wheat produced per person increase?
  - Why did productivity increase in the simulation?

Slide 2.12

Debriefing the Simulation

- **Economic growth** is an increase in the output of goods and services per person.
  - How did using capital goods affect economic growth?
  - How does economic growth affect the standard of living?

LESSON 3

THE NEOLITHIC AGRICULTURAL REVOLUTION

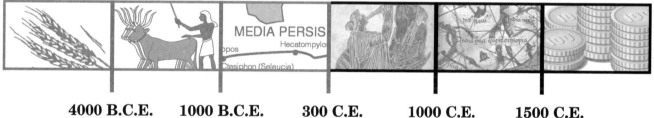

| 4000 B.C.E. | 1000 B.C.E. | 300 C.E. | 1000 C.E. | 1500 C.E. |

LESSON 3
THE NEOLITHIC AGRICULTURAL REVOLUTION

LESSON DESCRIPTION

Students read about and discuss the impact of the invention of the wooden plow on agricultural output, farmers, and consumers. They will use the wooden plow example to identify the potential relationships between agricultural innovations and food output, improved standards of living, and the population of ancient societies.

Students then study a multi-tiered timeline showing key agricultural innovations in ancient times and suggest impacts on agricultural output, farmers, and consumers. From the multi-tiered timeline, students can draw conclusions about the impact of increased agricultural output on individuals and societies. Finally, students participate in a simple simulation that illustrates how the introduction of a new technology can increase labor productivity.

As an assessment, students read a fictional story and answer questions about a farming family in the Fertile Crescent of Mesopotamia around 4000 B.C.E.

INTRODUCTION

A multi-tiered timeline illustrates a series or multiple sets of events or activities that occur over a time period. In some cases, the multi-tiered timeline can show events in multiple locations or in multiple categories. Students can use a multi-tiered timeline illustrating dates, world population, and important agricultural innovations to better understand the relationships between these factors.

The timeline in this lesson spans ancient civilizations from about 10,000 B.C.E., the Neolithic Revolution, to 500 B.C.E. The timeline identifies the agricultural innovations that contributed to improvements in food production and economic growth during each period of time.

Historians generally identify two historical eras as agricultural revolutions. During the Neolithic Revolution, people began to settle in villages and plant their food supplies. Using simple tools such as wooden plows and irrigation ditches enabled hunter-gatherers to settle in one place and eventually freed some people from the need to work in agriculture, which allowed them to specialize in producing other goods and services for the small villages. As food production increased, so did the population.[1]

Some historians debate whether or not the Neolithic Revolution and settled agriculture actually allowed standards of living and health to improve. Some argue that settled agriculture actually affected health negatively, and poor conditions in larger settlements increased the spread of disease.[2]

The second agricultural revolution began in the 1700s, when better tools, new power-driven machines, and innovative systems significantly increased productivity and output of farm labor. The steel plow allowed a farmer to break up hard soil much more efficiently. A horse-drawn reaper could harvest far more wheat than many workers using hand tools. New systems of crop rotation, irrigation, fertilization, and crop breeding increased the production of food.

The history of the United States over the past 220 years provides a good illustration of the impact of innovation on agricultural productivity and output. In 1790, when the United States had a population of just four million, farmers were 90 percent of labor force. By 1880, the U.S. population had reached 50 million, and farmers made up 49 percent of the workforce. By 2008, the population had reached 300 million, and only 2.1 percent of the population consisted of farmers. In the 1940s, it took about 20 farmers

---

[1] Cameron, Rondo, and Neal, Larry, *A Concise Economic History of the World*, New York: Oxford University Press, 2003.Pages 23–26. Roberts, J.M., *History of the World*, New York: Penguin Books, 1997. Pages 48–49.

[2] Diamond, Jared. *Guns, Germs, and Steel*, New York: W.W. Norton & Co., 1999. Pages 204–205.

to produce the food for 100 people. Today, it takes just two farmers to grow food enough for a hundred people.[3]

A third agricultural revolution, the Green Revolution, began in the 1940s (and may still be under way). During this time, advances in technology and plant and animal science greatly increased world food output. Rapid population and economic growth in some regions has greatly increased the demand for food commodities.

During revolutionary periods such as those discussed here, less reliance on agricultural labor freed more people to specialize in the production of other goods and enabled changes affecting family structures and social organization. Cities grew when a stable food supply was available in regional markets. Egypt was the "bread basket" of ancient Rome. Today, thanks to more efficient distribution systems, food markets are global and just about any food product people want is available in a modern grocery store.

CONCEPTS

Innovation

Invention

Production

Productivity

Revolution

Standard of living

Technological changes

OBJECTIVES

Students will be able to:

- Use a multi-tiered timeline to compare and draw conclusions about world population growth and agricultural innovations.

- Identify specific inventions and innovations that contributed to increases in agricultural production and productivity.

[3] "A History of American Agriculture," *Growing a Nation: The Story of American Agriculture, Agriculture in the Classroom*, U.S. Department of Agriculture, 2006.

- Suggest how improvements in agriculture and food production impacted individuals and societies in ancient times.

CONTENT STANDARDS

National Voluntary Content Standards in Economics, 2nd edition

- **Standard 15:** Students will understand that: Investment in factories, machinery, new technology, and in the health, education, and training of people can raise future standards of living.

World History Content Standards

Era 1: The Beginnings of Human Society

- **Standard 2:** The processes that led to the emergence of agricultural societies around the world.

Era 2: Early Civilizations and the Emergence of Pastoral Peoples, 4000–1000 B.C.E.

- **Standard 2:** How agrarian societies spread and new states emerged in the third and second millennia B.C.E.

- **Standard 4:** Major trends in Eurasia and Africa from 4000–1000 B.C.E.

Era 3: Classical Traditions, Major Religions, and Giant Empires, 1000 B.C.E.–300 C.E.

- **Standard 5:** Major global trends from 1000 B.C.E.–300 C.E.

TIME REQUIRED

50 minutes

MATERIALS

- Slides 3.1–3.8

- Activity 3.1, *The Agricultural Revolution*, 1 copy for each student

- Activity 3.2, *Timeline of Agricultural Innovation and World Population—10,000 to 500 B.C.E.*, 1 copy for each student

- Activity 3.3, *Assessment, Nurishtar Invents the Ard*, 1 copy for each student

- Scissors for half the students

- 8 ½" × 11" sheets of paper (new or recycled), 5 sheets per student

- Timer or clock with a second hand

PROCEDURE

1. Tell students that they will learn about a revolution. Ask the students, "What is a revolution?"

   (The students will typically refer to a political revolution—a violent overthrow of a government, such as the American or French revolutions.)

2. Explain that the term **revolution** is also used in history to describe times of relatively rapid change, often due to the use of new technologies.[4] In this case, "rapid" is a relative term—referring to a long period of time within a much longer period of human history.

3. Introduce the term "Neolithic Revolution," a revolution in which humans changed from being primarily hunter-gatherers to living in communities and depending on farming for their food supply. Explain that the Neolithic Revolution unfolded over thousands of years, but, in terms of change, it "revolutionized" people's lives. It is unlikely that any society made a dramatic switch from hunter-gatherer to settled

agriculture within a few years or a generation or two.[5]

4. Distribute copies of Activity 3.1, *The Neolithic Agricultural Revolution*, to students. Review the description of the Neolithic Agricultural Revolution:

   - Between 10,000 and 3000 B.C.E., people developed new agricultural technologies, machines and processes.

   - During this time, people also began the slow domestication and development of both crops and animals.

   - The results of these changes made agricultural production much more efficient.

5. Tell the students that the Neolithic Agricultural Revolution had many impacts on society. The results of these are shown on the bottom of Activity 3.1. Discuss these points:

   - Agricultural innovation greatly increased food production output and created a surplus beyond what people needed for survival.

   - Producing more food freed people's time from agricultural work. Some people continued to work in agriculture, while others did other forms of work.

   - People could specialize in work other than agriculture. The amount of nonagricultural goods produced increased.

---

[4] A **revolution** (from the Latin word *revolutio*, meaning "turn around") is a fundamental change in power or organizational structures that takes place in a relatively short period of time. In this case, a fundamental change in the methods of agricultural production that took place over thousands of years within the much longer period of human history.

[5] As Jared Diamond puts it in his book, *Guns, Germs and Steel*, in the Fertile Crescent "as late as 9000 B.C.E. people still had no crops and domestic animals, and were entirely dependent on wild foods. But, by 6000 B.C.E., some societies were almost completely dependent on crops and domestic animals." This transition, because of what Diamond calls the "road to domestication," was gradual. The wild precursors of modern crops had very low caloric yields and thousands of years of gradual modification of these crops by humans was required before they yielded enough to make settled agriculture viable.

- With more food available and temporarily better nutrition, population increased. Often, a population increased at a faster rate than an area's resources were capable of sustaining, and nutrition per person returned to its original level.

- As families and the number of potential workers grew, food production could increase even more.

6. Define **technological changes** as improvements in a firm's ability to produce due to improved processes, methods and machines. Apply the definition to agriculture in ancient times by giving examples of a machine such as a wooden plow, and processes, such as irrigation or crop rotation.

7. Define **production** as a process of manufacturing, growing, designing, or otherwise using productive resources to create goods or services used to satisfy a want. Tell the students that improvements in agriculture, such as the plow, enabled an individual or a group to produce more food in less time. This is an example of improved **productivity**. Define **productivity** as the amount of output (goods and services) produced per unit of input (productive resources) used.

8. To connect this lesson to the present, ask students to think about the "technology revolution" of the 1990s and 2000s. Ask the students to describe how using smart phones, mini-computers, MP3 players, TIVO, etc. has shaped their lives. How would their lives be different without these technologies?

(Answers will vary.)

9. Ask students the following questions to introduce timelines:

a. What is a timeline?

(A timeline shows a series of events over some time period.)

b. What is a multi-tiered timeline?

(A multi-tiered timeline shows several series or multiple sets of events or activities happening over a specified time period. In some cases, the multi-tiered timeline can show events in multiple locations or categories.)

10. Explain that the next part of the lesson will look at a multi-tiered timeline. The timeline shows ancient agricultural innovations and how they affected people's lives. It includes the first agricultural revolution. The tiers of this timeline are world population, years and agricultural innovations.

11. Show Slide 3.1, *Agricultural Innovation and World Population*, and distribute copies of Activity 3.2, *Timeline of Agricultural Innovation and World Population*.

12. Review the timeline components:

- Left column: World Population Estimates

- Center column: Years—Chronology

- Right column: Agricultural Innovations

13. Explain that the term "innovation" in this lesson includes innovations and inventions. The distinction between the two is often confusing and not important for the purposes of this lesson. Innovation is a more inclusive term. Define the following:

- **Innovation**—a new idea or method. It can be the use of an existing idea or method for a new production process or product.

- **Invention**—a new process, application, machine, or article of application.

14. Show Slides 3.2–3.4, which complete the timeline. Ask students what they find interesting or surprising about the sequence of events.

(Answers will vary.)

15. Ask students the following questions about the timeline:

    a. As the years from 10,000 B.C.E. to 500 B.C.E. passed, what happened to world population?

    (World population gradually increased from 1–5 million in 10,000 B.C.E. to 100 million in 500 B.C.E.)

    b. Look at the right-hand column, Agricultural Innovations. What is the relationship between the innovations and population growth?

    (As there was more innovation and thus more food, world population grew.)

16. Explain to students that they will engage in an experiment to see if using new technology increases productivity, such as what occurred during the agricultural revolution. Review the definition of productivity, if needed.

17. Divide the class into two groups. Distribute a pair of scissors to each student in one group. The other group will do the activity without scissors. Distribute five sheets of 8 ½" × 11" recycled/scrap paper to each student in both groups.

18. Explain that the five sheets of paper represent an acre of land. Each student's goal is to plow his or her acre of land so that it can be planted.

19. Explain that in this activity, plowing means cutting or tearing the paper—one sheet at a time—into rows (strips) no larger than about an inch wide and 8½ inches long. Because the land (paper) is to be planted in rows, it is important that the furrows (strips) be as straight and uniform in size (about an inch wide) as possible.

20. Explain that the students without scissors must plow the acre of land by hand—tearing the paper into strips. The students with scissors will plow their acre of land by cutting the paper into strips with the scissors.

21. Give the students three important reminders:

    • Cut or tear the paper across the short (8½") side of the paper.

    • Tear or cut only one strip of one piece of paper at a time.

    • The strips should be straight and about an inch wide.

22. When each student has paper and half of the students have scissors, tell the students that they will have two minutes to plow (cut or tear) their land (paper).

23. Announce the time to start production (plowing) by saying "Go!" Encourage both groups to work as fast as they can but to make sure the rows (paper strips) are uniformly about one inch wide and 8½ inches long.

24. Time the two-minute production period, then call "time," and have students stop plowing (cutting or tearing).

25. Collect the scissors and ask the students to lay the strips of paper out on their desks.

26. Have students report the number of rows each one could plow in two minutes. Determine the average number of rows each group (those with scissors and those without) produced in two minutes.

    (Normally, the average number of rows for the group with scissors will be much more than those who tore the paper by hand.)

27. Review with the students the definition of productivity.

28. Debrief the activity by asking the following questions.

    a. Ask the students to comment on the quality of the strips that were torn by hand compared to those that were cut by scissors.

    (Normally, the cut strips will be much straighter and more uniform in size.)

b. Which group, on average, produced more strips (plowed more rows)?

(Use the two groups' average number of strips (rows) to compare.)

c. Which group was more productive?

(Students should identify the most productive group as those who plowed the most land—cut the most strips—using two minutes of labor.)

d. Why was one group more productive?

(The group that produced more strips used technology to improve the productivity of their labor.)

29. Refer again to Activity 3.2, *Timeline of Agricultural Innovation and World Population*, which is also given in Slides 3.1–3.4.

30. Ask the student to identify agricultural inventions or innovations that may have improved agricultural productivity. As they name each innovation, ask them to identify how that innovation improved productivity.

Some of the many examples in the timeline:

- *Use of the **ard**, a crude wooden plow, improved crop output in Mesopotamia and the Nile River Valley around 6000 B.C.E. The plow enabled a farmer to till and plant more land. Prior to this time, farmers used sharp sticks and other simple digging tools. Note: Slides 3.5 and 3.6 show illustrations of the ancient plow.*

- *The **mouldboard plow** (with an iron V-shaped cutting edge) enabled Chinese farmers in 500 B.C.E. to work their land in much less time or to work more land in the same amount of time. The curved blade turned the soil. These early plows worked fairly well in the light, dry soils of the Middle East, but not so well on the heavier, wetter soils of other regions.*

- ***Irrigation systems** enabled Egyptian farmers in 3000 B.C.E. to farm more land and increased output per acre. More water helped the crops grow.*

- ***Domestication of animals** resulted in a greater food supply and made some animals available to work in the fields pulling plows. Domesticated dogs protected both people and animals.*

31. Define **standard of living** as the level of subsistence of a nation, social class or individual with reference to the adequacy of necessities and comforts of daily life. In other words, it refers to how well people are doing.

32. Ask students if they believe the innovations improved people's standard of living.

(Answers will vary, but most likely the answer will be that improved innovations and productivity result in a higher standard of living.)

CLOSURE

33. Ask students to identify modern innovations that have improved food production and productivity and standards of living.

(Examples: Chemical fertilizers and pesticides have improved crop output. Modern machines—harvesters, tractors, etc.—work more land, faster. GPS positioning is used to efficiently distribute seeds and fertilizer. Genetic modifications have created stronger crops.)

34. Ask students to speculate on how these innovations might affect today's society.

(New technologies and innovations protect food production, preparation, and delivery systems from disease and pests—improving food quality. More and better quality food can increase health, population, and life expectancy. Students might note that increased population growth has not reduced standards of living to basic levels.)

35. Show Slide 3.7. Ask students if they believe that the agricultural innovations they describe will generate enough food to keep pace with population growth.

(Answers will vary, but remind the students that mankind is very resourceful: many recent revolutions have resulted in a higher standard of living.)

ASSESSMENT

Multiple Choice

1. What agricultural innovation enabled farmers in ancient times to plant more land in a given period of time?

    a. Crop rotation

    b. Domesticated sheep

    c. Irrigation system

    d. **Wooden plow**

2. Increased productivity of workers means that _____ has increased.

    a. time

    b. total production

    c. output per worker

    d. number of workers

Constructed Response

1. Distribute copies of Activity 3.3, *Nurishtar Invents the Ard*. Show Slide 3.8, which depicts the Fertile Crescent region. Direct students to read the story about Nurishtar and complete the questions on page 2 of Activity 3.3. *(Answer key provided.)*

SOURCES

Ancient Agriculture

Cameron, Rondo, and Neal, Larry. 2003. *A Concise History of the World*, New York: Oxford University Press.

Diamond, Jared. 1999. *Guns, Germs, and Steel*, New York: W.W. Norton & Co.

Roberts, J.M. 1997. *History of the World*, London: Penguin Books Ltd.

Agriculture Timeline

Cameron, Rondo, and Neal, Larry. 2003. *A Concise History of the World*. New York: Oxford University Press. Pages; 3—Neolithic Revolution; 25—plow and farming techniques.

Diamond, Jared. 1999. *Guns, Germs, and Steel*. New York: W.W. Norton & Co. Pages: 88—plow, manure; 100—crop domestication; 167—animal domestication.

Morton, W. Scott, and Lewis, Charlton M. 2005. *China: Its History and Culture*. New York: McGraw-Hill, Inc. Page 27—mouldboard plow.

Roberts, J.M. 1997. *History of the World*. London: Penguin Books Ltd. Page 36: plow.

U.S. Census Bureau, "International Data Base, Historical Estimates of World Population," http://www.census.gov/population/international/data/idb/worldhis.php.

CONNECTIONS: COMPARING TO OUR WORLD TODAY

As a result of studying population growth in ancient times, students may be interested in the history of world population growth. Show Slide 3.7, *World Population Growth*. Discuss how the population growth rates seemed to increase more rapidly in each era until recent times. The time it takes to add one billion people to the total population has stabilized at 12 or 13 years. For teacher resources on world population, visit http://www.worldof-7billion.org/teacher_resources

One more factor that can be added to the timeline is life expectancy. For an article on increases in life expectancy, visit http://www.historyforkids.org/learn/people/life expectancy.htm

ACTIVITY 3.1

The Neolithic Agricultural Revolution

Between 10,000 and 3000 B.C.E., people in several areas around the earth developed new agricultural methods and machines, such as the plow pulled by horses or oxen. During this time, people also began the slow domestication and development of both crops and animals. The results of these changes made agricultural production much more productive. Food output increased. More land could be farmed by fewer people or in fewer hours. This resulted in greatly improved production and increased the availability of food.

RESULTS:

1. Agricultural innovation greatly increased food production output and created a surplus beyond what was needed for survival.

2. Producing more food freed people's time from agricultural work. Some people continued to work in agriculture, while others did other forms of work.

3. People could specialize in work other than agriculture. The amount of non-agricultural goods produced increased.

4. With more food and temporarily better nutrition, population increased. Often, a population increased at a faster rate than an area's resources were capable of sustaining it, and nutrition per person returned to its original level.

5. As families and the number of potential workers grew, food production could increase even more.

Activity 3.2
Timeline of Agricultural Innovation and World Population – 10,000 to 500 B.C.E.

World Population	Year	Agricultural Innovation
1–5 million	10,000 B.C.E.	Neolithic Revolution begins in Southwest Asia and other areas. Climate change resulted in longer dry seasons and the end of a 100,000-year ice age. Abundance of wild grains enabled hunter-gatherers to settle in villages. Domestication of dogs begins in Asia and North America.
	9500 B.C.E.	The "founder crops" of agriculture appear: wheat, barley, peas, lentils, bitter vetch, chickpeas, and flax.
8–10 million	8000–6000 B.C.E.	Nomadic hunter-gatherers begin to grow food and domesticate animals: Rice in China, 7500 B.C.E. Squash in Mexico, 7000 B.C.E. Wheat in Mesopotamia, 8500 B.C.E. Cattle in SW Asia and India, 7000 B.C.E. Domestication of sheep, goats and pigs begins in SW Asia. Irrigation systems introduced.
	7000–6000 B.C.E.	Domestication of cattle begins in Southwest Asia, Pakistan, and India.
	6000–3000 B.C.E.	A wooden plow, the ard, used in Mesopotamia and Egypt. Permanent villages established in the Fertile Crescent. Farming established on the banks of the Nile River.
	5000–3000 B.C.E.	Domestication begins of horses in Ukraine, donkeys in Egypt, and water buffalo in China. Corn (maize) production in Mexico.
14–20 million	3000 B.C.E.	Irrigation systems and dams built on the Nile River. Crop production increases trade and spread of agriculture. Potatoes domesticated in Peru.
	2000 B.C.E.	Iron plow developed in China.
50 million	1000 B.C.E.	Manure used as fertilizer. Iron plows widely used in China and Southwest Asia.
100 million	500 B.C.E.	Mouldboard plow with a V-shaped iron cutting edge developed in China.

ACTIVITY 3.3

Nurishtar Invents the Ard

Directions: *Read this fictional story about a farmer named Nurishtar, who lived in the Fertile Crescent of Mesopotamia around 4000 B.C.E. After reading the story, complete the assessment by answering the questions.*

Nurishtar was the eldest son in a very large family of farmers who grew grain used to make bread called bappir. Bappir was made from starch extracted from wild grains. Bappir was spread on a flat rock, placed over a fire and cooked into a primitive form of flatbread. Bappir could be stored for a long time.

Nurishtar and his five brothers spent over 60 days in the spring each year tilling the soil on their small plot of land. They used long pointed wood spikes to work the soil by hand. It was very hard work. Each year, they grew just enough grain to produce the bappir the family would eat for the year. If the weather was good, they might have enough bappir to trade a small surplus of grain to others. If the weather was bad, they risked periods of hunger and had to forage for other food.

One day, Nurishtar had an idea: If he could attach the spike to one of the cows they raised, the cow could pull the spike through the hard soil. He designed a tool he called an ard. He attached the spike to a frame that was harnessed to the cow. The cow dragged the ard through the soil, creating furrows in which to plant seeds. Nurishtar or one of his brothers put their weight on the frame to sink the spike into the ground. It took a long time to determine the right way to use the new tool and to train the cow to pull the ard.

By using this **innovation**—the ard, pulled by the cow—Nurishtar and his brothers could work their plot of land in far less time and increase their **productivity**. Because they saved so much time, some of the brothers could spend their time making a new harness for the cow or building an irrigation ditch to bring more water to their land. When they had more water, they could plow a larger plot of land and grow more grain to make more bappir. They increased their **production** of grain and bappir.

With some of the brothers free to work on other jobs, they built better homes and more tools. With a more abundant and sure food supply, they could have more children and enjoyed better health. Their **standard of living** improved, and they made a major contribution to the **Neolithic Agricultural Revolution.**

ACTIVITY 3.3, CONTINUED
Nurishtar Invents the Ard – Assessment

Fill in the blanks with the correct economic term (bolded in the reading).

1. When Nurishtar and his brothers were able to plow their land in a shorter period of time, they improved their _____.

2. The ard was a/an _____ that made farming easier.

3. When Nurishtar's family could consume more food and build better homes, they improved their _____.

4. Because Nurishtar could work more land with the ard, he was able to increase his _____ of grain.

5. The invention of the ard was an important part of the

   _____.

SHORT-ANSWER QUESTION

What resulted when ancient farmers like Nurishtar created new tools, such as the ard, and used new systems of farming?

_____

_____

_____

_____

_____

_____

ACTIVITY 3.3, KEY
Nurishtar Invents the Ard – Assessment

Fill in the blanks with the correct economic terms.

1. When Nurishtar and his brothers were able to plow their land in a shorter period of time, they improved their ____*productivity*____.

2. The ard was a/an ____*innovation*____ that made farming easier.

3. When Nurishtar's family could consume more food and build better homes, they improved their ____*standard of living*____.

4. Because Nurishtar could work more land with the ard, he was able to increase his ____*production*____ of grain.

5. The invention of the ard was an important part of the ____*Neolithic Agricultural Revolution*____.

SHORT-ANSWER QUESTION

What resulted when ancient farmers like Nurishtar created new tools, such as the ard, and used new systems of farming?

Sample Answer:

Using innovations such as the ard and irrigation increased the productivity

of farmers and enabled then to produce more food. When they were able to

produce more food, they were able to do other jobs and improve their lives.

The agricultural revolution increased food production and the world's

population grew.

SLIDE 3.1

Agricultural Innovation and World Population – 10,000 to 500 B.C.E.

Population	Year	Agricultural Innovation
1–5 million	10,000 B.C.E.	Neolithic Revolution begins in Southwest Asia and other areas. Climate change resulted in longer dry seasons and the end of a 100,000-year ice age. Abundance of wild grains enabled hunter-gatherers to settle in villages. Domestication of dogs begins in Asia and North America.
	9500 B.C.E.	The "founder crops" of agriculture appear: Wheat, barley, peas, lentils, bitter vetch, chick peas, and flax.

SLIDE 3.2

Agricultural Innovation and World Population – 10,000 to 500 B.C.E.

Population	Year	Agricultural Innovation
8–10 million	8000 – 6000 B.C.E.	Nomadic hunter-gatherers begin to grow food and domesticate animals: Rice in China, 7500 B.C.E. Squash in Mexico, 7000 B.C.E. Wheat in Mesopotamia, 8500 B.C.E. Cattle in SW Asia and India, 7000 B.C.E. Domestication of sheep, goats, and pigs begins in SW Asia. Irrigation systems introduced.
	7000 – 6000 B.C.E.	Domestication of cattle begins in SW Asia, Pakistan, and India.

SLIDE 3.3

Agricultural Innovation and World Population – 10,000 to 500 B.C.E.

Population	Year	Agricultural Innovation
8–10 million	6000 – 3000 B.C.E.	A wooden plow, the "ard," used in Mesopotamia and Egypt. Permanent villages established in the Fertile Crescent. Farming on the banks of the Nile River.
	5000 – 3000 B.C.E.	Domestication begins of horses in Ukraine, donkeys in Egypt, and water buffalo in China. Corn (maize) production in Mexico.

SLIDE 3.4

Agricultural Innovation and World Population – 10,000 to 500 B.C.E.

Population	Year	Agricultural Innovation
14–20 million	3000 B.C.E.	Irrigation systems and dams built on the Nile River. Crop production increases trade and spread of agriculture. Potatoes domesticated in Peru.
	2000 B.C.E.	Iron plow developed in China.
50 million	1000 B.C.E.	Manure used as fertilizer. Iron plows widely used in China and SW Asia.
100 million	500 B.C.E.	"Mouldboard" plow with a V-shaped iron cutting wedge developed in China.

SLIDE 3.5

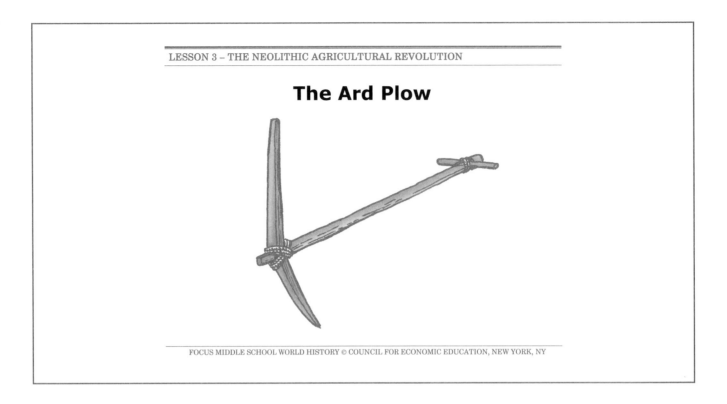

SLIDE 3.6

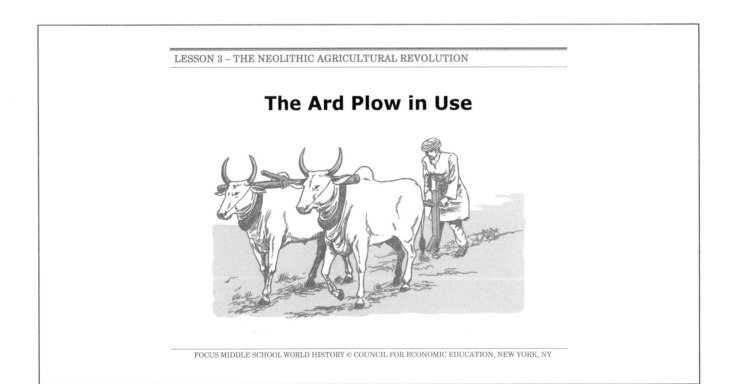

SLIDE 3.7

World Population Growth

Years Elapsed	Year	World Population
---	10,000 B.C.E.	5–10 Million
10,000	1 C.E.[1]	170 Million
1,800	1800[2]	1 Billion
130	1930	2 Billion
30	1960	3 Billion
15	1975	4 Billion
12	1987	5 Billion
12	1999	6 Billion
13	2012	7 Billion*
13	2025	8 Billion*

Source: U.S. Census Bureau, International Data Base
[1] Neolithic Revolution
[2] Industrial Revolution

SLIDE 3.8

The Fertile Crescent

LESSON 4

GREAT CIVILIZATIONS DEVELOP AROUND RIVERS

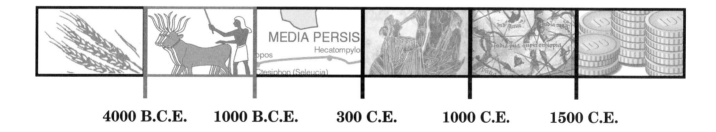

4000 B.C.E.   1000 B.C.E.   300 C.E.   1000 C.E.   1500 C.E.

LESSON 4
GREAT CIVILIZATIONS DEVELOP AROUND RIVERS

LESSON DESCRIPTION

This lesson illustrates how rivers such as the Tigris, Euphrates, Nile and Indus rivers increased the flow of resources, goods, services and ideas in the great civilizations from 4000 to 1000 B.C.E. In this lesson, students assume the role of producers in a three-round production simulation. They must produce (draw with markers or crayons) three distinct items—a hoe, a staff and a spear—in order to feed themselves and their families. In Round One, they are self-sufficient and must complete all of their work without access to other markets. In Round Two, they divide the responsibilities of production based on specialized skills. Trade is now permitted, but geographic barriers to trade obstruct it. In Round Three, the barriers are removed to represent the greater connectivity of markets made possible by rivers. Students experience how the improved flow results in surplus production and specialization, which brought many benefits to all those involved in voluntary trade.

INTRODUCTION

During the period of recorded human development from 4000 to 1000 B.C.E, great civilizations emerged around rivers, especially the Tigris, Euphrates, Nile, and Indus. People concentrated and settled on the rich lands near these waters. The rivers and the settlements around them lowered the costs of transportation and expedited the flow of goods, services and resources. Relatively easy access to markets and fertile land broadened opportunities for specialization and growth in production and trade in Mesopotamia, Egypt and the Indus Valley.

Mesopotamian (Tigris and Euphrates river systems), Egyptian (Nile river system), and Indus (Indus Valley river system) civilizations gave people viable alternatives to nomadic or self-sufficient lives and contributed to economic growth. Much of the growth arose from expanded trade and other commercial activity that took place along the great rivers. These rivers helped reduce the cost of exchange, which in turn released scarce resources for other uses. People moved resources, goods, services and ideas to those who valued them most. Some trade occurred locally, and some exchange of goods occurred among civilizations because of the rivers. As trade expanded, populations grew, urbanization proceeded and innovation occurred. Specialization and trade make it possible for societies to build wealth and prosper, especially around river settlements.

CONCEPTS

Scarcity

Productive resources

Human resources

Capital resources

Natural resources

Specialization

Surplus

Trade

OBJECTIVES

Students will be able to:

- Identify the three key resources used to produce goods and services during the historical period of study from 4000 to 1000 B.C.E.

- Measure total production.

- Show that the costs of moving resources, goods, services and ideas can be reduced (are less) along rivers and through the use of other modes of transportation, releasing resources to produce more goods and services.

- Show that when individuals, regions and nations can trade with relatively low transportation costs, both production and consumption may increase for the people involved.

CONTENT STANDARDS

Voluntary National Content Standards, 2nd edition

- **Standard 6:** When individuals, regions and nations specialize in what they can produce at the lowest cost and then trade with others, both production and consumption increase.

World History Content Standards

Era 2. Early Civilizations and the Emergence of Pastoral Peoples, 4000–1000 B.C.E.

- **Standard 1:** The major characteristics of civilization and how civilizations emerged in Mesopotamia, Egypt and the Indus Valley.

- **Standard 3:** The political, social and cultural consequences of population movements and militarization in Eurasia in the second millennium B.C.E.

TIME REQUIRED

75 minutes. Procedures 1–11, 30 minutes on the first day. Procedure 12 to the end of the lesson on the second day, 45 minutes.

MATERIALS

- 9 large pieces of paper 11" × 13" or equivalent

- 9 markers or crayons—three each of red, blue and green

- Black marker

- Slides 4.1–4.6

- Activity 4.1, three copies

PROCEDURE

1. Prepare students for the "Not-So-Great to Great Civilization" activity. Ask students to imagine going back in time. Invite them to picture how the people living in 4000 to 1000 B.C.E in Mesopotamia, Egypt and the Indus

Valley produced food for their families. Ask for a couple of students to describe what they imagine.

(Accept a variety of historically accurate responses—i.e., no dinosaurs.)

2. Show Slide 4.1. Explain that everyone in the world confronts **scarcity**. Explain that just like today, the people of this historical era made choices. Limited productive resources could not provide everything they wanted. Some self-sufficient families and individuals chose to produce everything themselves without relying on others. Others traded specialized goods they made for goods and services that they needed or wanted but did not make.

3. Show Slide 4.2. Define the three key productive resources used to produce goods and services. **Natural resources** are "gifts of nature." Examples include rivers, land, and mineral deposits. **Human resources** refer to human effort. **Capital resources** are goods made and used to produce other goods and services. Examples of capital resources include buildings, machinery, tools and equipment. Explain that, in this historical period, farming grain was common. Grain was used to make bread and other products. Discuss how productive resources allow society to produce goods like food.

4. Ask students to think about a self-sufficient family, which is a family that produces everything it needs to survive: food, clothing, shelter, etc. Ask them to discuss the challenges of producing everything without relying on people outside the family circle.

(Accept a variety of responses, but most students will suggest that people have difficulty producing everything by themselves.)

5. Ask the students to think about a family that specializes in producing one thing well and trades its **surplus**—extra beyond what is needed to survive—for

other items. Ask them to discuss the challenges of specializing and **trading** with others.

(Accept a variety of responses, but students may suggest that relying on trading for goods means you are dependent on others.)

6. Ask students to describe the pros and cons of self-sufficiency versus trading specialized goods with others.

(Accept a variety of responses.)

7. Refer to Slide 4.2. Provide an overview of how resources are used to produce things that people need or want such as food, clothing, shelter and other goods and services.

8. Ask for volunteers to identify each of the three key resources in the image in Slide 4.2. Have them describe how—in the context of an Egyptian farming family—each resource is used to produce wheat.

(The image shows human resources (the workers harvesting wheat), capital resources (their tools) and natural resources (the land and the sunlight).)

9. Show Slide 4.3. Explain the concept of **specialization** to students: Specialization is when individuals choose work based on their relative talents. Provide examples of specialization in this historical period, such as a potter producing pottery or a baker making bread. Note that each person did so because they believed they could do so at a relatively lower cost than others.

10. Show Slide 4.4. Tell students that specialization increases productivity by each person. This increase in productivity makes it possible for specialized workers to produce surplus goods for trade. Ask students how the potter and baker help each other produce surpluses for trade.

(Because they can trade, they can specialize, which increases productivity and leads to surplus.)

11. Show Slide 4.5. Discuss with the students other ways to increase productivity. Human capital is a term used to describe the education and skills training of workers.

12. **Class period two:** In preparation for the production activity, do the following:

- Gather 9 large pieces of 11" × 13" paper or their equivalent.

- Find 9 thick markers or crayons—three each of green, blue and red.

- Draw one big circle on each of the 9 pieces of paper with the one black marker. Separate the papers into 3 sets of 3 posters.

- Write in black marker one of the following titles on each poster in each set: A. Farming, B. Herding, and C. Hunting.

- Using Slide 4.6 as a guide, draw a miniature graphic to the right of each title. Use the appropriate marker to:

  ◆ Draw a **green** hoe (as shown in the slide) to the right of the farming label.

  ◆ Draw a **blue** staff (as shown in the slide) to the right of the herding label.

  ◆ Draw a **red** spear (as shown in the slide) to the right of the hunting label.

- Tape each set of circles (A. Farming, B. Herding, and C. Hunting) on the walls in three areas of the classroom, as distant from one another as possible.

- Important: Place barriers or obstacles, such as students' desks and chairs, in the classroom to make moving from one set of circles to the next difficult for students. This will simulate a trading environment hindered by geographical obstacles similar to hills or valleys or tough terrain to cross when traveling. So, you may want to place student desks, chairs and other large items in the paths going from one set to another set of posters. (Alternatively, once students are seated at the start of the class period, you could ask students to arrange their desks to obstruct the flow of people moving from one set of posters to another.)

13. After setting up the classroom, ask students to imagine going back in time again. Ask them to assume the roles of family members dependent on the head of their family for production and trade in the Great Civilizations of Mesopotamia, Egypt and the Indus Valley.

14. Divide the class into three groups. Consider each group a family and ask for each family to choose its head. After they have chosen, tell the students that the family head is personally responsible for producing barley by using the hoe, wheat by using the herding staff (the family uses animals to help with the farm work) and meat by using the spear.

15. Tell the students that one unit each of barley, wheat and meat are required to feed the family throughout a year. Any surplus (more than one unit in each category) can be traded.

16. Explain that each family head is responsible for sharing the fruits of his or her labor with the members of the family. If the family head does not produce enough, family members suffer. If the family head produces beyond what is required to sustain the family, family members can acquire luxury goods and services by trading surplus grains and meat.

17. Give each family head three colored markers. Tell them that they can only have one marker in their hands at a time. (They may keep the other markers where they can conveniently grab a different color.)

18. Show Slide 4.6. Explain that in the "Not-So-Great Civilization," each family head produces a good by drawing a picture of a tool needed to produce a certain good. The picture of the tool needs

to be drawn in the correct color. The family head will need a **green** hoe for farming barley, a **blue** staff for raising animals that help produce wheat, and a **red** spear for hunting. These pieces of capital are used to farm grains and meat. Show the family heads the examples you have drawn above the circles.

19. Tell the family heads that each item must be produced and production order does not matter. Family heads may **not** specialize by producing all the hoes, then all the staffs, and then all the spears. Tell them this ensures that families get one of each item, which is needed for survival. If time permits, they can start the drawing process again. Emphasize that quality *does* matter. Family heads are producing for their families, and poorly drawn items will be not count.

20. Ask the heads of the families to prepare to "feed" their families for a year. Ask them to pick up a marker and prepare to start production when they hear 1-1000. Ask the rest of the students to help mark a year. Announce that a year is defined by the class clapping and counting from 1 to 20 using the 1-1000, 2-1000, 3-1000 method of counting. The year will end at 20-1000.

21. **Conduct Round 1** when everyone is ready to begin. Start by clapping and saying 1-1000. Signal to students that they should join in at 2-1000. After reaching 20-1000, stop.

22. At the end of Round 1 (the year), ask each family head to count how many units of hoes, staffs and spears can be used to produce equal units of barley, wheat and meat for family consumption. Review the drawings and throw out items of poor quality, those that are incorrectly colored, and those that are otherwise "inconsumable." Be picky in this first round.

23. Distribute a copy of Activity 4.1 to the family heads. Ask each family to determine the total output in each

production area (one hoe is equivalent to one unit of barley, one staff is equivalent to one unit of wheat, and one spear is equivalent to one unit of meat).

24. Now ask students the following questions:

    a. Is there a reason for these families to trade?

    (No, not really. Each family is self-sufficient and producing a little bit of everything.)

    b. How do you think that the families could help each other by reorganizing the way they do things?

    (The students should suggest specialization.)

    c. Would the output of staffs, spears and hoes increase if the same person produced the same thing over and over again?

    (Yes, it should.)

    d. Who do you think should specialize in the drawing of the staff, spear and hoe?

    (Typically some students will possess drawing talent. Guide students into assigning production responsibilities based on ability to draw. At this point in the exercise, students will not be thinking about the obstacles to trade that you created earlier. Focus their attention on highlighting the benefits of specialization of the item he or she produces best.)

25. Ask students to choose which family head is the best candidate for specializing in producing **one** of the three items. Assign the responsibility of producing that item to the "specialized" family head. Make sure that each family head has one unique, specialized item to produce for all families.

26. In preparation for Round 2, instruct each family head to take the correct colored marker and move to the poster of the family to their right. Tell the family

heads that they will produce their specialized item for each of the three families. The family heads will need to move quickly from each production site in order to produce what is needed for their families plus what other families need.

27. Be clear that these specialized producers will produce (draw) only their product. *Because they are specialists, they may produce more than one item in one location before moving to the next location.*

28. Remind family heads that, by the end of the round, each family head should have tried to produce more than in the self-sufficiency round. Tell the students that this voluntary cross-family arrangement should benefit everyone.

29. **Conduct Round 2.** Again, lead the class by clapping and counting to 20-1000. In this round, students should have fun moving through the obstacles set before them, especially if the obstacles were forgotten. Encourage the family head to speed up production, challenge them to move through the obstacles and remind them of their responsibility to produce for all families.

30. At the end of Round 2, record and note the differences in output between rounds. (The students should count only the marks made in Round 2. You may want to have students separate the marks from the first and second rounds) Debrief the round:

    a. Ask the students if their family's output increased, decreased or stayed the same.

    (Answers and results will vary.)

    b. Ask students to raise their hands if they thought production would increase as a result of specialization.

    (Most students should.)

    c. Ask the students to explain their results.

    (The students should realize that total output may increase, decrease

or not change depending on the types of barriers created and the speed of the specialists. While specialization should increase output, the obstacles may have prevented this from happening.)

d. Ask the students to think about the obstacles in remote areas that separate them from other areas. Ask them to speculate why people in remote areas may tend not to specialize.

(Living in remote areas reduces people's ability to trade with others, forcing residents of such areas to produce everything themselves.)

31. Tell students they will have one more round to increase production. Ask them how they might be able to increase production.

(Students will want to remove the barriers for the next round.)

32. Allow the students to rearrange the desks. The new arrangement should allow the family heads to move quickly from production circle to circle. Compliment the students on their ingenuity. Be sure to call the new paths "rivers."

33. **Conduct Round 3.** Again, lead the class in clapping and counting to 20-1000. At the end of Round 3, total output should have increased significantly over output in Round 2. Further discuss the benefits of using specialized skills and easy transportation outlets to boost production, increase productivity and create possible surpluses to trade.

34. Ask students to summarize the benefits of living near a river or having access to one by another means of transportation.

(Rivers provide water, food, transportation and excellent soil for growing food. They increase the productivity of workers; expand trading possibilities; and

improve the flow of resources, skills, talents, goods, services and ideas between communities.)

35. Ask students to explain—in economic terms—why families and other groups moved to the lands along rivers.

(The fertile land and the river offered new production and consumption opportunities and lower transportation costs, which outweighed the benefits of staying put.)

CLOSURE

36. To close, ask students to summarize the economic value of a river in a society. Have them describe why a river may be beneficial to society and helpful in connecting people once self-sufficient in all that they produced.

(Students will quickly point out that when there are no rivers or other viable modes of transportation, the likelihood of a family or group of people being self-sufficient in production is high. So surpluses for trade will likely be small, if there are any at all. By contrast, a river that allows the flow of resources, specialized skills, goods, services and ideas will encourage each family or group to build surpluses and trade a wide variety of goods.)

ASSESSMENT

Multiple Choice

1. Which of the following benefits is commonly associated with specialization?

    a. Overall labor productivity decreases and the quality of work falls.

    b. Work becomes very difficult for the specialized workers.

    c. **Output increases and the overall quality of work may improve.**

    d. The total output produced by all workers decreases.

2. What is an example of increased productivity or output per worker?

a. **In Mesopotamia, irrigation boosts the amount produced by each worker.**

b. A nomad spends longer hours working and gets less from his herds.

c. An Egyptian artisan hires another person and the amount of pots they create drops.

d. A farmer's land is flooded and fewer crops are harvested.

Constructed Response

1. In many ways, the Internet is like a river. It increases the flow of information and helps connect people living in different parts of the world. Explain how the Internet, like the rivers of the Great Civilizations, has helped increase the value of specialization and trade in today's society.

   (Like a river, the Internet may decrease the cost of exchange and improve the flow of resources, goods, services and ideas. Both can increase specialization and trade.)

CONNECTIONS: TRADING, RIVERS AND OTHER THINGS THAT MATTER

1. During the period of the Great Civilizations, people who lived along the Nile River used it for agriculture and transportation. That hasn't changed. Ask students to research and compare how the methods of agriculture and transportation have changed over time along the Nile. Identify what the methods have in common in terms of helping the people specialize and trade while living along the Nile.

2. The world's longest river is the Nile. It is 4,160 miles long. The U.S. has the world's fourth-longest river at 3,870 miles—the Mississippi River, a river system that includes the Missouri River flowing in from the Rocky Mountains. Ask students to research methods of agriculture and transportation along the Mississippi-Missouri River network. Explain how these rivers help reduce transportation costs and increase people's ability to exchange their specialized goods in markets in the U.S. and around the world. Pay special attention to the amount of goods exported from and imported to the U.S. through the mouth of the Mississippi in the Gulf of Mexico.

3. Ask students to research other ways that Mesopotamia, Egypt and the Indus Valley increased per-person and total output through improved processes, techniques or machines. In economics, this is called technological innovation. Some methods of improving output included the use of canals and irrigation systems in Mesopotamia and drainage and irrigation systems that boosted production on land between the Tigris and Euphrates rivers.

ACTIVITY 4.1

Family Output Recording Sheet

Family _____

	Total Output (Number of Units Produced Each Year)		
	Hoe – Barley	Staff – Wheat	Spear – Meat
Round 1: Self-Sufficient			
Round 2: Specialization			
Round 3: Specialization with Rivers			

SLIDE 4.1

Key Concepts

- **Productive resources** include natural resources, human resources and capital. These resources are used to produce goods and services like food, clothing and shelter.

- All productive resources are **scarce**. Therefore, producers must choose which resources will produce the highest amount of goods and services given the costs.

SLIDE 4.2

Three Key Productive Resources

Natural Resources
"Gifts of nature" used to produce goods and services; for example, fields of land, water, minerals, and forests.

Human Resources
The human effort available to produce goods and services.

Capital Resources
Goods made and used to produce other goods and services. Examples include buildings, machinery, tools, and equipment.

Key Concepts

- **Specialization** involves a situation in which people produce a narrower range of goods and services than they consume. Specialization increases productivity; it also requires trade and increases interdependence.

Key Concepts

- **Productivity** is the amount of a good or service that can be produced with a given amount of natural resources, human resources, and capital resources. It is measured by taking total output and dividing it by the number of productive units used (typically the amount of labor).

Ways to Increase Productivity

- In addition to specialization, productivity can be increased through:
  - o Improved technology (new tools, irrigation)
  - o More capital or human capital (education and skills training)
  - o Innovation (new idea on how to reorganize the way labor is used)
  - o Discovery of better resources (new minerals are discovered)

Capital Increases Agricultural Output

Wooden Hoe Used to prepare the earth for the planting of seeds or to weed.	
Herding Staff Used to guide animals helping with farm work.	
Hunting Spear Helped in harvesting the animal used to feed individuals.	

LESSON 5

ENTREPRENEURS IN MESOPOTAMIA

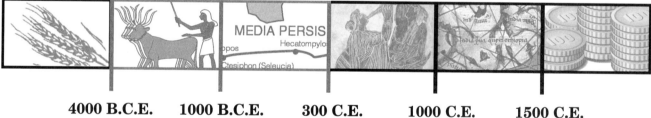

4000 B.C.E.   1000 B.C.E.   300 C.E.   1000 C.E.   1500 C.E.

LESSON 5
ENTREPRENEURS IN MESOPOTAMIA

LESSON DESCRIPTION

In this lesson, students read a one-page description of entrepreneurship in the Neo-Babylonian Empire (626 to 539 B.C.E.). They learn about entrepreneurship and the profit motive for entrepreneurs. The students, working in groups, participate in an entrepreneurial production activity in which they design, produce, and sell textiles as Babylonian entrepreneurs. After selling their textiles, the groups calculate their profits or losses.

INTRODUCTION

America's leading entrepreneurs, like Bill Gates (Microsoft), Mark Zuckerberg (Facebook), and Steve Jobs (Apple), are constantly in the news. They have joined a host of entrepreneurs such as Cornelius Vanderbilt, John Rockefeller, Andrew Carnegie, and Henry Ford, who transformed American life. We might think that entrepreneurship is modern and American, but it is ancient and global.

For almost a century, from 626 to 539 B.C.E., the Neo-Babylonian Empire thrived in Mesopotamia. Its capital was Babylon, a city on the Euphrates River near present-day Baghdad, Iraq. The powerful Neo-Babylonian Empire controlled large parts of the Near East. One of the famous Babylonian rulers during this period was Nebuchadnezzar, who carried out extensive projects to improve and expand the city of Babylon and extend an irrigation system throughout his realm. In 538 B.C.E., Cyrus the Great of Persia conquered Babylon. During the rule of Nebuchadnezzar and Cyrus, important entrepreneurial families, such as the Egibi and Nur-Sin families, helped ancient Babylonian society become wealthy as its population grew. During the Neo-Babylonian Empire and in the early years of Persian rule, Babylonian entrepreneurship developed, beginning in the temples, which were important religious and economic centers. The temples owned considerable land, but often lacked enough workers and draft animals to work the land. Eventually, the temples rented some of their land to farmers, who worked the land in exchange for paying a fixed amount of goods, cash, or both to the temple. These entrepreneurial rent farmers usually took on considerable personal risk by investing in equipment needed to farm the land they rented from the temples or wealthy families.

Entrepreneurship also developed in other areas of the Babylonian economy. In the sixth century B.C.E., entrepreneurs began to play an essential role in bringing agricultural products and other goods from the rural areas in the Babylonian empire to the cities. These entrepreneurs, who specialized in transport and marketing, were essential in bringing much-needed commodities to the cities in exchange for the money needed by rural people to pay taxes, rent, and irrigation fees and to buy the goods and services that they couldn't produce locally—thus improving their standard of living. Other entrepreneurs produced and sold food products and textiles.

In Babylonian society, entrepreneurs were well respected members of the community. Just as in the modern age, it was possible in ancient Babylon to rise from humble beginnings to a position of influence in the community by becoming an entrepreneur. Entrepreneurs were risk-takers, some of whom became very successful, others of whom faced economic ruin when their businesses failed. Entrepreneurial activity in the Neo-Babylonian Empire and beyond brought about new ways of doing things. Those new ways of doing things resulted in significant improvement in people's standard of living.

CONCEPTS

Entrepreneur

Entrepreneurship

Profit

OBJECTIVES

Students will be able to:

- Define entrepreneurs.

- Explain that entrepreneurs compare the expected benefits of entering a new enterprise with the expected costs.

- Identify whether an entrepreneur is earning a profit or suffering a loss, given simple production cost and selling price data.

- Explain that entrepreneurs earn profits when the price they sell their product for exceeds the costs of producing that product.

CONTENT STANDARDS

Voluntary National Content Standards in Economics, 2nd edition

- **Standard 14:** Entrepreneurs take on the calculated risk of starting new businesses, either by embarking on new ventures similar to existing ones or by introducing new innovations. Entrepreneurial innovation is an important source of economic growth.

World History Content Standards

Era 2: Early Civilizations and the Emergence of Pastoral Peoples, 4000–1000 B.C.E.

- **Standard 1:** The major characteristics of civilization and how civilizations emerged in Mesopotamia, Egypt, and the Indus valley.

Era 3: Classical Traditions, Major Religions, and Giant Empires, 1000 B.C.E–300 C.E.

- **Standard 1:** Innovation and change from 1000–600 B.C.E.: horses, ships, iron, and monotheistic faith.

TIME REQUIRED

60–75 minutes

MATERIALS

- Slide 5.1

- One copy of Activity 5.1 for each student and one for the teacher

- Seven copies of Activity 5.2

- One copy of Activity 5.3, cut apart

- Seven copies of Activity 5.4

- Six sheets of white construction paper

- Six sets of markers

- Six glue sticks

- Six rulers

- Six pairs of scissors

- Sufficient stickers, buttons, and yarn for students to decorate their textile design samples

PROCEDURE

1. Introduce the lesson by asking the following questions:

   a. Do you know anyone who ever started or owned his or her own business?

   (Answers will vary.)

   b. Why do you think that person started his or her own business?

   (Answers will vary, but the students are likely to say to earn a profit, because they wanted to work for themselves, because they had an idea for a great new product that they thought would be useful or helpful to people, etc.)

   c. When do you think that people first began opening their own businesses?

   (Answers will vary.)

2. Explain to students that people have been starting their own businesses for thousands of years, but in this lesson they are going to learn about a specific period when people started creating their own businesses in ancient Mesopotamia.

3. Distribute one copy of Activity 5.1, *Entrepreneurship in Ancient Mesopotamia,* to each student. Have the students read the activity.

4. After the students have finished the reading, discuss the following questions:

   a. What is an **entrepreneur**?

   (An entrepreneur starts businesses, assuming the risk of organizing productive resources to produce goods and services.)

   b. Who are some successful entrepreneurs in the modern world?

   (Answers will vary, but the students will likely name famous entrepreneurs like Henry Ford, Levi Strauss, Bill Gates, etc.)

   c. Why did **entrepreneurship** develop in Babylon's temples?

   (The temples had a lot of land and didn't have enough people to work the land.)

   d. What risks did rent farmers take on when they chose to become entrepreneurs?

   (They had to invest some of their own money to purchase equipment to farm the land they rented. If crops failed, they might not have enough money to pay rent to the temple for the land and cover the costs of the equipment they had to purchase to farm that land.)

   e. Why did rent farmers choose to rent the land from the temples despite the risks?

   (They expected to make money.)

   f. What did other entrepreneurs in Babylon do?

   (Some entrepreneurs in Babylon specialized in transportation and marketing, serving an essential role in the Babylonian economy by facilitating trade between rural and urban areas. Other entrepreneurs produced and sold food products and textiles.)

   g. What was the social position of entrepreneurs in Babylon?

   (They were respected members of the community.)

5. Discuss the following points with the students:

   • Just as in ancient Babylon, **entrepreneurs** today are individuals willing to take risks, develop new products, and start new businesses. They recognize opportunities, like working for themselves, and accept challenges.

   • Entrepreneurs often are innovative. They attempt to solve problems by developing and marketing new or improved products or ways of doing things. In ancient Babylon, entrepreneurs developed new ways of trading, farming, and producing goods and services. These developments improved the lives of people who lived in Babylon and beyond.

   • Entrepreneurs compare the expected benefits of beginning a new enterprise with its expected costs. If an entrepreneur believes the benefits of starting a new business will exceed the costs, she or he is likely to decide to start the business. But, if the individual expects that the benefits won't exceed the costs, she or he is likely to decide not to start or expand the business.

   • Starting a new business involves significant risks for entrepreneurs. Entrepreneurs will accept the risks if they believe they will make a profit. **Profit** is the income entrepreneurs receive in exchange for their skills and risk-taking. Profit is calculated by subtracting a business's total costs from its total revenues. In other words, profit is what is left of a business's income after all its costs of production have been paid.

   • Entrepreneurs and other sellers earn profits when buyers purchase the product they sell at prices high enough to cover the costs of production. Entrepreneurs and other sellers incur losses when buyers do not purchase the products they sell at prices high enough to cover costs of production.

6. Explain to the students that they are going to work in groups on an activity

that will help them to learn more about entrepreneurship. Divide the class into six groups.

7. Remind students that some entrepreneurs in ancient Babylon engaged in the production and sale of textiles. Explain that each group of students will represent a textile production business. Each group will create a textile design and produce one sample unit of their textile design on a piece of paper that you will distribute to each group.

8. Show the students the various supplies and tools available for them to use in the production of their textile. Emphasize to the students that they should plan their textile design very carefully before beginning work on their textile sample.

9. Explain that they must account for each supply or tool that they use in producing their textile sample on their Textile Production Worksheet. Explain that a shekel is an ancient measure of weight for gold and silver.

10. Distribute one copy of Activity 5.2, *Textile Production Worksheet*, to each group. Read the worksheet to the students and ensure that the students understand the textile sample planning and production process as outline on the activity.

11. Ask the students the following questions:

    a. What is an entrepreneur's goal?

       (To earn a profit)

    b. What is the amount that each group expects to earn when it sells each unit of textile?

       (45 shekels)

    c. In order to earn an expected profit on each unit of textile sold, what is the amount below which each group must keep its costs of production per unit?

       (At or below 44 shekels)

12. Give the groups time to plan their textile design. As each group finishes discussing its design, distribute to it one piece of paper and the resources they need to complete their textile sample

(i.e., buttons, glue sticks, markers, rulers, scissors, stickers, and yarn). Give the groups time to complete their textile sample, complete the costs table, and answer questions 1–3 on Activity 5.2.

13. After all the groups have created their textile sample and completed Activity 5.2, have each group present their textile sample and their calculation of the total cost to produce each unit to the rest of the class.

14. Tell students to assume that each group went on to produce multiple textile units and to sell them in markets across the Babylonian empire. Each unit was produced for exactly the amount that each group calculated. Emphasize to students that in reality, the price a good sells for is not determined by chance but by factors such as how much consumers want the good and how many units of the good producers are willing and able to sell at different prices. However, in this activity, each group will draw a Textile Price Card to determine the price of their textile.

15. Shuffle the cards created from Activity 5.3, *Textile Price Cards*, and have a representative from each group draw a card from the deck. Explain to the students that the price on their group's card is the price that they sold each unit of the textile for in the markets in Babylonia.

16. Distribute one copy of Activity 5.4, *Textile Profit Worksheet*, to each group. Ask the groups to calculate per-unit profit or loss by completing the worksheet.

17. Ask each group to tell you its per-unit cost of production, selling price, and profit or loss. Record them in the appropriate columns on the form on Slide 5.1, *Profits and Losses by Group*. Complete the last column by entering "Profit" if the group made a per-unit profit, "Loss" if the group suffered a loss, and "Broke Even" if the group neither earned a profit nor suffered a loss.

18. Ask the students the following questions:

a. How many groups earned a per-unit profit?

(Answers will vary.)

b. Why did those groups earn a per-unit profit?

(Buyers purchased the textiles they sold at prices higher than their costs of production.)

c. How many groups suffered a per-unit loss?

(Answers will vary.)

d. Why did some groups suffer a per-unit loss?

(Buyers did not purchase the textiles at prices high enough to cover production costs. Point out that these losses usually occurred because the groups expected to earn 45 shekels and sold each unit for less when they reached the market, as represented by the card they drew in Step 15.)

e. How many groups earned smaller profits than they expected?

(Answers will vary.)

f. Why did those groups earn smaller profits than they expected?

(They sold each textile unit for less than they had expected to sell it for.)

g. How many groups earned larger profits than they expected?

(Answers will vary.)

h. Why did those groups earn larger profits than they expected?

(They sold each textile unit for more than they expected to sell it for.)

i. Knowing what you know now about the final selling price, how would you have done things differently?

(Answers will vary, but some groups may say that they would have produced a textile with lower production costs.)

j. How often do you think that real entrepreneurs misjudge how much their product will sell for?

(Answers will vary.)

k. If entrepreneurs could see into the future, would they start business ventures even if they knew they would suffer a loss?

(Not likely)

CLOSURE

19. Review the important points taught in the lesson by discussing the following:

a. Who are entrepreneurs?

(Entrepreneurs are risk-takers who draw upon their skills and initiative to launch new businesses with the aim of making a profit.)

b. What two things would a smart entrepreneur be sure to compare when deciding whether to start a business?

(Expected costs and expected benefits from that business)

c. If the expected benefits of a business exceed the expected costs of that business, what is an entrepreneur likely to do?

(Start or invest in that business)

d. Why do entrepreneurs accept risks in organizing productive resources to produce goods and services?

(They expect to earn a profit.)

e. When do entrepreneurs earn profits?

(When buyers purchase their products or services at prices higher than the entrepreneurs' costs of production)

f. When do entrepreneurs suffer losses?

(When buyers purchase their products or services at prices lower than the entrepreneurs' costs of production)

g. What do we mean when we say that entrepreneurs are innovative?

(They attempt to solve problems by developing and marketing new or improved products and services.)

ASSESSMENT

Multiple Choice

1. Entrepreneurs

   a. are people who work for farmers and pick crops.

   b. **assume the risk of organizing productive resources to produce goods and services.**

   c. make profits by working for the government.

   d. describe rulers in Babylonia.

2. An entrepreneur is likely to start a new business when

   a. the government instructs her to do so.

   b. the number of workers she can hire exceeds the amount of work she has for them to do.

   c. **she expects to earn a profit.**

   d. the expected production cost for each unit her business will produce exceeds the expected price each unit will sell for.

Constructed Response

1. Assume that you are trying to decide whether to become a rent farmer in ancient Babylon. You expect that your annual costs of production will be as follows:

   Rent paid to landlord for land: 1,345 shekels of silver

   Wages paid to farm workers: 762 shekels of silver

   Costs of equipment: 239 shekels of silver

   Costs of seeds: 131 shekels of silver

   Costs for irrigation: 201 shekels of silver

   If you expect to earn 2,789 shekels of silver after planting, cultivating, harvesting, and selling grain as a rent farmer, will you choose to go ahead and become a rent farmer? Why or why not?

   (Yes, because you expect to earn a profit of 111 shekels of silver.)

   Assume that you become a rent farmer. If after harvesting and selling the grain from your rented land, you have earned 3,015 shekels of silver, have you earned a profit or suffered a loss? How big is that profit or loss?

   (Profit of 337 shekels of silver)

CONNECTIONS: ENTREPRENEURSHIP THROUGH U.S. HISTORY

Throughout history, entrepreneurs have taken risks to start businesses and, by doing so, have helped to fuel economic activity in countries the world over. In the United States, entrepreneurs such as Henry Ford, Bill Gates, Steve Jobs, and Ray Kroc started businesses that developed into huge, successful corporations. Countless other entrepreneurs—local barbers, restaurateurs, retailers, farmers, and contractors—have started small businesses that constitute the majority of commercial enterprises in the United States.

Suzanne Gallagher wrote a lesson for middle school, "U.S. History: Inventors & Entrepreneurs,"[1] that tells about important characteristics of U.S. entrepreneurs and inventors and how the two groups differ. In the lesson, students consider the invention of the electric light bulb, the airplane, the telephone, and the lightning rod, and the achievements of entrepreneurs who brought soda, Eskimo Pies, and potato chips to market.

[1] Suzanne Gallagher. "U.S. History: Inventors & Entrepreneurs" (Council for Economic Education) http://www.econedlink.org/lessons/index.php?lid=62&type=educator

ACTIVITY 5.1

Entrepreneurship in Ancient Mesopotamia

For almost a century, from 626 to 539 B.C.E., the Neo-Babylonian Empire thrived in Mesopotamia. Its capital was Babylon, a city on the Euphrates River near present-day Baghdad, Iraq. The Neo-Babylonian Empire was very powerful and controlled large parts of the Near East. Nebuchadnezzar was a famous Babylonian ruler during this period. He carried out extensive projects to improve and expand Babylon. For example, he worked on improving irrigation throughout his realm.

Entrepreneurs assume the risk of organizing productive resources to produce goods and services, drawing upon their skills and initiative to launch new businesses with the aim of making a profit. Entrepreneurs are risk-takers. Entrepreneurs have been around for thousands of years. Throughout the Neo-Babylonian Empire and the early years of Persian rule over Babylon, entrepreneurship thrived in the Babylonian economy. Ancient entrepreneurs invented businesses such as banking, renting, contracting, and investing.

Babylon needed entrepreneurs to survive, because it had few natural resources. Almost all building materials had to be imported. The soil in Babylon was good for crops, but the area lacked adequate rainfall. Babylonian farmers depended on irrigation canals to bring water from the Tigris and Euphrates Rivers to grow crops. The Babylonian kings were responsible for having the irrigation canals dug and maintained.

Entrepreneurship in Babylon began in the temples, which were important religious and economic centers. The priests were also entrepreneurs. That's because most temples owned a lot of land but lacked enough workers and draft animals to make the land productive. The temples rented some of their land to farmers, and the farmers worked the landed in exchange for a fixed payment in goods or cash. These farmers were entrepreneurs who usually took on considerable personal risk by investing in equipment needed to farm the land they rented.

Entrepreneurship developed elsewhere in the Babylonian economy. In the sixth century B.C.E., entrepreneurs carried agricultural products and other goods from rural areas into the cities. These entrepreneurs specialized in transport and marketing. They brought needed raw materials to the cities and paid money to rural people who needed it to pay for goods and services, taxes, rent, and irrigation fees. During this period in history, other entrepreneurs were engaged in producing and selling food products and textiles.

In Babylon, entrepreneurs were well-respected members of the community. Many entrepreneurs did not belong to rich and influential families—just as in the modern age, an entrepreneur in ancient Babylon could rise from humble beginnings to a position of influence in the community.

Also similar to today, entrepreneurs in Babylonian society took significant risks to set up businesses. Many entrepreneurs were very successful and made significant profits. Other entrepreneurs faced economic ruin when their business ventures failed. However, entrepreneurs in the Neo-Babylonian Empire discovered new ways of doing things that improved the lives of the people who lived in those times and beyond.

SOURCE

Wunsch, Cornelia. "Neo-Babylonian Entrepreneurs." In *The Invention of Enterprise: Entrepreneurship from Ancient Mesopotamia to Modern Times*, edited by David S. Landes, John Mokyr, and William J. Baumol, pp. 40–61. Princeton, NJ: Princeton University Press, 2010.

ACTIVITY 5.2

Textile Production Worksheet

Price you expect to sell your textiles for: 45 shekels of silver per textile unit

PLAN your design BEFORE you do anything with the paper or other resources!

You are entrepreneurs in ancient Babylonia! Your group will design a sample textile and decide how many of those textiles you are going to produce. Use the sheet of paper you are given and the materials listed in the following table. As entrepreneurs, you need to produce an enticing textile that people will want to buy. Pay attention to the costs involved in producing each textile unit and the price you expect to sell each unit for. Account for all materials and tools you use in producing your sample textile by completing the table below.

Resource	Cost	Number Used	Total Cost
Paper	5 shekels	1	5 shekels
Buttons	5 shekels per button		
Glue stick	5 shekels per textile		
Markers	3 shekels per color		
Ruler	4 shekels per textile		
Scissors	5 shekels per textile		
Stickers	1 shekel per sticker		
Workers (your group)	5 shekels per textile	1	5 shekels
Yarn	1 shekel per foot		
TOTAL COST OF EACH TEXTILE UNIT			

After you have accounted for all of the materials you used to make your textile sample, enter the total cost in the box at the bottom of your table.

Answer the following questions:

1. How much do you expect each unit of your textile will cost to produce? ____ shekels of silver

2. How much do you expect to sell each unit of your textile for? ____ shekels of silver

3. What do you expect your profit will be on each unit of your textile you sell? ____ shekels of silver

ACTIVITY 5.3

Textile Price Cards

35 shekels of silver	**47 shekels of silver**
45 shekels of silver	**33 shekels of silver**
50 shekels of silver	**37 shekels of silver**

Activity 5.4

Textile Profit Worksheet

Now that you have produced and sold your textile, answer the following questions:

From your Textile Production Worksheet:

1. How much did it cost to produce each unit of your textile? ____ shekels of silver

2. How much did you expect to sell each unit of textile for? ____ shekels of silver

3. What did you expect the profit for each unit sold to be? ____ shekels of silver

---

From the Textile Price Card you drew:

4. How much did each of the units of your textile that you produced sell for? ____ shekels of silver

---

Carry out calculations to answer these questions:

Subtract the costs of producing each unit of your textile (Question #1) from the amount that each textile unit actually sold for (Question #4) to get your profit or loss per unit of textile.

5. Did you earn a profit or suffer a loss on each unit of textile you produced? _____

6. How much was your profit or loss? _____ shekels of silver

SLIDE 5.1

Profits and Losses by Group

GROUP	Cost per Textile Unit	Selling Price per Textile Unit	Profit or Loss?	Amount of Profit or Loss per Textile Unit
Group 1				
Group 2				
Group 3				
Group 4				
Group 5				
Group 6				

FOCUS MIDDLE SCHOOL WORLD HISTORY © COUNCIL FOR ECONOMIC EDUCATION, NEW YORK, NY

LESSON 6

INDIA AND THE CASTE SYSTEM IN 200 B.C.E.

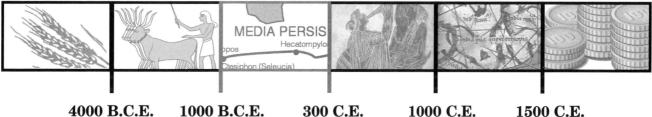

4000 B.C.E.   1000 B.C.E.   300 C.E.   1000 C.E.   1500 C.E.

LESSON 6
INDIA AND THE CASTE SYSTEM IN 200 B.C.E.

LESSON DESCRIPTION

Students examine the Indian culture and economy in the year 200 B.C.E., and explore the traditional institution of castes that defined people's lives and the Indian economy of that era. Students read about the caste system and how it organized the Indian society.

The students then compare the characteristics of the Indian economy in 200 B.C.E. to the general characteristics of market, command, and traditional economic systems in order to better understand the Indian economy. They answer the question, "What kind of economic system existed in India in 200 B.C.E.: a market economy, a command economy, a traditional economy, or a mixture of several kinds of economies?

INTRODUCTION

About 1500 B.C.E., Aryans (Indo-Europeans) from the north invaded the Indus Valley. The Aryans brought with them the beginnings of the caste system—a social order that divided people into groups with different statuses and legal rights. The caste system, because it determined people's occupations and economic relationships, also allocated resources, controlled markets, and distributed wealth.

The caste system was a strong social force in India in 200 B.C.E., and remains influential in India today. In 200 B.C.E., there were four primary castes or *varnas*.[1]

The ***Brahmins*** were the priests.

The ***Kshatriya*** were the relatively small group of rulers and warriors.

The ***Vaishyas*** were farmers, merchants, and traders—a large middle class group with many sub-castes.

The ***Shudras*** were typically servants and farm workers, including mixed-race people and those who had different religions.

An additional category of people, the ***Dalits*** (outcasts or untouchables) were not recognized as members of a caste. They were the lowest status group in the Indian society. Slavery did exist at times in some regions.

During this period in history, India enjoyed what may have been the highest standard of living in the world. India experienced rapid population growth—increasing its population density to one of the highest in the world.

Discrimination against the Dalits (outcasts) and most of the restrictions of the caste system were made illegal by the Indian Constitution in 1950. Despite this, the caste system remains a strong social and economic force in India today, especially in rural areas.[2]

Even the most developed market-oriented economies adhere to traditional customs and beliefs that may limit individual economic opportunities and markets. All market economies have some government powers that both protect and regulate markets. The vast majority of national economies are mixtures of the characteristics of market, command, and traditional economic systems.

Ancient India is a good example of a mixed economic system. The ancient Indian economy consists of active private markets, a strong government, and the traditional value system that has dominated Indian the culture and economy for centuries—the caste system.

CONCEPTS

Caste system

Command economy

Discrimination

Economic system

Market economy

---

[1]Keay, John. *India: A History*, New York: Grove Press, 2000. Pages 52–54.

[2]Appleby, Joyce. *The Relentless Revolution: A History of Capitalism*, New York: W.W. Norton & Co., 2010. Page 388.

Mixed economy

Mores/norms/customs

Traditional economy

OBJECTIVES

Students will be able to:

- Describe the characteristics of the caste system in India in about 200 B.C.E.

- Explain how the caste system affected markets in India in about 200 B.C.E.

- Explain how the characteristics of a traditional tribal economy, such as those found in India in 200 B.C.E. affect individual opportunities and a society.

CONTENT STANDARDS

Voluntary Content Standards in Economics, 2nd edition

- **Standard 3:** Different methods can be used to allocate goods and services. People acting individually or collectively must choose which methods to use to allocate different kinds of goods and services.

World History Content Standards

Era 3: Classical Traditions, Major Religions, and Giant Empires, 1000 B.C.E.–300 C.E.

- **Standard 3:** Major developments in East Asia and Southeast Asia in the era of the Tang dynasty, 600–900 C.E.

- **Standard 7:** Major global trends from 300–1000 C.E.

TIME REQUIRED

60 minutes

MATERIALS

- Slides 6.1–6.4

- Activity 6.1, one copy per student

- Activity 6.2, one copy per student

- Activity 6.3, one copy per student

PROCEDURE

1. **Optional Preparatory Activity**. To prepare the students for a discussion about castes, it may be helpful for them to briefly experience a caste-like system. One day prior to the lesson, divide the class into three groups. They can be divided arbitrarily or by some criteria such as clothing color or letter of first name. Explain that the three groups are castes.

   For the day (at school only) or just during the class period, the students should only associate with other members of their caste. In class, separate the castes and treat each group differently based on a hierarchy you create. Give more privileges to one caste than other castes. Assign specific responsibilities to each of the castes.

   After their experience living in a caste system, discuss their observations about caste systems. How did their behaviors change?

   (Answers will vary.)

   How did members of the higher and lower castes feel?

   (Higher castes members may have enjoyed their status; lower castes may not have.)

   How did the caste system affect the class as a whole?

   (Answers will vary.)

   How might such a system affect their lives over a longer period of time?

   (Answers will vary.)

2. Introduce the lesson by discussing situations in which social customs, norms, and mores affect personal economic decisions. For instance, ask students where their families buy groceries?

   (Answers will vary. There are many choices among grocery stores in most areas.)

   If needed, define customs, norms, and mores. **Mores** and **norms** are a society's virtues or values. Mores and norms are enforced by social pressures, but not strictly enforced or put into law. **Customs** are traditional ways of doing things.

3. Ask the students what their family would do if a new grocery store opened in their area?

   (Answers will vary. Some would continue shopping at the old stores and some would try the new store. They have choices.)

   Remind the students that in a market economy, the consumer chooses where to buy goods.

4. Ask the students the following questions.

   a. What is the occupation of your parents (or guardians or other relative)?

      (Answers will vary. They will name a variety of occupations.)

   b. Will you have the same profession as your parents?

      (Most will probably say no.)

   Remark to the students that they live in a market society where they have the opportunity to determine their careers.

5. Tell the students that in some societies, these decisions are made differently. In some societies, mores and customs determine these things. In some societies, these social "rules" can even determine your social status, whom you can associate with, and your occupation. In some cases, these rules allow discrimination against social, ethnic, religious, or other groups.

6. Ask the class to identify situations where individuals or groups discriminate in their economic choices, limiting their buying or selling to others in their group.

   (This discussion will normally bring out the word "discrimination." Examples may include racism, sexism, student cliques, "buy local" campaigns, or other

preferential treatment within or against ethnic, social, economic, or political groups.)

Keep the discussion at a nonpersonal level.

7. Define **discrimination** as prejudicial treatment of individuals based solely on their membership in a certain group or category. Discrimination can be positive behavior towards members of one's own group or negative behavior toward those of another group. It may include restricting members of one group from opportunities or relationships that are available to others.

   Note: "Discrimination" is such a loaded word in our society that use of it may immediately lead students to consider the caste system as a "bad" system, while for millennia its practitioners considered it a natural way of doing things.

8. Explain that the caste system, as it was historically practiced in India was a social, political, and economic structure that allowed and even required legal discrimination and separation among population groups. Define the **caste system** as a social structure, socially or legally enforced, that separates people on the basis of inherited social status. Within a caste system, people are expected to marry and interact only with people of the same social status.

9. Distribute copies of Activity 6.1. Have the students read about the history and structure of the Indian caste system. Students should keep their copies of Activity 6.1, as they will be used again later in the lesson. Show Slide 6.1, *India and the Caste System,* during the discussion to focus on the four major castes.

10. Ask the students to identify the main points of the reading.

    (Possible answers:

    • *The caste system defined social groups with different levels of power and wealth.*

- *There were four primary castes plus the Dalits (untouchables or outcasts).*

- *Interaction between castes was discouraged or not allowed.*

- *People's social and economic relationships were controlled by their caste.*

- *The caste system made discrimination legal in 200 B.C.E., and the impact of the historical caste system still exists in many ways.)*

11. Ask the following questions to bring out further the main points:

a. What was the caste system?

(The definition is found above.)

b. How did the caste system start?

(Around 1500 B.C.E.)

c. What were the primary groups in the caste system?

(The Kshatriyas were rulers and warriors. The Brahmans were the priests. The Vaishyas were small-business owners, commercial workers, and traders. The Shudras were the laborers.)

d. How did the caste system affect individuals?

(Answers will vary.)

e. Does the caste system exist today?

(Not officially or legally, although it influences many aspects of Indian life today, especially in rural areas.)

12. Explain that one important "rule" of the caste system was that individuals should interact primarily, if not solely, with others of their caste. If someone wanted to purchase food, it should be from someone of their caste or at the same caste level. Only those of a specified caste could do certain kinds of jobs. In some cases, only members of one family could provide a service to produce a good in a local area. Of course,

some contact among caste levels was necessary in daily commerce.

13. Ask the students what are possible results of caste-based limits on buying and selling?

(Students may suggest that there were fewer options for both buyers and sellers. This may limit competition and raise prices, or it may increase cooperation within a group and reduce prices. Generalize that any factor, such as a caste system or discrimination that limits producers or consumers, individuals or groups from free access to all markets will somehow limit growth in an economy.)

14. Explain that the caste system resulted from several factors, including religious beliefs (the *Vedas*), dominance by a powerful group, the Aryans[3], and an economically diverse population. This strong set of norms, mores, and customs that were enforced socially and legally created a unique economic system in India.

15. Ask the students if the caste system had any positive influences on the economy of the time.

(If the result was that everyone was clearer about their economic status and relationships, it had a stabilizing effect. Some economic historians argue that India's stability and relatively high standard of living at the time was due to the caste system and the lack of wide-spread opposition. The system was strongly enforced at the local level and provided benefits in those markets,

---

[3]The Aryans were a somewhat nomadic group from Central Asia who spoke an archaic Indo-European language, who were thought to have settled in prehistoric times in ancient Iran and the northern Indian subcontinent. The light-skinned Aryans invaded and conquered ancient India from the north. During their dominance in India, their literature, religion, and modes of social organization defined the Indian culture, especially the Vedic religion, a precursor to Hinduism.

such as reducing competition in local industries.)

16. Distribute copies of Activity 6.2. Show Slides 6.2–6.4 which describe the three types of economic systems. Use the slides to discuss the three types of economic systems individually.

17. Review the three general types of economic systems—market, command, and traditional—using the definitions below. Review the ways that the three types answer the three basic economic questions.

   - **Economic systems** are the institutional frameworks of formal and informal rules that a society uses to determine what to produce, how to produce, and how to distribute goods and services.

   - A **market economy** relies on a system of interdependent market prices to allocate goods, services, and productive resources and to coordinate the diverse plans of consumers and producers, all of them pursuing their own self-interest.

   - A **command economy** is an economy in which most economic issues of production and distribution are resolved through central planning and control.

   - A **traditional economy** relies on customs and habits to resolve most economic issues of production and distribution.

18. Tell the students that most economic systems are mixed economies. Define a **mixed economy** as an economy with some combination of the characteristics of the three types of economic systems. Use the following examples of **mixed economic systems** that are primarily identified as one the three types:

   - **Market example**: Throughout its history, the United States has been primarily a market-oriented economy, with a substantial government sector that commands or plans some

economic activities. In the United States, free markets are the dominant goal within the limits of what the Constitution calls the "general welfare."

   - **Command example**: Since 1949, China has had a strong one-party political system that closely controls the economy, but since the reforms of Deng Xiaoping in the 1980s, it has increasingly allowed market forces to exist under its control. The Chinese Constitution identifies the socialist goals of the nation and how private decisions are allowed only when appropriate to achieve those goals.

   - **Traditional example**: In the remote jungle of the Amazon River Valley lives a group of people who have no contact with outside groups. They eat only the food found locally and go about their daily lives in much the same way as their ancestors did. Because they have no new technologies or sources of information, any kind of social change is rare.

19. Ask students why the United States is not a pure market economy.

   (Answers will vary, but lead the student to the idea that the U.S. has some government involvement in its economy (command) and that some decisions are made by tradition.)

20. Reinforce the idea that almost all of the world's economies today are mixed. Some economic decisions are made by individuals and private firms. Other decisions are made by government officials, either through rules and regulations or government-owned firms. Still other economic decisions are determined by traditional value systems.

21. Ask students how Indian society in 200 B.C.E. answer the three basic economic questions of what to produce, how to produce, and for whom to produce.

(Accept a number of answers. See Activity 6.3, Sample Answers.)

22. Distribute copies of Activity 6.3, *What Kind of Economic System?* to each student. Have students work in pairs to complete an activity about the characteristics of the Indian economy in 200 B.C.E. Allow pairs of students 10 minutes to complete Activity 6.3.

23. Ask student pairs to share their lists. Using an overhead transparency of Activity 6.3 or on the chalk- or whiteboard, combine the students' ideas into one list. As students suggest an item in each category, they should explain how it is characteristic of the three economic systems described in Activity 6.3.

24. Through discussion of the students' lists, generalize about the Indian economy in 200 B.C.E., referring often to the importance of the caste system in the economy. Again, reinforce the meaning of a mixed economy.

    Note: If the caste system existed because it was the tradition and was enforced by religion and social norms, it might be classified as a "traditional" economic system. On the other hand, if the caste system was enforced by law, India's economic system of the time may be better classified as a "command" economic system. This is an example of how economies may not fit neatly into the definition of any one type of system.

CLOSURE

25. Review the role that the caste system played in the Indian economy in 200 B.C.E. Ask students if there are any traditional characteristics in the U.S. economy.

    (Examples: Many businesses close on Sundays, traditionally male- and female-dominated occupations exist, cultural definitions of marriage and family guide behavior, traditional holi-

days of dominant religious groups are observed.)

26. Ask the students how these "traditional" characteristics affect people.

    (They may limit when or where you can do business, influence personal relationships, and determine ethical values and economic opportunities.)

27. Reinforce the idea that the United States has a mixed economic system, just as India had in 200 B.C.E., and as most nations in the world have today. Although we typically say the United States has a market economy, it also has characteristics of traditional and command types of systems.

ASSESSMENT

Multiple Choice

1. Which of the Indian castes included small business owners, commercial workers, and traders?

    a. Kshatriyas

    b. Brahmins

    c. **Vaishyas**

    d. Shudras

2. What characteristic of Indian society in 200 B.C.E. was representative of a traditional economic system?

    a. **Castes**

    b. Legal codes

    c. Private businesses

    d. Markets

3. What is a mixed economic system?

    a. An economy with no clearly defined characteristics or central values

    b. An economy with equal parts of the three types of economic systems

    c. **An economy with some combination of the characteristics**

of the three types of economic systems

d. An economy dominated by the characteristics of one of the types of economic systems

Constructed Response

1. In what ways did the caste system help to define India in 200 B.C.E. as a traditional economy?

   (Student responses should identify the caste system as a tradition in India that controlled individual economic relationships and in some ways defined the economy as a whole. It determined occupations, families, and many daily economic decisions, based on customs and religious beliefs.)

SOURCES

Appleby, Joyce. 2010. *The Relentless Revolution: A History of Capitalism*. New York: W.W. Norton & Co. Page 388.

Cameron, Rondo, and Neal, Larry. 2003. *A Concise History of the World*, New York: Oxford University Press.

Keay, John. 2000. *India: A History*. New York: Grove Press.

Roberts, J.M. 1997. *History of the World*. London: Penguin Books Ltd.

Szczepanski, Kallie. 2011. "History of India's Caste System," About.com "Asian History," http://asianhistory.about.com/od/india/p/indiancastesystem.htm

"Indian People," Kidipede. 2011. http://www.historyforkids.org/learn/india/people/

CONNECTIONS: FURTHER STUDY OF CASTES

Literature. *Turning the Pot, Tilling the Land*, by Kancha Ilaiah, is the first children's book published in India that looks openly at the caste system and how it has affected the lives of the lower caste members and untouchables in modern India. (Navayana Publishing, 2007.)

Activity 6.1

India and the Caste System in 200 B.C.E.

About 1500 B.C.E., Aryans from the north invaded the Indus Valley. They brought with them the beginnings of the **caste system**, a social order that divided people into groups. Each group had a different status and different rights. In 200 B.C.E., there were four primary castes, called *varnas*.[1] The order of the castes, as laid out in early religious texts, was as follows:

- The ***Brahmins*** were the priests.

- The ***Kshatriya*** were the relatively small group of rulers and warriors.

- The ***Vaishyas*** were farmers, merchants, and traders—a large middle class group with many sub-castes.

- The ***Shudras*** were typically servants and farm workers, including mixed-race people and those who had different religions.

An additional category of people, the ***Dalits*** (outcasts or untouchables) were not recognized as members of a caste. They were the lowest status group in Indian society, although, at times, slavery did exist.

Within the larger castes were many smaller sub-castes. Sub-castes were usually based on families, geography, or some other common characteristic. A sub-caste might be restricted to one occupation. Castes often functioned like guilds or labor unions. By 500 to 200 B.C.E., castes controlled the local production of certain goods.

Caste played a large role in people's lives. A person's caste was determined by their parents' caste. Caste often determined a person's occupation. Castes influenced with whom people could trade and work. Marriage between people of different castes was not allowed.

The *Vedas*, Sanskrit texts brought by the Aryans that were the basis of Hindu scripture, reinforced the power of the system of castes.[2] Supporters of the caste system saw it as a way to organize society based on common religious beliefs and an established social structure. Those who opposed the caste system at this time in history faced strong social and legal pressure to conform to the system.

During the period of British rule of India, 1857–1947, many customs concerning the lower castes were found to be discriminatory. Discrimination against the Dalits and the restrictions of the caste system were banned by the Indian Constitution in 1950.[3] But the caste system is still a social influence in India today, especially in rural areas.

[1] Keay, John. *India: A History*, New York: Grove Press, 2000. Pages 52–54.

[2] Ibid, Keay. Pages 52–54.

[3] Appleby, Joyce. *The Relentless Revolution: A History of Capitalism*, New York: W.W. Norton & Co., 2010. Page 388.

ACTIVITY 6.2

Characteristics of Economic Systems

All nations have economic systems—ways of producing and distributing goods and services. Each has unique characteristics. Economic systems answer three basic economic questions: What goods and services are to be produced? How are goods and services to be produced? For whom are goods and services to be produced? Each economy has different ways to answer these questions. They include characteristics of market-oriented, command or planned, and tradition-based economic systems. Most economies are some combination of the three main types. In their pure states—which may not exist in today's world—market, command, or traditional economies have these general characteristics.

TYPE OF SYSTEM	WHAT TO PRODUCE?	HOW TO PRODUCE?	FOR WHOM TO PRODUCE?
MARKET ECONOMY	Businesses produce goods and services that consumers are willing and able to buy for prices that will yield profits for the businesses.	Seeking profits, business owners decide what resources they will use to produce goods and services. Individuals decide what occupations they will seek in the labor market.	Finished goods and services are distributed to individuals willing and able to buy them.
COMMAND ECONOMY	A central planning authority (government agency) decides what and how much of goods and services will be produced.	A central planning authority (government agency) decides what combinations of productive resources will be used to produce goods and services. The government may assign people to jobs.	A central planning authority (government agency) decides who will receive the goods and services that are produced.
TRADITIONAL ECONOMY	The goods and services produced today are the same goods and services that were produced in previous generations.	The productive resources used are the same as in past generations. Occupations are determined largely by tradition and families.	Finished goods and services are traded within the group or distributed based on tradition.

ACTIVITY 6.3

What Kind of Economy?

Directions: From the information in Activity 6.1, *India and the Caste System in 200 B.C.E.*, identify the characteristics of the Indian economy in 200 B.C.E. that represented the three basic types of economic systems. List the characteristics of the Indian economy in 200 B.C.E. in the appropriate columns.

- What characteristics of India in 200 B.C.E. were those of a market economy?

- What characteristics of India in 200 B.C.E. were those of a command economy?

- What characteristics of India in 200 B.C.E. were those of a traditional economy?

Market Economy Characteristics	Command Economy Characteristics	Traditional Economy Characteristics

ACTIVITY 6.3, SAMPLE ANSWERS
What Kind of Economy?

Directions: From the information in Activity 6.1, *India and the Caste System in 200 B.C.E.*, identify the characteristics of the Indian economy in 200 B.C.E. that represented the three basic types of economic systems. List the characteristics in the appropriate columns.

• What characteristics of India in 200 B.C.E. were those of a market economy?

• What characteristics of India in 200 B.C.E. were those of a command economy?

• What characteristics of India in 200 B.C.E. were those of a traditional economy?

Market Economy Characteristics	Command Economy Characteristics	Traditional Economy Characteristics
Possible answers: *Markets determined production.* *Private ownership of resources and businesses* *Trade was used to distribute goods.*	*Legal codes enforced the social norms and mores.* *Government recognition of the caste system*	*Castes determined opportunities and relationships.* *Strong religious influence* *Occupations were inherited.* *Marriage within castes* *Limited movement between castes*

SLIDE 6.1

The Caste System in Ancient India

- The **Brahmins** were the priests.
- The **Kshatriya** were the relatively small group of rulers and warriors.
- The **Vaishyas** were farmers, merchants, and traders.
- The **Shudras** were typically servants and farm workers, including mixed-race people and those who had different religions.
- The **Dalits**, the outcasts or untouchables, were not recognized as members of a caste.

SLIDE 6.2

Characteristics of Economic Systems

Market Economic System	
What to produce?	Businesses produce goods and services that consumers are willing and able to buy for prices that will yield profits for the businesses.
How to produce?	Seeking profits, business owners decide what resources they will use to produce goods and services. Individuals decide what occupations they will seek in the labor market.
For whom to produce?	Finished goods and services are distributed to individuals willing and able to buy them.

SLIDE 6.3

Characteristics of Economic Systems

Command Economic System

What to produce?	A central planning authority (government agency) decides what and how much of goods and services will be produced.
How to produce?	A central planning authority (government agency) decides what combinations of productive resources will be used to produce goods and services. The government may assign people to jobs.
For whom produce?	A central planning authority (government agency) decides who will receive the goods and services that are produced.

FOCUS MIDDLE SCHOOL WORLD HISTORY © COUNCIL FOR ECONOMIC EDUCATION, NEW YORK, NY

SLIDE 6.4

Characteristics of Economic Systems

Traditional Economic System

What to produce?	The goods and services produced today are the same goods and services that were produced in previous generations.
How to produce?	The productive resources used are the same as in past generations. Occupations are determined largely by tradition and families.
For whom to produce?	Finished goods and services are traded within the group or distributed based on tradition.

FOCUS MIDDLE SCHOOL WORLD HISTORY © COUNCIL FOR ECONOMIC EDUCATION, NEW YORK, NY

LESSON 7

THE SILK ROAD

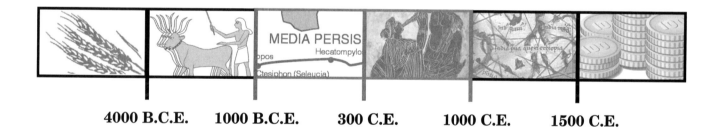

4000 B.C.E.   1000 B.C.E.   300 C.E.   1000 C.E.   1500 C.E.

LESSON 7
THE SILK ROAD

LESSON DESCRIPTION

This lesson explores the Silk Road from Chang'an, China, to Rome, sometime during the second century C.E. Students learn to think as traders in six cities along the Silk Road, bartering with traders from neighboring cities. As the silk moves west toward Rome and gold moves east toward Chang'an, students will see changes in the values of the goods they trade.

After an introductory reading about the Silk Road, the students will use economic reasoning to calculate the prices for goods along the Silk Road. They will then learn if a trade is a good deal or a bad deal. Finally, the students decide if it is beneficial to take other routes to China.

INTRODUCTION

During the Han Dynasty in China, 206 B.C.E. to 220 C.E., a period of relative stability was established across China. One result of political and social stability was an increase in trade between the far-flung cities of the dynasty's region.[1] Trade eventually spread to regions that are now India, Pakistan, Iraq and Iran, and as far as the Mediterranean Sea to Rome.[2] Commodities such as silk had become known to people in Rome through regional trade within the empire as it spread west. Silk was a highly desired commodity in cities like Rome and very profitable for producers in China. Romans demanded it for clothing and decoration.

The Silk Road connected the West with the East through cities like Alexandria Eschate (Alexandria the Furthest) in what is now Tajikistan, founded by Alexander the Great in 329 B.C.E.[3] The Han Dynasty's capital, Chang'an (now spelled Xi'an), in central China was the primary city at the eastern end of the Silk Road.

Rather than just one route, the Silk Road was a series of roads extending north and south. At times, sea routes carried this trade, as maritime technologies improved or when violence threatened the land traders. When pirates and other perils faced the merchants on the sea routes, trade increased on the land routes.

Along the routes of the Silk Road, other regions offered commodities such as dates, copper, herbs, and finished goods. Magnetic compasses, silk, gunpowder, and ceramics were traded from Chinese cities to the west. All along the trade routes, gold was a common form of money for trading.

The Silk Road carried not only goods and commodities but also cultural characteristics, ideas, languages, customs, and scientific knowledge. One additional impact was the spread of diseases such as the bubonic plague, which spread across Central Asia into China and resulted in the Black Death in Europe by the fourteenth century.[4]

The end of the Han Dynasty resulted in greater social and political conflict and lowered trade levels for some time. Later dynasties revived trade for periods of time. The end of the ancient Silk Road began with the disintegration of the Mongol Empire in the late 1300s. In the late Middle Ages, land trade declined as sea routes expanded with the use of new navigation

[1]Roberts, J. M., *History of the World*, 3rd edition, London: Penguin Books, 1997. Pages 430–432.
Liu, Xinru, *The Silk Road in World History* (e-book version), New York: Oxford University Press, 2010. Pages 24–26.
[2]Ibid, Liu, 2010. Page 61.

[3]"Alexander the Great." Encyclopædia Britannica. Encyclopædia Britannica Online. Encyclopædia Britannica, 2011. Web. 11 Jul. 2011. http://www.britannica.com/EBchecked/topic/14224/Alexander-the-Great.
[4]Wade, Nicholas, "Europe's Plagues Came From China, Study Finds", *New York Times*, October 31, 2010.

technologies that reduced the costs and perils of sea trade.[5]

Over its history, the Silk Road saw periods of increase and decrease in trade, depending on political conflict and stability, changes in technology, ever-changing consumer wants, and competitive forces. Consequently, changes in the relative prices of the various resources and goods affected trading activities along the Silk Road.

CONCEPTS

Barter

Markets

Product

Relative price

Trade

OBJECTIVES

Students will be able to:

- Identify the time span, regions, and cities involved in trade along the Silk Road.

- Identify the types of resources and goods that were traded along the Silk Road.

- Explain factors that influenced the relative prices of the products.

- Determine if a trade is a good trade based on relative prices.

CONTENT STANDARDS

Voluntary Content Standards in Economics, 2nd edition

- **Standard 5:** Voluntary exchange occurs only when all participating parties expect to gain. This is true for trade among individuals or organizations within a nation and among individuals or organizations in different nations.

- **Standard 8:** Prices send signals and provide incentives to buyers and sellers.

---

[5]Major, John S., Joan Barnatt and John Bertles, "Silk Road Encounters Sourcebook," Boston: The Silk Road Project, 2011. Page 15. URL: http://www.silkroadproject.org/Portals/0/Uploads/Documents/Public/sourcebook.pdf

When supply or demand changes, market prices adjust, affecting incentives.

World History Content Standards

Era 3: Classical Traditions, Major Religions, and Giant Empires, 1000 B.C.E.–300 C.E.

- **Standard 3:** How major religions and large-scale empires arose in the Mediterranean basin, China, and India, 500 B.C.E.–300 C.E.

- **Standard 5:** Major global trends from 1000 B.C.E.–300 C.E.

Era 4: Expanding Zones of Exchange and Encounter, 300–1000 C.E.

- **Standard 7:** Major global trends from 300–1000 C.E.

TIME REQUIRED

60 minutes

MATERIALS

- Slides 7.1–7.4

- Activity 7.1, 1 copy per student

- Activity 7.2, 1 copy per student

- Activity 7.3, 1 copy

- Activity 7.4, 1 copy per student

- Scissors

- Wall map of Europe and Asia (physical map with national boundaries—current period)

PROCEDURE

1. Briefly introduce the history of the Silk Road by having the students read Activity 7.1, *Introduction to the Silk Road*. Explain that the purpose of trade was for people in different regions to be able to consume goods they could not produce themselves.

2. Define **trade** as the exchange of goods and services for money or other goods and services and provide examples of its use in local everyday transactions and with people from other nations.

---

3. Show Slide 7.1 or distribute copies of the map of the Silk Road (Activity 7.2). Using a classroom wall map that includes physical features of Europe and Asia, review the geographic features of the Silk Road routes by comparing the physical map to the map of the Silk Road. Point out that trade routes typically follow flat areas, valleys, and rivers. Specifically point out where the deserts meet the mountainous areas and where the trade routes converge between mountains.

4. Note: More maps of the Silk Road can be found at the Silk Road Project website: http://www.silkroadproject.org/Education/TheSilkRoad/HistoricSilkRoadInfoandExternalLinks/SilkRoadMaps/tabid/177/Default.aspx

5. Ask students why the trading routes generally follow the valleys and rivers.

(Travel is easier.)

6. Ask students to identify why the northern, southern, and middle routes followed certain paths. Point out the mountain ranges and river valleys along the routes.

(Students should recognize the easiest routes to travel and the forms of transportation the traders might have used—camels, donkeys, and boats.)

7. Explain that the Silk Road generally extended from East Asia to Europe. Specifically point out the route that extends from Chang'an, China (map coordinates 34°16′ N, 108° 54′ E), to Rome, Italy (map coordinates 41° 58′ N, 12° 40′ E).

8. Explain that other routes on the Silk Road began in other cities in China and ended in other cities in Europe. The most recognized route is that from Chang'an to Rome. Note: Chang'an is spelled Xi'an on modern maps of China.

9. Explain that the students will pretend to trade along the southern route of the Silk Road from Chang'an in Eastern China to ancient Rome. Along the way,

trades will also be made in the cities of (modern location):

Chang'an	(Eastern China)
Khotan	(Western China)
Kashgar	(Western China)
Alexandria Eschate	(Tajikistan)
Damascus	(Syria)
Rome	(Italy)

10. Explain that in each city is a market where goods are exchanged. Traders meet in the markets to barter for other products. Define **markets** as places, institutions or technological arrangements where or by means of which goods or services are exchanged. Define **barter** as trading a good or service directly for another good or service without using money or credit.

11. Explain that many products were traded along the Silk Road. Give the students a brief overview of the following products that might have been traded:

- **Silk**: People wanted silk because clothing made of wool and linen were heavier and had rougher textures. Silk was highly prized by women in Rome for warm-weather attire. Some Romans objected to silk clothing because it was so sheer and revealing.

- **Jade**: Green-colored gemstone used for decoration.

- **Herbs**: People valued herbs to make their food taste better. Herbs were widely traded as commodities and sold in local markets.

- **Copper**: Copper was important for making cooking pots, jewelry, tools and other objects. It could be alloyed with other metals to make artwork and tools.

- **Dates**: Dates could be dried for long journeys. They were a food staple in the Middle East.

- **Gold**: Gold was valued for producing jewelry and other ornamental objects. It often served the function of money because it was universally accepted in trade.

12. Draw a diagram across the entire board as shown below:

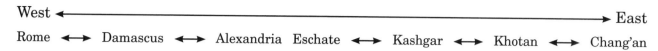

West ◄——————————————————————————————————► East

Rome ◄——► Damascus ◄——► Alexandria Eschate ◄——► Kashgar ◄——► Khotan ◄——► Chang'an

13. Tell students the diagram on the board shows cities on the Silk Road from west to east.

14. Tell students that they will be doing an exercise that will illustrate how relative prices might have changed along the Silk Road.

15. Define **relative price** as the price of one good in relation to the price of another good. It is a measure of opportunity cost, which is what is given up to obtain something. Therefore, it is the price that affects economic decision-making. Example: A relative price is the number of one product traded for some number of another product such as two oranges for one apple.

16. Tell students that traveling the Silk Road was rough. Many obstacles faced traders, including taxation and thieves. Traders who hired help to transport the goods also had to pay their workers.

17. Ask a student to stand in front of the Chang'an part of the board. Give the student a copy of Activity 7.3, a box consisting of 32 squares. (Cut top, bottom and side margins off.) Tell the student that each square represents a bolt of silk cloth. Tell the student that he or she wants to take the silk to Rome.

18. Tell the student to start the trip by going to Khotan. As the student moves to the next point on the board, tell the student that due to taxes, thieves and paying workers, the amount of silk has decreased. Tell the student that you will reduce the amount of silk by half. With the scissors, cut 16 squares out, and give the remainder to the student.

19. Tell the students that half might be a bit high, but it makes the calculations easier for the example.

20. Ask the student to continue the journey to Rome. At each city, cut half of the remaining squares out. Mark how many squares the student has left at each city on the board.

21. When the student arrives in Rome, the student will just have one square.

22. Ask the student if it is expensive to travel along the Silk Road. *(Most likely the answer will be yes.)* Ask the student if he or she will want a lot of gold for their trip. *(Again, yes.)*

23. Tell students that traders might trade their goods at any city along the road and that the goods may change hands many times along the Silk Road.

24. Tell the students that they will calculate the relative prices of goods along the Silk Road. Hand out Activity 7.4 to each student. Have students work in pairs.

25. Tell students that each city produces one good. Show Slide 7.2. Gold is made in Rome. Dates are grown in Damascus. Copper is produced in Alexandria Eschate. Herbs are grown in Kashgar. Jade is produced in Khotan. Silk is made in Chang'an. Tell students that the shaded squares in the table will help them remember what is produced in each city. Note: Many of these goods in the activity may have been produced in cities other than the ones specified; the activity simplifies things by assuming products are made in only one city.

26. Show Slide 7.3. Tell students that the columns of the table show the amount of one good it takes to barter for units of another good. For example, in Alexandria Eschate, it takes four gold coins to buy

eight baskets of dates. It takes four gold coins to buy four bolts of silk. Tell students that right now, they only know the trading prices in Alexandria Eschate, but once they fill out the table, they will know the relative prices of all goods in all places.

27. Ask students the following questions to see if they understand the concepts presented:

    a. In Alexandria Eschate, what good(s) buy more units of other goods?

       (Gold and silk—both will buy twice the units of dates, copper, or jade; both will buy four times the number of units of herbs.)

    b. Why do dates buy twice the number of herbs, even though both come from neighboring cities?

       (Many answers could apply, including differences in tastes for dates and herbs. Or the size of the baskets might differ.)

28. Tell students that they can apply the example demonstrated by the student who traveled from Chang'an to Rome to this activity. Tell them that as a good is moved from city to city, half of the good is lost to traders, thieves and taxes. For example, if 32 silk bolts begin in Chang'an and are sent west, only 16 bolts arrive in Khotan. If the 16 bolts are sent west from Khotan, only eight bolts arrive in Kasgar. Have the students fill in the numbers on the bottom row.

29. Remind students that products move **away** from where they are produced, so that if eight copper coins go from Alexandra Eschate to Damascus, only four copper coins will arrive. But the same is true if the coins were sent from Alexandra Eschate to Kashgar—only four copper coins will arrive.

30. Have students complete the rest of the table by filling in the rows and answering the questions in Part I.

31. After the student pairs have finished Part I, have them check their answers in the table by showing Slide 7.4.

    (The answers for questions are:

    1. Kashgar, 32

    2. 16 gold coins

    3. 1 gold coin

    4. Rome. As the silk travels further, it becomes more costly. Also, gold is produced in Rome, so it is not very costly.

    5. Chang'an, 64 bolts of silk.)

32. Emphasize to students that in this activity, the cost of things depends a lot on the cost of shipping the goods from place to place.

33. Ask students if they think they would make good traders.

    (Answers will vary.)

34. Tell students to try to answer the questions in Part II. Go over the answers.

    (1. Good trade; 2. Bad trade; 3. Good trade, if you take advantage of the small child; 4. Bad trade)

35. Conclude the activity by noting that travel by sea might lower the costs of travel. Have the students complete Part III, in which they are given the opportunity to travel to Chang'an for a low cost.

    (The students should elect to travel. They arrive in Chang'an with two gold coins. They can buy 128 bolts of silk in Chang'an with their gold. As they travel to Rome with their silk, they lose some of their silk to thieves, taxes and payments for workers. They start with 128 bolts of silk, but end up with four bolts of silk. Happily, a bolt of silk is worth 16 gold coins in Rome, so they will finish their journey with 64 gold coins.)

CLOSURE

36. Briefly review the purpose, history and geography of the Silk Road. Students should be able to explain that Silk Road

trade routes moved goods east and west between Europe and Asia.

37. Ask students why silk was so expensive in Rome.

    (Costs of travel made silk expensive to import. Some students might say that silk was popular in Rome, which is another reason it could have been so expensive.)

38. Ask students what is meant by relative price.

    (A price that is expressed in comparison to another good.)

ASSESSMENT

Multiple Choice

1. The Silk Road connected what two regions?

    a. China and Southwest Asia

    b. **China and Europe**

    c. Europe and India

    d. Europe and Japan

2. Relative price means

    a. the prices of two products that are used together.

    b. the price after a good that is purchased and resold.

    c. **the amount of one good traded for another good.**

    d. the change in the price when something is purchased.

Constructed Response

1. Why was silk so expensive in ancient Rome?

    (Romans valued silk for clothing and other items and were willing to pay a high price. The cost of transporting the silk from Chang'an to Rome was high, making the costs of obtaining silk high as well.)

SOURCES

"Alexander the Great." Encyclopædia Britannica Online. 2011. http://www.britannica.com/EBchecked/topic/14224/Alexander-the-Great.

Cameron, Rondo, and Neal, Larry. 2003. *A Concise History of the World*. New York: Oxford University Press.

Major, John S., Barnatt, Joan, and Bertles, John. "Silk Road Encounters Sourcebook," Boston: The Silk Road Project, 2011. Page 15. http://www.silkroadproject.org/Portals/0/Uploads/Documents/Public/sourcebook.pdf

Morton, W. Scott, and Lewis, Charlton M. 2005. *China: Its History and Culture*. New York: McGraw-Hill Inc.

Liu, Xinru. 2010. *Silk Road in World History* (e-book). New York: Oxford University Press.

Roberts, J. M. 1997. *History of the World*. London: Penguin Books Ltd.

Waugh, Daniel C. 2011. "Silk Road Narratives: A Collection of Historical Texts," Silk Road Seattle, Walter Simpson Center for the Humanities at the University of Washingtonhttp://depts.washington.edu/silkroad/index.html

CONNECTIONS: OTHER TRADING ROUTES AND THE SILK ROAD PROJECT

Several examples of historically important trading routes can be found throughout history:

Saharan Africa to Western Africa through Timbuktu

Native American routes across the South and Midwest

The "Spanish Trail" connecting New Mexico and southern California

Sea trade between Rome and India

The "Ambassador's Road" across mainland China

The Appian Way in Italy

Maritime spice routes from Asia to Africa

The trade of salt and gold between North and West Africa is the focus of Lesson 3 – *Trade In Africa: 9th to 12th Centuries A.D.*, published in *Focus on Economics: World History*, Council for Economic Education, 1996. Order #: 0490 ISBN: 1-56183-490-4.

The Silk Road Project

The Silk Road Project, Inc. provides a variety of resources about the Silk Road, including music and the arts, and YouTube videos. http://www.silkroadproject.org/Education/SilkRoadConnect/tabid/455/Default.aspx

The Silk Road Project also offers more maps of the Silk Road at http://www.silkroadproject.org/Education/TheSilkRoad/SilkRoadMaps/tabid/177/Default.aspx

ACTIVITY 7.1

Introduction to the Silk Road

During the Han Dynasty in China, 206 B.C.E. to 220 C.E., a period of stability was established across China. One result of this stability was an increase in trade between the cities of the dynasty's region. This trade spread to regions that are now India, Pakistan, Iraq and Iran, and as far as the Mediterranean Sea to Rome.

Commodities such as silk had become known to people in Rome through regional trade within their empire as it spread west. Silk was highly desired in cities like Rome, where people wanted it for clothing and decoration. Silk was very profitable for producers in China.

The Silk Road connected the West with the East through cities like Alexandria Eschate (Alexandria the Furthest) founded by Alexander the Great in 329 B.C.E. The Han Dynasty's capital Chang'an (now spelled Xi'an) in central China was the main city at the eastern end of the Silk Road.

The Silk Road was actually a series of roads extending north and south. People used these roads to carry goods between Rome and Chang'an. At times, sea routes carried this trade, as maritime technologies improved or when violence threatened land traders. When pirates and other perils faced the merchants on the sea routes, trade increased on the land routes.

Along the routes of the Silk Road, different regions offered goods such as dates, copper, herbs, and finished products. Goods such as the magnetic compass, silk, gunpowder and ceramics were traded from Chinese cities to the west. All along the trade routes, gold was a common form of money for trading. The Silk Road also spread cultures: ideas, languages, customs, and scientific knowledge. One additional impact was the spread of diseases such as the bubonic plague that spread across Central Asia into China and resulted in the Black Death in Europe.

Over its history, the Silk Road saw periods of increase and decrease in trade. The amount of trade depended on conflict or stability along the road as well as new technologies, changing consumer wants, and competitive forces. The price of goods changed along the Silk Road, depending on consumer wants and the cost of transporting the goods over long distances.

ACTIVITY 7.2

Map of the Silk Roads

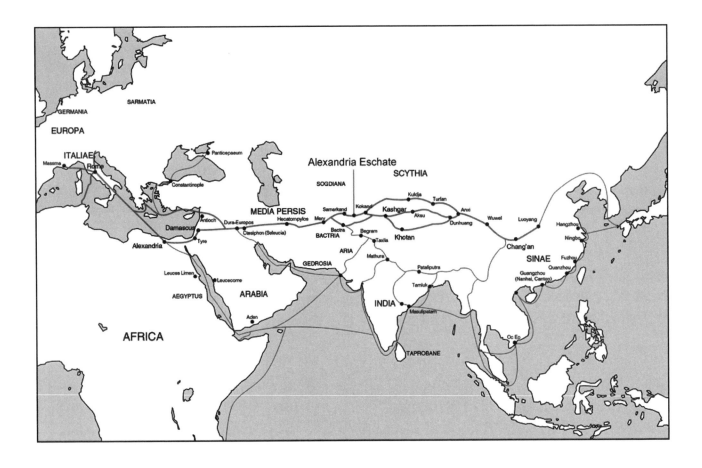

ACTIVITY 7.3

Bartering

ACTIVITY 7.4

Bartering along the Silk Road

The table below shows six cities and six goods. The cities listed across the top of the table are the cities you would visit if you traveled the Silk Road from west to east.

| Good | West ← —————— Cities —————— → East | | | | | |
	Rome	Damascus	Alexandria Eschate	Kashgar	Khotan	Chang'an
Gold (coins)			4			
Dates (baskets)			8			
Copper (coins)			8			
Herbs (baskets)			16			
Jade (boxes)			8			
Silk (bolts)			4			32

In this example, each good is made in only one city: gold is made in Rome; dates are grown in Damascus; copper is produced in Alexandria Eschate; herbs are grown in Kashgar; jade is produced in Khotan; and silk is made in Chang'an. (You can see where each product is from by using the shaded squares.)

If you read up and down the columns, the table shows what amount of one good it takes to barter for units of another good. For example, in Alexandria Eschate, it takes four gold coins to buy eight baskets of dates. It takes four gold coins to buy four bolts of silk.

It costs a lot to transport goods along the Silk Road. The path is rough and traders demand payment for the time and trouble of taking goods along the road. Many obstacles stand in traders' way, such as taxes and thieves.

In this example, as a good is moved from city to city, half of the goods are lost to pay traders as well as to encounters with thieves and paying taxes. For example, if 32 silk bolts begin in Chang'an and are sent west, only 16 bolts arrive in Khotan. If the 16 bolts are sent farther west from Khotan, only 8 bolts arrive in Kashgar.

Part I: Trading along the Silk Road

1. Fill in the rest of the table using the information above. (Hint: Be sure to know which way the goods are traveling along the road.) If 16 baskets of herbs arrive in Alexandria Eschate, where did they come from? _____ How many baskets of herbs were originally shipped from that city to Alexandria Eschate? _____

2. In Rome, how many gold coins does it take to buy one bolt of silk? _____

3. In Alexandria Eschate, how many gold coins does it take to buy one bolt of silk? _____

4. Are bolts of silk worth more in gold coins in Rome or Alexandria Eschate? Why is this true?
    _____

5. In which city does a gold coin buy the most silk? _____ How much silk will a gold coin buy in this city? _____

Part II: Good Trade?

For each of the following, determine whether the trade is a good trade or a bad trade, based on information in the table. Check the appropriate column.

The trade:	Good Trade	Bad Trade
1. A man in Damascus offers to sell you three baskets of herbs for one copper coin.		
2. A woman in Kashgar offers to sell you three boxes of jade for one basket of dates.		
3. A small child in Rome to offers to sell you one copper coin for 6 gold coins.		
4. An old man in Chang'an offers to sell you 12 baskets of herbs for one gold coin.		

Part III: What Would You Do?

You are an ambitious young person living in Rome. You have 16 gold coins in your pocket. An odd ship captain approaches you and offers to take you to Chang'an along a new oversea route. The total cost of travel to Chang'an will be 14 gold coins—one way. Once in Chang'an, the only way to travel back to Rome is along the Silk Road. Would you go to Chang'an with the captain? (Assume information in the table still applies.) Explain what you would do to return to Rome and become a rich person.

_____

_____

_____

_____

_____

SLIDE 7.1

Map of the Silk Road

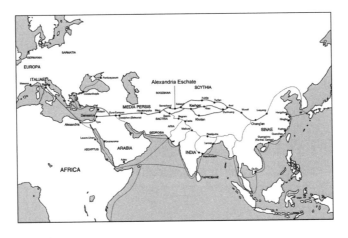

SLIDE 7.2

Silk Road Cities and Products

Chang'an	Silk
Khotan	Jade
Kashgar	Herbs
Alexandria Eschate	Copper
Damascus	Dates
Rome	Gold

SLIDE 7.3

Bartering along the Silk Road

Good	West ←		Cities		→ East	
	Rome	Damascus	Alexandria Eschate	Kashgar	Khotan	Chang'an
Gold (coins)			4			
Dates (baskets)			8			
Copper (coins)			8			
Herbs (baskets)			16			
Jade (boxes)			8			
Silk (bolts)			4			32

FOCUS MIDDLE SCHOOL WORLD HISTORY © COUNCIL FOR ECONOMIC EDUCATION, NEW YORK, NY

SLIDE 7.4

Bartering along the Silk Road - Key

Good	West ←		Cities		→ East	
	Rome	Damascus	Alexandria Eschate	Kashgar	Khotan	Chang'an
Gold (coins)	16	8	4	2	1	.5
Dates (baskets)	8	16	8	4	2	1
Copper (coins)	2	4	8	4	2	1
Herbs (baskets)	4	8	16	32	16	8
Jade (boxes)	2	4	8	16	32	16
Silk (bolts)	1	2	4	8	16	32

FOCUS MIDDLE SCHOOL WORLD HISTORY © COUNCIL FOR ECONOMIC EDUCATION, NEW YORK, NY

Lesson 8

Athens and Sparta—Imagine the Possibilities

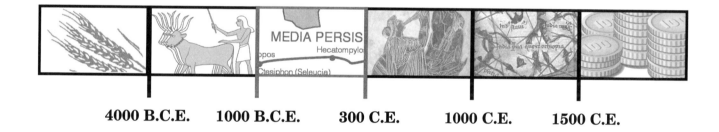

4000 B.C.E.   1000 B.C.E.   300 C.E.   1000 C.E.   1500 C.E.

LESSON 8
ATHENS AND SPARTA—IMAGINE THE POSSIBILITIES

LESSON DESCRIPTION

In this lesson, students learn about important similarities and differences between two key Greek city-states, Athens and Sparta. The students will read a passage about each society and complete a compare-and-contrast activity using a Venn diagram. Next, students learn about the economic concepts of scarcity, choice, and opportunity cost in the context of a *production possibilities frontier*. Finally, using the concept of opportunity cost and the production possibilities frontier, students answer a key historic question: Why did Athens and Sparta, while similar in many ways, develop into such different economic systems?

INTRODUCTION

Athens and Sparta were both prominent Greek city-states in ancient times. They had much in common. For example, they spoke the same language (Greek), had the same religion, and both faced a problem at a pivotal time in their respective histories—the rough terrain did not produce enough food to feed their growing populations. They solved their food shortage problems differently. Sparta conquered its neighbors, the Messenians, and enslaved them. Athens turned to trade. For each city-state, their decision largely determined their direction as a society. The Spartans, fearing a slave revolt, established a militaristic society that dominated all aspects of Spartan life. Because resources were limited, the Spartans' use of resources meant that they had to forgo other opportunities, such as the art, architecture, theater, and philosophy that their contemporaries were developing in Athens. This lesson uses basic economic reasoning to explain the stark differences between these two storied city-states.

CONCEPTS

Scarcity

Choice

Opportunity cost

Production possibility frontier

OBJECTIVES

Students will be able to:

- Compare and contrast the ancient Greek city-states of Athens and Sparta.

- Define the economic concepts of scarcity and opportunity cost.

- Use a production possibilities frontier to describe the economic concepts of scarcity and opportunity cost.

- Explain the differences in economies using the production possibilities frontier as an economic reasoning tool.

CONTENT STANDARDS

Voluntary Content Standards in Economics, 2nd Edition

- **Standard 3**: Different methods can be used to allocate goods and services. People acting individually or collectively must choose which methods to use to allocate different kinds of goods and services.

- **Standard 1:** Productive resources are limited. Therefore, people cannot have all the goods and services they want; as a result, they must choose some things and give up others.

World History Content Standards

Era 3: Classical Traditions, Major Religions, and Giant Empires, 1000 B.C.E.–300 C.E.

- **Standard 2:** The emergence of Aegean civilization and how interrelations developed among peoples of the eastern Mediterranean and Southwest Asia, 600–200 B.C.E.

TIME REQUIRED

60 minutes

MATERIALS

- Slides 8.1-8.9

- One copy of Activity 8.1 for half the class

- One copy of Activity 8.2 for half the class

- One copy of Activity 8.3 for half the class (only 1 copy of answer key portion is needed)

- One copy of Activity 8.4 for half the class

PROCEDURE

1. Ask students the following questions:

   a. In the United States, 11 towns are named Sparta. Why would so many towns be named that?

      (Answers will vary. Sparta was the name of an ancient Greek city-state. Many towns are named Sparta because it was a very important city-state and important to the study of world history.)

   b. Likewise, in the United States, 19 towns are named Athens. Why would so many towns have that name?

      (Answers will vary. Athens was also the name of an ancient Greek city-state. Many towns are named Athens because it was a very important city-state and important to the study of world history.)

2. Ask students if they know what a city-state is.

   (Answers will vary.)

   Tell the students that a city-state is a city and surrounding region that is also an independent nation. Tell students to imagine their own city as an independent nation with its own army, currency, laws, and elected leaders. Imagine nearby cities were also independent nations. Tell the students the city-states of ancient Greece could be described like this.

3. Give half the students Activity 8.1, *Athens' Choices*, and the other half Activity 8.2, *Sparta's Choices*, and have them read their passages.

4. After they have finished reading, have students pair off with a class member who has the other reading. Tell students they are to teach each other about their respective city-state.

5. Give each pair of students a copy of Activity 8.3 and Activity 8.4. Show Slide 8.1 on an overhead screen. If students have not used a Venn diagram, briefly describe how to use one. Tell the pairs of students to correctly place each numbered statement in their copy of a Venn diagram (or just write the number of the statement). While they work, draw a Venn diagram on the whiteboard.

6. Call the pairs of students to the front of the class and have them write the description on the correct part of the Venn diagram on the whiteboard. Have the students check their own Venn diagrams as the statements are being placed. Discuss the actions of students and correct as needed, using the Activity 8.3 Answer Key.

7. When you have finished, discuss the following with students:

   a. How did the Athenians solve their food problems?

      (They traded products such as olive oil and wine for grains.)

   b. Why couldn't the Athenians produce enough food on their own?

      (The soil was infertile, so grain did not grow well, but olives and grapes did. They produced olive oil and wine from the olives and grapes and traded for grain.)

   c. What did the Athenians value?

      (Because Athenians enjoyed a large degree of freedom, there was not a single focus for society. Remind students that the Athenians developed democracy, had a large degree of individual freedom of expression, produced timeless art, literature, and philosophy and developed a sophisticated trade network.)

d. Ask students how the Spartans solved their food problems.

(The Spartans conquered the neighboring Messenians and made them agricultural slaves known as helots.)

e. What did the Spartans value?

(Strength, duty, and discipline, which resulted in a strong military)

f. Ask students what evidence leads them to think that the military was the focus of Spartan society?

(Answers will vary. Several possible reasons include babies were inspected for worthiness as soldiers, boys left home to start military training at age seven, and women were encouraged to be fit and strong so they could bear strong children who would grow into strong soldiers.)

g. Why did the Spartans need such a strong military?

(They feared a helot revolt. Because they needed the helots to grow food for them and because the helots outnumbered them 8-to-1, they justified the need for a strong military.)

8. Tell students that the goal is to answer a key historic question: Why did Athens and Sparta, similar in many ways, develop into such different societies?

9. Tell students that economists have developed theories and tools that help explain human behavior, both by individual people and entire societies. Tell the students that they will be using economic concepts and a key economic tool to explain how Athens and Sparta developed differently.

10. Show Slide 8.2. Read through the definition of **scarcity** with students. Ask students to give an example of scarcity.

(Answers will vary. For example, their list of birthday wishes is probably longer than their parents' ability or desire to fulfill. Perhaps students want to go to

a basketball game but must study for a test instead.)

11. Why do all people face the problem of scarcity?

(We can't always have what we want because our wants are greater than our resources.)

12. Read the definition of productive resources from Slide 8.2. Ask students to think about the types of resources Athens and Sparta had.

(Answers will vary, but lead the discussion toward natural resources, human resources, and capital resources.)

13. Read the definitions for natural resources and human resources from Slide 8.3. Ask students:

a. What are some examples of natural resources from Athens and Sparta?

(The most notable natural resource is the land each city state used to grow food crops. Both societies had difficulty feeding their growing populations by farming the rocky soil.)

b. What are some examples of human resources from Athens and Sparta?

(Students are likely to note that both Athens and Sparta relied heavily on slave labor. Much of the nonslave labor in Sparta was devoted to the military. In Athens, labor resources—both slave and nonslave—were devoted to a variety of tasks, including farming and manufacturing.)

14. Read the definition of capital resources from Slide 8.4. Ask students for some examples of capital resources from Athens and Sparta.

(Both Athens and Sparta used tools to produce goods and services. For example, Spartan soldiers used spears and shields to make war. Athenian blacksmiths used hammers to beat hot iron into shields.)

15. Conclude the discussion of resources by asking the following questions:

    a. Who determined how the resources would be used in Sparta?

       *(In Sparta, government determined how natural, human, and capital resources would be used. It chose to use its resources to build a strong military. Individuals had little freedom to pursue their own goals. Economists call this a **command economy** because the government commands how the resources will be used.)*

    b. Who determined how the resources would be used in Athens?

       *(In Athens, people had considerable freedom to pursue their own interests; they produced what they wanted to produce. This kind of system, where individuals decide how resources are used, is called a **market system**.)*

    c. Does the United States use a system more like the Spartan command system or the Athenian market system?

       (Answers will vary, but most will suggest that the market and freedom of Athens more closely resembles the U.S. economic system.)

16. Read the economic problem on Slide 8.5 with students. Tell students that scarcity forces people to make **choices** from among the various things we want. For example, because of scarcity, workers (human resources) used for one purpose cannot be used for another. A blacksmith working in a workshop is a human resource unavailable for farming.

17. Read the definition for **opportunity cost** from Slide 8.5 with students. Tell students that whenever people make a choice they give something up. The thing that is given up is a lost opportunity or an *opportunity cost*. Ask students: Can you provide an example of opportunity cost?

(Answers will vary. The opportunity cost of being in school is the lost opportunity to sleep. The opportunity cost of going to the football game tonight is the lost opportunity to go to the movies.)

18. What is the opportunity cost of using Athenian land to grow olives?

    (The land cannot be use to grow grapes.)

19. Explain to students that economists sometimes use a tool called a **production possibilities frontier** to illustrate how societies use resources. Read the definition for production possibilities frontier from Slide 8.6. Tell students that the graph is also used to illustrate the economic concepts of scarcity and opportunity cost.

20. Tell the students to imagine a society that only produced two goods—grapes and olives. All of their resources are devoted to producing these two goods. Refer students to the graph on Slide 8.7.

21. Ask the students what the word *frontier* means.

    (A general definition of the word could be "the farthest-out point." For example, space is called the last frontier. The pioneers were headed for the frontier, the farthest-out point.)

22. Tell students that the curved line on the graph is called a frontier because it represents the maximum production for the society if it uses all of its resources. The society can produce anywhere along the frontier. Society's preferences determine at what point it will produce. Its preferences may change over time. Ask students the following questions about Slide 8.7:

    a. If the society chooses to produce at point A, how much of each good will it produce?

       (It will produce nine grapes and three olives.)

b. What will happen if the society wants six olives instead?

(It will have to give up some grapes. In fact, if it produces six olives, it will have only enough resources to produce seven grapes. So, producing three more olives means giving up two grapes.)

c. If society starts at point A, what is the opportunity cost of producing the three more olives?

(Two grapes)

d. Suppose society chooses to produce at point B. How much of each good will it produce?

(It will produce three grapes and nine olives.)

e. What will happen if society wants six grapes instead?

(It will have to give up some olives. In fact, if it produces six grapes, it will have only enough resources to produce seven olives. So, producing three more grapes means giving up two olives.)

f. If society starts at point B, what is the opportunity cost of producing three more grapes?

(Two olives)

g. How does a production possibilities frontier demonstrate opportunity cost?

(If you are producing on the frontier, producing more of one thing [such as olives] means that you must give up some of the other [such as grapes].)

23. Direct students' attention back to Athens and Sparta. Explain that economists use the production possibilities frontier to talk about the decisions that societies make.

24. Show Slide 8.8. Tell students that a graph will help them examine the decisions made by Athens and Sparta using a concept referred to as *guns versus*

butter. Societies must decide between using resources for guns (military goods and services) or butter (civilian goods or services). We will assume that Athens and Sparta had similar resources and technology.

25. Explain to the students that the words "guns" and "butter" are not literal; rather, they stand for something else. In this case, the word "guns" stands for resources used to produce goods and services for the military. The word "butter" stands for resources devoted to the production of civilian (nonmilitary) goods or services.

26. Show Slide 8.9. Tell students that one graph represents Athens and the other graph represents Sparta. Both graphs show the trade-off between guns and butter. Ask students: Which letter probably most closely represents the choice made by Athens?

(Students should choose "A" because it shows production focused on butter or civilian goods and services. Have them explain why the other choices are not likely. Both "B" and "C" are unlikely—while Athens had a military, it represented a smaller part of its total resources.)

27. Ask students if they think these choices changed over time.

(Yes. For example, when a nation goes to war it chooses to use more resources for military and national defense. In this case, Athens would move closer to "B" or even "C" during war and, in times of peace, would likely have shifted back toward "A.")

28. Ask students: Which letter probably most closely represents the choice made by Sparta?

(Students should choose "C" because it shows production focused on guns, or military goods and services. Both "A" and "B" are unlikely because almost all of Sparta's resources were devoted to the Spartan military.)

29. Athens and Sparta were both Greek city-states and had many things in common, such as religion, language, and geography. However, the two city-states developed in dramatically different ways. Athens is remembered for its economic activity as well as its achievements in art, architecture, literature, government, and philosophy. Sparta, on the other hand, is remembered for its military fanaticism. Ask the students to answer the historic question posed at the beginning of the lesson: Why did these city-states that were so similar develop in such different ways?

(Answers will vary. The students should speculate that it is due to differences in preferences or government.)

30. To clarify, ask the students the following questions:

   a. Why did the Spartans choose to use their resources for military power?

   (Because Spartans feared a helot revolt.)

   b. Why were the helots necessary to the Spartans?

   (The helots were enslaved to grow food for the Spartans.)

   c. Sparta thrived as a military power, but did not achieve much beyond that. What was the opportunity cost of the Spartan focus on military security?

   (While it did not have exactly the same resources as Athens, the resources Sparta devoted to the military meant that those resources could not be used to build great buildings or to produce philosophy, artwork, or literature. So, the opportunity cost of Sparta's decision to achieve military greatness was the lost opportunity to pursue the cultural and social achievements that made Athens great.)

   d. How did Athens choose to use its resources differently?

(Resources were used to develop democracy and produce magnificent temples, art, literature, and philosophy.)

   e. What was the opportunity cost of the Athenian choice to devote its resources to "butter"?

   (Because Athens chose to devote most of their resources to "butter" they were vulnerable to Spartan military power. In fact, they were defeated by Sparta during the Peloponnesian War in 404 B.C.E.)

CLOSURE

31. Ask students the following questions to review the historical content:

   a. What common problem was each city-state forced to solve early in their history?

   (The city-states had to decide how to feed a growing population.)

   b. How did Sparta choose to increase its food production?

   (It conquered and enslaved its neighbor, Messenia.)

   c. How did Athens choose to increase its food production?

   (It grew olives and grapes and produced olive oil and wine, which it traded for grain.)

   d. What was the focus of Spartan society and why?

   (Military strength; Sparta feared a helot revolt.)

   e. What was the focus of Athenian society?

   (There was no single focus; instead, people were free to pursue their own interests. The result was a civilization that achieved greatness.)

32. Ask students the following questions to review the economic content:

a. Why does scarcity exist?

(Scarcity exists because human wants exceed the capacity of available resources to satisfy those wants.)

b. What is opportunity cost?

(The highest-valued alternative given up when a choice is made)

c. What is a production possibilities frontier?

(A table or graph that shows the various combinations of two goods it is possible to produce with a given amount of resources)

d. How do economists use the phrase *guns versus butter*?

(The phrase refers to the trade-off that nations face when they make choices about devoting resources to military or civilian goods and services.)

e. Using these economic tools, how do you explain the vast differences between Athens and Sparta?

(Sparta chose to use its resources for its military. This left few resources for pursuing literature, art, and philosophy. Sparta chose guns at the expense of butter.)

ASSESSMENT

Multiple Choice

1. Which of the following was **not** characteristic of ancient Athens?

   a. It used direct democracy as a form of government.

   b. Trade was encouraged.

   c. **Women had considerable freedom.**

   d. Craftsmen built magnificent temples.

2. Which statement best reflects the choices made by Athens and Sparta?

   a. **Athens devoted more resources to *butter*, the opportunity cost was *guns*.**

   b. Athens devoted more resources to *guns*, the opportunity cost was *butter*.

   c. Sparta devoted more resources to *butter*, the opportunity cost was *guns*.

   d. Athens and Sparta made similar guns and butter decisions.

Constructed Response

1. Imagine you are the economic adviser to the king of Olivia, a Greek city-state. The king has contacted you regarding the city-state's use of resources. Olivia has neither the cultural achievement of Athens nor the military might of Sparta. Your task is to write a short report describing the current use of productive resources and draw a "guns versus butter" production possibilities frontier that illustrates current production. You should compare Olivia's resource use to Athens and Sparta. Your king is a bit jealous of Athenian achievements, so include your recommendations for how Olivia can model itself after Athens.

(The report should describe the current resource allocation as somewhere between Athens and Sparta. The production possibilities frontier should have "guns" on one axis and "butter" on the other with the Olivia point on the frontier line somewhere in the middle of the two axes. Students should advise the king to reduce the size of the military; this will free some of Olivia's most talented people to pursue "butter" activities. On the production possibilities frontier this would move the point along the curve closer to the "butter" axis.)

SOURCES

Beck, Roger B., Black, Linda, and Krieger, Larry S. 2001. *McDougal Littell World History: Patterns of Interaction*. Evanston, IL: McDougal Littell.

Durant, Will. 1939. *The Life of Greece*. New York: MJF.

Esler, Anthony, and Ellis, Elisabeth Gaynor. 2001. *World History: Connections to Today*. Upper Saddle River, NJ: Prentice Hall.

Nardo, Don. 2000. *Life in Ancient Athens*. San Diego, CA: Lucent.

Waterfield, Robin. 2004. *Athens: a History: from Ancient Ideal to Modern City*. New York: Basic Books.

FOR FURTHER STUDY

Recent research by Stephen Hodkinson states that the traditional interpretation of Sparta's economy is distorted. He argues that the economic system was not as closed as conventional thought would propose—Spartans were not banned from buying and selling, they were not forbidden from possessing gold and silver (except in the early fourth century B.C.E.), and private ownership of land existed.

Historical ideas, like in the other social sciences, develop over time and it is important to discuss with students the difficulties of understanding events from so long ago. History is rife with competing interpretations. Hodkinson's research may well change the way we view Sparta.

Hodkinson, Stephen. 2009. *Property and Wealth in Classical Sparta*. Swansea: Classical of Wales.

CONNECTIONS: U.S. HISTORY

Compare the freedom of Spartan women to the freedom experienced by women during World War II in America. In both cases, women gained additional freedom and responsibilities because the nation was using more resources for the military. Specifically, a large part of the male population was used for military purposes, which gave women more opportunities in their absence.

ACTIVITY 8.1

Athens' Choices

Athens was located in one of the least fertile areas in ancient Greece. Its unproductive land could not grow the grain necessary to feed the growing city-state. It solved its problem by growing olives and grapes, which it used to produce olive oil and wine. Athenians traded olive oil, wine, and other goods for grain from other locales. Athens' dependence on trade led to the building of the Athenian fleet, which went everywhere in the Mediterranean, from Spain in the west to the Black Sea in the east.

Athenians built magnificent temples, such as the Parthenon, but lived in very simple homes built of sun-dried brick. Houses had no plumbing, and light was provided by olive-oil lamps. Marriage and family were important to Athenian life. Marriages were arranged by parents. Girls usually were married at about the age of 14 to an older man—sometimes twice her age. Women did not have much freedom in Athens. Although they were citizens, they could not own or inherit property. Women were to remain at home and manage the household and slaves. They could appear in public only with permission from their husbands. Men did much of the shopping at the market. Girls did not usually receive a formal education; most stayed home and learned from their mothers how to manage a household. Boys usually went to school at the age of seven, where they were taught reading, writing and grammar, music, and gymnastics. Instead of paper and pencil, students wrote on wax-covered wooden tablets. At age 18, a boy received a year of military training.

Most Athenian families of the citizen class owned at least one slave. The most common use of slaves was in farming, the main industry in Athens. Slaves also worked in the homes of Athenian citizens, and some conducted trade for their masters or accompanied them on trips. Female slaves cooked, cleaned, and made clothing. Slaves who worked in the silver mines probably endured the worst conditions.

The arts were celebrated in Athens, and great works of art, literature, and drama became the standard by which such works are judged even today. In addition, some of history's greatest thinkers and philosophers walked the streets of this city-state. Among them were the philosophers Socrates, Plato, and Aristotle. Various forms of Athenian government eventually evolved into direct democracy. Athens is remembered as one of the most advanced civilizations of ancient times and the birthplace of democracy.

ACTIVITY 8.2

Sparta's Choices

As Sparta grew, it could not feed its growing population. Sparta solved its food shortage by conquering neighboring Messenia around 725 B.C.E., taking over Messenian land and enslaving the Messenians to serve as agricultural slaves called *helots*. They forced the helots to grow crops for Sparta. The helot population grew and they outnumbered the Spartans by almost 8-to-1. In 600 B.C.E., the helots revolted and were nearly successful in putting down their Spartan rulers. The Spartans responded by reforming their society into one focused on military strength. They formed a government that exerted total control. In fact, every newborn baby had to be presented to rulers who decided whether the baby had the potential to be a great soldier or the mother of strong children. Those who failed the test were abandoned to die.

For men, daily life was focused on the military. At age seven, boys left home and moved into military barracks. Their schooling involved marching and training during the day and sleeping on hard benches at night. To encourage stealthiness, they were fed poorly and encouraged to steal food—but they were warned that if they were caught stealing food, they would be beaten. The goal was to make soldiers who were tough and ready to fight. It is said that when Spartan sons went off to war, their mothers told them to come back carrying their shields (victorious) or upon them (dead).

Spartan women had considerable freedom compared to women living in other Greek city-states. For example, women took on responsibilities such as managing the family estates. Spartan women could even inherit property, a right that was rare in the ancient world. Girls were encouraged to be fit and strong—they ran, wrestled, and played sports. It was thought that strong Spartan women would produce strong Spartan men for military service.

The Spartan government included two kings, a council of elders who advised the kings, and an assembly that approved major decisions. The assembly chose five *ephors* who ran the day-to-day affairs of the people, and wielded the real power in Spartan society.

Spartan society isolated itself from other Greeks. Except during wars, the people were not permitted to travel. Trade was discouraged. Money was made of iron bars to make economic transactions difficult. Free expression was discouraged and the arts and philosophy that flourished in nearby city-states did not occur in Sparta. Spartan society valued strength, duty, and discipline over individual worth and freedom. From this society, we get the English word *Spartan,* which means simple, frugal, or austere. Other Greeks were amazed at the military power of Sparta, but wondered if "Spartans are willing to die for their city because they have no reason to live."

ACTIVITY 8.3

Characteristics of Society

1. Travel was forbidden.

2. Trade was discouraged.

3. Military power was the focus of society.

4. Slavery existed.

5. Citizens lived in a city-state.

6. Great works of art were created.

7. Philosophy grew.

8. Government was a democracy.

9. Women had considerable freedom.

10. Women had few freedoms.

11. Trade was encouraged.

12. Enslaved helots were used to grow food.

13. Boys learned literature, music, and gymnastics.

14. Boys lived in military housing and trained for war.

15. Government consisted of 2 kings, assembly, and 5 ephors.

ACTIVITY 8.3

Characteristics of Society – Key

1. Travel was forbidden.

    (Sparta)

2. Trade was discouraged.

    (Sparta)

3. Military power was the focus of society.

    (Sparta)

4. Slavery existed.

    (both Athens and Sparta)

5. Citizens lived in a city-state.

    (both Athens and Sparta)

6. Great works of art were created.

    (Athens)

7. Philosophy grew.

    (Athens)

8. Government was a democracy.

    (Athens)

9. Women had considerable freedom.

    (Sparta)

10. Women had few freedoms.

    (Athens)

11. Trade was encouraged.

    (Athens)

12. Enslaved helots were used to grow food.

    (Sparta)

13. Boys learned literature, music, and gymnastics.

    (Athens)

14. Boys lived in military housing and trained for war.

    (Sparta)

15. Government consisted of 2 kings, assembly, and 5 ephors.

    (Sparta)

ACTIVITY 8.4

Athens   **Sparta**

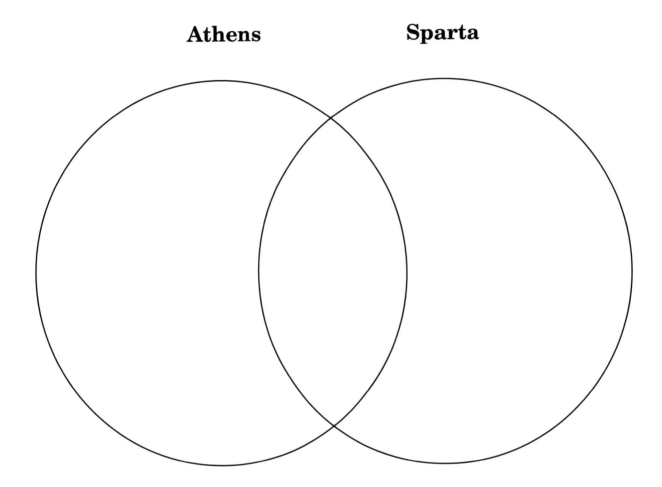

SLIDE 8.1

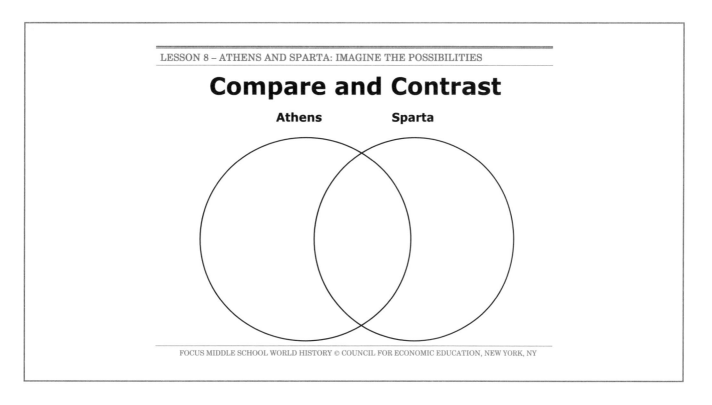

SLIDE 8.2

LESSON 8 – ATHENS AND SPARTA: IMAGINE THE POSSIBILITIES

Societies must make choices because of scarcity.

Scarcity: The condition that exists because human wants exceed the capacity of available resources to satisfy those wants.

Productive Resources: Natural resources, human resources, and capital resources used to make goods and services.

FOCUS MIDDLE SCHOOL WORLD HISTORY © COUNCIL FOR ECONOMIC EDUCATION, NEW YORK, NY

SLIDE 8.3

Productive resources include:

➤**Natural Resources** — "Gifts of nature" that can be used to produce goods and services; for example, oceans, air, mineral deposits, forests, and fields of land.

➤**Human Resources** — The health, education, experience, training, skills, and values of people; for example, doctors, teachers, and farmers.

SLIDE 8.4

Productive resources include:

➤**Capital Resources** — Goods made and used to produce and distribute goods and services; examples include tools, machinery, and buildings.

SLIDE 8.5

Societies must make choices because of scarcity.

Choices: Because our wants are greater than our resources, people must make choices. When you choose one thing, you must give up something else, which means there is an opportunity cost.

Opportunity Cost: The highest valued alternative that is given up when a choice is made.

SLIDE 8.6

Production Possibilities Frontier

Production Possibilities Frontier: A table or graph that shows the various combinations of two goods it is possible to produce with a given amount of resources.

Imagine a society that used all of its resources (natural, human, and capital) to produce two goods: olives and grapes. We can illustrate their choices on a production possibilities frontier, shown on the next slide.

SLIDE 8.7

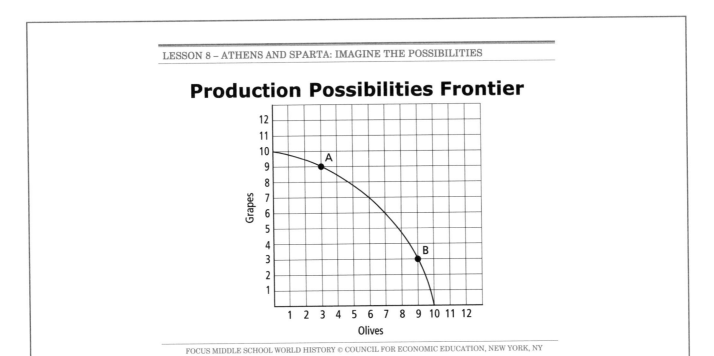

LESSON 8 – ATHENS AND SPARTA: IMAGINE THE POSSIBILITIES

Production Possibilities Frontier

FOCUS MIDDLE SCHOOL WORLD HISTORY © COUNCIL FOR ECONOMIC EDUCATION, NEW YORK, NY

SLIDE 8.8

LESSON 8 – ATHENS AND SPARTA: IMAGINE THE POSSIBILITIES

Guns vs. Butter

Guns vs. Butter: A phrase that refers to the trade-off that nations face when choosing to devote more or fewer resources to military or civilian goods and services.

Guns: Resources devoted to the production of military goods or services.

Butter: Resources devoted to the production of civilian goods or services.

FOCUS MIDDLE SCHOOL WORLD HISTORY © COUNCIL FOR ECONOMIC EDUCATION, NEW YORK, NY

SLIDE 8.9

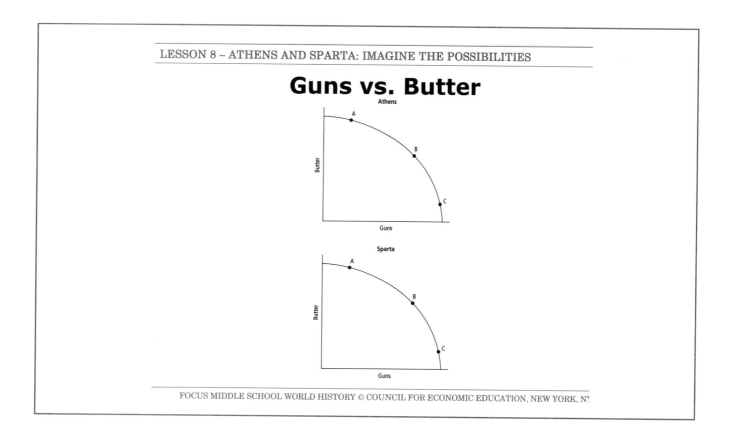

LESSON 9

ATHENS AND OLIVE OIL

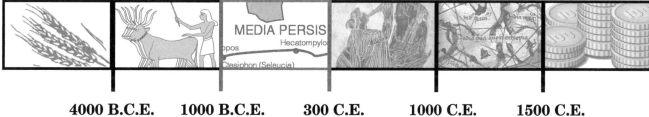

4000 B.C.E.   1000 B.C.E.   300 C.E.   1000 C.E.   1500 C.E.

LESSON 9
ATHENS AND OLIVE OIL

LESSON DESCRIPTION

In this lesson, students participate in a hypothetical Athenian assembly to discuss the Athenian trade policy with Egypt. While Athenian farmland does not grow the wheat necessary to sustain the population, it is conducive to growing olives, which are used to produce olive oil—a valuable trade commodity. The Athenian assembly decides to send a trade delegation to Egypt to discuss trade terms with Egyptian merchants. Students learn that both parties can benefit by specializing and trading.

INTRODUCTION

Athens was surrounded by substandard farmland that was not productive enough to grow the grains necessary to feed its population. In spite of the poor quality of the land, it was conducive to growing olives, which were used to produce olive oil. Olive oil had many uses in the ancient world and was very valuable. Athens had what economists would call a comparative advantage in olives and olive oil. It specialized in olives and olive oil and traded for wheat. Egypt had a comparative advantage in growing wheat, but its land was not very conducive to olive production. Egypt would specialize in wheat and trade for olive oil. Trade between Athens and Egypt allowed both to benefit.

CONCEPTS

Opportunity cost

Voluntary exchange

Absolute advantage

Comparative advantage

Production possibilities frontier (optional activity)

OBJECTIVES

Students will be able to:

- Determine opportunity cost of producing a good.

- Determine when a person or country has a comparative advantage in producing a good.

- Realize that trade benefits both sides in a transaction.

- (Optional) Construct and interpret a production possibilities frontier.

CONTENT STANDARDS

Voluntary Content Standards in Economics, 2nd edition

- **Standard 5:** Voluntary exchange occurs only when all participating parties expect to gain. This is true for trade among individuals or organizations within a nation, and among individuals or organizations in different nations.

- **Standard 6**: When individuals, regions, and nations specialize in what they can produce at the lowest cost and then trade with others, both production and consumption increase.

World History Content Standards

Era 3: Classical Traditions, Major Religions, and Giant Empires, 1000 B.C.E.–300 B.C.E.

- **Standard 2:** The emergence of Aegean civilization and how interrelations developed among peoples of the eastern Mediterranean and Southwest Asia, 600–200 B.C.E.

TIME REQUIRED

45 minutes; 60 minutes with optional activity

MATERIALS

- Two plastic cups, one marked "yes" and the other "no"

- Small pebbles or paperclips, one per student

  FOCUS: MIDDLE SCHOOL WORLD HISTORY © COUNCIL FOR ECONOMIC EDUCATION, NEW YORK, NY

- Slides 9.1–9.7

- Activity 9.1, one copy for each student

- Activity 9.2, one copy for each student

- Activity 9.3, four copies with the pages printed back-to-back on one sheet of paper

- Activity 9.4, four copies with the pages printed back-to-back on one sheet of paper

Additional materials for optional activity:

- Activity 9.5 and 9.6, one for each student

- Slides 9.8–9.12

- Rulers or straight edges, one per student

PROCEDURE

1. Ask students the following questions:

    a. Does your family make everything you use? Why not?

    (No. The students should say that their family uses earnings from working at jobs to buy what they use as opposed to trying to make everything they use.)

    b. Ask students if nations make everything they use. Why not?

    (Nations generally import quite a lot. In the same way that families do not make everything they use, countries do not make everything they use.)

    c. Do you hear people complain that it seems that very little is made in the United States? Why do they see that as a problem?

    (They may think the United States is dependent on those nations with which it trades.)

    d. Why do people trade?

    (To get goods and services they don't have or can't produce efficiently.)

    e. Are people better off or worse off because of trade?

    (Answers will vary, but let the students know that this is a question this lesson will answer.)

2. Ask students what they know about olive oil.

    (Students may have used olive oil in cooking or dipped bread in olive oil instead of using butter.)

3. Ask students if they know of other uses for olive oil. *(Answers will vary.)* Tell students that the ancient world had many uses for olive oil.

4. Distribute a copy of Activity 9.1 to each student. Ask students to read Activity 9.1 to find out more about olives and olive oil. Ask students the following questions:

    a. Why was olive oil called liquid gold?

    (It had many uses and was very valuable.)

    b. What were some of the many uses for olive oil?

    (It was used for food, medicine, fuel for lamps, and as a cosmetic, among other things).

    c. Although the Athenians had olive oil, what food problem did they have? Why?

    (The Athenians could not grow the food necessary to feed their growing population because their farm land was rocky and suited to growing very few crops.)

    d. Ask the students if they can think of a solution to this problem.

    (Answers will vary. Students may suggest trade, because the Athenians had a valuable good to trade.)

5. Tell students that the class will be traveling back in time to visit the Athenian assembly and listen to a discussion

that might have taken place. Tell the students you need some volunteers. Assign students the roles listed at the top of Activity 9.2. Give Activity 9.2 to each student who volunteers. You may also want to give a copy of Activity 9.2 to the rest of the class so that they can follow along. In addition, give the four students who play the part of Athenian slaves a copy of Activity 9.3. Give the four students who play the part of Egyptian slaves a copy of Activity 9.4. Finally, give each student a pebble or paper clip. (At the end of **Part A**, students will vote by dropping pebbles or paper clips into one of two plastic cups marked *yes* or *no*.)

6. Have the students perform Part A of the Activity 9.2 dialogue: The Athenian Assembly. It might be beneficial in creating the atmosphere of the assembly if students stand in different parts of the classroom to give their oration.

7. After the students have finished reading Part A, discuss the following:

    a. Why doesn't Pericles grow his own food?

    (He does not grow his own food because he finds it more beneficial to work as a blacksmith and buy his food at the market. The time required to grow food would take away from his work as a blacksmith.)

    b. Why does Themistocles grow food but not make his own tools and weapons?

    (He finds it more beneficial to farm and take the profit to buy tools and weapons.)

    c. Compared to Pericles, is Themistocles better at farming or blacksmithing?

    (He is better at both farming and blacksmithing.)

    d. If he is better at both, why doesn't he do both?

(He would give up too much farm production by spending time blacksmithing. Even though he is good at both, his farm production benefits him more.)

8. Show Slides 9.1 and 9.2. Go over terms **voluntary exchange**, **absolute advantage**, **comparative advantage**, and **opportunity cost** with the students. Make sure students understand the difference between absolute and comparative advantage by explaining the following:

    • Explain that absolute advantage is when one person or country is better at a task than another, and can produce more with the same resources (or produce the same amount with fewer resources).

    • Explain that comparative advantage exists when a certain person or country has a lower opportunity cost of doing something. Opportunity cost is the highest valued alternative given up when a choice is made—in other words, what is given up to obtain something.

9. As an example, tell students you are cleaning the house tonight. You are better at vacuuming and washing dishes than anyone else in your family. Ask students:

    a. What kind of advantage do you have in vacuuming and washing dishes?

    (Absolute advantage)

    b. Does this mean that you should do all the work and not ask for any help from your children? Why?

    (No. You will be able to finish more quickly if your children help, even if they are not as good at it as you.)

    c. Assume that, although you are much faster at both tasks, your children can wash dishes fairly well but have a hard time pushing the heavy vacuum cleaner. In which task do your children have a comparative advantage?

(Your children have a comparative advantage in washing dishes.)

10. Tell students you are returning to Athens. Ask the following questions:

    a. Who has an absolute advantage in farming, Pericles or Themistocles?

    (Themistocles has the absolute advantage in farming.)

    b. Who has an absolute advantage in blacksmithing, Pericles or Themistocles?

    (Themistocles also has an absolute advantage in blacksmithing.)

    c. If Themistocles has an absolute advantage in both farming and blacksmithing, does that mean he should do both?

    (No. Even though one person is better at both, he should specialize in that which has the lowest opportunity cost. Therefore, Themistocles should produce what he has a comparative advantage in, which is farming. Themistocles notes he would give up too much farming to do blacksmith work. The cost of farming is low in that he does not give up as much in blacksmith work.)

11. Direct students back to Athens and Egypt. Ask the following questions:

    a. According to the discussion, who is better at growing wheat, Egypt or Athens?

    (Egypt has the climate and fertile soil for wheat production. Egypt has an absolute advantage in growing wheat.)

    b. Who is better at growing olives and producing olive oil?

    (The Athenians believe they make the best olive oil in the world, though a few members of the assembly discussed the possibility that Egypt

would also be very productive at growing olives and producing olive oil. Athens has an absolute advantage in producing olive oil.)

12. While Athens is the more productive olive oil producer, some speculate whether Egypt could be better at producing both wheat and olive oil. Does Demetrios think they can find an opportunity to trade, even in that case? Why?

(Yes. Just as Themistocles buys his tools instead instead of making them because he would give up too much farm production, it will still benefit the Egyptians to specialize in wheat and trade for olive oil, because growing olives would mean giving up too much wheat, which they are very productive at growing. In economic terms, the opportunity cost is too high.)

13. Have students read **Part B** of Activity 9.2. After the dialogue, ask the following questions:

    a. What are the terms of trade for the two sides?

    (One bushel of wheat will be traded for one jar of olive oil.)

    b. Does it seem like Athens will benefit from this trade? Why?

    (Yes, they can have more than they could without trade. In the play, Athens gained two bushels of wheat by trading.)

    c. Does it seem like Egypt can benefit from this trade? Why?

    (Yes, they can have more than they could without trade. In the play, Egypt gained three jars of olive oil by trading.)

    d. So even if a country can produce many things, can it benefit from specializing in some goods and **voluntarily exchanging** these goods for others?

    (Yes, because of comparative advantage a country can have more of

many goods by specializing in producing some and trading for others.)

e. Which items should they produce?

(They should produce the goods with the lowest opportunity cost. In other words, they should produce the goods in which they have a comparative advantage.)

14. Show Slide 9.3. Tell the students that countries should produce where they have a comparative advantage. Consider Athens, where producing olive oil means they had to give up only 0.5 bushels of wheat for every jar of olive oil. Now consider Egypt, where producing one jar of olive oil means giving up producing four bushels of wheat.

15. Using the definition of comparative advantage and the questions on Slide 9.4, ask the students:

a. Which country has the lower opportunity cost of producing olive oil?

(Athens has a lower opportunity cost, giving up only 0.5 bushels of wheat instead of the 4 bushels that Egypt would give up.)

b. Which country has the comparative advantage in producing olive oil?

(Because Athens has a lower opportunity cost, it has a comparative advantage in olive oil.)

c. Who should produce olive oil?

(Athens should produce olive oil and trade for wheat.)

16. Show Slide 9.5. Consider Egypt, where producing a bushel of wheat means giving up 0.25 jars of olive oil. Now consider Athens, where producing a bushel of wheat means giving up two jars of olive oil.

17. Using the definition of comparative advantage and the questions on Slide 9.6, ask the students:

a. Which country has the lower opportunity cost of producing wheat?

(Egypt has a lower opportunity cost, giving up only 0.25 jars of olive oil instead of the 2 jars of olive oil that Athens would give up.)

b. Which country has the comparative advantage in producing wheat?

(Because Egypt has a lower opportunity cost, it has a comparative advantage in wheat.)

c. Who should produce wheat?

(Egypt should produce wheat and trade for olive oil.)

Note: Optional activity directions for a graphical activity follow the Closure section.

CLOSURE

18. Ask the following questions to review the lesson:

a. Are people better or worse off because of trade?

(People trade because they will be better off or they wouldn't have traded in the first place.)

b. What benefit did trade have for Athens?

(Trade allowed Athens to have more goods than it would have had without trade.)

c. In what way did trade benefit Egypt?

(It also had more goods than it would have had without trade.)

d. How does opportunity cost help determine what one group should produce and trade?

(People should produce and trade goods for which they have a lower opportunity cost.)

e. When does a person or country have a comparative advantage in producing a good?

(When they have a lower opportunity cost than another for producing that good.)

19. Show Slide 9.7. Ask students the following questions about trade in Athens:

   a. What do the quotes from Isocrates and Thucydides tell you about trade in Athens?

      (Trade in Athens led to a large variety of goods in Athens. Athens became a city-state where people had access to goods from all over the world.)

   b. How would trade allow for this variety of goods?

      (Athenians specialized in producing where they had a comparative advantage and were able to use their trade network to trade for goods from all over the Mediterranean.)

   c. In what way do these quotes remind you of the United States today?

      (The United States specializes and trades. As a result, it has access to a huge variety of goods from all over the world.)

OPTIONAL ACTIVITY

A. Give the students Activity 9.5 and Activity 9.6. Read the definition of **production possibilities frontier** with students from Slide 9.8. Students can use the production cards from the play to produce a production possibilities table and frontier. Have the "slaves" who are holding the production cards return to the front of the class to participate.

B. Both the Athenian and Egyptian slaves should start with their cards turned to the wheat side. Have students begin with the production possibilities table.

C. Tell students they will now construct a production possibilities frontier (PPF) for Athens. In the first column, the amount of wheat should be 4 and quantity of olive oil should be 0. Have the slaves flip their cards over one by one. As slaves flip their cards, a different combination of wheat and olive oil is shown. Have students write each combination in the appropriate column. Use Slide 9.9 as a guide.

D. Have students graph the information from the Athens production table by plotting a point at each of the coordinates from the table and connecting the dots to form a line. Use Slide 9.10 as a guide.

E. Tell students they will now construct a PPF for Egypt. In the first column, the quantity of wheat should be 16 and the quantity of olive oil should be 0. As slaves flip their cards one by one, the numbers will change so that in the last column, Egypt produces 4 olive oil and 0 wheat. Again, with each flip, the students should see a different combination of wheat and olive oil that could be produced. Have the students write each combination in the appropriate column. Use Slide 9.11 as a guide.

F. Have students graph the information from the Egypt production table by plotting a point at each of the coordinates from the table and connecting the dots to form a line. Use Slide 9.12 as a guide.

G. Tell students that the production possibilities frontier is a useful tool for showing the production possibilities of each civilization.

H. Tell the students to examine Activity 9.5. Refer to Slide 9.10 and ask the students: Can Athens by itself produce 4 bushels of wheat and 4 jars of olive oil?

   (No, if they want to have 4 jars of olive oil, they can only produce 2 bushels of wheat.)

I. Based on the lesson, is there a way for Athens to have more wheat and olive oil than what appears on this chart and frontier?

   (Yes, they can produce where they have a comparative advantage (olive oil) and trade for wheat. They will end up with more than they could produce on their own. In fact, using the terms of trade in the activity, by specializing in olive oil

and trading, Athens could have 4 bushels of wheat and 4 jars of olive oil.)

J. Tell students to examine Activity 9.6. Refer to Slide 9.12 and ask the students: Can Egypt produce 12 bushels of wheat and 4 jars of olive oil?

(No, if they want to have 12 bushels of wheat, they can produce only 1 jar of oil.)

K. Based on the lesson, is there a way for Egypt to have more wheat and olive oil than what appears on this chart and frontier?

(Yes, they can produce where they have a comparative advantage (wheat) and trade (for olive oil)—they will end up with more than they could produce on their own. In fact, using the terms of trade in the activity, by specializing in wheat and trading, Egypt could have 12 bushels of wheat and 4 jars of olive oil.)

ASSESSMENT

Multiple Choice

1. To figure who has the comparative advantage in a good, one must know about

   a. price.

   b. incentives.

   c. **opportunity cost.**

   d. absolute advantage.

2. Ancient Athens produced

   a. wheat, because its land was flat and fertile.

   b. olive oil, because it had an absolute advantage in producing it.

   c. wheat, because it had a comparative advantage in producing it.

   d. **olive oil, because it had a comparative advantage in producing it.**

Constructed Response

1. Athens had an advanced trade fleet and traded for many goods all over the Mediterranean Sea region. Explain how life in Athens might have been different if it had decided that it did not want to be dependent on other nations and should no longer trade for goods.

   (Athens was able to produce and consume more with trade than it would have without trade. So, a reversal of trade policy would have meant less of everything—including food—in terms of quantity and variety.)

CONNECTIONS: NAFTA

The North American Free Trade Agreement (NAFTA) is a trade agreement that created a North American trade bloc among the United States, Canada, and Mexico. In the period prior to its signing on December 8, 1993, much discussion focused on whether free trade would be beneficial to the United States. Economists stated then and continue to argue that comparative advantage allows all parties to benefit in voluntary exchange.

ACTIVITY 9.1

Agriculture in Athens

The 630,000 acres of land in Attica, the region in which Athens was located, were rocky and unproductive. In fact, one-third of it was not suitable for any kind of farming. Even with careful land management and irrigation, the region only produced 675,000 bushels of grain per year—hardly enough to supply a quarter of its population. Without imported food, Athens would have starved.

Although the terrain of Attica was not well suited for growing grain, it was well-suited for olives. An olive tree took 16 years of growing to produce use-able olives and 40 years to reach full productivity. Olive trees were so valuable in Athens that cutting one down was a crime punishable by exile or death. While the olive tree and its leaves became symbols of peace, wisdom, and victory, it was **olive oil** that was the source of Athens' wealth. Olive oil was considered liquid gold, and Greek olive oil was considered the finest in the ancient world. The oil had many uses: as a food and in cooking, in religious ceremonies, as lamp fuel for lighting homes, as a skin conditioner and a cleanser instead of soap, and as a medicine. Hippocrates, the father of medicine, referred to it as "the great therapeutic" with more than 60 uses as a medicine. Olive oil was applied to the skin of Olympic athletes before competitions.

www.istockphoto.com/ninette_luz

Olive oil was as valuable to the ancient world as petroleum oil is to the modern world. In Greek mythology, olives and olive oil were considered gifts from the goddess Athena to the Athenian people. Because of her gift of olives, one myth says, Athena was selected as the city's patron saint over Poseidon (god of the sea).

SOURCES

Durant, Will. 1939. *The Life of Greece.* New York: MJF.

Waterfield, Robin. 2004. *Athens: A History, from Ancient Ideal to Modern City.* New York: Basic Books.

ACTIVITY 9.2

CAST OF CHARACTERS

Aescylus

Ares (Greek god of war)

Athenian Trade Representative #1–abbreviated "Athenian T.R. #1"

Athenian Trade Representative #2–abbreviated "Athenian T.R. #2"

Athenian Trade Representative #3–abbreviated "Athenian T.R. #3"

Demetrios

Egyptian Merchant #1

Egyptian Merchant #2

Hermes (Greek god of trade)

Narrator

Pericles

The Archon

Themistocles

4 Greek Slaves

4 Athenian Slaves

PART A: THE ATHENIAN ASSEMBLY, AROUND 408 B.C.E.

Narrator:	The Athenian assembly has been called to discuss trade policy. Let's listen in on the discussion.
Aescylus:	Athens is a mighty city-state. I don't think we should be dependent on trading with other nations for food.
Pericles:	I agree! We defeated the mighty Persians; we should not have to be dependent on others for food!
Demetrios:	We have been trading for food for centuries. Why would we stop now? What do you propose?
Pericles:	The Persians control Egypt. Now they have entered into an alliance with Sparta against us. They would like nothing better than to punish us by cutting off our food supply.

Ares:	*(Whispering into the ear of Aesculus)* We defeated the Persians once before – maybe we should be planning war!
Aescylus:	Perhaps we should invade Egypt instead of trading. They have lots of grain. We defeated the Persians; we can conquer the Egyptians.
Ares:	*(Louder, more excitedly)* Conquer the Egyptians!
Hermes:	*(Whispering into the ear of Demetrios)* Why do we need war? We have the best olive oil in the world. We can trade for the grain.
Demetrios:	No, how about we continue to **trade** with the Egyptians?
Ares:	*(To Aescylus)* What?! Trade is for weak countries that grow dependent on others!
Aescylus:	We are Greeks; we don't need to depend on the Egyptians.
Demetrios:	*(Laughing)* If we don't trade we can only consume what we produce. With trade, we end up with more.
Pericles:	Do you think that trade is some sort of trick of the gods?
Demetrios:	No, but tell me, Pericles, what do you do for a living?
Pericles:	I am a blacksmith. I make tools and weapons out of hot metal.
Demetrios:	Do you grow your own food?
Pericles:	No. I spend my workday in my workshop. I take the profit and go to the market to buy my food.
Demetrios:	Why wouldn't it be worth your time to take part of your day and grow some food behind your workshop?
Pericles:	I can make enough money in a day in my workshop to buy food for many days. If I were to grow my own garden, I would give up time in my workshop. I wouldn't be nearly as well off.
Demetrios:	But aren't you dependent on the farmers who sell at the market?
Pericles:	What's with all the questions? Do you think you're Socrates or something? *(Laughing; the assembly also laughs)*
Demetrios:	Very funny. Socrates is a good friend of mine. But tell me, aren't you dependent on the farmers who sell at the market?
Pericles:	I guess I am.

Demetrios:	Isn't trading with Egypt the same? We are good at growing olives and we make the best olive oil in the world. The Egyptians love our olive oil. I think we are better off spending our time and effort growing olives and producing olive oil and continuing to trade for grain from the Egyptians.
Pericles:	Maybe. I'm not sure. What if the Egyptians decide to cut us off and grow their own olives and produce their own olive oil?
Demetrios:	They are just as dependent on us for olive oil as we are on them for wheat. Why would they stop trading with us if it benefits them, too?
Pericles:	They have very rich farmland and irrigation provided by the Nile. They can probably grow wheat **and** olives better than we can. If they grow their own olives and produce their own olive oil, they won't need to trade with us.
Demetrios:	I doubt anyone could grow olives as well as Athens. It is the fruit of the olive tree, given to us by Athena, the goddess of our great city. But, I will humor you. Tell me Pericles, from whom do you buy your food at the market?
Pericles:	I buy most of my food from Themistocles.
Demetrios:	Is Themistocles here?
Themistocles:	I am here.
Demetrios:	Tell me Themistocles, why do you spend your time farming?
Themistocles:	I inherited good farmland from my father. He taught me the skills I need. I make a good living growing food and selling it in the market.
Demetrios:	Do you ever buy tools or weapons from Pericles?
Themistocles:	Yes, he makes great tools.
Demetrios:	Why don't you take some time away from the fields and make your own tools?
Themistocles:	As it turns out, I am a very talented blacksmith. Some say I am even better than Pericles.
Pericles:	I admit, he is a better blacksmith. I am fortunate he spends his time farming.

Themistocles:	Thank you for the compliment, Pericles. I choose to farm because my farm is so productive. Every hour I would spend making my own weapons and tools is an hour that I cannot farm. I would be giving up too much in terms of farm produce if I spend my time making tools. It is more benefit to me to farm and take my profits and buy my tools from Pericles.
Demetrios:	So you are an excellent farmer and blacksmith, maybe the best in Athens in both tasks; but you still choose to spend all your time farming and buy your tools from Pericles?
Themistocles:	Yes. Even though I am very good at both, I am better off farming.
Demetrios:	Would you ever think of not trading with Pericles?
Themistocles:	Why would I? I benefit from our trade, too.
Demetrios:	So tell me, citizens of Athens, could it be possible that even if the Egyptians could grow olives very well, they would still trade with us?
Hermes:	*(To Demetrios)* If the Persians and Spartans continue to make our lives difficult, it will be important to have a strong trade partner. I think Greece can arrange a trade deal with Egypt— maybe even get a better deal than we are getting now!
Demetrios:	I think Greece should look into trade with Egypt. Let's send a trade ship of olive oil to Egypt with some of our finest traders from the market. Let's see if we can find a way that will benefit both of us.
The Archon:	Let's put it to a vote. The question is: shall we send a trade delegation to Egypt to strengthen our trade partnership. You will be given one pebble, put it in either the "yes" jar or the "no" jar.
Narrator:	All members of the assembly vote by putting their pebble in one of the two jars. All but Aeschylus (who under advice from Ares still wants war) vote to send the trade delegation.
The Archon:	The assembly had decided to send a trade mission to Egypt. Their goal is to bring back a trade agreement that benefits Athens.
Aeschylus:	Darn, I was hoping for war.
Ares:	*(Disappointed)* So was I.

PART B: TRADE MEETING IN EGYPT

Note: Behind each delegation, four slaves now stand with cards. Behind Egypt, the cards have 4 wheat on one side and 1 olive oil on the other side. Behind Athens, cards have 1 wheat on one side and 2 olive oil on the other side. In the beginning, two Athenian slaves have the wheat side of their card showing and two have the olive oil side of their card showing. In Egypt, three slaves have the wheat side showing and one slave has the olive oil side showing.

Narrator:	The scene is now in Egypt, where Egyptian merchants are meeting with the Athenian trade merchants.
Athenian T.R. #1:	Thank you for meeting with us today. We have a ship loaded with our finest Athenian olive oil in the harbor. We want to work out a trade agreement for the olive oil in our ship and for olive oil in the future.
Egyptian Merchant #1:	We like your olive oil. It is the best in the Mediterranean. What are you proposing? What—in terms of wheat—will we have to pay for your olive oil?
Athenian T.R. #1:	We are prepared to pay one jar of olive oil for each bushel of wheat.
Athenian T.R. #2:	Wait, can we talk privately for a minute?

Each side huddles to discuss the terms of trade.

Athenian T.R. #1:	What's the matter, #2?
Athenian T.R. #2:	Are you sure that we benefit from that deal? One jar of our finest olive oil for one bushel of wheat?
Athenian T.R. #1:	Let's see. *(Pointing to the Greek slaves.)* Currently, two bushels of wheat and four jars of olive oil are being produced. If you have the slaves produce only olive oil, how much would you have?
Athenian T.R. #2:	*(To the Greek slaves)* Produce only olive oil. *(The slaves should turn their cards to olive oil.)* I can produce eight jars of olive oil.

Athenian T.R. #1:	And if you produce only wheat, how much can you produce?
Athenian T.R. #2:	*(To the Greek slaves)* Produce only wheat. *(The slaves should turn their cards to wheat.)* I can produce only four bushels of wheat.
Athenian T.R. #1:	So, if you were to produce eight jars of olive oil—*(To Greek slaves)* go back to eight oil—and trade one for one, you could have eight bushels of wheat, or twice as much as you could have if you grew it. Or you could trade four olive oil jars for four units of wheat—you would have the same amount of olive oil as before trade, plus gain two bushels of wheat—you would have four bushels of wheat instead of the two you had with no trade!
Athenian T.R. #2:	Wow, it's like a gift from Hermes, the god of trade!
Hermes:	You're welcome!
Athenian T.R. #1:	Well #3, what do you think?
Athenian T.R. #3:	Sounds like we will benefit from the deal. Let's do it.

Meanwhile, over in the Egypt huddle …

Egyptian Merchant #1:	Can we benefit from a one-bushel-of-wheat-for-one-jar-of-olive-oil trade?
Egyptian Merchant #2:	Egyptian farmers can grow as much as 16 bushels of wheat …

Egyptian slaves flip cards so all are showing wheat.

Egyptian Merchant #2:	Or produce as many as four jars of olive oil.

Egyptian slaves flip cards so all are showing olive oil.

Egyptian Merchant #2:	Currently, the Egyptian farmers produce about 12 bushels of wheat and one jar of olive oil.

Three Egyptian slaves show the wheat side of their card, one shows the olive oil side.

Egyptian Merchant #1:	We could increase production of wheat by four bushels.

The Egyptian slave showing olive oil flips to wheat, so all are showing wheat.

Egyptian Merchant #1:   The four bushels of wheat could be traded to the Greeks for four jars of olive oil—we would have the same amount of wheat, 12 bushels, but have more olive oil, four jars instead of one!

Egyptian Merchant #2:   Yes, we can benefit from this trade deal.

Huddles break up and representatives meet in the middle of the space.

Athenian T.R. #1:   Again, we would like to trade with you on the following terms: one jar of olive oil for one bushel of wheat.

Egyptian Merchant #1:   You have a deal.

They shake hands. The Athenian traders can be seen doing arm pumps and giving high-fives as they leave. Egyptians look at each other and shrug.

Hermes: I love it when a plan comes together!

ACTIVITY 9.3

Production Card: Athens

www.istockphoto.com/bigredlynx

ACTIVITY 9.3, CONTINUED
Production Card: Athens

www.istockphoto.com/ninette_luz

ACTIVITY 9.4

Production Card: Egypt

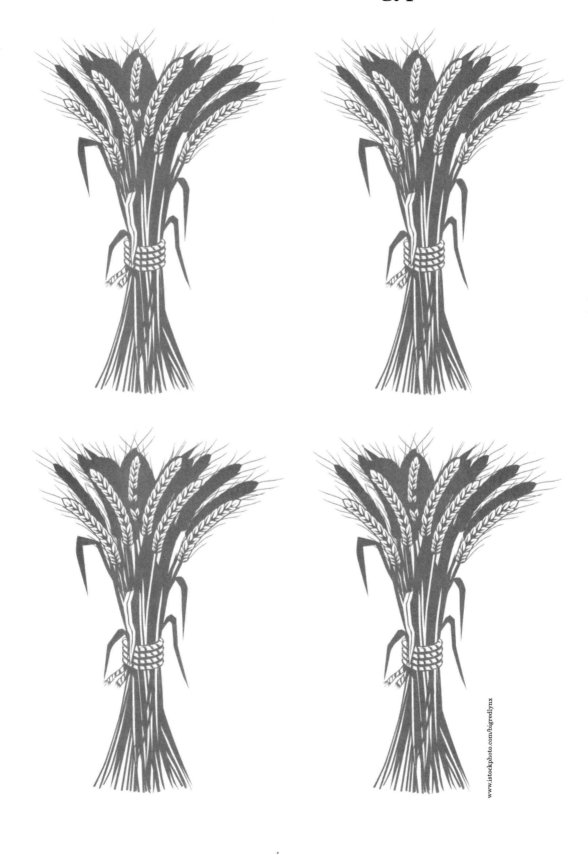

www.istockphoto.com/bigredlynx

ACTIVITY 9.4, CONTINUED

Production Card: Egypt

www.istockphoto.com/ninette_luz

ACTIVITY 9.5

Athens (optional activity)

Production Possibilities Frontier – A table or graph that shows the various combinations of two goods it is possible to produce with a given amount of resources.

Athens	All cards wheat	Flip one card	Flip second card	Flip third card	Flip last card
Wheat					
Olive Oil					

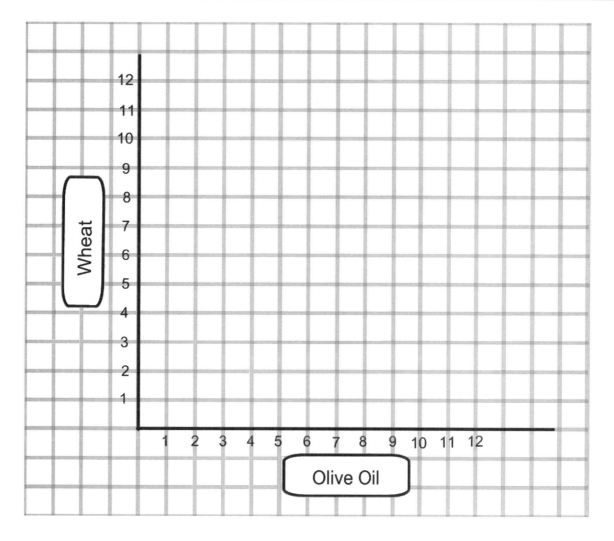

ACTIVITY 9.6

Egypt (optional activity)

Production Possibilities Frontier – A table or graph that shows the various combinations of two goods it is possible to produce with a given amount of resources.

Egypt	All cards wheat	Flip one card	Flip second card	Flip third card	Flip last card
Wheat					
Olive Oil					

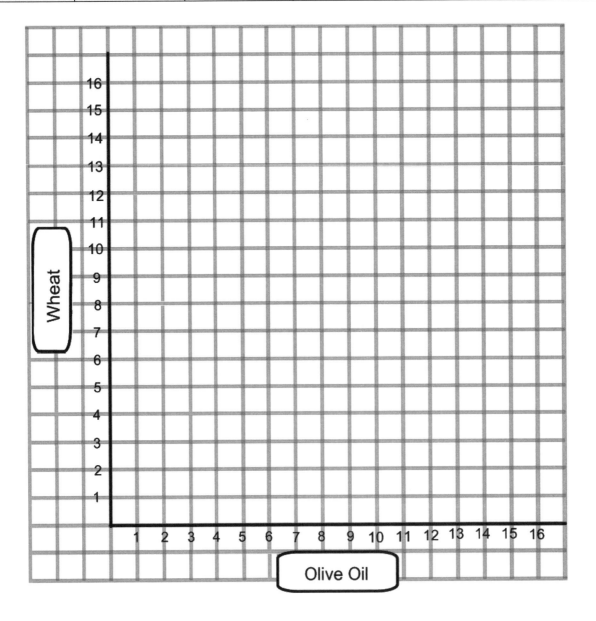

S<small>LIDE</small> 9.1

Vocabulary

Voluntary Exchange: Trading goods and services with other people because both parties expect to benefit from the trade.

Absolute Advantage: The ability to produce more units of a good or service than some other producer, using the same quantity of resources.

S<small>LIDE</small> 9.2

Vocabulary

Comparative Advantage: The ability to produce a good or service at a lower opportunity cost than some other producer. This is the economic basis for specialization and trade.

Opportunity Cost: The highest valued alternative that is given up when a choice is made.

SLIDE 9.3

In Athens:
Producing one jar of olive oil meant giving up one-half bushel of wheat.

The opportunity cost of is

In Egypt:
Producing one jar of olive oil meant giving up four bushels of wheat.

The opportunity cost of is

SLIDE 9.4

Comparative Advantage: *The ability to produce a good or service at a lower opportunity cost than some other producer.*

Which country has the lower opportunity cost of producing olive oil?

Which country has the comparative advantage in producing olive oil?

Therefore, who should produce olive oil?

SLIDE 9.5

LESSON 9 – ATHENS AND OLIVE OIL

In Egypt:
Producing one bushel of wheat meant giving up one-fourth jar of olive oil.

The opportunity cost of is

In Athens:
Producing one bushel of wheat meant giving up two jars of olive oil.

The opportunity cost of is

SLIDE 9.6

LESSON 9 – ATHENS AND OLIVE OIL

***Comparative Advantage:** The ability to produce a good or service at a lower opportunity cost than some other producer.*

Which country has the lower opportunity cost of producing wheat?

Which country has the comparative advantage in producing wheat?

Therefore, who should produce wheat?

SLIDE 9.7

The articles which it is difficult to get, one here, one there, from the rest of the world, all these it is easy to buy in Athens.

—Isocrates, Greek Orator (436–338 B.C.E.)

The magnitude of our city draws the produce of the world into our harbor, so that to the Athenian the fruits of other countries are as familiar a luxury as those of his own.

—Thucydides, Greek Historian (460–395 B.C.E.)

SLIDE 9.8

Vocabulary

Production Possibilities Frontier: A table or graph that shows the various combinations of two goods it is possible to produce with a given amount of resources.

SLIDE 9.9

Athens' Production Possibilities Table

Athens	All cards wheat	Flip one card	Flip second card	Flip third card	Flip last card
Wheat	4	3	2	1	0
Olive Oil	0	2	4	6	8

SLIDE 9.10

Athens' Production Possibilities Graph

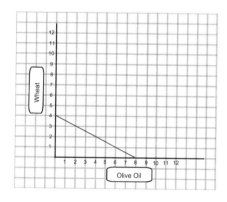

SLIDE 9.11

Egypt's Production Possibilities Table

Egypt	All cards wheat	Flip one card	Flip second card	Flip third card	Flip last card
Wheat	16	12	8	4	0
Olive Oil	0	1	2	3	4

SLIDE 9.12

Egypt's Production Possibilities Graph

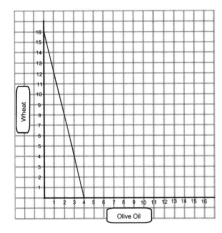

LESSON 10

FALL OF ROME

4000 B.C.E.   1000 B.C.E.   300 C.E.   1000 C.E.   1500 C.E.

LESSON 10
FALL OF ROME

LESSON DESCRIPTION

This lesson highlights the economic role of government in the period leading up to the fall of Rome. Like most lessons on government, it emphasizes the beneficial aspects. However, unique to this lesson, it investigates some of the weaknesses of government by focusing on some of the governmental decisions that contributed to the fall of Rome. This investigation helps students understand why governments, like markets, can and do fail. Specifically, this lesson discusses how even well-intentioned government officials may make decisions that are not in the best economic interests of citizens.

In the lesson, the teacher provides payment for student work throughout a designated class period. Students receive a payment of paper clips for attending class, obeying the rules of the classroom, and participating in class discussions. Taxes are collected to represent the government's desire to raise revenue to pay for roads, military defense, and special programs like circuses or gladiator competitions. Students, representing Roman taxpayers, are asked to discuss the benefits and costs associated with government spending and to vote on whether to pay for a gladiator competition. Throughout this activity, the economic benefits of each government project are compared to their costs across voting and taxpaying groups. Students see that the benefits of government spending on things like roads outweigh the costs. But they also see that the costs of special programs like a gladiator competition can outweigh the benefits, even when the majority of voters determine what is funded. This comparison of public projects highlights the possibility of government failure.

INTRODUCTION

When Rome was at the center of the Western world's wealth around 117 C.E., its economy was driven largely by agriculture. Farmers, olive oil producers, shepherds and other agriculturalists accumulated wealth by providing the goods and services others valued in the marketplace. Rome built up surpluses and traded with other nations possessing non-agricultural skills and resources. During this period, some large-scale businesses in manufacturing emerged. Bustling urban centers surfaced. Sanitation advanced. Education spread. Public parks provided places for people to wander and enjoy themselves. Attracted by economic opportunities, immigrants came to Rome, making more development possible. Civil order and respect for both individual rights and private property in Rome prevailed for free individuals, though not for slaves. Early on, Roman government protected individuals' rights and supported free trade. Taxes and tariffs were relatively low and the benefits of Roman government spending largely outweighed the costs in different areas. Free Romans gained wealth. Consequently, the trading of goods, services and resources was brisk. But eventually, trade slowed and progress stalled. The Western Roman Empire collapsed in the fifth century.

Popular explanations cite various causes of the collapse as external military threats, people fleeing diseases and plagues, climate change, rapid inflation, the spread of Christianity, and moral decay. But a closer investigation of the fall of Western Rome indicates that the Roman government itself played a role. During the third and fourth centuries, government spending expanded and was unpredictable, taxes rose, and money devaluation occurred. Each of these government choices contributed to the weakening of the overall economy. For these reasons and others, the Roman Empire collapsed in 476 C.E.

CONCEPTS

Government expenditures

Government failure

Public goods and services

Subsidy

Taxes

Tax revenue

Wages

OBJECTIVES

Students will be able to:

- Explain how tax dollars are used to provide national defense, school education, and roads.

- Show that public goods and services provide benefits to many people. Their use cannot be restricted to those people who can or are willing to pay.

- Give examples that show that the benefits of government can outweigh the costs.

- Explain why the costs of government policies can also exceed the benefits.

- Identify some of the economic and political factors contributing to the decline of the Roman Empire.

CONTENT STANDARDS

Voluntary Content Standards in Economics, 2nd edition

- **Standard 16:** There is an economic role for government in a market economy whenever the benefits of a government policy outweigh its costs. Governments often provide for national defense, address environmental concerns, define and protect property rights and attempt to make markets more competitive. Most government policies also have direct or indirect effects on peoples' incomes.

- **Standard 17:** Costs of government policies sometimes exceed benefits. This may occur because of incentives facing voters, government officials and government employees, because of actions by special interest groups that can impose costs on the general public, or because social goals other than economic efficiency are being pursued.

World History Content Standards

World History Era 4. Expanding Zones of Exchange and Encounter, 300–1000 C.E.

- **Standard 1:** Imperial crises and their aftermath, 300–700 C.E.

- **Standard 7:** Major global trends from 300–1000 C.E.

TIME REQUIRED

60 minutes

MATERIALS

- Approximately 40 paper clips per student. Macaroni noodles or something similar may be substituted for paper clips.

- Slides 10.1–10.5

- A piece of blank paper for each student

- Activity 10.1, 5 copies

- Activity 10.2, 5 copies

- Activity 10.3, 5 copies

PROCEDURE

1. Tell students that they will play the role of Roman citizens. Place 20 paper clips on each student's desk. Tell them that the paper clips in their possession will determine the number of points awarded at the end of this activity. Identify yourself as the Roman emperor. You may want to dress the part, with a sheet draped around you, toga style.

2. Explain the role-playing activity:

   - The 20 paper clips on the students' desks represent their property, payments for completed work, and rewards for respecting the rules of the empire and cooperating with others.

   - The citizens of the empire can earn additional paper clips throughout the class period by answering questions, cooperating with others, and obeying the rules of the "empire" (classroom).

3. Illustrate how the role-play works by taking away 5 paper clips from the citizens (students) who arrived after class officially starts or were not quiet at the start of the class. Explain that only government, not business, has the right to take away income from the people of the empire. In your capacity as emperor, remove the clips from the desks of students who are absent.

4. Explain that the citizens of the empire must fund their government through **tax revenues**. Tell the students that a 10 percent tax will be charged on the property held by each citizen. Ask the class what is owed by each citizen if the tax rate is 10 percent. *(2 is 10 percent of 20.)* A tax of 2 paper clips per 20 paper clips must be collected.

5. Tell students that taxes are needed by the empire to fund **government expenditures**. Give examples of these expenditures, using your school as an analogy for the Roman Empire: to provide schools (the class), build and repair roads (school hallways), provide a legal system (school rules), and provide national defense (school and student protection from outside forces).

6. Ask one student to work for the Roman government. For a payment of 10 paper clips, this public employee is responsible for policing, distributing payments on behalf of the Roman Emperor and government, collecting taxes and helping the emperor (you, the teacher) when called on. The tax collector is exempt from paying taxes. Make a big deal out of this. The employee's first task is to serve as tax collector.

7. Ask him or her to go around and collect the tax of 2 paper clips per students. After the tax collector completes this work, pay his or her government wage of 10 paper clips, and place the collected tax in a visible place.

8. Tell students that, as Roman citizens, they can work to earn paper clips. They do so by answering questions and participating in discussions throughout class.

Note: At your discretion, give students from 2 to 20 paper clips for providing correct answers or making meaningful contributions to class discussions. At appropriate times throughout this activity, announce that it is time to pay taxes. Send the tax collector to collect the 10 percent tax (rounding up).

9. Ask students to define (remembering to reward those who answer):

- **wages**

- **taxes**

*(**Wages** are direct payments made by employers to workers for voluntarily providing services that help businesses produce goods and services. Wages can be consumed, saved, or invested by the wage earner. **Taxes** are compulsory payments to the government. People have to pay them or risk penalty.)*

10. Ask students (remembering to reward those who answer):

a. Who benefits from earning a wage?

(The wage earner receives the direct benefits of the wages, given the sacrifice made to work. A person works when the additional benefits of working exceed the costs of working elsewhere, spending time with family, relaxing, or indulging in recreational activities. Otherwise, the worker will not work. It doesn't make sense to work when there is more benefit from doing something else. The worker is free to choose to work or not to work. The employer is free to choose to employ the worker or not.

b. Who benefits from taxes?

(Taxes are required by the government to pay for running the government, upholding laws, building schools and bridges, maintaining welfare, and supporting government-sponsored programs. The people who benefit from taxes are those who benefit from the programs funded by the government. While some government programs benefit everyone, some

government programs benefit a small portion of the population.)

11. Remind students that everything discussed today is related to the Roman Empire:

    - At times, the Roman Empire was ruled by one person with unlimited power, who made all of the governmental decisions on his own.

    - At other times, the ruler made decisions on things like what taxes or spending programs to set in place under the influence of special groups of people. Some of these groups were called assemblies. Other groups formally swayed the emperor in an official capacity, such as the Roman Senate.

    - For the sake of discussion, this lesson focuses on the period when the Roman Empire was ruled by an emperor whose power was kept in check by a Senate that represented the peoples' assemblies.[1] People in government wanted to stay in government and pleasing the people supporting them was a way to do that.

    Note: There is considerable debate about the level of influence of the peoples' assemblies and the Senate on the emperor over time. For the point of discussion, we assume that the influence of the Senate and peoples' assemblies was significant. This signals that the will of the people mattered and guided some of the choices made by the government.

12. Tell students that for the rest of the class, they will be divided into groups representing towns and cities of the Roman Empire. Divide the students into five groups of nearly equal size. Name them one of the following: Rome,

Naples, Pompeii, Herculaneum, and Capreae. Ask each group to choose a leader to relay the group's answers to questions. The group's answer can be determined by consensus or majority rule when there are different views on issues.

13. Tell the students that governments have certain economic roles. Tell the students that Rome provides an opportunity to study four of these roles. Beginning with Slide 10.1, review these four key roles of government:

    - Support a legal system and protect property rights

    - Provide public goods

    - Maintain competition in markets

    - Redistribute income through tax collection and government programs

14. At Slide 10.2, note that economists have a special meaning for a public good. A public good is:

    - Shareable (nonrival in economist-speak)—which means that many people can enjoy the good at the same time. National defense, flood control projects, and firework displays are examples of goods that many people can enjoy at the same time without diminishing other people's enjoyment of the good.

    - Not excludable—which means that, once the good is made available, people cannot be prevented from enjoying it. For example, once national defense is provided, everyone benefits, regardless of whether they have paid.

15. Tell students that the government provides public goods because private businesses can't get people to pay for them.

16. Continue reviewing the slides with the students, show Slides 10.3 and 10.4.

17. Distribute Activity 10.1 to each group. Ask each group to look over the different types of spending programs of the Roman Empire. Ask students to classify

---

[1]Gibbon, Edward. 1782 (Written) and 1845 (Revised). *History of the Decline and Fall of the Roman Empire.* 7 volumes. Public Domain Books (November 1, 1996).

each program. (Again, reward individuals or groups who participate.)

(Suggested answers: Roman road – might best be considered a public good, although toll roads—common in Roman times—were not available to all and some roads became too crowded for everyone to use. Another idea might be that roads promoted competition because they allowed trade between cities. Roman military – public good. Subsidized bread – redistribution of income through a government program. Roman law – legal system. Aqueducts – redistribution of income through a government program (providing "free" water for people) or a public good (assuming that the water was available to all and that enough water was available for everyone). Note: Finding examples of pure public goods is difficult; national defense is the best example. The correctness of the example depends on how "shareable" and "not excludable" the good is.)

18. With a lot of enthusiasm, ask students, as citizens of the Roman Empire, if they would like to see horse and chariot races—also known as a Roman circus. By a show of hands, take a class vote. *(The majority of students will probably vote yes!)* Announce that the circus will go on! Pause and then ask the "citizens" how they will pay for this government-sponsored program. *(Someone should eventually answer taxes.)*

Remember to pay for answers.

19. Announce that the Senate has decided to raise taxes to fund the circus. Everyone must pay 5 paper clips. Direct the tax collector to take 5 paper clips from each citizen.

20. Once the taxes are gathered, point to the group of students assigned the city of Rome and enthusiastically say, "Only the people of Rome can see the circus! This is where, I, the emperor, want to see the chariot races. Because the viewing area is limited, I choose the citizens

living in my city! They support me most!" Discuss with the citizens of other cities how they feel about having to pay taxes benefiting only those living in the city of Rome.

(Accept a variety of responses. Encourage dissatisfied students to say that they are frustrated, mad, or angry with the government. What is happening is unfair and not beneficial to everyone. Some students may even say they want to revolt against the government.)

Again, remember to pay students joining the discussion.

21. Hand out Activity 10.2. Ask students to look at the table and determine whether their group should vote in favor of the government sponsoring a gladiator competition. Ask them to explain their vote using the golden rule of economics: Do something if the benefits outweigh the costs!

(Using the appropriate data in each row, students across groups should weigh the benefits against the costs. The groups representing Rome, Naples, and Pompeii should vote in favor of the gladiator event because the benefits of the competition exceed the costs; the others should oppose it because the costs exceed the benefits.)

22. Ask each group leader to vote with a "thumbs up" or "thumbs down."

(The gladiator competition should be funded due to majority vote; three out of five of the groups should vote "yes.")

Enthusiastically announce that the gladiator competition, like the circus, will go on! Remember to collect taxes from each group and to reward the groups who benefit from the gladiator competition with paperclips.

23. Ask students in Herculaneum and Capreae to discuss the impact on their cities. Points to discuss:

- Government-sponsored goods or services can be provided to certain groups at no direct money cost to them. Nevertheless, they are not free. They have to be funded. Tax dollars fund the costs of these government-sponsored programs.

- **Government failure** can occur. Programs whose costs are higher than the benefits may be implemented if enough voters benefit from the program.

24. Ask students why they think wasteful programs occurred in ancient Rome and what the effects were.

   (Roman emperors, senators, and their supporters liked taking credit for providing "free circuses" or "free entertainment," which was misleading because they were not free. The entertainment was paid for by citizens, many of whom received no benefit. Rome, in its later stages, suffered greatly from wasteful spending by government officials.)

25. Hand out Activity 10.3. Ask student groups to look at the list of goods. Have them weigh overall benefits to overall costs to the Roman Empire. Groups will need to speculate a bit. Have them write yes or no in the first column. Review their answers.

   (The students will likely say that the roads, laws, and aqueducts have benefits greater than the costs of providing them. They are likely to suggest that the gladiator fights have costs greater than the benefits. Finally, the subsidized bread program was very expensive for Rome; the benefits were visible but likely smaller than the costs.)

26. Finally, ask each group to vote whether they want the program. Tell groups to decide which programs they will support and enter their choices in the second column (yes or no).

27. Read down the list and ask the group leaders to (simultaneously) give each program a "thumbs up" or a "thumbs down," based on their group's decision.

   (Of course, results will vary. It is very likely that roads, laws, and aqueducts will be voted in, based on the benefits

relative to the costs. Bread subsidies may or may not be voted in, depending on the importance students place on helping the poor relative to the costs of the program. Finally, given the distribution of the benefits of the gladiator fights, it is unlikely this will be voted in.)*

28. Tell students that a corrupt and wasteful government was only one of many reasons Rome fell. Show Slide 10.5 and review some of the other reasons that may have contributed to Rome's fall.

29. Bring the activity to an end. Ask students to count their paper clips. Ask them to place their name on a clean sheet of paper and state their total on it. Ask your assistant to check and collect their work along with the clips. Reward the students based on how many paper clips they have. Rewards might include extra-credit points or classroom privileges.

CLOSURE

30. Ask the students the following questions:

   a. What are four economic roles of government?

      (Provide legal system, provide public goods, maintain competition, and redistribute income.)

   b. Why do government programs whose costs are greater than their benefits get passed?

      (The programs benefit enough people to be approved by politicians trying to please voters. Or, in the case of Rome in its later stages, emperors who were trying to cling to power tried to implement popular, but inefficient, programs.)

   c. Which Roman projects do you think were good for the Roman Empire in the long run?

      (Answers will vary.)

31. Conclude by summarizing the lesson as follows: As the Roman government funded more and more projects, it

misused more and more of the empire's resources. The economy of the Roman Empire suffered. On one hand, projects such as roads and aqueducts helped Rome grow and expand; on the other hand, as special programs increased, the government's poor spending choices wasted resources, frustrated taxpayers, and discouraged overall cooperation and harmony in markets.

ASSESSMENT

Multiple Choice

1. Which one of the following is an example of a public good?

   a. Olives

   b. **Fireworks display over a large lake**

   c. Katy Perry concert in an arena

   d. Cable television

2. When is a program whose overall costs are greater than its overall benefits most likely to be approved by elected officials?

   a. **When the large costs of the program are on a few people and the benefits go to many people.**

   b. When the small benefits go to a small number of people and the larger costs are paid by a large number of people.

   c. When the costs are paid equally and the benefits are enjoyed by all.

   d. When the costs are less than twice the benefits for everyone.

Constructed Response

1. Use an example drawn from the Roman Empire to explain how government can fail to help individuals.

   (When government intervenes and chooses programs whose costs exceed the benefits for the entire citizenry, resources are wasted. Problems arise and individuals resist having governmental decision-makers use their tax dollars to spend on unproductive projects. Students are likely to use the activity involving the gladiator competition to illustrate this point. However, they can also use the examples of the circuses, amphitheatre productions, and the like.)

CONNECTIONS: MORE ON ROME: INFLATION AND MONEY

Most history textbooks discuss how inflation problems weakened the economy of Western Rome. Instructors can now connect the Roman expansion in money and the devaluation of its currency to spending on subsidy programs and entertainment. Because the spending did not support overall business expansion and encouraged waste, the Roman Empire could not rely on an expanding tax base from increased business activity and higher incomes. Government had to turn to methods like making coins with less gold and silver in them and producing more of the less-valuable coins. Prices rose, and excessive budget deficits (annual government expenditures exceeding tax revenues) surfaced. Creative public financing was needed to pay off public debt (accumulated deficits) and fueled inflation. People became upset and frustrated as prices rose. By issuing more money (devaluing the country's currency), the government caused an increase in the demand for goods and services. But because the country's production of goods and services depended on the quality and quantity of its resources and its technology—two elements that have not changed in this scenario—too many units of currency chased too few goods and services continued to push prices upward.

ACTIVITY 10.1

Government Programs and the Role of Government

Names: _____

Roman Government Program	Legal Framework or Property Rights	Public Good	Promote Competition	Redistribute Income via Taxes or Programs
Roman Roads				
Roman Military				
Subsidized Bread (Government pays to the baker part of cost of producing bread)				
Roman Law				
Aqueducts (Channels built to allow water to flow to everyone for safe drinking and washing)				

ACTIVITY 10.2

Analyzing the Benefits and Costs of Government Programs

Names: _____

Costs and Benefits of Government Spending on a Gladiator Competition denarius, a unit of Roman currency NOTE: denarius, plural denarii		
		Tax Plan Payment per GROUP
City	**Benefits Received per GROUP** (paper clips ~ denarii)	**Taxes** (paper clips ~ denarii)
Rome	20	15
Naples	20	15
Pompeii	20	15
Herculaneum	0	15
Capreae	0	15

ACTIVITY 10.3

Weighing the Benefits and Costs

Names: _____

Roman Government Program	Overall Benefits > Overall Costs?	Will you vote for the program?
Roman Roads throughout Empire		
Gladiator Competitions in Rome and Naples		
Subsidized Bread for the Poor		
Roman Law		
Aqueducts throughout Empire		

SLIDE 10.1

Examples of the Roles of Government

1. Support a legal system and protect property rights
   - Rome had an extensive system of laws created to protect the rights of free people.
   - Roman law influenced legal systems well after Rome's fall.

SLIDE 10.2

Examples of the Roles of Government

2. Provide public goods (such as national defense)
   - Rome's military was an important aspect of the Empire's success.
   - Through taxpayer support, the military was designed to protect all Roman citizens from outside forces.
   - Public goods have two characteristics:
     - Shareable
     - Not excludable

SLIDE 10.3

Examples of the Roles of Government

3. Maintain competition in markets
   - Early Rome encouraged free trade.
   - The Roman government protected private individuals so they could decide how to use their income and profits. Competition lowered prices and helped increase the variety and amount of goods, services, and resources available.

SLIDE 10.4

Examples of the Roles of Government

4. Redistribute income through tax collection and government programs
   - Programs like bread production were subsidized or partly paid for by all taxpayers, but only a small group could get the subsidized bread.
   - Horse and chariot races (also called circuses) and gladiator competitions were sponsored by the government. For a variety of reasons, only a few citizens actually participated.

SLIDE 10.5

Other Causes of Fall of Rome

- External military threats
- People fleeing the Empire due to the invasion of diseases and plagues
- Climate change
- Rapid inflation
- The spread of Christianity
- Overall moral decay

LESSON 11

ECONOMIC SYSTEMS OF THE INCAS AND AZTECS

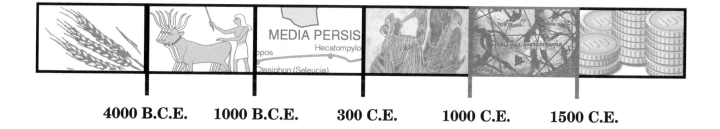

4000 B.C.E.   1000 B.C.E.   300 C.E.   1000 C.E.   1500 C.E.

Lesson 11
Economic Systems of the Incas and Aztecs

LESSON DESCRIPTION

Groups of students produce jewelry in one of three economic systems. Groups share how they answered the three basic economic questions. The class then determines the type of economic system in which they produced. From a reading on pre-Columbian societies, students determine which economic system the Incas and Aztecs were most like.

INTRODUCTION

All societies face the same fundamental economic problem of scarcity, because societies have limited resources and unlimited wants. Because of scarcity, every society must answer the basic economic questions of what to produce, how to produce, and for whom to produce. How a society or nation allocates its human, capital, and natural resources depends on the type of economic system it uses. In market economies, most resources are privately owned. Consumer sovereignty directs resources for the production of goods and services. By spending their dollars, consumers indicate their preferences for goods and services. Producers compete for consumer dollars and use this information to decide which goods and services to offer for sale in the marketplace. Producers decide how a good is produced based on the costs of production. They decide how much to supply by comparing the cost of producing the product to the price they expect to receive for it. Command economies generally have a group of central planners who make allocation decisions based on goals they have established or have been given by the country's political leaders. These planners determine what is produced, the mix of resources used to produce the goods and services, and the prices, which are often set below market price, creating shortages. In traditional economies, the basic economic questions of what to produce, how to produce, and for whom to produce are answered based on a society's traditions and customs.

Governments play a role in all economies. In a pure command economy, all economic activity would be directed by government planners or leaders. Government would answer the basic economic questions and own all property. In a pure market economy, economic activity is organized through markets with a very limited role for government. In reality, how much of a role governments play in the economy falls somewhere between these two extremes.

CONCEPTS

Economic system

Command system

Market system

Traditional system

OBJECTIVES

Students will be able to:

- List the three economic questions every society must answer.

- Explain how the three basic economic questions are answered in a command, traditional, and market economy.

- Identify characteristics of command and market economics in Incan and Aztecan societies.

CONTENT STANDARDS

Voluntary Content Standards in Economics, 2nd edition

- **Standard 3:** Different methods can be used to allocate goods and services. People acting individually or collectively must choose which methods to use to allocate different kinds of goods and services.

World History Content Standards

World History Era 5. Intensified Hemispheric Interactions, 1000–1500 C.E.

- **Standard 6:** Expansion of states and civilizations in the Americas, 1000–1500 C.E.

TIME

90 minutes: Procedures 1–8, 45 minutes on the first day. Procedures 9–26, 45 minutes on the second day.

MATERIALS

- Slides 11.1–11.5

- Activity 11.1, two copies, cut apart

- Activities 11.2, 11.3, and 11.4, one per student

- 2 sticky notes per pair of students and 1 for the teacher

- Small balls of string or yarn, one per group

- Ruler, 1 per group

- Scissors, 2 per group

- Markers, 2 per group, each marker a different color

- Bag or bowl of small tubular macaroni, one per group

PROCEDURE

1. Tell students that they will participate in a simulation to learn about different economic systems. Explain that all societies must determine how to use their scarce resources. Show Slide 11.1. Review the definition of **economic systems**. Point out that because of scarcity, all societies must answer three basic economic questions: What goods and services will be produced? How will these goods and services be produced? Who will consume them? Tell students that how these questions are answered determines the type of economic system a society has.

2. Divide students into groups of four or five students. From Activity 11.1, distribute one of the three production instructions (labeled A, B, and C) to each group. Group B must consist of five students. Groups A and C may be four or five students. Be sure that at least one group has one type of instruction (A, B, or C). Tell students they will produce jewelry made from macaroni following the instructions given to their group.

3. Show Slide 11.2. Review with students the production specifications for making bracelets and necklaces. Point out that the product specifications displayed in Slide 11.2 apply to all groups but that each group will also have additional directions specific to their group.

4. Give the students time to read their production instructions and organize their groups. Circulate among the groups to make sure groups understand their tasks. From Group A, select one student who will use the supplies first to make bracelets.

5. Distribute the macaroni, string, scissors, 2 markers, and a ruler to each group.

6. Allow 15 minutes for groups to produce jewelry. After 15 minutes, stop production.

7. Show Slide 11.3. Tell the students that the value of a necklace is $10 and that the value of a bracelet is $5. Have each group—beginning with Group A, then Group B, and then Group C—report how many bracelets and necklaces they produced and the value of their production. Debrief all groups according to the following:

   - When Group A reports, tell them that it is tradition that the men in the group divide the bracelets equally among themselves. Record the value of their production. Have group divide the bracelets equally among the men.

   - If Group B reports more than five bracelets or any necklaces, note that the extra output will go to the central planners. Record an amount earned equal to $5 per bracelet for up to five bracelets. As the central planner, seize the extra products. Tell the group that as central planner, you will distribute five bracelets as a reward for meeting the quota—give the bracelets to group members in any way you wish.

   - When Group C reports, tell them they will be paid the value of their output. They can use the money to pay for goods. Write the value of their output in the table. Do not actually sell the bracelets or necklaces, but ask if they can buy more than the other groups received.

(It will depend on the group's output, but it is likely.)

8. Discuss the following.

   a. What is different about the production output of the groups?

   (Group A should produce the fewest; Group B should produce at least five bracelets. Some groups may produce more but the extras are distributed as deemed desirable by the central planner, the teacher. Group C should produce the most and may produce necklaces.)

   b. What might explain the differences in output?

   (Answers will vary but might include different supplies, skills of workers, or method of production, rewards system. Students may not know that all groups had the same supplies and that different groups had different instructions. Do not point this out at this time.)

   c. What is different about the value of what the groups produced?

   (Group A should have the least; Group B may produce more than five but will only be paid for five; Group C should earn the most, because they probably produced the higher priced necklaces.)

   d. What might explain this?

   (Answers will vary. Students may say that the group had better tools, a better method of production, more workers, more supplies, or they produced necklaces instead of bracelets, etc. Accept all answers but give no explanation at this time.)

9. Tell students that each group will have an opportunity to share how they produced their bracelets and necklaces. Ask

one member of each group to tell the class how the group determined:

- what to produce
- how to produce it
- what job each member of the group would have
- who would get the final products

10. Show Slide 11.4. Ask the students to listen to the presentations and think about how each group answered the basic economic questions.

11. Ask a representative from Group A to present. Discuss the following and record answers on Slide 11.4.

    a. How did Group A decide what to produce?

    (Traditional ways, custom)

    b. How did Group A assign jobs and determine how to produce and how much to produce?

    (Traditional ways, custom)

    c. How did Group A determine who would get the bracelets?

    (Tradition – the men, custom)

12. Ask a representative from Group B to present. Discuss the following and record answers on Slide 11.4.

    a. How did Group B determine what to produce?

    (Central planners determined what was needed. The group produced what the central authority told it to produce.)

    b. How did Group B assign jobs and determine how to produce and how much to produce?

    (Central authority wanted the group to produce efficiently. Each member was assigned a job and the group was told how to set up the production process using an assembly line. Individuals could not choose their job. They were randomly assigned. The group was told to produce five

bracelets. If the group met this quota, each member of the group would be rewarded.)

c. How did Group B determine who would get the jewelry?

(Central planners (the teacher) declared who was in need of the bracelets.)

13. Ask a representative from Group C to present. Discuss the following and record answers on Slide 11.4.

a. How did Group C determine what to produce?

(The group produced whatever it wanted. They were motivated to select what they felt would be most profitable.)

b. How did Group C determine how to produce and how many to produce?

(The group was free to organize any way it chose. It chose a method group members thought would be efficient and least costly. Group members produced as many items as they could, given the skills and education of the workers.)

c. How did Group C determine who would get the jewelry?

(The jewelry went to individuals willing to pay the highest price.)

14. Show Slide 11.5. Review the definitions for three types of economic systems, **traditional system, command system,** and **market system**.

15. Return to Slide 11.4. Ask students which economic system they represented in the jewelry production simulation.

(As students identify their economic system, cross off the letters for each group on Slide 11.4 and write the type of economic system each group represented. A was traditional; B command; and C market.)

16. Return to Slide 11.3. Ask students why the groups produced different

amounts of jewelry and earned different amounts.

(Those in the market system produced more and earned more. Members of group C got to keep all that they earned, which was an incentive other groups didn't have. Group B was rewarded only for meeting their quota, which was to produce five bracelets. Anything over five went to the central planners, and workers were not rewarded for these. There was no incentive to produce more. Group A followed custom and wasn't motivated to produce any other way.)

17. Distribute a copy of Activity 11.2 to each student. Tell students that the reading is about different economic systems in Latin America during the pre-Columbian period. Ask students to read Activity 11.2, *Economic Systems of the Incas and Aztecs,* and think about the type of economic systems that existed in Latin America.

18. Write the word *Traditional* on the board. Draw a continuum on the board like the one below for *Command* and *Market*.

Traditional   Command------------Market

19. Discuss the following:

a. What is the domestic mode of production?

(Economies that were self-sufficient. Individual families produced and gathered all they needed to survive. All families engaged in the same economic activities. Men hunted, fished, produced stone tools, and engaged in war. Women were in charge of weaving, food preparation and cooking, water collection, and ceramic production. These economies continued until about 1600 B.C.E. in Mesoamerica and 2400 B.C.E. in South America.)

b. What type of economic system is the domestic mode of production most like? Explain.

(Traditional. Production was carried out by families, based on tradition.)

c. Place a sticky note with the letters DMP (domestic mode production) on it under Traditional on the board.

20. Assign students to work in pairs. Give each pair two small sticky notes. Ask them to label one A for Aztecs and one I for Incas. After discussion among the pairs, ask pairs to come to the board and place their sticky notes on the diagram under the type of system they think the Aztecan and Incan economic systems were most like.

21. Discuss the following.

a. Why did so many of you put your sticky note for the Incas under command?

(Most economic activity was controlled by central authority.)

b. How did the Incas answer the three basic economic questions?

(Inca state owned the land, the products of the land, and the output of labor. The state controlled the craft specialists and what they produced. The state determined how production would be allocated. Central markets did not exist in many parts of the empire. Trading was controlled by the state and done through barter.)

c. Why did so many of you put your sticky note for the Aztecs under market?

(Nobles owned most of the land, communal and private. Land was allocated to commoners in exchange for military service and for labor and food for the noble household. Once farm output increased due to the construction of chinampas, Aztec people no longer had to grow their own crops. They could specialize and trade for the goods they did not produce. The Aztecs facilitated exchanges through the use of commodity money, such as cacao beans and quills.)

d. What is commodity money?

(Commodity money is a good that has value as money and as a good.)

e. How would trade using commodity money be easier than using barter?

(With barter you have to find someone who has what you want and wants what you have. With commodity money, currency equivalents can be established.)

Give an example.

(At Aztec markets, cotton cloaks were worth 65, 80, or 100 cacao beans depending on quality. A small rabbit cost about thirty cacao beans.)

f. Why did some of you put your sticky notes between the command and market?

(Some students may realize that neither was a pure command nor market economy.)

22. Point out to students that both the Aztecs and the Incas had some aspects of command and market economies but the level of government control varied. Ask students to what extent government control existed in Aztecan and Incan states?

(The Incan state provided all of the needs for the residents and controlled land, production, and distribution. Both used military conquest to expand their land and increase the labor supply. The government also collected tributes from those they conquered. Incans used these tributes to finance the state. Aztecs used tributes to support the military but did allow individuals to receive tributes, which they could exchange for more practical items. Aztecs regulated the markets and it was illegal to exchange outside the markets. A portion of goods brought to market was paid to the ruler.)

23. Summarize that, in general, the Aztec Empire was most like a market economy and the Inca Empire a command economy.

CLOSURE

24. Ask students what three economic questions all societies have to answer.

(What, how, and for whom to produce)

25. Distribute a copy of Activity 11.3 to each student. Have them work with a partner to complete the activity.

26. Review student answers.

(Traditional 3, 9, 12; Command 1, 6, 7, 8, and 10; Market 2, 4, 5, 11)

ASSESSMENT

Multiple Choice

1. Jose has an idea for starting a business. He wants to open a cleaning business. He uses his savings and borrows money from the bank to start his business. He is quite successful and makes a small profit the first year. Jose most likely lives in a

   a. traditional economy.

   b. developing economy.

   c. command economy.

   d. **market economy.**

2. Anna lives in a country with a command economy. In Anna's country the decision of what goods and services to produce would most likely be made by

   a. consumers.

   b. **central planners.**

   c. elders.

   d. producers.

Constructed Response

1. Misha is a new student at your school. He was born in a country with a command economy. He is amazed at all the goods and services produced for the American consumer. He is very excited about a new pair of blue jeans he bought. He tells you that in his country he, his friends, and other teenagers could only dream of owning blue jeans. Even if they had the money, there were never any available for sale in the shops. You ask why producers in Misha's country didn't produce blue jeans, if teenagers wanted to buy them.

To help students organize their answers, distribute a copy of Activity 11.4. Review the components of the RAFT handout.

Role: Tell students that they may answer the question from the following perspectives: Misha, a government leader in Misha's country, a government reporter from Misha's country, or a student in the United States who has studied command economies.

Audience: For this assignment, the audience will be the students in the class.

Format: Tell students they may write their response as an essay, letter to the class, newspaper article, or another format approved by the teacher.

Topic: Tell students that everyone will be writing an answer to the question: Why did producers in Misha's country not produce blue jeans, if teenagers wanted to buy them?

CONNECTIONS: ECONOMIC SYSTEMS TODAY

Assign students one of the following countries or groups: Singapore, United States, Canada, North Korea, Cuba, Belarus, Kalahari Bushmen, Inuit, Amish. Have students research life in these countries or groups to determine how they answer the basic economic questions. Ask them to determine which economic system their assigned country or group is most like and why.

Activity 11.1

Group A Production

Your group values the way things were done in the past. Tradition dictates the way you do things. You produce what your ancestors did and in the same way. Your ancestors produced bracelets so you will produce bracelets.

Each member of the group makes an entire bracelet. The teacher will give the macaroni, markers, scissors, and ruler to one member of the group. This member will make one complete bracelet, pass it around for the other group members to admire, and then pass the production material to the next group member. Tradition dictates that each group member makes only one bracelet.

Group B Production

Your group lives in a country where the central leadership makes decisions. It determines what the people need and how resources are used. The leadership values efficient use of time and resources.

You produce what the central leadership wants. The central planners have determined that five bracelets are needed immediately and that you are to produce bracelets.

Your group will specialize and divide up the labor. You cannot choose your job. The tallest member of the group will be the string cutter. Going clockwise around the group, the next person will draw dots on the macaroni. The third person will string the macaroni alternating the different-colored dots. The fourth person will tie the knot, and the fifth will trim the knot.

If you fill your quota of five bracelets, your group will be rewarded by the central planner with bracelets. If you produce more than five bracelets, any extra bracelets will go to the central planners. If you produce necklaces, the central planners will take all the necklaces.

Group C Production

Individuals in your country produce whatever brings the highest price and can be produced in the least costly method. Your group can produce whatever jewelry it wants and organize group members any way it chooses. Your goal is to produce as many pieces of quality jewelry as possible in the time you have.

You do not have to trim knots neatly. Your group will be paid for as many pieces of jewelry as it can produce. Your group will be paid $5 for every bracelet and $10 for every necklace.

Activity 11.2
Economic Systems of the Incas and Aztecs

Many societies before the Incan and Aztecan societies in Pre-Columbian Latin America followed a "domestic mode" of production. These groups were self-sufficient. They produced and gathered everything they needed. The men did the fishing, hunting, producing stone tools, and engaging in warfare. Women were responsible for weaving, cooking, gathering food and collecting water. Men and women worked together in agriculture and house construction.

The Incan Society (early 1200 C.E. to late 1500 C.E.)

In the Incan society, all land, the products of the land, and the output of labor belonged to the state. The central authority collected resources and large amounts of goods that were stored in warehouses and then redistributed. Incan administrators kept track of these goods using the *khipu*, a system of knotted strings. Inca controlled all craft specialists and what they produced. The centralized Incan state provided all of the needs—material and spiritual—for its people. The Inca Empire lacked currency and had few central markets. Trading was controlled by the state and accomplished through barter, the direct exchange of goods for goods without use of money.

Military conquest and expansion were important to the Incans; conquests resulted in more subjects for labor and tributes. Tributes were goods that provinces were required to pay, similar to taxes. Tributes were important for state financing.

The Aztec Society (1200 C.E. to 1500 C.E.)

In the Aztec Empire, communal and private land was usually controlled by nobles. Communal land was allocated to commoners in exchange for military service and for labor and food for the noble household. The Aztec people created *chinampas*, which were artificial islands or floating gardens. Raising crops on chinampas created a surplus of farm goods, which meant Aztecs did not have to grow their own crops. Aztec workers could fully specialize in other areas of production. Specialized production became quite extensive in the Aztec Empire. Specialists such as feather workers, paper makers, wood carvers, charcoal makers, obsidian tool-makers, and hide tanners achieved a guild-like status.

Markets were central to the Aztecan economy at all levels. Towns held daily markets selling basic and luxury goods. Many farmers and merchants came to the market to sell their produce and products. Even commoners could exchange their surplus goods. It was illegal to exchange outside the markets. A portion of goods brought to market was paid to the ruler. About 60,000 people came into the markets daily to buy food, firewood, slaves, clothing, jewelry, feathers, and more, using commodity money. Commodity money consists of items that served as currency and could be consumed, such as cacao beans and quills. Currency equivalents were available to make exchange easier. For example, cotton cloaks were worth 65, 80, or 100 cacao beans, depending on quality. A small rabbit cost about 30 cacao beans. Merchants were in charge of administering the markets, enforcing fair prices, and handling complaints.

Military conquest was also important to the Aztecs. The Aztecan system also used tributes to support the military but allowed individuals to receive tributes of luxury items as payments or rewards. Individuals could exchange the tributes in the marketplace for more practical items.

SOURCE

Bulmer-Thomas, V., Coatsworth, J., and R. Cortes Conde (eds.) *The Cambridge Economic History of Latin America: Vol. I: The Colonial Era and the Short Nineteenth Century. Chapter 3: The Pre-Columbian Economy* by Rebecca Storey and Randolph Widmer. New York: Cambridge University Press, 2006.

ACTIVITY 11.3

Economic Systems Review

Read each statement and put a check mark under the type of economic system it represents.

Characteristics	Tradition	Command	Market
1. Central authority or government determines what to produce			
2. Individuals choose their jobs			
3. Custom determines jobs			
4. Goods distributed to highest bidder			
5. Produce by the least costly method			
6. Government determines what is needed			
7. Goods distributed based on those declared in need			
8. Production process determined by central authority			
9. Produce the way ancestors produced goods			
10. Government determines jobs			
11. Demand and profit determine what is produced			
12. Custom determines what to produce			

ACTIVITY 11.4

RAFT Form

Role	Audience
Format	Topic

SLIDE 11.1

Economic System Definition

- **Economic System:** The institutional framework of formal and informal rules that a society uses to determine what to produce, how to produce, and how to distribute goods and services.

SLIDE 11.2

Production Specifications

Production Steps	One Bracelet	One Necklace
Cut piece of string	10 inches long	16 inches long
Draw dots on macaroni using two different color markers—use one color per piece of pasta	10 pieces of macaroni—5 with each color dot	16 pieces of macaroni—8 with each color dot
Place macaroni on string	10 pieces of macaroni—alternate color dots	16 pieces of macaroni—alternate color dots
Knot string	Knot two ends of string together to create a bracelet	Knot two ends of string together to create a necklace
Trim knot using scissors	Trim knot	Trim knot

SLIDE 11.3

Production Recording Sheet

Group	# of Group Members	# Produced		Value of Production
		Bracelets	Necklaces	

SLIDE 11.4

Economic Systems

Group	What to Produce	How to Produce	For Whom to Produce
A			
B			
C			

SLIDE 11.5

LESSON 11 – ECONOMIC SYSTEMS OF THE INCAS AND AZTECS

Systems Definitions

- **Command System:** An economy in which most economic issues of production and distribution are resolved through central planning and control.

- **Market System:** An economy that relies on a system of interdependent market prices to allocate goods, services, and productive resources and to coordinate the diverse plans of consumers and producers, all of them pursuing their own self-interest.

- **Traditional System:** An economy in which customs and habits from the past are used to resolve most economic issues of production and distribution.

LESSON 12

MANSA MUSA: INFLATION THEN AND NOW

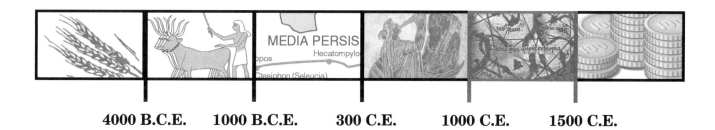

4000 B.C.E.   1000 B.C.E.   300 C.E.   1000 C.E.   1500 C.E.

LESSON 12
MANSA MUSA: INFLATION THEN AND NOW

LESSON DESCRIPTION

Students participate in two auctions to gain an understanding of the concept of inflation. They use what they've learned about inflation to explain the impact Mansa Musa had on Egypt during his hajj, or pilgrimage, to Mecca. Finally, students look at a Middle School Consumer Price Index for two time periods and draw conclusions about how inflation can affect consumers.

INTRODUCTION

Inflation is a rise in the general or average price level of all the goods and services produced in an economy. Inflation occurs in an economy when the money supply increases faster than the growth of output of goods and services. During periods of inflation, money loses value. Goods and services become more expensive because the purchasing power of money is reduced. If incomes don't increase at the same rate as inflation, people are worse off. They are able to purchase fewer goods and services with the same income.

Mansa Musa, King of Mali from 1312–1337, made a hajj, a holy pilgrimage, to Mecca in 1324. His caravan had 80–100 camels each carrying 300 pounds of gold. During his stay in Egypt, his generous gifts and numerous expenditures depressed the value of gold and caused its price to fall. Prices for goods and services rose. This example teaches students about inflation and how it reduces the value of money using a historical context.

CONCEPTS

Inflation

Purchasing power

Consumer price index (CPI)

OBJECTIVES

Students will be able to:

- Define inflation and purchasing power.

- Explain how inflation reduces the value of money.

- Explain the relationship between inflation and purchasing power of money.

CONTENT STANDARDS

Voluntary Content Standards in Economics, 2nd edition

- **Standard 11:** Money makes it easier to trade, borrow, save, invest, and compare the value of goods and services. The amount of money in the economy affects the overall price level. Inflation is an increase in the overall price level that reduces the value of money.

- **Standard 19:** Unemployment imposes costs on individuals and the overall economy. Inflation, both expected and unexpected, also imposes costs on individuals and the overall economy. Unemployment increases during recessions and decreases during recoveries.

World History Content Standards

World History Era 5. Intensified Hemispheric Interactions, 1000–1500 C.E.

- **Standard 4:** The growth of states, towns, and trade in sub-Saharan Africa between the 11th and 15th centuries.

TIME REQUIRED

90 minutes. Procedures 1–12, 45 minutes on first day. Procedures 13–22, 45 minutes on the second day.

MATERIALS

- Slides 12.1–12.3

- Activity 12.1, one per student

- Activity 12.2, one per student

- Activity 12.3, one for every group of three students

- Large supply of gold paper clips (approximately 400) or small pieces of gold paper

- 2 bags of goldfish crackers

- 2 cupcakes or other baked goods made with flour

- 2 bags of round chocolate candies

PROCEDURE

1. Tell students they are going to learn about inflation. Explain that inflation has occurred throughout history, an excellent example being a trip taken by Mansa Musa, a King of Mali, in the 14th century. Explain briefly who Mansa Musa was, if he has not been previously discussed. Explain that inflation can reduce one's ability to buy goods and services. Distribute a copy of Activity 12.1 to each student. Point out to students that the two key concepts in the lesson they will participate in are inflation and purchasing power. Tell students they will complete this activity as they participate in the lesson.

2. Tell students they are going to play the role of Egyptians during Mansa Musa's time. They will buy "Egyptian" goods using special money—gold paper clips. Remind students that money is anything accepted as final payment for goods and services. Distribute a small handful of gold paper clips to each student. Ensure that students receive different amounts of paper clips.

3. Display a small bag of goldfish crackers, a cupcake or other baked good, and a bag of small round candies. Tell students that the crackers represent dried fish, the cupcake represents wheat, and the small round candies represents broad beans, staples in the Egyptian household.

4. Explain to students that they will be able to purchase these items using the gold paper clips. Ask students to determine how many paper clips they have to spend.

5. Draw the table below on the board, but do not put the title "Auction Round 2"

or "Price in Gold Paper Clips" in second column until later. Auction the three items and record the auction price for each item in the Auction Round 1 column. Collect the appropriate amount of paper clips from the highest bidders for each item.

Item	Auction Round 1	Auction Round 2
	Price in Gold Paper Clips	Price in Gold Paper Clips
Goldfish crackers		
Cupcake		
Small candies		

6. Discuss:

    a. How many students were able to purchase items in Round 1?

    (Three)

    b. What do students think might improve their ability to purchase items if the auction is held a second time?

    (Most likely, students will say more paper clips or money.)

    c. Ask students why they think more money results in an improved chance to obtain one of the three items.

    (Most students will think they now have more to spend without recognizing that everyone in the class will have more money to spend.)

7. Tell students that they will have an opportunity to participate in a second auction and bid on a second set of items identical to those auctioned in Round 1. Write "Auction Round 2" and "Price in Gold Paper Clips" in second column of the table.

8. Announce that you have heard their complaints about wanting more gold paper clips. Tell them that because you are a generous teacher, you will give them more gold paper clips to use in this round of the auction.

9. Parade through the class, lavishly distributing handfuls of gold paper clips to the students. Conduct Round 2, auctioning each item to the highest bidder. Record the auction price for each item in the Auction Round 2 column.

10. Discuss the following questions:

    a. What happened to the price of items auctioned in Round 2?

       (Price went up.)

    b. What happened to the money supply in Round 2?

       (It increased.)

    c. Why did the price go up?

       (Students had more money to spend in Round 2 than in Round 1, but the goods available for auction remained the same.)

    d. Were students better off in Round 2, when they received additional money?

       (No. Only three students were able to outbid their classmates for the items, and they had to pay a higher price.)

    e. Were the gold paper clips worth more or less in Round 2?

       (Less)

    f. Why were paper clips worth less than in the first round?

       (More gold paper clips were available to purchase the same items auctioned for less in Round 1.)

11. Show Slide 12.1. Tell students that what they experienced is called **inflation**. Explain that inflation is defined as a rise in the general or average price level of all the goods and services produced in an economy. Tell students that inflation is not a one-time event and, during times of inflation, the prices of almost all goods and services rise continuously. Have students write the economic definition for inflation, a definition in their own words, draw a picture, and use inflation in a sentence on their copies of Activity 12.1.

12. Tell students that inflation is a concern in today's economy as it was a concern in the past.

13. Distribute a copy of Activity 12.2 to each student. Have students read Activity 12.2. Note that as current gold prices change, the prices for gold in this reading should be adjusted. Look up the most recent price of gold and calculate the current cost of Mansa Musa's gold as follows.

    (100 camels × 300 pounds) + (500 slaves × 4 pounds) = 32,000 pounds of gold.

    (80 camels × 300 pounds) + (500 slaves × 4 pounds) = 26,000 pounds of gold.

    1 pound = 14.5833 troy ounces

    32,000 pounds × 14.5833 troy ounces/ pound = 466,665.6 troy ounces of gold.

    26,000 pounds × 14.5833 troy ounces/ pound = 379,165.8 troy ounces of gold.

    Plug in the latest price of an ounce of gold and multiply it by 379,165.8 for 80 camels and 466,665.6 for 100 camels.

14. Discuss the following questions.

    a. Who was Mansa Musa?

       (King of Mali from 1312 to 1337)

    b. What were Mansa Musa's achievements?

       (Expanded the kingdom of Mali, promoted trade, brought peace and order to Mali, promoted education, and made Mali known throughout Europe and the Muslim world.)

c. Why did he want to make a pilgrimage to Mecca?

(Making a trip to Mecca is one of the five duties of a devout Muslim.)

d. Why is Mansa Musa's pilgrimage remembered?

(His caravan consisted of thousands of people, 80 to 100 camels carrying 300 pounds of gold each, and 500 slaves each carrying a gold staff weighing four pounds.)

e. What did Mansa Musa do with the millions of dollars of gold he brought with him on his pilgrimage?

(He gave it as gifts and spent it.)

f. How did Mansa Musa's spending affect the price of gold in Egypt?

(The price of gold fell.)

g. How did this affect Egyptians' standard of living?

(Because it took more gold to buy the same goods individuals bought before Mansa Musa came to Egypt, their purchasing power declined. Egyptians who saved gold were worse off and had a lower standard of living.)

h. What did the gold paper clips represent in the auction activity?

(Bars of gold)

i. What happened to your purchasing power during the two rounds of the auction? (It declined.) Explain.

(In Round 2, it took more gold paper clips to buy the same items that sold for a lower price in Round 1.)

j. How were Mansa Musa's spending and giving gifts of gold similar to the auction activity?

(He put so much gold into circulation, the value of gold decreased, and it took more gold to purchase goods. In the auction, with an increase in the supply of gold paper clips, goods became more expensive in terms of paper clips.)

15. Divide students into groups of three. Show Slide 12.2. Distribute a copy of Activity 12.3 to each student. Explain that the chart shows a Middle School Consumer Price Index. Tell students that a **consumer price index** measures the cost of a fixed basket of consumer goods and services and compares the cost of this basket in one time period with its cost in some base period.

16. Explain that each student receives a weekly allowance of $12. Listed are some items each would like to buy. Group members should determine how to spend their $12, using 2005 prices. They must each agree to buy the same items and quantities. ***Tell the students not to worry about the 2010 prices right now, because they might have a different allowance in the future.***

17. Discuss the following questions:

a. What items did you purchase?

(Answers will vary.)

b. Were you able to buy everything you wanted? *(Some may say no.)* Why not?

(Didn't have enough allowance.)

c. Did you save any of your allowance? How much?

(Answers will vary.)

18. Explain to students that they are to repeat the activity and try to buy the same items as they purchased with the 2005 prices but this time they are to use 2010 prices. Ask the partners to decide who will be a "1," a "2," or a "3" for this portion of Activity 12.3. Tell the 1's they still have a weekly allowance of $12, the 2's will get $13 a week, and the 3's will get $14 a week.

19. Ask the groups to predict what will happen when they spend their allowances. Have groups share their predictions.

(Answers will vary.)

20. Allow time for the students to complete the activity.

21. Discuss the following questions:

    a. What happened to prices between 2005 and 2010?

    (They increased.)

    b. What is this called?

    (Inflation)

    c. How many of the 1's were able to buy and save in 2010 exactly what they bought and saved in 2005?

    (None.)

    d. How might you be able to buy the same quantity of goods?

    (Use some of their savings.)

    e. How many of the 2's were able to buy and save in 2010 exactly what they bought and saved in 2005?

    (Some should have been able to buy the same items and save the same amount, but some might not, based on what they purchased.)

    f. Why were some groups of 2's able to buy the same goods and quantities that they bought in 2005?

    (The prices of some of the goods they bought didn't go up as much as other goods. Some goods, like pizza, increased as little as 4 percent and others, like cola, increased as much as 12 percent.)

    g. How many of the 3's were able to buy in 2010 exactly what they purchased in 2005?

    (All should have been able to buy what they did with the 2005 prices.)

    Why do you think this was the case?

    (Their increase in allowance was enough to cover the higher prices charged in 2010.)

    h. Show Slide 12.3. Tell students that **purchasing power** means the amount of goods and services that a fixed dollar amount of income can buy. Ask students what happened to their purchasing power between 2005 and 2010.

    (For the 1's, it decreased because their income stayed the same; for the 2's it may have increased or decreased. The 3's should have been able to purchase and save the same amount and have some money left over, because their income increased from $12 to $14. Their purchasing power went up because their income increased faster than prices.)

    i. How does inflation affect purchasing power?

    (It causes it to decline. People are able to buy fewer goods with the same income.)

    j. What do you think happened to the purchasing power of gold during Mansa Musa's stay in Egypt?

    (It lost value.)

    k. How did inflation affect the standard of living for Egyptians?

    (The standard of living would have declined for Egyptians who had saved gold. People would have been able to purchase less with the gold they had.)

22. Ask students to take out their copies of Activity 12.1. Have them add the definition for purchasing power. Give them time to write a definition in their own words, draw a picture and use the word in a sentence. Have students work in pairs to check their definitions, explain their pictures, and share their sentences.

CLOSURE

23. Discuss the following questions:

    a. What is inflation?

    (A rise in the general or average price level of all the goods and services produced in an economy.)

    b. What caused prices to rise in the auction?

    (An increase in the money supply or gold paperclips.)

c. How did Mansa Musa create inflation in Egypt?

(He gave many gifts of gold and spent large quantities of gold. This increased the amount of gold in Egypt causing it to lose value.)

d. What is purchasing power?

(The amount of goods and services that a fixed dollar amount of income can buy.)

e. What is the relationship between inflation and purchasing power?

(During periods of inflation, money loses value. Goods and services become more expensive. People are not able to buy as much with the income they have.)

ASSESSMENT

Multiple Choice

1. What does inflation mean?

   a. Rise in production of most goods

   b. Increase in unemployment

   c. Increase in interest rates

   d. **Rise in most prices**

2. What happens during times of inflation?

   a. Consumers increase the amount they save.

   b. **Purchasing power of fixed income declines.**

   c. Money gains value.

   d. Workers lose jobs.

Constructed Response

1. You have heard on the news that the inflation rate is expected to increase. You decide to ask your parents for a raise in your allowance. Use what you know about inflation and purchasing power to write an argument on why you need a raise in your allowance.

   (Answers should reflect that the allowance should increase by the rate of inflation. Students may argue for a higher increase in their allowance if they want to increase their purchasing power. Other students may argue that the goods they typically buy have increased faster than inflation; therefore, their allowance should increase by a rate higher than inflation.)

CONNECTIONS: INFLATION IN U.S. HISTORY

Ask students to interview someone 60–69 years old and ask them about grocery prices when they were teenagers. Have them compare the groceries that could be purchased with $10 then with those that can be purchased with $10 today.

U.S. Gold Rush – The California Gold Rush of 1849 resulted in an increase in the country's money supply, which was based on gold. From 1850 to 1855, the wholesale price levels of goods increased 30 percent.

Source: Whaples, Robert. *"California Gold Rush."* EH. Net Encyclopedia, edited by Robert Whaples. March 16, 2008. http://eh.net/encyclopedia/article/whaples.goldrush

ACTIVITY 12.1

What Do These Words Mean?

Word	Economic definition	Definition in your own words	Picture	Use in a sentence
Inflation				
Purchasing power				

ACTIVITY 12.2

Mansa Musa—Ruler of Mali (1312–1337)

Mansa Musa became king of Mali in 1312. During his rule, he expanded his kingdom, promoted trade, brought peace and order, promoted education, and made Mali known throughout Europe and the Muslim world.

One of the five duties of a devout Muslim is to visit the holy city of Mecca. In 1324, Mansa Musa set out on a hajj, a holy pilgrimage. He left Timbuktu with a great caravan. According to al-Umari, a 14th century Arab historian, the caravan had 80 to 100 camels, each loaded with 300 pounds of gold. Today, this would be valued at $583 to $718 million. Mansa Musa took thousands of his subjects: bearers to carry his personal effects, soldiers, officials, and dignitaries. Five hundred slaves rode in front of the king, each carrying a gold staff weighing four pounds.

Mansa Musa stayed for months in Egypt and his trip was remembered for centuries for his generous gifts and expenditures. Twelve years later, when historian al-Umari visited Cairo, he wrote that Mansa Musa gave large quantities of gold to all dignitaries, those who held a royal office, and others he met. He gave away so much gold that it lost its value.

By the time Mansa Musa left Egypt, the value of gold had fallen 10 to 25 percent. When he left Egypt to return home, he was penniless and had to borrow gold to travel back to Mali.

SOURCES

Landes, D. 1998. *The Wealth and Poverty of Nations: Why Some Are So Rich and Some So Poor.* New York: W.W.Norton & Company, Inc.

Boahen, A., Ajayi, J., and Tidy, M. 1986. *Topics in West African History.* England: Longman Group Limited.

ACTIVITY 12.3

Middle School Consumer Price Index

Item	2005 Price	2010 Price
Bag of potato chips (1.875 oz.)	$ .88	$ .93
Chocolate candy bar (1.55 oz.)	$ .79	$ .86
Bottle of cola (20 oz.)	$ 1.46	$ 1.64
1 movie ticket	$ 8.04	$ 8.80
Package of gum (15 sticks)	$ 1.22	$ 1.28
Hamburger, fries, and a small drink	$ 2.68	$ 3.01
Small (10-inch) pizza	$ 4.46	$ 4.64

You receive an allowance of $12 per week. Listed above are some items you would like to buy and the price of each. You don't have to spend all your allowance; you may save some.

Using 2005 prices, decide with your partners how to spend your weekly allowance. All group members must agree on the items and quantities to purchase. List the items you wish to buy. Determine the quantity you plan to purchase. Find the cost of the items and enter the information in the appropriate column below. For savings, enter the dollar amount you wish to save. The total amount you spend added to the amount you save should equal your allowance.

Item	Quantity	Cost (2005 prices)	Cost (2010 prices)
		$	$
		$	$
		$	$
		$	$
		$	$
		$	$
Savings		$	$
Total allowance		$ 12.00	$

SLIDE 12.1

Inflation

- A rise in the general price level of all the goods and services produced in an economy.

SLIDE 12.2

Middle School
Consumer Price Index

Item	2005 Price	2010 Price
Bag of potato chips (1.875 oz.)	$ .88	$ .93
Chocolate candy bar (1.55 oz.)	$ .79	$ .86
Bottle of cola (20 oz.)	$1.46	$1.64
1 movie ticket	$8.04	$8.80
Package of gum (15 sticks)	$1.22	$1.28
Hamburger, fries, and small drink	$2.68	$3.01
Small (10-inch) pizza	$4.46	$4.64

SLIDE 12.3

LESSON 12 – MANSA MUSA: INFLATION THEN AND NOW

Purchasing Power

- The amount of goods and services that a fixed dollar amount of income can buy.

LESSON 13

PAPER MONEY OF THE SUNG, YUAN, AND MING DYNASTIES

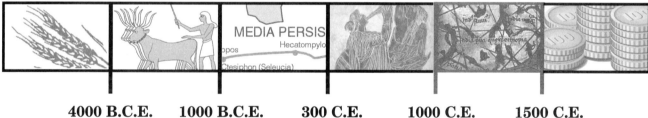

4000 B.C.E.   1000 B.C.E.   300 C.E.   1000 C.E.   1500 C.E.

LESSON 13
PAPER MONEY OF THE SUNG, YUAN, AND MING DYNASTIES

LESSON DESCRIPTION

In this lesson, students participate in a trading activity using play paper money. They learn about the characteristics and functions of money. The students identify how the paper money in the trading activity demonstrates each of money's three functions. The students complete a reading about the adoption and abandonment of paper money in China during the Sung, Yuan, and Ming dynasties. Finally, the students work in groups to evaluate different commodities' ability to function as money using spider graphs.

INTRODUCTION

In the 800s, the Chinese became the first civilization to use paper money. In 1024 C.E., the Chinese imperial government became the first government to monopolize the issuing of paper money. It's not surprising that the Chinese, inventors of both paper and printing, would be the first to realize that paper notes could be used to represent economic value. As long as people were required to use those notes to make transactions, a monetary system based on paper money could result in a more efficient market. What is perhaps surprising is that the Chinese, around 1430, were also the first to stop using paper money.

The use of money expanded rapidly during the Sung dynasty (960–1279). During this time, trade within China and among the Chinese and their neighbors increased significantly. During the Sung dynasty, paper money and copper cash coins were both in use. The Sung dynasty fell to the Mongols in 1279. The Mongol invaders ruled China for nearly 90 years as the Yuan dynasty (1279–1368). Like the Sung rulers before them, the Yuan made extensive use of paper money. Unlike the Sung, the Yuan established a paper money system with both large- and small-denomination notes. The Yuan established strict rules that forced people to use paper money for commercial transactions. The strict rules included harsh punishments for those who tried to

circumvent the rules. Counterfeiting was a capital offense. The universal requirement that people use paper money as well as the ever-expanding economy during the period ensured that the paper money issued during the Yuan period was highly successful. European visitors to China, such as Marco Polo, returned home with stories about the Chinese successfully using paper money. These stories amazed Europeans, who still used precious metals and commodity monies. Europeans were intrigued that something with so little intrinsic value as a piece of paper, not backed by silver or gold, could be used to represent economic value.

During the early years of the Ming dynasty, paper money was also used extensively. However, the Ming rulers were not nearly as strict about the use of paper money as their Yuan predecessors had been. The acceptability of paper money gradually declined in China, in part due to the fact that people had more acceptable substitutes such as silver coins and in part due to the fact that counterfeiting increased under the Ming. As demand for paper money slumped, so did its value. By 1430 C.E., the paper money issued by the Ming government was practically worthless and government-issued paper money was not issued again until the modern period.

CONCEPTS

Money

Characteristics of money

Functions of money

Legal tender

Medium of exchange

Store of value

Unit of account

OBJECTIVES

Students will be able to:

- Define money as anything widely accepted as final payment for goods and services.

- Evaluate an item's usefulness as money based on the three functions of money.

- List the three functions of money: medium of exchange, store of value, and unit of account.

CONTENT STANDARDS

Voluntary National Content Standards in Economics, 2nd edition

- **Standard 11:** Students will understand that money makes it easier to trade, borrow, save, invest, and compare the value of goods and services. The amount of money in the economy affects the overall price level. Inflation is an increase in the overall price level that reduces the value of money.

World History Content Standards

Era 5: Intensified Hemispheric Interactions, 1000–1500 C.E.

- **Standard 1:** The maturing of an interregional system of communication, trade, and cultural exchange in an era of Chinese economic power and Islamic expansion.

- **Standard 3:** The rise of the Mongol empire and its consequences for Eurasians, 1200–1350 C.E.

TIME REQUIRED

60–75 minutes

MATERIALS

- Slides 13.1–13.4

- 1 copy of Activity 13.1, cut apart (laminate, if possible)

- 6 copies of Activity 13.2, cut apart (laminate, if possible)

- 1 copy of Activity 13.3 for each student and the teacher

- 8 copies of Activity 13.4 for group activity, plus one copy for each student to use during assessment activity

- 1 copy of Activity 13.5, cut apart

- 8 quart-size plastic food-storage bags with zippers

- 26 tea bags in their wrappers

- 200 fish crackers (Swedish fish can be used as a substitute)

- 100 paper clips

- 10 pairs of disposable wooden chopsticks (20 pencils can be used as a substitute)

- Permanent marker for writing on plastic bags

- 8 sheets of white construction paper

- 8 markers or colored pencils

- Masking tape

- 8 plastic shopping bags

PROCEDURE

Preparation Before Class

1. Using the plastic food-storage bags, teabags, fish crackers, paper clips, chopsticks, cards from Activity 13.1, *Trading Cards,* and paper money from Activity 13.2, *Paper Money,* assemble sets of materials for each group of students. The table below shows what goods and amounts of paper money should be placed in each food-storage bag. Mark the group's number on the outside of each bag with a permanent marker.

Group Number	Goods	Paper Money	Group Number	Goods	Paper Money
1	11 tea bags	12 strings	5	25 paper clips	16 strings
2	15 tea bags	5 strings	6	75 paper clips	5 strings
3	75 fish crackers	18 strings	7	4 pairs of chopsticks	16 strings
4	125 fish crackers	9 strings	8	6 pairs of chopsticks	9 strings

In Class

2. Introduce the lesson by explaining to the students that they will be learning about the functions of money and about the first paper money, issued by the Chinese government in 1024 C.E.

3. Explain to students that they will participate in a role-play activity to show how people use paper money in their daily lives. In this activity, the students will work in groups to buy and sell products based on trading instructions that will be provided to them. The trading instructions will tell students how much they should sell their products for as well as what items they want to buy in the market.

4. Divide the class into eight groups. Explain to the students that the classroom will serve as the marketplace. Assign each of the groups a section of the classroom to serve as their market stall. Allow students to rearrange the desks to create their selling spaces. Within each group, students should split up the work of buying and selling; some should specialize in selling their goods at the stall, while others should work at buying the goods the group wants.

5. Show the students one of the eight prepared bags. Explain that each bag contains the goods they will be selling, some currency, and their trading instructions.

6. Explain that the four commodities used in this activity are related to China. The four commodities are tea bags, fish crackers, chopsticks, and paper clips.

   • Tea has been popular in China since at least the Qin dynasty (221–206 B.C.E.). In this lesson, tea bags will be used. Tell students not to take the tea bags out of their wrappers.

   • Fish is a food staple for many Chinese and has been for thousands of years. In this lesson, fish crackers represent fish. Tell students not to eat the fish crackers.

   • The Chinese have been using chopsticks since the Shang dynasty (1600–1046 B.C.E.). Tell students that the chopsticks must be bought and sold in pairs.

   • Metal tools have been in use in China since 3100 B.C.E. In this lesson, paper clips represent metal tools.

7. Explain to students that before the trading activity they will complete a reading about the use of paper money in ancient China. Distribute one copy of Activity 13.3, *Paper Money in China (1024 C.E. to 1430 C.E.)* to each student; have students read it. Give the students time to read the activity.

8. Ask the students the following questions:

   a. Marco Polo observed paper money being made in China. What did he see?

   (Marco Polo saw the Chinese make paper made from mulberry tree bark. When the paper was ready, each sheet was cut into pieces of different sizes. Each piece of paper money was marked with officials' signatures and the official seal of the emperor.)

   b. According to Marco Polo, everyone in China was willing to use paper money. Why was this so?

   (Because they knew that they would be able to buy the goods and services they wanted with it because the government had declared that it had to be accepted for payment.)

   Explain to students that when a government declares that a form of money must be accepted for payment, it is called **legal tender**.

   c. During the Sung dynasty, what two forms of money were most common?

   (Paper money and copper coins)

   Which form of money had the largest denominations?

   (Paper money)

d. During the Yuan dynasty, what denominations of paper money did the government print?

(Both large and small denominations)

e. What caused the Ming dynasty to stop issuing paper money?

(Paper money had lost most of its value.)

f. Why did paper money lose most of its value during the Ming dynasty?

(The Ming rulers were not as strict about making people use paper money as their counterparts in the Yuan dynasty had been. The Ming rulers were also not as careful as the Yuan rulers had been about punishing counterfeiters. Therefore, counterfeit money became more common. Because the people no longer faced harsh punishments for using other things like silver coins as money, they switched from using paper money to using coins. Once the demand for paper money dropped as a result of people using it less, it lost its value.)

9. Distribute one of the preassembled plastic storage bags and one of the plastic shopping bags to each of the groups. Ask the groups to remove their trading instructions from their bags. Explain to the students that each group's trading instructions tell them the minimum amount that they are willing to sell their commodity for; explain that they should try to get as much as possible for each unit of goods that they sell. At the same time, they should be mindful of the fact that they should strive to sell all of their goods by the end of the 10-minute trading period.

10. Explain to students that the trading instructions also indicate how many goods they want to purchase in the market from the other groups. Explain to the students that they should strive to purchase all of the items on their

shopping list at the lowest cost possible while keeping in mind that they need to try to buy all the goods on their list during the 10-minute trading period. As they purchase items in the market, they should put them in their shopping bag. Emphasize to the students that their goal for this activity is to sell their goods at the highest price possible, buy the goods they want for the lowest price possible, and have as much money left over at the end of the activity as possible.

11. Distribute one sheet of construction paper and a marker to each group of students and instruct them to create a sign for their stall. The sign should tell prospective buyers what they are selling and their group number. Have them tape the sign where everyone can see it.

12. Explain to students that they will use paper money representing strings of copper coins. Emphasize that, for all trading, they must use paper money. Just as during the Yuan dynasty, there are strict punishments for those who do not use paper money for all of their transactions. Explain that you will confiscate the goods of any group caught bartering—trading goods for other goods.

13. Tell students to begin trading. Allow 10 minutes for trade. Give the students five-minute, two-minute, and one-minute warnings before the trading period ends. After the trading period, ask the following questions:

a. Which groups were able to sell all of the goods and buy all of the goods that they wanted to buy?

(Answers will vary.)

b. If some groups were not able to buy all of the goods they wanted, why not?

(Answers will vary, but some groups may say they didn't have enough money or that they had trouble finding buyers for their own goods.)

c. When you ran out of money, what did you have to do in order to purchase more of the goods that you wanted?

(Sell more of their group's goods.)

14. Explain that for something to serve well as a form of money, it must perform three functions. Show Slide 13.1, *Functions of Money.* Explain the three **functions of money** as follows:

    • **Medium of exchange**: Money acts as a go-between to make it easier to buy and sell things. Sellers agree to accept it in exchange for a good or service. In this way, money functions as a medium of exchange.

    • **Store of value**: As a store of value, money makes it easier for people to save and defer consumption until the future. Money holds its value until people want to exchange it for a good or service.

    • **Unit of account**: Money serves as a way to measure and compare the value of goods and services in relation to one another. When comparing prices, individuals can determine if one good is a better buy than another. Money also allows people to keep accurate financial records. As a unit of account, money is used to compare the market value of different goods and services.

15. Ask the students the following questions:

    a. How do you know that money was used as a medium of exchange in the trading activity?

    (Because when goods were bought or sold, the buyer exchanged money for the good.)

    b. Why were sellers willing to accept the money in exchange for their goods?

    (The sellers knew that they would be able to use the money they received in exchange for the sale of their

goods to buy goods from other sellers in the market.)

    c. What was the unit of account in the trading activity?

    (Strings of copper cash coins)

    d. How do you know that money was used as a unit of account in the trading activity?

    (Prices were denominated in strings of copper cash coins. Buyers were able to make decisions about which and how many goods to buy using the price information, which was all denominated in strings of copper cash coins.)

    e. How do you know that money was used as a store of value in the trading activity?

    (Sellers were able to sell their goods in exchange for paper money. That paper money retained the value of the goods that the sellers sold. When the sellers subsequently purchased the goods they wanted, they were able to do so using paper money. Therefore, the paper money acted as a store of value.)

16. Explain that in order for money to perform its functions well, it must possess six characteristics. Show Slide 13.2, *Characteristics of Money.* Explain each of the **characteristics of money** as follows:

    • Acceptable—Money must be acceptable to everyone in exchange for goods and services.

    • Divisible—Money must be easily divided into small parts (or already in small pieces) so that people can purchase goods and services at any price.

    • Durable—Money must be able to withstand the wear and tear of many people using it.

    • Portable—Money must be easy to carry.

- Scarce—Money must be hard for people to obtain.

- Stable in value—Money's value must remain relatively constant over long periods of time.

17. Explain to students that for money to perform each of its functions well, it must exhibit most, if not all, of the characteristics listed above. Explain each of the following:

    - If money is not accepted by everybody in exchange for goods and services, money will not function well as a medium of exchange. It would not be possible to buy something in a store if the storekeeper wouldn't accept the money you offer for payment.

    - If money is not divisible, it will not be a good medium of exchange, store of value, or unit of account. Buyers and sellers have to be able to make change, which would be difficult, if not impossible, if money is not divisible. Likewise, in order for money to be an effective unit of account, there has to be a way for money to be divided to express different prices. Money will not be a good store of value if you can't divide it so that you can save some and spend some.

    - If money is not durable, people will be much less willing to accept it as a medium of exchange. Money that will rot or disintegrate is not a good store of value.

    - If money is not portable, it will be hard to use it as a medium of exchange. Anything that is heavy or bulky will be difficult to carry from one place to another to make payments.

    - If money is not relatively scarce, it will not be a good medium of exchange or a store of value. Money that is not scarce will lose its value, because people will be able to get more money easily. Money that loses

its value will not be widely accepted as a medium of exchange because sellers won't want to take chances selling goods in exchange for money that might lose value.

- If money is not stable in value, it is hard to use as a medium of exchange, store of value, or unit of account. Money that is not stable in value will lose its value because people will be unwilling to accept it as a medium of exchange or hold on to it as a store of value. Similarly, money that is not stable in value will be a bad unit of account because changes in value of the money will make it difficult to express prices.

18. Show Slide 13.3, *Functions of Money Spider Graph*. Explain that a spider graph is a chart that allows us to plot three or more different types of data on one graph. Explain that students will work in their groups to analyze how good an item would be at meeting the functions of money. Show students how each of the three axes of the spider graph represents one of the three functions of money.

19. Show Slide 13.3, *Spider Graph Examples*. Explain to students that the graph on the left was created for bricks and the graph on the right was created for Brussels sprouts. The person who created these graphs thought about the characteristics of good money and ranked each item on a scale of 1 to 5 as to how well it would work as a medium of exchange, a store of value, and a unit of account. Ask the students the follow questions:

a. Why do you think that the person who created these spider graphs rated bricks 5 and Brussels sprouts 1 for store of value?

(Answers will vary, but students may say that bricks are very durable, whereas Brussels sprouts will rot and are therefore not very durable. Items that are not durable will not

serve as good stores of value. Also, while bricks could be made to have a unique pattern that would thwart counterfeiting, people could simply grow Brussels sprouts. If people grew lots of them, Brussels sprouts would no longer be relatively scarce and would not retain their value in terms of the amounts of other goods and services that people could buy with them.)

b. Why do you think that the person who created these spider graphs rated bricks 2 and Brussels sprouts 4 for unit of account?

(Answers will vary, but students may say that Brussels sprouts, because they are relatively small, can be divided into many different denominations. Bricks are large and heavy and not easily divisible. Therefore, Brussels sprouts are likely to be a better unit of account than bricks.)

c. Why do you think that the person who created these spider graphs rated bricks 3 and Brussels sprouts 4 for medium of exchange?

(Answers will vary, but students may say that Brussels sprouts are easier to carry than bricks. Therefore, people would be more likely to use the Brussels sprouts than bricks as a medium of exchange.)

20. Distribute one copy of Activity 13.4, *Functions of Money Spider Graph,* to each group. Have each group draw one card from the deck made from Activity 13.5, *Commodities as Money Cards.* Tell the groups to consider how well their commodity meets the characteristics of good money. Based on their understanding of the characteristics of their commodity, they are to evaluate on a scale of 1 to 5 the degree to which they believe that their commodity functions as a medium of exchange, store of value, and unit of account, where 5 is "functions extremely well" and 1 is "functions

extremely poorly." Then, they will complete the spider graph in Activity 13.5 to reflect their decisions about how well their commodity functions as money and answer the questions at the bottom of the activity.

Note: This activity uses higher-order thinking skills. Different students will make different decisions about the degree to which each of the items will function as money. These differences are highly acceptable as long as the students can demonstrate that they used solid reasoning for evaluating their items as they did.

21. Distribute markers or colored pencils to the groups for graphing. Give the groups about five minutes to do the spider graph activity. After the groups completed their spider graphs, have them each come to the front of the classroom and present their conclusions to the class. Each group should:

• Explain what their commodity is.

• Show their spider graph.

• Explain why they ranked it the way that they did with respect to each of the three functions of money.

• Give their recommendation on whether their commodity could be used as a form of money.

22. Ask the students the following:

a. Which commodities were recommended by the groups to be used as a form of money?

(Answers will vary.)

b. What characteristics of money do those commodities have in common?

(Answers will vary.)

c. What characteristics of money did the commodities that weren't recommended lack?

(Answers will vary.)

CLOSURE

23. Review important points in this lesson by discussing the following:

   a. Based on your experience during this lesson, what is **money**?

   (Money is anything widely accepted as final payment for goods and services.)

   b. What are the three functions of money?

   (Medium of exchange, store of value, and unit of account)

   c. Would a horse or a thimble work as a better medium of exchange?

   (Thimble) **Why?** *(Answers will vary, but students may say that thimbles are smaller and therefore more portable.)*

   d. Would a horse or a thimble work as a better store of value? *(Thimble)* **Why?** *(Answers will vary, but students may say that thimbles are more durable than horses and therefore would be a better store of value.)*

   e. Would a horse or a thimble work as a better unit of account? *(Thimble)* **Why?** *(Answers will vary, but students may say that thimbles are smaller and therefore would be better able to be used to denote different values.)*

ASSESSMENT

Multiple Choice

1. Money is

   a. the resource that an economy uses to produce goods and services.

   b. **anything widely accepted as final payment for goods and services.**

   c. anything of value.

   d. never scarce.

2. Which of the following three functions of money makes it easier for people to save their money?

   a. Medium of exchange

   b. Interchangeability of denomination

   c. **Store of value**

   d. Unit of account

Constructed Response

1. Distribute a copy of Activity 13.4 to each student. Ask students to complete the activity using the following information:

   Caps from plastic bottles are plentiful and difficult to recycle. Consider whether you would recommend that a country adopt plastic bottle caps as money. Complete the spider graph and answer the questions below the graph.

   (Answers will vary, but should focus on whether bottle caps have the characteristics of money and would function well as money.)

CONNECTIONS: MONEY THROUGH TIME

Throughout history, societies have used a vast array of things as money, including huge stones, shells, elephant-tail bristles, gold and silver coins, furs, salt, whales' teeth, and of course, pieces of paper. Niall Ferguson in *The Ascent of Money* provides an overview of the development of early money.[1]

Benjamin Franklin, one of the nation's greatest thinkers, was also one of the earliest to write about how paper money worked in colonial America. Farley Grubb, in his essay, "Benjamin Franklin and the Birth of a Paper Money Economy,"[2] summarizes Franklin's observations about early American paper money and describes how paper money developed in the new nation. The essay is accompanied by a lesson that is highly adaptable to the middle grades.[3]

One of the most remarkable forms of money in the world is the so-called Yap stones, which were used on a few islands in Micronesia. Michael Bryan, in his essay "Island Money" describes how these stones, often weighing hundreds of pounds, were used as money.[4]

[1] Ferguson, Niall. 2008. *The Ascent of Money*. New York: Penguin Press. Pages 17–31.

[2] Grubb, Farley. "Benjamin Franklin and the Birth of a Paper Money Economy." Federal Reserve Bank of Philadelphia. http://www.philadelphiafed.org/publications/economic-education/ben-franklin-and-paper-money-economy.pdf.

[3] Hill, Andrew. "A Lesson to Accompany 'Benjamin Franklin and the Birth of a Paper Money Economy'." Federal Reserve Bank of Philadelphia. http://www.philadelphiafed.org/education/teachers/lesson-plans/benjamin-franklin.pdf.

[4] Bryan, Michael F. 2004. "Island Money." Federal Reserve Bank of Cleveland. http://www.clevelandfed.org/Research/commentary/2004/0201.pdf

Activity 13.1

Trading Instructions

Group 1 – Tea Merchants

You are a family of tea merchants. Your goal is to sell all your tea bags for *at least*:

2 strings of copper coins for each tea bag

SHOPPING LIST – You want to purchase:

- 1 pair of chopsticks
- 25 fish
- 12 paper clips

Group 2 – Tea Merchants

You are a family of tea merchants. Your goal is to sell all of your tea bags for *at least*:

4 strings of copper coins for each tea bag

SHOPPING LIST – You want to purchase:

- 2 pairs of chopsticks
- 35 fish
- 18 paper clips

Group 3 – Fishmongers

You are a family of fishmongers. Your goal is to sell all of your fish for *at least*:

1 string of copper coins for 10 fish

SHOPPING LIST – You want to purchase:

- 1 pair of chopsticks
- 6 tea bags
- 15 paper clips

Group 4 – Fishmongers

You are a family of fishmongers. Your goal is to sell all of your fish for *at least*:

1 string of copper coins for 5 fish

SHOPPING LIST – You want to purchase:

- 2 pairs of chopsticks
- 2 tea bags
- 21 paper clips

Activity 13.1, continued

Trading Instructions

Group 5 – Tool Producers

You are a family of tool-makers. Your goal is to sell all of your tools (represented by paper clips) for *at least:*

1 string of copper coins for 2 paper clips

SHOPPING LIST – You want to purchase:

- 2 pairs of chopsticks
- 8 tea bags
- 35 fish

Group 6 – Tool Producers

You are a family of tool-makers. Your goal is to sell all of your tools (represented by paper clips) for *at least:*

1 string of copper coins for 3 paper clips

SHOPPING LIST – You want to purchase:

- 2 pairs of chopsticks
- 4 tea bags
- 45 fish

Group 7 – Chopstick Producers

You are a family of chopstick makers. Your goal is to sell all of your chopsticks for *at least:*

3 strings of copper coins for 1 pair of chopsticks

SHOPPING LIST – You want to purchase:

- 12 paper clips
- 4 tea bags
- 30 fish

Group 8 – Chopstick Producers

You are a family of chopstick makers. Your goal is to sell all of your chopsticks for *at least:*

4 strings of copper coins for 1 pair of chopsticks

SHOPPING LIST – You want to purchase:

- 20 paper clips
- 2 tea bags
- 30 fish

ACTIVITY 13.2

Paper Money

Good for **1 string** **of copper cash coins**	**Good for** **1 string** **of copper cash coins**
Good for **1 string** **of copper cash coins**	**Good for** **1 string** **of copper cash coins**
Good for **1 string** **of copper cash coins**	**Good for** **1 string** **of copper cash coins**
Good for **1 string** **of copper cash coins**	**Good for** **1 string** **of copper cash coins**
Good for **1 string** **of copper cash coins**	**Good for** **1 string** **of copper cash coins**
Good for **1 string** **of copper cash coins**	**Good for** **1 string** **of copper cash coins**
Good for **1 string** **of copper cash coins**	**Good for** **1 string** **of copper cash coins**
Good for **1 string** **of copper cash coins**	**Good for** **1 string** **of copper cash coins**

ACTIVITY 13.3
Paper Money in China (1024 C.E. to 1430 C.E.)

The Chinese were the first people to use paper money beginning in the 800s. The Chinese government began issuing paper money in 1024 C.E. Beginning that year, only the Chinese government was allowed to issue paper money. The Chinese continued to use paper money through the Sung dynasty (960–1279), the Yuan dynasty (1279–1368), and the beginning of the Ming Dynasty (1368–1644). Around 1430 C.E., the Chinese were the first to stop using paper money.

During the Sung dynasty, paper money and copper coins were both used. The copper coins had a hole in the middle that allowed them to be threaded onto a string. These strings of copper coins could then be transported from place to place and used to buy goods and services. During the Sung dynasty, the paper money issued by the government was in large denominations (amounts) only. Individual copper coins were used when people wanted to pay for something of small value. However, many copper coins could be exchanged for paper money. Money became more important in China during the Sung dynasty, because the amount of trading that the Chinese did among themselves and with neighboring peoples increased rapidly.

During the Yuan dynasty, paper money was issued by the government in both large and small denominations. The government during the Yuan period ensured that everyone accepted the paper money in exchange for goods and services. Merchants who refused to accept paper money for payment were punished severely. Counterfeiting—the printing of fake money—was punishable by death.

European visitors to China in those days were amazed that the Chinese used paper money that wasn't backed by silver or gold. One such visitor to China was Marco Polo, trader and merchant from Venice. From 1271 to 1295, Marco Polo traveled extensively throughout China. When he returned to Venice, he wrote a book about his travels. One story explained how the Chinese produced paper money. Polo described how the Chinese used the bark of mulberry trees to make paper. When the paper was ready, it was cut into different sizes. The smaller sizes had lower value than the larger sizes.

Marco Polo explained how a number of officials were appointed by the Yuan emperor to supervise the production of the paper money. These officials would sign each piece of paper money and the chief official would stamp the emperor's seal on In this way, each piece of paper money was marked to indicate that it was authentic government money (legal tender).

Marco Polo also described how everyone in China was willing to accept paper money in exchange for goods and services because they knew that they, in turn, could buy the goods and services with the paper money. The Chinese government had declared that paper money had to be accepted as payment. He described how people could bring their worn-out paper money to the mint to exchange for new paper money.

During the early years of the Ming dynasty, paper money was used extensively. But, by the beginning of the 1400s, paper money in China had lost most of its value because most people stopped using it. People stopped using paper money during the Ming dynasty for many reasons. First, the Ming rulers did not have strict rules and harsh punishments to force people to use paper money and to stop them from printing counterfeits. Counterfeiting increased during the Ming dynasty and people began to distrust paper money and refuse to accept it in exchange for goods and services. They began to use more silver coins. As the demand for paper money decreased, so, too, did its value. Paper money eventually became practically worthless, so the Ming government stopped issuing it around 1430.

SOURCES

Chen, Chau-Nan and Shikuan Chen. 1995. "The Sung and Ming Paper Monies: Currency Competition and Currency Bubbles." *Journal of Macroeconomics*, 17 (Spring), pp. 273–288.

Tullock, Gordon. 1957. "Paper Money—A Cycle in Cathay." *The Economic History Review*, New Series, 9, pp. 393–407.

ACTIVITY 13.4

Functions of Money Spider Graph

Would _____ be good to use as money?

enter your commodity here

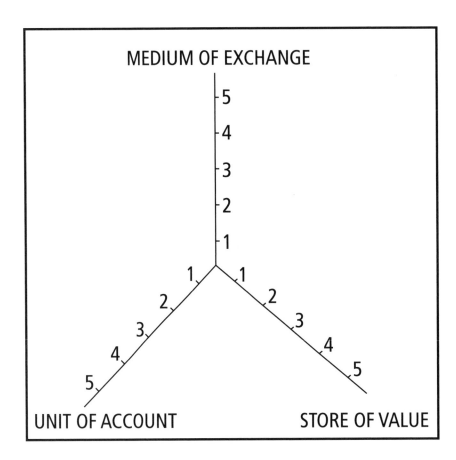

1. Based on your spider graph analysis of your commodity, would you recommend that it be used as money?

2. What characteristics of your commodity contributed to your recommendation?

ACTIVITY 13.5

Commodities as Money Cards

Rice	**Silk**
Carrots	**Paper**
Paintbrushes	**Oxen**
Pebbles	**Porcelain figurines**

SLIDE 13.1

Functions of Money

Medium of Exchange Money acts as a go-between to make it easier to buy and sell things.

Store of Value Money holds its value until people want to exchange it for a good or service.

Unit of Account Money serves as a way to measure and compare the value of goods and services in relation to one another.

SLIDE 13.2

Characteristics of Money

Acceptable Money must be acceptable to everyone in exchange for goods and services.

Divisible Money must be easily divided into small parts (or already in small pieces) so that people can purchase goods and services at any price.

Durable Money must be able to withstand the wear and tear of many people using it.

Portable Money must be easy to carry.

Scarce Money must be hard for people to obtain.

Stable in value Money's value must remain relatively constant over long periods of time.

SLIDE 13.3

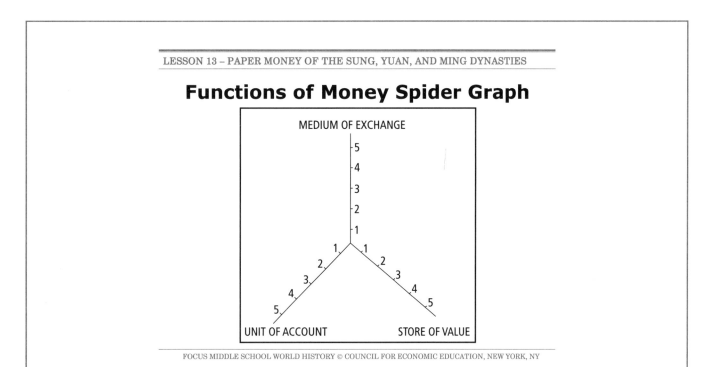

SLIDE 13.4

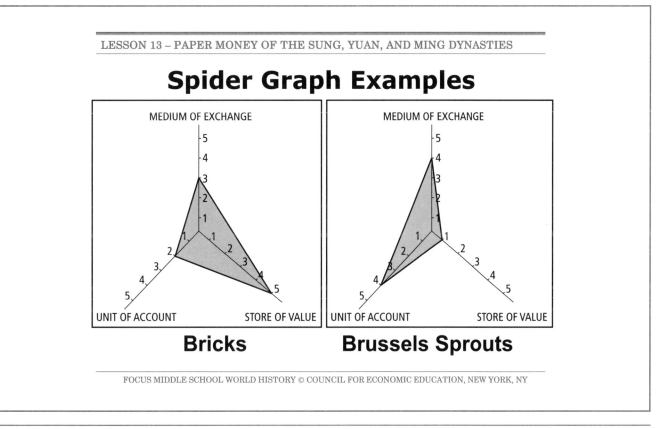

LESSON 14

THE ECONOMIC SYSTEM OF MEDIEVAL EUROPE

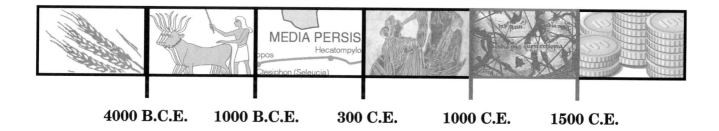

4000 B.C.E.   1000 B.C.E.   300 C.E.   1000 C.E.   1500 C.E.

LESSON 14
THE ECONOMIC SYSTEM OF MEDIEVAL EUROPE

LESSON DESCRIPTION

Working in groups, students, as serfs, play three rounds of a simple production activity to experience life in a manorial system. In the third round, new technology and incentives are introduced. Students learn about new capital goods, techniques, and the importance of private incentives that promoted economic growth during the Middle Ages. Finally, students answer the three economic questions that people in every society face and determine what type of economic system the manorial system was most like.

INTRODUCTION

Beginning in the late 700s C.E., large numbers of invaders raided and pillaged much of Europe, causing political and economic systems to collapse. Frankish kings needed warriors to protect their empires. Without an effective means of collecting taxes and, for all practical purposes, the lack of a stable money system, the kings created a system of political and military relationships called feudalism. They gave some of their land to warriors, called knights or lords, in exchange for protection. Residents on the land were peasants known as serfs, who were required to produce goods and services for the lords. In exchange for the serfs' labor, the lord maintained order, provided protection, and administered justice. The lords collected rent in the form of goods and services to support their material existence. In exchange, the serfs had access to protected land on which to grow crops to support their families. This economic arrangement was known as the manorial system.

The manorial system lasted for centuries and was characterized by instability, declining specialization and commercial activity, primitive production techniques, and a low standard of living. The Middle Ages, 500–1500 C.E., has long been considered a period of stagnation during which little economic growth occurred. However, new technology and incentives emerged over time as serfs were given more freedom and rewarded for production and investment decisions.

CONCEPTS

Economic incentives

Economic system

OBJECTIVES

Students will be able to:

- Explain how incentives change behavior.

- Explain the impact of inventions and technology on output.

- Answer three basic economic questions for the manorial system.

- Explain what economic system or systems existed in the Middle Ages and justify their answers.

CONTENT STANDARDS

Voluntary Content Standards in Economics, 2nd edition

- **Standard 3:** Different methods can be used to allocate goods and services. People acting individually or collectively must choose which methods to use to allocate different kinds of goods and services.

- **Standard 4:** People usually respond predictably to positive and negative incentives.

World History Content Standards

World History Era 5. Intensified Hemispheric Interactions.

- **Standard 2**: The redefining of European society and culture, 1000–1300 C.E.

TIME REQUIRED

90 minutes. Procedures 1–17, 45 minutes on the first day. Procedures 18–41, 45 minutes on the second day.

MATERIALS

- Slides 14.1–14.7

- Activities 14.1 and 14.2, one copy per student

- Activity 14.3, cut apart

- Small candies, homework passes, or other incentives

- Large supply of scrap paper

PROCEDURE

1. Distribute a copy of Activity 14.1 to each student. Ask students to read the activity.

2. Discuss the following questions:

   a. How did the raids of the large number of invaders impact Europe beginning in the late 700s?

      (Collapse of law and order, a decline in trade, and collapse of local economies)

   b. What is feudalism?

      (Medieval form of government, a system of military and political relationships)

   c. Why did feudalism emerge?

      (Kings needed protection. They gave portions of their estates to warriors in exchange for 40 days of military service in times of peace and more during times of war.)

   d. What did the lords and knights receive in exchange for their military service?

      (Estates or manors that came with peasants called serfs)

   e. What responsibilities did the knights and lords have?

      (Provide serfs with protection, order, and enforcement of manorial rules and laws.)

   f. What did the serfs owe the lord?

      (Their labor, which produced food and other goods the lord needed to maintain his lifestyle.)

3. Tell students that you are a powerful lord and they are powerless serfs. Explain that during the Middle Ages in medieval Europe, serfs lived in villages on the lord's manor and farmed his land. Divide the students into five groups. Explain that they will be working as serfs producing an agricultural product by planting seeds. Assign each of the groups one of the following: barley, wheat, rye, oats, or vegetables.

4. Show Slide 14.1. Crumble several pieces of scrap paper and put them on a desk. Tell students that these wads of paper represent seeds. Demonstrate, or have a student demonstrate, how to produce one unit of an agricultural product following the steps on Slide 14.1. Place a piece of scrap paper on your desk. Standing, put your hands on your shoulders, reach down to the desk and select one crumbled piece of paper from an imaginary bag by bringing your elbows together, reach down to the floor, plant the seed by releasing your elbows, sit down at your desk, and write the word of your assigned product on the piece of scrap paper that will be used to keep track of the number of seeds planted.

5. Distribute 50–60 pieces of scrap paper. Ask students to crumble the paper and place it on a desk. Have each student write on the top of a piece of scrap paper the name of the agricultural product their group is assigned to produce. Tell students they will have three minutes to plant as many seeds as possible. Note to the students that in this first round, they will be working for you, the lord of the manor, so there is no reward for doing the best they can, though very slow workers may be punished.

6. Allow three minutes for students to produce their crops.

7. Ask each group to count how many seeds they planted. (This is equal to the number of times they wrote the name of their product on the scrap piece of paper—provided they "planted" the seed

according to the rules.) Ask students to determine the average number of seeds planted per minute by dividing the group's total number of seeds planted by three. Note: If the groups are of different sizes, have the larger groups use the same number of students as the smaller groups by dropping the necessary number of students' results from the total (group's choice).

8. Show Slide 14.2. Record the average number of seeds planted per minute for each group in the column labeled Round 1.

9. Tell students they will work for three more minutes. Tell students these are the new rules of the game. Unlike in Round 1, everything they plant in this round belongs to them. Everyone in their group must agree on what to produce—wheat, barley, rye, oats, vegetables, or some combination of these. Allow time for students to determine what they will plant. Everyone in the group must agree on what to plant.

10. Tell students that the goal is to plant as many seeds as possible so their families will have food to eat.

11. Have groups pick up the seeds (crumbled paper) planted in Round 1 and place them on their desks.

12. Allow three minutes for students to plant.

13. Ask students to count the number of seeds planted and determine the average number of seeds planted each minute by dividing the group's total number of seeds planted by 3.

14. Record the average number of seeds planted per minute by each group on Slide 14.2 in the column labeled Round 2.

15. Show Slides 14.3–14.6. Make the following points:

    • Under feudalism in medieval Europe, the economic system was the manorial system.

• An **economic system** is the institutional framework of formal and informal rules that a society uses to determine what to produce, how to produce, and how to distribute goods and services.

• Point out to students that every society must answer these three economic questions.

• Organization of manorial work was a mixture of cooperation and coercion on the manors. Depending on the manor, serfs worked three to four days a week for the lord. Everything produced during that time belonged to the lord.

• Tell students that there was no such thing as a typical manor but all manors consisted of land, buildings, and people.

• The lord's land consisted of 25 to 30 percent of the arable land of the manor plus the manor house, barns, stables, workshops, gardens, mills, and ovens.

• Serfs were bound to the land. Lords might leave, but serfs stayed with the land.

• Serfs' land was in large fields divided into strips. A peasant household may have had 24 strips of land scattered throughout the manor's fields. Serfs had to agree on what and when to harvest and who would do what. This was called communal farming. Often oxen were needed and families were unlikely to have had more than one ox so they had to combine resources to plow their fields. By working together, families shared the risk if crops failed.

• Serfs planted only half their fields each year. The other half were left fallow each year to preserve soil fertility. This was called two-field crop rotation.

• Few markets existed where lords could buy goods and services; lords relied on serfs to produce what they needed.

- Serfs had to pay a fee to grind their grain in the lord's mill and bake bread in the lord's oven.

- Serfs had to pay other fees that were collected on a regular basis or on special occasions. Fees could be as high as 50 percent of the goods a serf produced.

16. Point out to students that the manorial system flourished mainly in the fertile grain-growing regions of Europe – e.g., not so much in pastoral regions, mountainous areas, or drier areas. Also note that within the manorial economy, there was a lot of variance in how the system worked. Free workers (who didn't owe labor but paid rent) often existed side by side with serfs.

17. Divide the class into pairs of students. Distribute a copy of Activity 14.2 to each student. Have student pairs complete the cloze activity. Review their answers.

18. Discuss the two rounds of the production activity:

    a. In Round 1 of the production activity, what did the three minutes of production represent?

    (Three days of labor working for the lord)

    b. What was the average output per day for your group in Round 1?

    (Answers will vary.)

    c. Who will get the products that grow from the seeds you planted in Round 1?

    (The lord will get them.)

    d. How might this affect your willingness to produce?

    (Less desire to produce)

    e. Why didn't the lord purchase goods and services instead of having serfs produce them?

    (Few markets existed.)

    f. In Round 2, what did the three minutes of production represent?

    (Days that serfs had to work their strips of land and produce goods for their families)

    g. What happened to output per day in Round 2? *(Increased)* Why? *(Greater desire to produce because the output was for the serfs and their families and not for the lord)*

    h. Many groups may have increased their output because they chose to produce rye rather than one of the other agricultural goods. Ask students why they chose rye.

    (They produced rye because it had the fewest letters to write when they recorded each seed planted. It took less time to record the seed planted which gave time to plant more seeds.)

    Point out that on the manor, serfs would have planted a variety of seeds to meet their needs.

19. Tell students that people respond to incentives. Define **economic incentives** as factors that motivate and influence the behavior of individuals and organizations, including firms and government agencies. Tell students that rewards are positive incentives that motivate people to do things. A reward makes people better off.

20. Ask students for examples of a reward for positive classroom behavior.

    (Answers will vary but may include earning points to spend at a school store or extra credit.)

21. Explain that penalties are negative incentives that deter people from doing something. Penalties make people worse off. Ask students for examples of penalties or negative incentives that discourage inappropriate behavior at home.

    (Answers will vary but might include loss of time with friends or use of cell phone if family rules are not followed.)

22. Ask students for an example of incentives that encourage students to change their behavior in the following examples and identify the incentive as positive or negative. Sample answers are provided for each example below.

    a. Read more books outside of class

       (Receive a raffle ticket for a chance to win a new electronic game, positive incentive)

    b. Return library books on time

       (Fine for late books, negative incentive; loss of library privileges, negative incentive)

    c. Get to school on time

       (Detention after school if late, negative incentive)

    d. Stop using cell phones in social studies class

       (For each week cell phone is not used, student receives points toward final grade in social studies, positive incentive. Cell phone is confiscated for two weeks if used in class, negative incentive.)

23. Discuss:

    a. What incentive did the serfs have to produce as much as possible for the lord on the days they worked his land?

       (Little to no incentive to work as hard as possible to produce for the lord. The lord took all that was produced.)

    b. What incentive might the lord have given to encourage greater output?

       (Answers will vary but might include reduced fees for use of lord's mill or oven or increase of the percentage of production serfs could keep and freely use.)

    c. What incentive did the serfs have to work harder on the days they worked on their land?

       (They could keep what they produced after paying a portion to the lord in fees. Even though this could be as high as 50 percent, serfs needed the output for their families to survive.)

24. Conduct a third round of production. The students will probably groan, so tell them you have good news: Because of the invention of the heavy-wheeled plow, they neither have to put their hands on their shoulders nor reach to the ground. They must only stand, pick up a paper "seed" with their elbows, and drop it on the floor before returning to their seats to write their product name.

25. Tell students their groups are to plant the same kinds of seeds as in Round 2. Their goal is to plant as many as possible in the three-minute period. If their output exceeds what they produced in Round 2, they will receive a reward. (The reward can be such things as candy, extra points toward their social studies grade or a homework pass for each group member.)

26. Allow students three minutes to produce.

27. Have students count how many seeds they planted and determine the average number of seeds planted per minute by dividing the group's total seeds planted by three. Record the average number of seeds planted per minute by each group on Slide 14.2 in the column labeled Round 2.

28. Discuss the following questions:

    a. What happened to the average number of seeds planted in Round 3 compared to Rounds 1 and 2?

       (Increased)

    b. Why were you able to plant more?

       (New production technique and rewards or incentives)

29. Explain that many lords and serfs were quite entrepreneurial when provided with incentives and found ways to increase output on their manors. Round 3 represented work on a manor with an

entrepreneurial lord. Provide each of the groups one of the cards from Activity 14.3. Tell groups to read their card and be prepared to tell the class about an innovation or incentive that changed the way work was done and what the lords and serfs gained.

Group 1 — heavy-wheeled plow

Group 2 — introduction of draft animals

Group 3 — watermill

Group 4 — three-field system

Group 5 — lord/peasant cooperation

30. Allow time for groups to present their reports.

31. Remind students that every society must answer the three economic questions of what to produce, how to produce, and for whom to produce. Explain that the "for whom" question means who will get the goods produced.

32. Show Slide 14.7. Explain the three types of economic systems.

- In a traditional economic system, the three economic questions are answered by custom or tradition: People do things the way they have always done them.

- In a command system, the three economic questions are answered by an individual or group in authority.

- In a market system, the answer to the question of *what* to produce is whatever is profitable, *how* to produce is the least costly method, and *for whom* is the consumer willing to pay the highest price.

33. Discuss the following questions:

a. How was the question of what to produce answered in the manorial system?

(The lord determined how the labor would be used for the production of his goods and services. The serfs

had to agree on what they would produce.)

b. How was the question of how to produce answered?

(At great deal of labor was used with limited tools and equipment. Some lords increased production by using heavy wheeled plows, draft animals, mills, and providing incentives for the serfs.)

c. How was the question of for whom answered?

(The lord took all that was produced from the labor of the serfs on the days they worked for the lord. Serfs kept what they produced during the remaining days of the week after paying fees.)

34. Ask students what kind of economic system they think the manorial system was most like.

(The manorial system had many characteristics of the command economy. The lord determined much of what was produced, how it was produced, and for whom. Peasants had some control over their land, but the decisions of what to produce were made as a group and the harvest was divided among them.)

CLOSURE

35. Review the following questions with the students:

a. What is feudalism and why did it evolve?

(A system of political and military arrangements between kings and lords. Kings needed protection from invaders. Without a means of taxation and a lack of a money system, they made arrangements for a military and protection with the lords.)

b. Describe the relationship between the lord and the king.

(The lord provided the king with at least 40 days of military service or more in times of war and, in return, the king gave the lord land.)

c. What was the manorial system?

(The economic system of the Middle Ages)

d. Describe the relationship between the lord and the serfs.

(The lords provided protection, order, and enforcement of manorial rules and laws. The serfs owed the lord their labor used to produce goods and services.)

e. What are economic incentives?

(Factors that motivate and influence the behavior of individuals and organizations, including firms and government agencies)

f. What incentives increased production for the lord?

(Special privileges, new capital goods, and paying a small rent in return for which peasants gained more control over the land and rights that resulted in personal freedom)

g. What inventions and technology increased production for the lord?

(Heavy-wheeled plow, horse collar, three-field system, and watermills)

Explain.

(The plow allowed more land to be plowed and used for planting thereby increasing the amount of crops produced. The horse collar allowed horses to be harnessed to pull plows; horses were stronger and faster than oxen, so fields could be cleared and tilled in less time. The three-field system yielded greater output from the soil; one-third more food crops could be planted. The watermill freed workers, mainly women, who were in charge of grinding grain, to work on other tasks.)

h. What is an economic system?

(The institutional framework of formal and informal rules that a society uses to determine what to produce, how to produce, and how to distribute goods and services)

i. What are the three economic questions all societies must answer?

(What to produce, how to produce, and for whom to produce)

j. What type of economic system is the manorial system most like?

(Command system)

Explain.

(The economic questions were answered by authority, the lord.)

ASSESSMENT

Multiple Choice

1. The lords needed the labor of the serfs to produce goods and services in order to maintain their lifestyle. In exchange for serf labor, lords provided _____.

   a. money

   b. churches

   c. **protection**

   d. festivals

2. The manor system was most like a _____.

   a. traditional economy

   b. **command economy**

   c. market economy

   d. modern economy

Constructed Response

1. A history museum has an exhibition on the Middle Ages. One of the exhibits is a diorama of a manor. Write a handout for visiting middle school students that explains the economic system of the manor.

SOURCES

Cameron, R. and Neal, L. 2003. *A Concise Economic History of the World*. 4th edition. Oxford University Press. Murray, J. 2010. "Entrepreneurs and Entrepreneurship in Medieval Europe." In *The Invention of Enterprise: Entrepreneurship from Ancient Mesopotamia to Modern Times*, David S.

Landes, John Mokyr, and William J. Baumol, editors. pp. 88-93. Princeton University Press.

North, D. and Thomas, R. 1973. *The Rise of the Western World: A New Economic History*. Cambridge University Press.

CONNECTIONS: TO OTHER TIMES

Have students explore the collective farm system of the former Soviet Union and compare it with the manor system of the Middle Ages.

ACTIVITY 14.1

Feudalism: What Is It and Why Did It Emerge?

Beginning in the late 700s C.E., large numbers of invaders raided villages throughout Europe. This resulted in a collapse of law and order, a decline in trade, and collapse of local economies. To counter these threats, Frankish kings needed warriors. They created a system of military and political relationships called feudalism.

Feudalism was the medieval model of government. Paying for troops was impossible because society at this time lacked a money system. Without a money system, collecting taxes was difficult. The kings offered land or estates to warriors, also called knights or lords, in exchange for military service. They agreed to 40 days of service each year in times of peace and more days in times of war.

The land given to knights or lords came with peasant farmers, known as serfs. The serfs provided the lords or knights with labor to produce food and other goods they needed to maintain their life-styles. The knights and lords were in charge of maintaining order, protection, and enforcing rules and laws on their estates or man-ors. In exchange, serfs were given protected land to grow crops to support their families. This economic arrangement was known as the manorial system.

ACTIVITY 14.2

Cloze Activity

Use the words in the box to complete the sentences below.

land	strips of land	markets	what	manorial
50%	what	economic system	lord	two-field crop rotation
for whom	communal	3-4 days	when	how	fee

In Medieval Europe, the economic system was the _____ system.

The institutional framework a society uses to answer the basic economic questions is called an _____.

The three economic questions every society must answer are _____to produce, _____ to produce, and _____to produce.

Serfs were bound to the _____ and worked for the lord _____ per week. Goods produced during this time belonged to the _____.

Serfs had _____scattered across the manor on which to grow food for their family.

Serfs of a manor all had to agree on _____ and _____ to harvest. This was called _____ farming.

Leaving half of the fields fallow each year to preserve soil fertility was called _____.

The serfs were required to produce goods and services for the lord because there were few _____.

Serfs were required to grind their grain at the lord's mill and bake bread in his ovens for a _____.

Fees collected by the lord could be as high as _____ of the goods a serf produced.

ACTIVITY 14.3

Innovations and Incentives

Heavy-Wheeled Plow

This iron plow allowed the peasants to turn the heavy soil of north-western Europe. Although expensive, lords invested in this capital good because it resulted in more fields being tilled and increased output per worker.

Draft Animals

Teams of two to four oxen were used to pull the heavy-wheeled plows. The invention of the horse collar and the practice of using horseshoes to protect horses' hoofs made it possible to use horses as draft animals. Horses were more expensive but were also stronger and faster than oxen. Draft animals made it possible to till more fields and increase output per worker.

Watermill

The lords provided watermills. In 1086, England had 6,082 mills. The watermill meant the women didn't have to mill grain by hand, and their labor could be used for other purposes. Eventually, mills were used to saw lumber and hammer metals.

ACTIVITY 14.3, CONTINUED

Three-Field Rotation

The two-field rotation method was a method in which half the land was planted each year and the other half was not used. The next year, farmers planted the fields that had lain fallow. If 600 fertile acres were available, 300 acres each year were not used. Under *three-field rotation*, the land was divided into three parts. Two fields were planted and the third was left unused. Every third year, a field would "rest" unplanted. If 600 fertile acres were available, 400 acres could be planted and harvested each year. In addition, the three-field system usually involved a crop that enriched the soil, e.g., peas, beans, and especially clover, which not only enriched the soil but also was a good forage crop for work animals.

Lord/Peasant Cooperation

To encourage peasants to move to the farther reaches of the manor and cultivate wasteland, lords provided special privileges, capital (tools and equipment) and incentives. In return for paying a small rent, peasants gained control over their land as well as rights that resulted in more personal freedom.

SLIDE 14.1

LESSON 14 – THE ECONOMIC SYSTEM OF MEDIEVAL EUROPE

Production Steps

1. Stand and put your hands on your shoulders.
2. Reach down to your desk and select a seed (crumbled piece of paper) from an imaginary bag by bringing your elbows together.
3. Reach down to the floor.
4. Plant the seed by releasing your elbows.
5. Sit down at your desk.
6. Write the word of your assigned product on the piece of scrap paper.
7. Continue planting seeds by repeating steps 1-6.

FOCUS MIDDLE SCHOOL WORLD HISTORY © COUNCIL FOR ECONOMIC EDUCATION, NEW YORK, NY

SLIDE 14.2

LESSON 14 – THE ECONOMIC SYSTEM OF MEDIEVAL EUROPE

Production Table

Group	Round 1	Round 2	Round 3

FOCUS MIDDLE SCHOOL WORLD HISTORY © COUNCIL FOR ECONOMIC EDUCATION, NEW YORK, NY

SLIDE 14.3

Manor System

- Under feudalism in Medieval Europe, the economic system was manorialism.
- An **economic system** is the way in which a group organizes to determine what to produce, how to produce, and for whom to produce.
- The lord's land consisted of 25 to 30 percent of the arable land of the manor plus the manor house, barns, stables, workshops, gardens, mills, and ovens.

SLIDE 14.4

Manor System

- Serfs were bound to the land. Lords might leave but serfs stayed with the land.
- Serfs' land was in large fields divided into strips. A peasant household had possibly two dozen strips scattered throughout the open fields.
- Serfs of a manor agreed on what and when to harvest. This was called communal farming.

SLIDE 14.5

LESSON 14 – THE ECONOMIC SYSTEM OF MEDIEVAL EUROPE

Manor System

- Serfs planted only half their fields each year. The other half were left fallow each year to preserve soil fertility. This was called two-field crop rotation.

- Serfs worked the land for the lord three to four days week. Few markets existed where the lord could buy goods and services. They relied on the serfs to produce most goods.

SLIDE 14.6

LESSON 14 – THE ECONOMIC SYSTEM OF MEDIEVAL EUROPE

Manor System

- Serfs had to grind their grain in the lord's mill and bake bread in the lord's oven for a fee.

- Serfs had to pay other fees collected on a regular basis or on special occasions. Fees could be as high as 50% of goods that the serf produced.

SLIDE 14.7

LESSON 14 – THE ECONOMIC SYSTEM OF MEDIEVAL EUROPE

Economic Systems

	Traditional	Command	Market
What to Produce	Custom	Central authority	Whatever is profitable
How to Produce	Custom	Central authority	Least costly method
For Whom to Produce	Custom	Central authority	Highest bidder

LESSON 15

WAGES AND THE BLACK DEATH

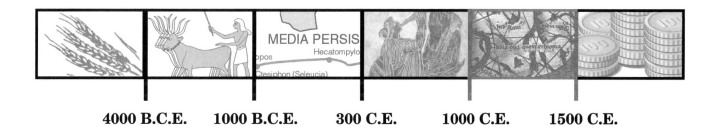

4000 B.C.E.   1000 B.C.E.   300 C.E.   1000 C.E.   1500 C.E.

LESSON 15
WAGES AND THE BLACK DEATH

LESSON DESCRIPTION

Students will learn that a plague called the Black Death caused a large decrease in the population of Europe in the 14th century as well as an increase in workers' wages. Students will also learn that efforts by European producers and governments to resist wage increases, such as the Statute of Laborers in 1351, were unsuccessful. As workers' wages rose, they experienced an increase in their standard of living. Producers switched to raising sheep and other activities that required less labor. Students will complete a sequence chart on which they will record the order of events after fleas and rats spread the plague throughout Europe. The final activity of the lesson is an imaginary trial in which the black rat is accused of responsibility for the Black Death. Selected students will read the testimony of the trial and the other students will serve as jurors and decide the guilt or innocence of the black rat.

INTRODUCTION

The Black Death struck Europe between 1347 and 1352. Historians believe the disease was a bubonic plague caused by the bacterium *Yersinia pestis*. The plague started in Asia and was carried to Europe in 1347 on merchant ships by black rats infested with fleas carrying the deadly bacteria. Although it was not the only plague that caused widespread sickness and death in Europe, the Black Death of 1347–1352 is notable for the estimated 20 million human deaths it caused and the terror it spawned. At least one-third of the total population of Europe died and many people also died in Asia. It took 500 years for the true cause of the plague to be identified. In the 14th century, physicians could do little to help or comfort those who contracted the bubonic plague. The plague had an economic impact with far-reaching results: The reduction in population led to a large decrease in the number of workers, which, in turn, resulted

in an increase in wages and better working conditions for peasant workers. As wages rose, workers achieved a higher standard of living and more freedom.

CONCEPTS

Costs of production

Labor

Labor market

Productive resources

Productivity

Scarcity

Standard of living

Wage

Workers

OBJECTIVES

Student will be able to:

- Explain the impact of a decrease in the number of workers on wages.

- Discuss why the Statute of Laborers was unsuccessful in preventing wage increases in the 14th century.

- Explain how an increase in wages can lead producers to change the goods they produce in order to reduce their labor costs.

CONTENT STANDARDS

Voluntary Content Standards in Economics, 2nd edition

- **Standard 8:** Prices send signals and provide incentives to buyers and sellers. When supply or demand changes, market prices adjust, affecting incentives.

- **Standard 13:** Income for most people is determined by the market value of the productive resources they sell. What workers earn primarily depends on the market value of what they produce.

 FOCUS: MIDDLE SCHOOL WORLD HISTORY © COUNCIL FOR ECONOMIC EDUCATION, NEW YORK, NY

World History Content Standards

World History Era 5. Intensified Hemispheric Interactions. 1000–1500 CE

- **Standard 5:** Patterns of crisis and recovery in Afro-Eurasia, 1300–1450.

- **Standard 7:** Major global trends, 1000–1500 C.E.

TIME REQUIRED

90 minutes. Procedures 1–10, 45 minutes on the first day. Procedures 11 to lesson's end, 45 minutes on the second day.

MATERIALS

- Slides 1 (optional), 2 and 3

- Activities 15.1, 15.2, 15.3, and 15.4, copies for each student

PROCEDURE

1. Distribute Activity 15.1. Ask students to read the passage and then describe the impact of the Black Death on those who survived it.

   (Responses will vary. Some students may mention that a lack of knowledge about the cause of the plague and the inability of physicians to cure the disease affected the behavior of the survivors. Those who lived during this period often became devoutly religious or indulged in worldly pleasures and spent their incomes rather than saving.)

2. Explain that **workers** are employed to produce goods and services and are paid a **wage** for their efforts. The large decrease in population caused by the Black Death reduced the number of workers, or the supply of labor, throughout Europe. This means that there was an increase in the scarcity of labor. **Scarcity** is the condition that exists because human wants exceed the capacity of available resources to satisfy those wants. Ask the students to describe the impact of a decrease in the number of workers on the remaining workers' living conditions.

   (Workers were able to demand higher wages and better working conditions. Workers had more freedom to choose to move from one job to another job that paid a higher wage).

3. **Optional**: Show Slide 15.1. (If Slide 15.1 is not shown, go to Procedure 4.) Tell students that **labor** represents the quantity and quality of human effort available to produce goods and services. In the graph on Slide 15.1, the quantity of labor varies along the horizontal axis; the quality of labor is assumed not to change. The graph shows the labor market with a labor supply and a labor demand curve. The intersection of these curves determines the equilibrium wage and the quantity of people who work at this wage. Emphasize that the supply changes because of the deaths of workers during the plague, which leads to higher wages.

4. Distribute Activity 15.2 to the students. Have the students read the passage, which is an excerpt from the Statute of Laborers (1351). European producers initially resisted paying workers higher wages, and some countries' rulers issued ordinances, or laws, to keep wages from rising. An example is England's Statute of Laborers. Workers who violated the Statute of Laborers risked being placed in stocks, pillories, or prisons and being branded.

5. Show Slide 15.2, which depicts a man in a pillory. Explain that a pillory or stock was a form of punishment used in medieval times. They were often located in public places so that anyone passing by would be aware who had violated laws. People were allowed to verbally abuse or assault people in stocks. Ask students why the statute was ineffective in preventing workers from demanding and producers paying higher wages.

   (Producers who did not meet workers' demands soon discovered that other producers would. Producers had to choose between paying higher wages and not producing anything. Although some

workers were punished for violating the statute, the government did not have enough resources to enforce it effectively. Local lords were responsible for enforcing the statute, but the lords also hired people to work for them. Some lords paid higher wages in spite of the statute and other lords avoided violating the statute by making in-kind payments to workers and offering workers fringe benefits.)

6. Tell students that although the plague killed many people, it did not destroy the tools, buildings, and machines workers used to farm and produce goods and services. Some cows, horses, and other work animals died because the plague killed the people who cared for the animals. Because each worker had more tools and animals to work with, productivity increased. **Productivity** is the amount of output (goods and services) produced per unit of input (productive resources). **Productive resources** are natural resources, human resources, and capital resources used to make goods and services. When worker productivity rises, producers can afford to pay higher wages.

7. Tell students that the increase in workers' wages raised standards of living. The **standard of living** is the level of subsistence of a nation, social class, or individual with reference to the adequacy of necessities and comforts of daily life.

8. Ask students how the increase in wages and the standard of living affected peasant workers.

(They were able to demand better working conditions from the lords who employed them. Workers had greater freedom to choose where they lived and worked. As their incomes rose, they were able to afford to buy more meat, fruit, clothing, and other goods that they could not have afforded before. Eventually, some peasants were able to buy their own land.)

9. Ask students to explain how producers responded to the decrease in the number of workers and higher wages which increased their **costs of production**.

(They began to produce goods that required less labor. Grain production, for example, required many workers. Production of grain decreased. Raising sheep did not require many workers. As more sheep were raised, the production of woolen clothing increased.)

10. Distribute Activity 15.3 to the students and show Slide 15.3. Tell the students to complete the sequence chart by placing the events listed on Slide 15.3 in the correct chronological order, beginning with the earliest event.

(The suggested order based on the reading: #5, #6, #2, #1, #8, #4, #7, #3. Alternatively, #4 could come after #7, #3.)

11. Distribute a copy of Activity 15.4 to each student. Tell students that they will hear testimony from the trial of Reginald ("Reggie") Rattus, a black rat who represents those accused of causing the deaths of more than 20 million people during the Black Death. Reggie's codefendant is Fiona Flea. The trial setting is the (fictional) Global Court of Justice in Geneva, Switzerland. Court reporters for the British Broadcasting Corporation (BBC) narrate the trial. The BBC is the principal public service broadcaster in the United Kingdom, and the largest broadcaster in the world.

12. Assign the nine speaking parts and tell students that those without speaking parts will serve as jury members. The jury will be responsible for determining whether the evidence presented during the trial is sufficient to find the accused guilty of causing the deaths of more 20 million people from the Black Death. You have the option of instructing the jury that a guilty verdict will result from a unanimous decision or a majority decision of the jury.

13. After the trial testimony has been read, ask the students to vote on the guilt of the rat.

CLOSURE
14. Review the following points with the students:

- An increase in workers' wages resulted from the large decrease in population and the number of workers caused by the Black Death.

- Fewer workers caused an increase in workers' wages and standard of living.

- Workers enjoyed greater freedom to choose where to work and bargained for better working conditions.

- Eventually, some workers were able to save enough income to buy their own land.

ASSESSMENT

Multiple Choice

1. Which of the following was a result of the Black Death of 1347–1352?

   a. **There was a decrease in the number of workers and an increase in wages.**

   b. European governments helped people find jobs and earn higher wages.

   c. Producers switched to producing goods and services that used less land and more workers.

   d. There was an increase in the number of workers and a decrease in wages.

2. Which of the following was *not* part of the Statute of Laborers issued in England in 1351?

   a. Every able-bodied man and woman under the age of 60 who did not have a craft or trade would have to work for anyone who wanted to hire them.

   b. Workers were required to accept wages that were no higher than the wages paid in 1346.

   c. **All vendors (sellers) of food items were allowed to charge any prices that wanted in order to sell their goods.**

   d. Workers who left the service of their employers before the end of the terms they agreed to work would be sent to prison.

Constructed Response

1. The Black Death led to higher wages and higher costs of production for food, clothing, and other goods. What was the government's response to higher wages? Why was this response ineffective?

   (Several European governments passed laws to keep wages from rising in order to prevent production costs, and the prices of goods that were produced, from rising. These efforts failed. Wages rose because the scarcity of labor increased. The lords who were supposed to enforce these laws also hired workers. To avoid violating the laws, they made in-kind payments to workers in addition to their legal wages, and gave workers other fringe benefits.)

ACTIVITY 15.1
The Economic Impact of the Black Death of 1347–1352

THE PLAGUE ENDS POPULATION GROWTH IN EUROPE

Between 1347 and 1352, the Black Death killed more than 20 million people in Europe. This was one-third or more of Europe's population.[1] The plague began in Asia and spread to Europe on trading ships. At the time, no one knew what caused the plague. Many years later, the source was found to be bacteria from black rats and fleas. The fleas infected rats, and the rats infected people after they hopped aboard ships and sailed to Genoa, Venice, Messina, and other European ports. From these cities, the plague spread quickly throughout Europe. "So lethal was the disease that cases were known of persons going to bed well and dying before they woke…. So rapidly did it spread from one to another that to a French physician … it seemed as if one sick person 'could infect the whole world.'"[2]

RULERS RESIST WORKERS' DEMANDS FOR HIGHER WAGES

The plague had an important effect on the relationship between the lords who owned much of the land in Europe and the peasants who worked for the lords. As people died, it became harder and harder to find people to plow fields, harvest crops, and produce other goods and services. Peasants began to demand higher wages.

European rulers tried to keep wages from rising. An English law in 1349 tried to force workers to accept the same wages they received in 1346. A similar law, the Statute of Laborers,[3] was issued in 1351. The statute said that every healthy unemployed person under 60 years old must work for anyone who wanted to hire him. Workers who violated the Statute of Laborers were fined and were put in stocks[4] as punishment for disobeying the statute. In 1360, punishments became worse. Workers who demanded higher wages could be sent to prison and—if they escaped—branded with the letter "F" (possibly for Fugitive) on their foreheads.

---

[1] Rondo Cameron and Larry Neal. *A Concise History of the World* (4th edition). 2003. New York: Oxford University Press, p. 16.

[2] Barbara Tuchman. *A Distant Mirror – The Calamitous 14th Century*. 1978. New York: Ballantine Books, pp. 92-93.

[3] The English spelling is "Labourers."

[4] Stocks were used in the medieval times as a form of punishment involving public humiliation. The stocks were often located in a public place, so that people who passed the victim would know he broke some law.

ACTIVITY 15.1, CONTINUED

GREATER SCARCITY OF LABOR RESULTS IN HIGHER WAGES

Although worker population decreased because of the plague, the amount of land and the tools did not change much. Some farm animals died when the people who took care of them died. Because the remaining workers had more tools and land to work, they became more productive, producing more goods and services. When workers are more productive, employers are willing to pay higher wages.

The Statute of Laborers and similar laws in other countries were not very effective. Some lords avoided violating the statute by making "in kind" payments—paying workers with food or other goods rather than wages—or providing other "fringe benefits." Some lords began to pay illegally high wages. Wages increased because there were fewer workers—labor had become more scarce.[5]

THE BLACK DEATH CHANGES EUROPEAN AGRICULTURE

Before the plague, the large population kept wages from rising. Most peasants did not consider leaving their villages to find work somewhere else. After the plague, workers asked for higher wages and better working conditions. Many lords agreed to these demands, and those who didn't soon found that other lords would. Lords began to realize they had less control over workers and began to change what they produced. Many workers were needed to grow and harvest grain, so some lords began to raise sheep instead. Raising sheep required fewer workers and there were more customers for the meat and for woolen clothing. As their incomes rose, people were able to buy more vegetables, fruits, and clothing. Production of these goods increased. Peasants eventually became free to move away from estates owned by lords; some were even able to buy their own land.[6]

The Black Death was a great tragedy. However, the decrease in population caused by the plague increased the wages of peasants. As a result, peasants began to enjoy a higher standard of living and greater freedom.

---

[5] Stephen Broadberry, et al., "British Economic Growth, 1270-1870," http://www2.warwick.ac.uk/fac/soc/economics/staff/academic/broadberry/wp/britishgdplongrun8a.pdf
[6] David Routt, "The Economic Impact of the Black Death," http://eh.net/encyclopedia/article/Routt.Black.Death.

ACTIVITY 15.2

The Statute of Laborers (1351)

… Because a great part of the people … has now died … some, seeing the straights of the masters and the scarcity of servants, are not willing to serve unless they receive excessive wages, and others … prefer to beg in idleness: We have seen fit to ordain: that every man and woman of our kingdom of England … who is able bodied and below the age of sixty years, not living from trade nor carrying on a fixed craft … shall be bound to serve him who has seen fit so to seek after him; and he shall take only the wages … which … were accustomed to be paid in [1346] … and if any man or woman … will not do this … he shall be taken and sent to the next jail.… And if a reaper or mower, or other workman or servant … who is retained in the service of any one, do depart from the said service before the end of the term agreed, without permission … he shall undergo the penalty of imprisonment.… Likewise let butchers, fishmongers … all other vendors of any [food], be bound to sell such [food] for a reasonable price … and if any one sell such [food] in another manner, and be convicted of it in the aforesaid way, he shall pay the double of that which he received to the party injured.… And because many sound beggars do refuse to labour so long as they can live from begging … giving themselves up to idleness and sins … let no one, under the … pain of imprisonment presume, … to give anything to such as can very well labour, or to cherish them in their sloth, so that thus they may be compelled to labour for the necessaries of life.

Statute of Labourers (1351)

http://avalon.law.yale.edu/medieval/statlab.asp

("Statutes of the Realm," vol. i p. 307.)

ACTIVITY 15.3

Sequence Chart

Name_____

Topic

Results of the Black Death

In the space provided below, list events in the order in which they occurred.

First:
Next:
Next:
Next:
Next:
Next:
Next:
Last:

ACTIVITY 15.4

The Trial of the (14th) Century

CHARACTERS:

Reginald ("Reggie") Rattus	The accused
Atticus Flinch	Attorney for the accused
Beatrice Berger	Prosecuting attorney
Oliver Wendell Huts	Presiding judge
Nigel Snoddy	BBC reporter
Valerie Bennett-James	BBC reporter
Dr. Mats Swenson	Witness
Dr. Jane Maynard Friedman	Witness
Bailiff	

Setting: The Global Court of Justice in Geneva, Switzerland

Nigel Snoddy: Well, good morning once again from the Global Court of Justice in Geneva, Switzerland. This is your BBC legal correspondent, Nigel Snoddy, along with Valerie Bennett-James. We are watching the second day of the trial that will determine the fate of those accused of causing the so-called "Black Death" of 1347-1352. Valerie, the first day of the trial had a surprise development, didn't it?

Valerie Bennett-James: Yes, Nigel. Yesterday Judge Huts announced that one of the accused, Fiona Flea, had flown. Both Reginald Rattus and Fiona Flea are accused of spreading the plague throughout Europe. Mr. Atticus Flinch, attorney for the rat, argued that because the flea had flown the charges against Mr. Rattus should be dropped. But, Nigel, Judge Huts disagreed.

Nigel: Yes, the judge agreed with Beatrice Berger that the trial of Reginald Rattus should continue. Fiona Flea will be tried when she is found. Ms. Berger explained, "Our prison cells cannot be expected to hold fleas. Fiona Flea slipped through the bars of her cell or maybe she jumped onto a guard or animal that walked by the cell. We have other fleas in custody who know where she is. We expect her arrest shortly. The trial of Mr. Rattus should go on."

Valerie: Nigel, the judge has just entered the courtroom. Let's listen.

Bailiff: All rise for the Honorable Oliver Wendell Huts.

Judge Huts: Please be seated. Bailiff, please announce the case before us.

Bailiff: Your Honor, the case is the people of Medieval Europe versus Reginald Rattus—representing *Rattus rattus*, the small black rat.

Judge Huts: Very well, is the prosecution ready?

Beatrice Berger: Yes, Your Honor.

Judge Huts: And the defense?

ACTIVITY 15.4, CONTINUED

Atticus Flinch:	Yes, Your Honor.
Judge Huts:	The prosecution may make an opening statement.
Ms. Berger:	Your Honor and ladies and gentlemen of the jury. Today we will present evidence that will show that *Rattus rattus* is guilty of infecting millions of Europeans with the plague bacteria in the 14th century. These infections led to terrible deaths. The defense claims that the rat is innocent. We disagree. The rat was aware of his role in this crime. In his greedy search for food—in garbage dumps, back alleys, and trading ships—he became a 14th century taxi for the flea. Together, they spread the plague all over Europe.
	Ladies and gentlemen, it has been nearly 700 years since the flea and rat caused the deaths of over 20 million people. Justice delayed is justice denied! We cannot try the flea, but we ask you to find the rat guilty of mass murder!
Judge Huts:	Mr. Flinch, you may make your opening statement.
Mr. Flinch:	Your Honor, ladies and gentlemen of the jury. I have come to defend Reginald Rattus, not to praise him. We will agree that *Rattus rattus*—black rats—spread the plague bacteria throughout Europe. But my client's ancestors did not realize this. We will hear testimony that the rats were victims of the plague. An economist will argue that, as terrible as the plague was, it led to an increase in the wages of workers who survived and improved their standard of living.
	Mr. Rattus is appearing here to seek justice for his fellow rats. You know that Fiona Flea escaped from her jail cell yesterday. Is this the action of an innocent flea? Members of the jury: I ask that you not allow any opinions you have of rats to affect your decision. Judge my client on the testimony you will hear today.
Judge Huts:	The prosecution may call its first witness.
Ms. Berger:	The state calls Dr. Mats Swenson to the stand.
Bailiff:	Do you swear that the testimony you are about to give will be the truth, the whole truth and nothing but the truth, so help you God?
Dr. Mats Swenson:	I do.
Ms. Berger:	Dr. Swenson, please state your occupation.
Dr. Swenson:	I am a professor of European history at the State University of Sweden. I specialize in the period of the Black Death from 1347 to 1352.
Ms. Berger:	Dr. Swenson, can you explain how the Black Death began?
Dr. Swenson:	Before the time you asked about, from 850 through early 1300 C.E., the population in Europe steadily increased. But by 1347, something terrible had happened. Historians believe the plague started in Asia. We know that in October 1347 trading ships from Genoa docked at Messina, Sicily. This is where the rat and flea began to murder more than 20 million innocent Europeans …
Mr. Flinch:	Objection, Your Honor! Dr. Swenson is assuming that my client is guilty of the charge against him!

ACTIVITY 15.4, CONTINUED

Judge Huts:	Yes, I agree. Objection sustained. Dr. Swenson, please comment only on the facts of the case.
Dr. Swenson:	I'm sorry, Your Honor.
Ms. Berger:	Dr. Swenson, please continue.
Dr. Swenson:	By January 1348, the plague had traveled to France and North Africa. From Italy, it crossed the Alps into Switzerland and moved eastward to Hungary. At the time, no one knew the source of the disease. This added to the terror people felt. Some 500 years passed before we learned that the killers were the flea and the rat! Fleas!! Too small for people to notice. Rats!! They carried the fleas with them on trading ships. The ships' crews were unaware of the deadly cargo they had on board. And …
Mr. Flinch:	Objection, Your Honor!
Judge Huts:	Sustained. Dr. Swenson, you must control yourself!
Dr. Swenson:	What? Oh, yes. I *am* sorry. I get carried away whenever I think of this awful tragedy. Uh, where was I?
Ms. Berger:	You described the spread of the bacteria throughout Europe by the flea and the rat.
Dr. Swenson:	Yes, I remember now. The bacteria lived in the stomach of the flea and the bloodstream of the rat. The disease was transferred to humans by the bite of both the rat and the flea. The rat was the black rat, *Rattus rattus*. This plague killed probably more than a third of the population of Europe.
Ms. Berger:	Thank you Dr. Swenson. I am finished with this witness.
Judge Huts:	Mr. Flinch?
Mr. Flinch:	I have no questions for this witness.
Judge Huts:	Dr. Swenson, you are excused. Ms. Berger, you may call your next witness.
Ms. Berger:	Your Honor, the state rests its case against the defendant.
Judge Huts:	Very well. Mr. Flinch, you may call your first witness.
Mr. Flinch:	I call to the witness stand Dr. Jane Maynard Friedman.
Bailiff:	Do you swear that the testimony you are about to give will be the truth, the whole truth and nothing but the truth, so help you God?
Dr. Friedman:	I do.
Mr. Flinch:	Dr. Friedman, isn't it true that you have studied the history of Europe during the Black Death?
Dr. Friedman:	Yes, I have.
Mr. Flinch:	In addition to the human cost of the plague, you have written about the economic impact. Can you summarize this impact for the jury?
Dr. Friedman:	Because so many people died there was a great decrease in the number of workers.
Mr. Flinch:	What was the result of this?

ACTIVITY 15.4, CONTINUED

Dr. Friedman:	Workers found out that they could demand higher wages. The lords who owned much of the land in Europe did not like it, but the price of labor— the wage rate— began to rise.
Mr. Flinch:	You say the lords didn't like paying higher wages?
Dr. Friedman:	Yes. In England and other countries laws were passed to keep wages from rising and to provide for punishment of workers who quit their jobs to work for someone else. But these laws did not work. Producers could not keep wages from rising.
Mr. Flinch:	So, Dr. Friedman, the plague led to an increase in workers' wages?
Dr. Friedman:	Workers also found that they could refuse to work if the jobs they were given were difficult or dangerous.
Mr. Flinch:	So, workers were better off after the plague?
Dr. Friedman:	The plague was a great tragedy, but it is true that workers who survived earned higher wages and better working conditions. Over time, peasants had greater freedom. Years later, some were even able to own their own land and start their own businesses.
Mr. Flinch:	I have no further questions of this witness.
Judge Huts:	Ms. Berger?
Ms. Berger:	I have no questions for the witness.
Judge Huts:	Thank you, Dr. Friedman. You are excused. Mr. Flinch, you may call your next witness.
Mr. Flinch:	The defense calls to the stand … Reginald Rattus!
	[Loud murmuring fills the courtroom]
Judge Huts:	*[pounds his gavel]* Order in this courtroom! Bailiff, wait until we have silence before the next witness is sworn in.
Nigel:	This is certainly a surprise announcement. Valerie, this is a risky move …
Valerie:	Nigel, I believe that Mr. Rattus wants to testify against his lawyer's advice. Now Ms. Berger will be able to cross-examine Mr. Rattus.
Judge Huts:	Bailiff, please swear in Mr. Rattus.
Bailiff:	Do you swear that the testimony you are about to give will be the truth, the whole truth and nothing but the truth, so help you God?
Reginald Rattus:	I do.
Mr. Flinch:	Mr. Rattus, you are testifying on behalf of all black rats accused in the deaths of 20 million Europeans between 1347 and 1352. Please explain why.
Mr. Rattus:	Mr. Flinch, please call me Reggie. I am here today on behalf of my fellow rats, who have been accused of this awful crime for over 600 years. Rats did spread the plague throughout Europe. We are really sorry about this, but we were victims of the plague, too. We had no idea that we were carrying the disease until it was too late, for people and for rats.

ACTIVITY 15.4, CONTINUED

I know what people think of us; dirty, grubby, hanging out in old buildings, raiding dumpsters. But what's a rat to do? We look for food where we can find it. Rats have made important contributions to humans. Many have given their lives for scientific research. And some rats are kept by humans as pets—would people keep rats as companions if they thought we were a threat to them? In China, people born in the Year of the Rat are said to have qualities including creativity, honesty, and ambition.

Some say we are nuisance, but in many ways, we are like you—all of you here in this courtroom. Hath not a rat eyes? Hath not a rat hands and organs? We eat the same food—at least that portion that people toss into dumpsters—and are subject to the same diseases, including the plague. If you prick us do we not bleed? If you tickle us—well, OK; I admit that few humans tickle rats, but if they did …

Ms. Berger:	*[interrupts]* Your Honor, we agree that rats have eyes and eat garbage.
Judge Huts:	Mr. Rattus, please comment only on the facts of this case.
Mr. Flinch:	Reggie, you said that rats were victims of the plague. Please explain what you meant.
Mr. Rattus:	The source of the bacteria was the flea, not rats. When fleas jumped onto rats they often bit us. It is true that we spread the disease, but only because fleas got into our fur. When the fleas bit us, we were infected. Many rats died from the plague. That's why I said we were also victims of the plague.
Mr. Flinch:	Thank you, Reggie. I have no further questions.
Judge Huts:	Ms. Berger, do you want to cross-examine the witness?
Ms. Berger:	Yes, Your Honor. Reggie, you claim that your fellow rats had no idea that they were carriers of the plague. But those rats died many years ago. How can you be sure that this is true?
Reggie:	Well, the story has been handed down by rats throughout the centuries. My grandparents told me about the plague.
Ms. Berger:	Members of the jury, this is not evidence from eyewitnesses. No one living today can know that rats were "innocent victims." Reggie, isn't it true that if rats had not transported infected fleas throughout Europe, the plague would not have spread beyond Asia?
Reggie:	Well, I suppose that's true, but …
Ms. Berger:	Thank you, Mr. Rattus. That will be all.
Judge Huts:	Reggie, you are excused. The defense may call its next witness.
Mr. Flinch:	Your Honor, the defense rests.
	The case now goes to the jury.

SLIDE 15.1

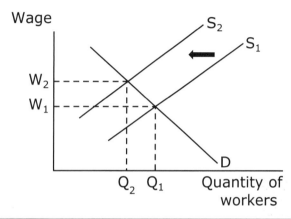

SLIDE 15.2

SLIDE 15.3

Results of the Great Plague

Place the statements in the correct order:

1. The Statute of Laborers is issued in England.
2. Workers begin to ask for higher wages.
3. Some peasants buy their own land.
4. To reduce their labor costs, some producers shift from growing grain to raising sheep.
5. Millions of Europeans die after being infected by the plague bacteria.
6. The supply of workers in Europe decreases.
7. The standard of living of peasant workers rises and they can choose where to work.
8. Producers begin to pay more "in kind" benefits and pay illegally high wages.

LESSON 16

BUSINESS IN THE MIDDLE AGES: WORKING IN A GUILD

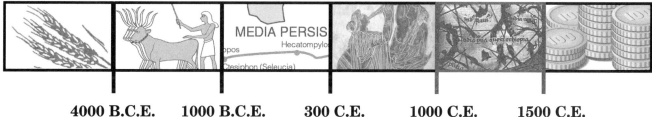

4000 B.C.E.   1000 B.C.E.   300 C.E.   1000 C.E.   1500 C.E.

LESSON 16
BUSINESS IN THE MIDDLE AGES: WORKING IN A GUILD

LESSON DESCRIPTION

Students take part in a production activity that emphasizes the importance of job skills and training, which were provided by guilds in medieval Europe. They are introduced to information about the organization and purposes of guilds and the effects of specialization and monopoly power. Finally, they inspect an adaptation of a document from the Hatters Guild of London in 1347 to draw conclusions about the roles of guild members and the Hatters Guild.

INTRODUCTION

Guilds in medieval Europe were business and social organizations designed to promote the interests of guild members. They were prolific throughout Europe during the Middle Ages. A significant part of the skilled labor force in cities was structured around guilds. The organization and structure of guilds were often sophisticated, extending into the families of masters, journeymen, and apprentices alike. Apprenticeships were generally arrangements between a master and an apprentice. The master provided education, room and board, and sometimes an extended family for apprentices. The education provided through the guild structure is a focus of this lesson.

Although guilds strove to function as monopolies and to restrict competition in their trades, guild members realized it was in their self-interest to produce high-quality products. Product quality and enforcing quality standards benefited both consumers and producers. Through records and contracts kept relating to guilds in medieval Europe, we have glimpses into that society as well as the market economies that were to come. This lesson about the Middle Ages gives middle school students some new economic vocabulary and introduces them to the concepts of specialization, monopoly, and the effects of education on production.

CONCEPTS

Production

Specialization

Productivity

Monopoly

OBJECTIVES

Students will be able to:

- Determine the impact of specialization and training on production.

- Define the terms medieval, Middle Ages, specialization, productivity, guild, trade, apprentice, journeyman, master, and monopoly.

- Describe the organization and purposes of guilds in medieval Europe.

- Analyze a historical document to identify the role of guild workers in the Hatters Guild in medieval London.

CONTENT STANDARDS

Voluntary Content Standards in Economics, 2nd edition

- **Standard 1:** Productive resources are limited. Therefore, people cannot have all the goods and services they want; as a result, they must choose some things and give up others.

- **Standard 6:** When individuals, regions, and nations specialize in what they can produce at the lowest cost and then trade with others, both production and consumption increase.

- **Standard 9:** Competition among sellers usually lowers costs and prices, and encourages producers to produce what consumers are willing and able to buy. Competition among buyers increases prices and allocates goods and services to those people who are willing and able to pay the most for them.

World History Content Standards

Era 5: Intensified Hemispheric Interactions 1000–1500 C.E.

- **Standard 2:** The redefining of European society and culture, 1000–1300 C.E.

TIME REQUIRED

One 45-minute class period for the production activity plus 30 minutes for analyzing the historical document. Analyzing the document may be done as homework.

MATERIALS

- Single newspaper pages, two sheets per student. Tear the pages apart at the vertical fold if necessary. Use full-sized newspapers.

- Several rolls of tape (transparent or masking), to be shared by students

- Slides 16.1–16.9

- One copy of Activity 16.1 for each group of five students

- One copy of the exercise in Activity 16.2 for each student

- One copy of the answer key for Activity 16.2 for the teacher

PROCEDURE

1. Before the class begins, write the following terms on the board: Medieval, Middle Ages, Guild, Specialization, Productivity, Trade, Apprentice, Journeyman, Master, Monopoly.

2. Tell students they are going to learn about working in a guild in medieval Europe. They will be learning about both history and economics. During this lesson, they will participate in a production activity and read some rules from a guild in London in 1347. They will learn or review the 10 terms on the board, which relate to history or economics. While you are making these statements, make a newspaper hat and put it on your head. Do not comment on making the hat while you are introducing the

lesson. The instructions for making the hat are in Activity 16.1.[1] (Be sure to practice making the hat before class!) Leave your hat on through Step 7.

3. Show Slides 16.1 and 16.2 and discuss the definitions of **medieval** and **guild**. Point out that workers in a guild produced only one type of product; they were specializing.

4. Show Slides 16.3 and 16.4 and discuss the definitions for **specialization** and **productivity**. Ask students why specializing would allow each worker to increase his or her productivity, which can be defined as how much of a good or service a worker can produce during a day. For example, why might a worker who specialized as a weaver be able to weave more cloth in a day than someone else?

   (Likely answers include that the person who specialized in weaving would have more practice and better skills and would know how to weave faster.)

5. Tell students that they will now discover some of the reasons why workers in cities in Europe during the Middle Ages often organized themselves into guilds. Tell the students that they are going to become hatters.

6. Distribute one sheet of newspaper to each student. Make tape available.

7. Tell students you will give them approximately two minutes to make a hat like the one you are wearing. Emphasize to students that hat quality is important. Tell them they cannot work together or talk to one another during this time. Tell the students to begin their work.

8. When students begin trying to make the hats, it may become clear that some know how to make them. If so, shorten

---

[1] Note that these instructions are for a simple triangular hat. If you think most of your students already know how to make this hat, you can find instructions for more complex hats on the Internet and adapt Activity 16.1 as appropriate.

the time period so that about five students can finish, but do not allow enough time for others to be able to copy them.

9. At the end of the time period, if there are any finished hats, inspect them to see if they are taped and folded like the model you made. Inform the class how many hats meet your quality standards. If there are no finished hats or none that meet your standards, ask students why they were not able to make any hats.

(Likely answers will include that they did not have instructions, they had not learned to make a hat, or there was not enough time for them to figure it out.)

10. Ask what could have helped them to be able to make a hat in the time period.

(Likely answers will include that you should have given them instructions or taught them how to make a hat, or [if applicable] you should have let the students who knew how to make hats help the others.)

11. Collect the unfinished hats and newspapers.

12. Tell students that learning a trade from others who had skills and experience was one of the benefits of belonging to a guild in the **Middle Ages**. Display Slides 16.5, 16.6, and 16.7 and discuss the roles of **apprentices**, **journeymen**, and **masters**. Make sure that students know that the word **trade** in this case refers to an occupation.

13. Tell the other students that they will now act as apprentices to the Hatters Guild of London in the 14th century. You will play the role of a master and teach them how to make hats. Following the instructions on Activity 16.1, demonstrate how to make a hat, carefully explaining each step.

14. Divide students into groups of five, and appoint one person in each group to be a master. If any students knew how to make hats in Step 8, appoint each of them to be a master and assign each

to a group. Give the masters a copy of Activity 16.1 for the group and one sheet of newspaper for each student in their group. Announce that they will again have about two minutes to make a hat. Tell them that they may ask questions of you, their master, or of each other during the two-minute period. They may also look at Activity 16.1.

15. At the end of the time period, ask the masters to check the quality of the hats in their group and to tell you how many hats were produced that meet the quality standards of the Hatters Guild. (This can be determined by comparing the hats to the picture on Activity 16.1 and to the model hat that you made.)

16. Compare the number of hats in the second round to the number from the first hat production exercise (Step 8). Ask the students why the number of "good" hats produced was greater this time?

(Likely answers will include that students had training, directions, and could learn from each other this time.)

17. Ask a few of the masters to comment on the quality of the hats produced in their group. *(Likely comments will include that students helped each other make quality hats and that, if they had been given more time, they could have made more.)* After this discussion, emphasize that enforcing the quality of the products produced in a guild was an important role for guilds.

18. Ask students who benefits from having high-quality products, such as hats.

(The likely answer will be that consumers benefit.) Encourage students to come up with the idea that producers will also benefit, because if producers produce high-quality hats, consumers will want to buy them and will be willing to pay a good price for them. If producers do not produce high-quality products, consumers would not want to buy them and producers would go out of business.

19. Show Slides 16.8 and 16.9 and discuss with students the purposes of guilds, some of which have been discussed earlier in the lesson. Emphasize the following ideas:

- Guild members provided training for apprentices and jobs and wages for journeymen. The training enabled people to learn how to produce quality products.

- Guilds provided day labor and wages for journeymen. Journeymen worked by the day and were paid wages by the day for working in their trade.

- Guilds set standards for the quality for the goods produced, which benefited both consumers and producers.

- When a guild in the Middle Ages had a monopoly, it did not have any competition. For example, the only people allowed to produce and sell hats would be those who worked in the Hatters Guild. If people wanted to buy a hat, they could not shop around for the best price; they would have to pay the price the Hatters Guild was charging. **Monopoly** is defined as a firm that is the single supplier of a good or service for which there are no close substitutes. Ask students to predict if prices would be higher or lower if there was more competition.

  (Students will likely respond that more competition should lead to lower prices. With competition, hat makers may have to lower prices in order to sell their hats.)

- Because workers in the guild had joined together, they were in a position to have more influence with the government than if they were not joined together. Guilds wanted to influence the government to set up rules or laws that would help the guild. This points to an important reason for the existence of guilds: When guild members acted together to influence the government, they could accomplish more than as unaffiliated individuals.

- Guild members often took care of each other's families in time of need. Also, it was often easier for the children of guild members to become apprentices and journeymen in guilds than for those outside guild families.

- Guilds also had religious purposes and encouraged members to attend church on Sundays. Guilds arranged for funerals and burials, and members prayed for the souls of deceased members. Guild members were expected to follow Christian religious ideals such as being truthful, working hard, and not gambling or stealing.

20. Explain to students that using original sources or documents from earlier times is an important way for historians to learn about the past.

21. Distribute a copy of Activity 16.2 to each student. Explain that this document was adapted from one written in 1347 that listed rules for the Hatters Guild in London. (It was adapted to simplify some of the Old English and to shorten and clarify some of the rules.) Call on six students to read each of the six rules.

22. Give students time to answer the questions in groups, and discuss the answers using the answer key that follows the activity. (If time is short, students may complete this assignment as homework.)

CLOSURE

23. Turn to the 10 definitions on the board and call on students to review the definitions.

24. Discuss the relationship of specialization, productivity, and monopoly on the structure of guilds in the Middle Ages by asking the following questions:

a. How did the guild system increase worker productivity?

(Workers specialized in a trade and received training from masters.)

b. Why did guilds result in higher-quality products?

(Guild members were trained. The guilds also inspected products to ensure high quality and that the products had been made by guild members.)

c. Why did guilds result in higher prices?

(Guilds acted as monopolists and restricted competition. If higher quality hats cost hatters more to produce, it resulted in higher prices.)

ASSESSMENT

Multiple Choice

1. One of the purposes of a guild in the Middle Ages was

    a. to compete with others making the same products.

    b. to study migration patterns of early humans.

    c. to encourage journeymen to get married.

    d. **to provide training for future workers.**

2. Who benefitted when guilds enforced standards to make high-quality products?

    a. Consumers only

    b. Producers only

    c. **Both consumers and producers**

    d. Neither consumers nor producers

Constructed Response

1. Write a paragraph explaining how someone could become a master in a guild in the Middle Ages. In your paragraph, explain the terms "apprentice," "journeyman," and "master."

    (Answers should follow information on Slides 16.5 to 16.7.)

SOURCES

Epstein, Steven A. 1991. *Wage Labor and Guilds in Medieval Europe*. University of North Carolina Press: Chapel Hill.

Richardson, Gary. 2010. "Medieval Guilds." Economic History Association. Net *Encyclopedia of Economic and Business History*. Retrieved online March 2011 at http://eh.net/encyclopedia/article/richardson.guilds

"The Articles of the Heaumers and of the Hatters" from *A Source Book of London History from the Earliest Times to 1800*, edited by P. Meadows, London: B. Bell and Sons, Ltd., 1914, pp. 44–45. Available at http://www.archive.org/stream/sourcebookoflond00mead#page/n5/mode/2up

CONNECTIONS: GUILDS TODAY AND IN OTHER CULTURES

Guilds Today

Guilds in the Middle Ages have many things in common with labor unions today. Labor unions consist of workers who join together to protect their common interests. They believe that they can gain more by bargaining collectively than independently.

Guilds in Other Cultures

Guilds, called *za*, also existed in Japan from the 12th through the 16th centuries. In addition to trade guilds, there were also guilds for performers. Za had connections with temples and shrines for both protection and agreements for selling goods.

Activity 16-1

Instructions for Making Hats

Step 1. Fold a newspaper page in half from top to bottom. Crease the folded edge.

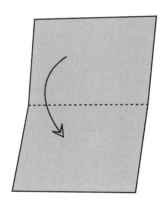

Step 2. Fold the two folded corners to the middle. This will make two triangles that are touching each other.

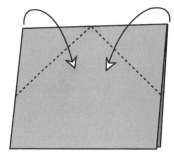

Step 3. Fold the bottom flap (the one on the top) up and in half, and then fold it up again.

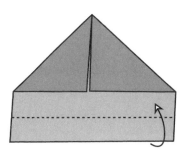

Step 4. Turn the hat over and repeat Step 3.

Step 5. Secure each side end with a small piece of tape.

Wear your hat with pride!

ACTIVITY 16.2

Year 1347 A.D.: The Rules of the Hatters of London[1]

These rules are accepted by Thomas Leggy, Mayor of London, at the request of the Hatters of London.

1. —In the first place, six of the most lawful men of the hatters trade shall be assigned to be Wardens. They will rule and watch the trade, in the same way that Wardens rule and watch other trades.

2. —Also, that no one shall make or sell any manner of hats within the city if he is not free and from the same city. If anyone is caught violating this rule he must give up the hats that he made or offered for sale.

3. —Also, that no one shall be made apprentice in the hatters trade for a term of less than seven years. Anyone who receives an apprentice in any other manner shall lose his freedom until he buys it back again.

4. —Also, that no one in the hatters trade shall take any apprentice, if he is not himself a freeman of London.

5. —Also, that the Wardens of the hatters trade shall search all the hats that are for sale in the area, as often as need be. And the Wardens shall have the power to take any hats that they find defective and bring them before the Mayor of London, so that those causing the defects found may be punished.

6. —Also, some workmen in the trade have made hats that are not high quality, and this deceives the common people and brings great scandal, shame and loss to the good folks of the hatters trade. Therefore no workman in the trade shall do any work by night, but only in clear daylight, when the Wardens may openly inspect their work. Anyone who does otherwise shall pay a fine to the Chamber of Guildhall for the first and second offense, and the third time he shall lose his freedom.

---

[1] Adapted from "The Articles of the Heaumers and of the Hatters" from *A Source Book of London History from the Earliest Times to 1800*, edited by P. Meadows, London: B. Bell and Sons, Ltd, 1914; pp. 44–45. Available at http://www.archive.org/stream/sourcebookoflond00mead#page/n5/mode/2up

ACTIVITY 16.2, CONTINUED

Name: _____

Learning from a Historical Document

After reading "The Rules of the Hatters of London" from 1347, answer the following questions:

1. What powers did the mayor of London have in 1347?

_____

_____

_____

_____

2. a. What was the role of the wardens in the Hatters Guild?

_____

_____

_____

_____

b. How did someone get to be a warden in the Hatters Guild?

_____

_____

_____

_____

3. How long would someone be an apprentice in the Hatters Guild in London in 1347?

_____

_____

_____

_____

ACTIVITY 16.2, CONTINUED

4. **Why does one of the guild's rules specify that "no workman in the trade shall do any work by night, but only in clear daylight"?**

_____

_____

_____

_____

_____

5. **What evidence is in the document that some people in London were not free in 1347?**

_____

_____

_____

_____

_____

6. **What kind of punishments existed in London in 1347 for not following the rules of the Hatters Guild?**

_____

_____

_____

_____

_____

ACTIVITY 16.2, ANSWER KEY
Learning from a Historical Document

Suggested answers:

1. What powers did the mayor of London have in 1347?

(The mayor had the power to approve (accept) the Hatters Guild's rules. Also, defective hats were brought before the Mayor and he appears to have been in charge of punishing those who caused the defects.)

2. a. What was the role of the wardens in the Hatters Guild?

(The wardens "rule and watch the trade." They examine all the hats for sale in the area and have the power to bring defective hats before the Mayor.)

b. How did someone get to be a warden in the Hatters Guild?

(If you were one of six of the most lawful men of the trade, you could be assigned to be a warden.)

3. How long would someone be an apprentice in the Hatters Guild of London in 1347?

(Seven years)

4. Why is there a rule saying that "no workman in the trade shall do any work by night, but only in clear daylight"?

(Rule 6 says that some workmen have made hats that are not of high quality, and this has caused "… scandal, shame and loss to the good folks of the hatters trade." Therefore, if hats can only be made in daylight, the wardens can inspect the work.)

5. What evidence is in the document that some people in London were not free in 1347?

(Rule 2 says that no one can make or sell hats in London if he is not free [and from London]. Rule 4 says that no one in the hatters trade can take an apprentice if he is not a freeman of London. If you took an apprentice for less than seven years, you would lose your freedom and have to buy it back. The third time a workman is caught working at night, he loses his freedom.)

6. What are some of the punishments that existed in London in 1347 for not following the rules of the Hatters Guild?

(Rule 2: Give up the hats he made or was selling; Rule 3: lose freedom until he buys it back; Rule 6: pay a fine to the Guildhall and lose one's freedom.)

SLIDE 16.1

LESSON 16 – BUSINESS IN THE MIDDLE AGES: WORKING IN A GUILD

FOUR IMPORTANT DEFINITIONS: #1

Medieval: Relating to the Middle Ages. The Middle Ages are often dated from the fall of the Roman Empire in the 5th century C.E. to the beginning of the Renaissance in the 15th century.

SLIDE 16.2

LESSON 16 – BUSINESS IN THE MIDDLE AGES: WORKING IN A GUILD

FOUR IMPORTANT DEFINITIONS: #2

Guild: A business group formed by workers in the same occupation to promote their interests. Guilds were common in medieval Europe between the 11th and 16th centuries. Carpenters, weavers, painters, goldsmiths, hat makers, and many other types of workers formed guilds.

SLIDE 16.3

LESSON 16 – BUSINESS IN THE MIDDLE AGES: WORKING IN A GUILD

FOUR IMPORTANT DEFINITIONS # 3

Specialization: A situation where people produce a narrower range of goods and services than they consume. Guilds involved specialization, since guild workers only produced one type of product. Specialization allows people to increase their productivity.

SLIDE 16.4

LESSON 16 – BUSINESS IN THE MIDDLE AGES: WORKING IN A GUILD

FOUR IMPORTANT DEFINITIONS # 4

Productivity: The productivity of a worker refers to the output for a worker in a certain time period, such as an hour or a day.

SLIDE 16.5

HOW GUILDS WERE ORGANIZED: Apprentices

An apprentice was a young person (most often male) who worked for a guild master while learning a trade. Apprentices often began at age 12 and were given room and board at the master's house, but earned no money. Apprenticeships could last for 2–7 (or more) years.

SLIDE 16.6

HOW GUILDS WERE ORGANIZED: Journeymen

After finishing the apprenticeship, the worker could become a journeyman. Journeymen, or day laborers, were paid wages by the day while working in the trade.

SLIDE 16.7

LESSON 16 – BUSINESS IN THE MIDDLE AGES: WORKING IN A GUILD

HOW GUILDS WERE ORGANIZED: Masters

A master (or master craftsman) was a full member of the guild and could start his own business.

To become a master and a full member of the guild, journeymen sometimes had to produce a "masterpiece" in their trade. If the masterpiece was accepted by the guild members, they could vote to accept the journeyman as a master in the guild.

It was an honor to be a guild member. Some masters were chosen to be inspectors to make sure that other guild members' products were of a high standard or quality.

FOCUS MIDDLE SCHOOL WORLD HISTORY © COUNCIL FOR ECONOMIC EDUCATION, NEW YORK, NY

SLIDE 16.8

LESSON 16 – BUSINESS IN THE MIDDLE AGES: WORKING IN A GUILD

SOME PURPOSES OF GUILDS

- Provided training for apprentices to learn to make the product.
- Provided day labor and wages for journeymen.
- Set standards for the quality of the goods produced.
- Established a monopoly and restricted competition in the trade occupation.
  - A *monopoly* is when there is only one seller of a product. If a guild had a monopoly, it could set a higher price than it could with competition.

FOCUS MIDDLE SCHOOL WORLD HISTORY © COUNCIL FOR ECONOMIC EDUCATION, NEW YORK, NY

SLIDE 16.9

LESSON 16 – BUSINESS IN THE MIDDLE AGES: WORKING IN A GUILD

SOME PURPOSES OF GUILDS

- Gained influence over local governments to be able to promote the interests of the guild members.
- Provided for the families of guild members in case of illness or death.
- Encouraged religious living following Christian practices.

LESSON 17

WHY DIDN'T CHINA DISCOVER THE NEW WORLD?

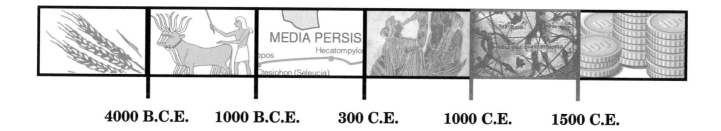

4000 B.C.E.   1000 B.C.E.   300 C.E.   1000 C.E.   1500 C.E.

LESSON 17
WHY DIDN'T CHINA DISCOVER THE NEW WORLD?

LESSON DESCRIPTION

Students read about two unnamed explorers and the resources they used. Using a graphic organizer, they learn about the huge differences between the explorers' available resources and technology. Based on this information, students will predict which explorer would be most likely to "discover" the New World. Students are most likely to choose Explorer B, who is revealed to be Zheng He, a Chinese explorer. Students may be surprised, because Christopher Columbus is given credit for discovering the New World. The question posed: With all its technology and resources, why didn't China discover the New World?

INTRODUCTION

While the European Age of Discovery gets much attention, the Chinese were more advanced in technology. Explorer Zheng He led a huge fleet nearly 90 years before Columbus's famous voyage across the Atlantic. This lesson explores the differences in technology, and the importance of incentives. Students discover that while Chinese explorers such as Zheng He had more resources and technology than Christopher Columbus, when the emperor cut off the funding, Chinese exploration stopped.

CONCEPTS

Incentives

Technology

CONTENT STANDARDS

Voluntary Content Standards in Economics, 2nd edition

- **Standard 4:** People usually respond predictably to positive and negative incentives.

National Standards for World History

Era 5: Intensified Hemispheric Interactions, 1000–1500 C.E.

- **Standard 1:** The maturing of an interregional system of communication, trade, and cultural exchange in an era of Chinese economic power and Islamic expansion.

OBJECTIVES

Students will be able to:

- Define incentive and give an example.

- Explain the role of incentives in exploration.

- Explain the role of technology in exploration.

TIME REQUIRED

45 minutes; 60 minutes with optional activity

MATERIALS

- Slides 17.1–17.5

- Activity 17.1, one copy for each student

- Activity 17.2, one copy for half the class

- Activity 17.3, one copy for half the class

- Activity 17.4, one copy for each student

For optional activity:

- Two meter sticks

- Two rolls of masking tape

- Two plastic cups

- Two jars of popcorn kernels or beans

PROCEDURE

1. Ask students to define the word *explorer*.

   (Answers will vary.)

   After discussing, define an explorer as someone who travels into little-known regions to discover trade opportunities, resources, or information.

2. Tell the students that, in many cases throughout history, governments (usually a king or emperor) funded exploration. Ask students:

   a. Why do you think most explorers in the 1400s had to rely on government support? Why didn't they pay for it themselves?

   (Sea exploration in the 1400s was very expensive and risky. Very few individuals could afford it and even fewer would risk their finances on such a voyage. Teacher note: While most explorers were government-supported, some were sponsored by for-profit companies like the Dutch East India Company.)

   b. Why were governments willing to finance exploration?

   (Discoveries can have huge benefits to the country that discovers a new land. For example, they might lead to national prestige, colonies, military advantages, new trade routes and relationships, and valuable resources such as gold and spices.)

3. Explain that a large part of the globe had not been explored in the 15th century. Before this time, sea exploration was dangerous because ships had to sail far away from the sight of land without good maps or navigation equipment. Many ships were not big enough or strong enough to withstand storms at sea. A series of advancements in sea navigation technology had occurred in the centuries leading to the age of exploration.

4. Using Slides 17.1 and 17.2, discuss sailing technology. Ask students how these advances made exploration more feasible, effective, and safe.

   (Each of these advances made it safer to sail in stormy seas and easier to navigate farther from the sight of land. For example, the axial rudder can be used to change directions, and multiple masts and sails allow a ship to sail into the wind.)

5. Tell students they are going to learn about two explorers funded by two different nations. Divide the students into two groups. Give half the class Activity 17.2 and the other half Activity 17.3. Distribute a copy of Activity 17.1, a graphic organizer, to each student. Tell the students in each group to read the information about their explorer and summarize their results on the graphic organizer.

6. After the students have had time to enter their information, have each student find a partner from the other group. Have the partners exchange the information necessary to complete their organizer. After the students have completed the exchange of information, have them return to their large groups.

   (If you do not wish to complete the optional activity, skip to Procedure 7.)

   Optional Activity: The following instructions are for an optional activity that can be used to show the relative size of the ships.

   A. Tell students you want to see the differences in resources the two explorers had in a more direct way. Give each group a roll of masking tape, a cup, and a jar of popcorn kernels or beans.

   B. Tell students they will be making a scale version of the largest ship that each explorer had. The scale they will use is 1 foot: 1 centimeter. On the chalkboard or whiteboard, draw a line that is one foot in length and another that is one centimeter. To illustrate scale, explain that if a students was five feet tall, a five-centimeter line would represent the student's height to scale, and draw such a line on the board.

C. Find an open area of the classroom or hallway and tell each half of the class to use a meter stick and the masking tape to make a scale version of the length of the largest ship their explorer used. Arrange ships so that they will be aligned next to each other when they finish.

D. After students have finished their models and their work has been checked, have them return to their groups. Discuss the following:

a. Which ship is larger?

(Explorer B's largest ship is more than five times as large as Explorer A's largest ship.)

b. How would these longer ships make sea travel easier?

(The larger ship allowed for a bigger crew and more supplies. It also made the ship better able to withstand storms.)

E. Compare the differences in the number of ships on the voyages, by having a student from each group put popcorn kernels or beans into the cup to represent the number of ships on their explorer's voyage. After students have finished, have them display their cups and then set the cup for their explorer on the floor next to the ship.

7. Continue with the lesson by asking the following questions:

a. How would more ships be beneficial?

(A greater number of ships would allow for more supplies and crew members. For example, Explorer B had water tankers in his fleet that carried fresh water for the crew.)

b. What was the size of the crew for each explorer?

(Explorer B had a crew of 28,000 while Explorer A's crew was a mere 90.)

c. How would the size of the ships affect the number of crew members?

(The fact that Explorer B had larger ships and more ships in his fleet also meant that more crew members were required.)

d. Based on the information you see, which explorer do you think had the best chances of discovering the New World?

(The evidence clearly points to Explorer B having more resources and more advanced technology; therefore, Explorer B is much more likely to discover the New World.)

8. Identify Explorer A as *Christopher Columbus* and Explorer B as *Zheng He.* Slides 17.3 and 17.4 review the answers with the appropriate explorer labeled.

9. Ask students who discovered the New World?

(Students will most likely say Christopher Columbus. Point out that the Native Americans were already in the Americas and note that Vikings also had landed in North America. However, from the European perspective, the voyages of Columbus led to European knowledge of the Americas and opened the way for a new age of exploration and discovery.)

10. Show Slide 17.5 and ask a student to read the definition of incentive. Tell the students that people are constantly responding to incentives. Ask the following questions:

a. Why don't you think that Zheng He and the Chinese-sponsored exploration arrived in the Americas first?

(Answers may vary.)

b. Did you read about any incentives for exploration in either of the passages about the explorers?

(Answers will vary.)

11. Discuss the following points about how incentives influenced the two explorers:

    • Columbus had the personal incentives of profits and prestige. Spain, which funded the voyage, also had an incentive of potentially lucrative trade routes and sites for colonies, which would expand their reach.

    • Zheng He earned great prestige from his efforts. His emperor gained power, wealth, and the prestige of neighboring countries.

12. Have students read Activity 17.4. Discuss the reasons the Chinese government ceased to sponsor voyages of exploration after 1433. Ask the following questions:

    a. How did the change in government policy change the incentives for Zheng He?

    (The government ban served as a disincentive to explore.)

    b. What are some of economic reasons that might explain the change in policy?

    (Government revenues were not adequate to fund expensive voyages in addition to other government expenses. Mongol attacks on China's north border further strained the government's resources.)

    c. What are some of the cultural reasons that might explain the change in policy?

    (Neo-Confucian philosophy discouraged trade and profits. Some Chinese were apprehensive about the influence foreign goods and ideas might have on their culture. Some students may note that some of these reasons deal with how the Chinese culture perceived economic issues. If so, note that economics is a social science and that culture always influences how societies view economics issues.)

    d. What might have happened if China had continued to explore and develop trade routes?

    (If Chinese explorers had continued to explore in the tradition of Zheng He, China is likely to have discovered and explored the New World before European explorers. It might be noted that Columbus was successful in discovering the New World because he was headed in the right direction as he tried to find a route to Asia. Zheng He was focused on exploring and trading in India, Persia, Arabia, and Africa because he considered the gains to be much greater in those regions than elsewhere.)

CLOSURE

13. Review the lesson by asking the following questions:

    a. How did technological advances make exploration more feasible, effective, and safe?

    (Each made it safer to sail in stormy seas and easier to navigate beyond the sight of land. In both cases, the technological advances made the success of the voyages more likely.)

    b. What is an incentive?

    (Any reward or benefit, such as money, advantage or good feeling that motivates people to do something)

    c. How does our discussion of incentives help answer the question, why didn't China discover the New World?

    (The Chinese Emperor forbade the building of ships for exploration. Also, there were cultural disincentives to exploration.)

ASSESSMENT

Multiple Choice

1. Which of the following is true of Zheng He?

    a. **He led seven voyages.**

    b. He discovered the New World.

    c. He financed his own expeditions.

    d. He did not have the resources or technology that was available to Columbus.

2. Which of the following theories has been used to explain why support for Chinese exploration evaporated?

   a. Neo-Confucian philosophy discouraged trade and profit.

   b. Mongols attacked the northern border of China.

   c. Tax revenues did not cover government expenses.

   d. **All of the above**

Constructed Response

1. Explain the relationship between changes in sailing technology and the age of exploration that followed.

   (The technology discussed in the lesson allowed explorers to venture far from the sight of land. For example, the magnetic compass allowed sailors to determine direction at sea. Other advances, such as the axial rudder, made navigation more precise, and multiple masts and sails enabled ships to sail into the wind. These technological advances made the voyages of Zheng He possible. Note that not all the technological advances listed were necessary for successful exploration—Columbus' ships had neither leeboards nor watertight hull compartments.)

SOURCES

Ignatius, Adi. "The Asian Voyage: In the Wake of the Admiral " *Breaking News, Analysis, Politics, Blogs, News Photos, Video, Tech Reviews.* TIME.com. 20 August, 2001. 17 March, 2011. http://www.time.com/time/world/article/0,8599,2054421,00.html.

Kristof, Nicholas D. "1492: The Prequel." *The New York Times - Breaking News, World News & Multimedia.* 1999. 17 March, 2011. http://www.nytimes.com/library/magazine/millennium/m3/kristof.html.

Levathes, Louise. 1994. *When China Ruled the Seas: the Treasure Fleet of the Dragon Throne 1405–1433.* New York: Simon & Schuster.

Menzies, Gavin. 2003. *1421: the Year China Discovered America.* New York: William Morrow.

Temple, Robert K. G., and Joseph Needham. 1986. *The Genius of China: 3,000 Years of Science, Discovery, and Invention.* New York: Simon and Schuster.

FOR FURTHER STUDY

A recent book, *1421,* by Gavin Menzies, speculates that China discovered America in 1421, which is refuted by many historians who think Menzies' book lacks evidence. Have students research and discuss or debate the possibility that Chinese explorers arrived in the Americas before European explorers.

Menzies, Gavin. 2003. *1421: the Year China Discovered America.* New York: William Morrow.

CONNECTIONS: EXPLORATION IN THE MODERN WORLD

Discuss with students how modern governments still fund exploration. Ask students: Do governments still sponsor exploration?

(Yes, government supports exploration and research. An example of modern exploration would be NASA, the agency that explores space. The benefits of space exploration include advances in aviation safety and medicine. For example, the devices used to track the health of astronauts in space are now used in hospitals to monitor patients. Other examples of government-sponsored exploration could include grants that support scientific research of the deep sea or medical research that leads to new treatments and medications.)

ACTIVITY 17.1

Resources

	Length of longest ship	Number of masts on longest ship	Number of ships in fleet	Number of crew members in fleet
Explorer A				
Explorer B				

When did each explorers' society develop the following technologies?

	Explorer A	Explorer B
Axial rudder	_____ century	_____ century
Multiple masts and sails	_____ century	_____ century
Watertight compartments in ship hulls	_____ century	_____ century
Leeboard	_____ century	_____ century
Magnetic compass	_____ century	_____ century

ACTIVITY 17.2

Explorer A

This explorer was seeking a better trade route. After looking to several governments to fund his expedition, he finally found enough financial support from one reluctant government and some private investors. If his expedition succeeded, he would be given many rewards, including the rank of Admiral of the Ocean Sea. He would also be appointed Viceroy and Governor of all the newly colonized lands. In addition, he would receive a portion of all profits from the expedition. Although the rulers financially supported him, they thought that the odds of his success were very low. It was a very risky venture. They were willing to take a chance because success would give them a trade advantage over neighboring countries. The goals of this voyage were exploration, wealth, alternative trade routes, spices, and gold. His first voyage used three ships and a crew of 90 men, the largest ship being 85 feet long, with three masts and a crew of 40.

Explorer A's society developed the following technologies:

Axial rudder	12th century
Multiple masts and sails	14th century
Watertight compartments in ship hulls	18th century
Leeboard	16th century
Magnetic compass	12th century

ACTIVITY 17.3

Explorer B

This explorer led seven expeditions. The ruler of his country funded his voyages in an effort to make the country more prosperous and powerful than it had been under other rulers. He also wanted to increase his own status as a regional leader. The voyages were also an effort to promote trade and collect tribute (taxes) from neighboring countries. The explorer's first expedition included over 300 ships with a crew of more than 28,000 men. His fleet included supply ships to carry horses, troop transports, patrol boats, warships, and tankers to carry fresh water. The largest ship in his fleet was reported to be 400 feet long, with nine masts and a crew of over 1,000 men.

During his seven expeditions, he explored the coasts of faraway places, visited many ports, and gained prestige for his accomplishments. As a result of his voyages, merchants from his country settled in busy trade centers. Surrounding countries feared this country's power and strength. The country had little desire to establish colonies; its focus was trade in goods that were not readily available at home.

Explorer B's society developed the following technologies:

Axial rudder	1st century
Multiple masts and sails	2nd century
Watertight compartments in ship hulls	2nd century
Leeboard	8th century
Magnetic compass	9th–11th centuries

ACTIVITY 17.4

Zheng He and Chinese Exploration

Between 1405 and 1433 C.E., the Chinese government sent seven naval expeditions south and west to India, Persia, Arabia, and Africa. The leader of these voyages was Zheng He, who sailed most of these voyages during the reign of Emperor Yung-lo (1403–1425). Many of these expeditions included several hundred ships and thousands of sailors and soldiers.

After 1433, the Chinese government launched no further naval expeditions. In 1436, the emperor forbade the building of ships for overseas voyages. Forty years later, the government destroyed the records of the voyages of Zheng He. While Spanish and Portuguese explorers claimed the lands of Central and South America, the Chinese withdrew from the seas.

Why did China not follow up on its technological superiority? There are several theories:

- The spending of Yung-lo's government greatly exceeded the tax revenue that could be collected. Although the Chinese system of taxation was the most advanced in the world, even the emperor could not continue to fund massive fleets on the scale of those used by Zheng He.

- In the mid-1400s, Mongols began frequent attacks on China's northern border. The attacks may have forced China to devote more resources to the defense of the border.

- Neo-Confucian scholars held many important government posts. Neo-Confucian philosophy encouraged the suppression of desire for worldly things. Trade and profits were held in contempt. Particularly after Yung-lo's death, the influence of the Neo-Confucian scholars grew.

- Some of the Chinese people at the time were concerned about the influence that foreign goods and ideas had on Chinese culture.

All of these reasons changed the incentives for exploration. Zheng He is said to have died returning from his final expedition in 1433 C.E.

"We . . . have beheld in the ocean huge waves like mountains rising sky high, and we have set eyes on barbarian regions far away hidden in a blue transparency of light vapors, while our sails, loftily unfurled like clouds day and night, continued their course [as rapidly as] a star, traversing those savage waves as if we were treading a public thoroughfare."

– Zheng He, 1432

Slide 17.1

Sailing Technology

Axial Rudder: An axial rudder is a vertical blade at the stern of a vessel that can be used to change direction.

Multiple Masts and Sails: A ship with multiple masts and sails can sail better into the wind.

Watertight Compartments in Ship Hulls: These compartments prevent water from filling the entire hull of a ship after it has been damaged.

Slide 17.2

Sailing Technology

Leeboard: A leeboard is a board that is lowered into the water to prevent a ship from drifting sideways.

Magnetic Compass: The magnetic compass allows sailors to determine the direction of the ship when navigators are out of sight of land. The magnetic compass made it possible to find direction at sea.

SLIDE 17.3

	Length of longest ship	Number of masts of longest ship	Number of ships in fleet	Number of crew members in fleet
Christopher Columbus (Explorer A)	85 feet	3 masts	3 ships	90
Zheng He (Explorer B)	400 feet	9 masts	300 ships	28,000

FOCUS MIDDLE SCHOOL WORLD HISTORY © COUNCIL FOR ECONOMIC EDUCATION, NEW YORK, NY

SLIDE 17.4

Resources and Technology

When did each of the explorer's society develop the following technology?

	Christopher Columbus	Zheng He
Axial Rudder	12th Century	1st Century
Multiple Masts and Sails	14th Century	2nd Century
Watertight Compartments in Ship Hulls	18th Century	2nd Century
Leeboard	16th Century	8th Century
Magnetic Compass	12th Century	9-11th Century

Temple, Robert K. G., and Joseph Needham. *The Genius of China: 3,000 Years of Science, Discovery, and Invention*. New York: Simon and Schuster, 1986.

FOCUS MIDDLE SCHOOL WORLD HISTORY © COUNCIL FOR ECONOMIC EDUCATION, NEW YORK, NY

SLIDE 17.5

Definition

Incentive: Any reward or benefit, such as money, advantage or good feeling, that motivates people to do something.

LESSON 18

CHRISTOPHER COLUMBUS, ENTREPRENEUR? QUEEN ISABELLA, VENTURE CAPITALIST?

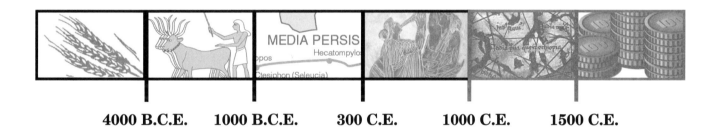

4000 B.C.E.　　1000 B.C.E.　　300 C.E.　　1000 C.E.　　1500 C.E.

LESSON 18
CHRISTOPHER COLUMBUS, ENTREPRENEUR? QUEEN ISABELLA, VENTURE CAPITALIST?

LESSON DESCRIPTION

This lesson uses reader's theater to explore economic elements of Columbus' first voyage. Students are introduced to reader's theater and to key economic concepts associated with this episode from history. Students read a short primer on the fundamentals of investing and a special category of investor—the venture capitalist. The lesson concludes with a "decision tree" activity used to determine whether Spain's decision to fund Columbus was a sound investment for venture capital.

INTRODUCTION

One of the most often told tales in American history is how "in 1492, Columbus sailed the ocean blue." Once hailed as a courageous hero who discovered a "new" land, history's view of Columbus and his voyage has changed over time. Indeed, Columbus is just as likely to be portrayed as a colonizer who brutally conquered an autonomous people (the Taino) as a romantic or heroic explorer. Who was Christopher Columbus? More importantly, why did he "sail the ocean blue"?

History books often misrepresent the story surrounding Columbus' voyages. For example, much has been written about Columbus' desire to prove that the Earth was not flat but round. But evidence shows that most educated and literate people of the time (and Columbus was one) believed that the Earth was round. In fact, many mapmakers (including Claudius Ptolemy, 90–168 C.E.) had produced world maps that clearly depicted the Earth as a sphere.

An equally popular myth is that Columbus' voyage was funded because Queen Isabella (or Ysabel) of Spain was secretly in love with the explorer—that her love so blinded her to the unlikeliness of Columbus' success that she funded it regardless. This story is embellished in part because Columbus' first attempt to secure funding was indeed a failure. He had approached King John (Joao) II of Portugal in 1484, and King John rejected Columbus' proposal. However, King John did not reject the offer because he thought the voyage impossible but, rather, because the Portuguese were already engaged in the exploration of their own route to the East around Africa's Cape of Good Hope. In addition, John found Columbus' proposal (i.e., that one-eighth of all profits should go to Columbus himself) unfavorable to Portugal.

If Columbus' contemporaries believed the world was indeed round, and his journey was not due to a romantic relationship with the queen, why did Spain choose to fund his voyage when Portugal had not? This lesson explores potential explanations for the Spanish decision to provide funding by examining the decision as one a modern venture capitalist might make in response to an entrepreneur's proposal. Entrepreneurs are individuals who take on the calculated risks associated with a new business venture. Entrepreneurs are motivated by the potential for financial reward as well as by the desire to be their own bosses. Columbus was motivated by both of these. Spain's decision depended on an expectation of positive return on its investment. Queen Isabella (as well as King Ferdinand) expected something in return for outfitting Columbus with three ships, the men to crew them, and supplies to last several months at sea. In this case, their expected rate of return was almost 90 percent of all wealth accumulated by Columbus on his voyage; seven-eighths of all the gold, silver, jewels, or other precious cargo returning home from the New World.[1] Investors expect their returns to reflect the risks

---

[1] The actual agreement between Columbus and Queen Isabella was more detailed; but seven-eighths reasonably approximates the terms of the agreement.

associated with an investment. In this case, the expected rate of return was quite high because the risks of failure (getting lost, storms at sea, starvation, etc.) were so high. Many of the King and Queen's advisers believed the voyage was much longer than Columbus estimated, and the true distance to Asia *was* longer than Columbus assumed. Some economics historians believe this risky venture succeeded only because the investors got lucky!

CONCEPTS

Entrepreneurship

Investment

Profit

Risk

OBJECTIVES

Students will be able to:

- Understand the terms entrepreneur, venture capitalist, risk, and reward.

- Determine whether Columbus was an entrepreneur and whether Queen Isabella was a venture capitalist.

- Debate the financial soundness of Queen Isabella's decision to support Columbus' entrepreneurial adventure to the New World.

CONTENT STANDARDS

Voluntary National Content Standards in Economics, 2nd edition

- **Standard 14:** Entrepreneurs take on the calculated risk of starting new businesses, either by embarking on new ventures similar to existing ones or by introducing new innovations. Entrepreneurial innovation is an important source of economic growth.

World History Content Standards

Era 5. Intensified Hemispheric Interactions, 1000–1500 C.E.

- **Standard 6:** The expansion of states and civilizations in the Americas, 1000–1500.

Era 6: Emergence of the First Global Age, 1450–1770.

- **Standard 2:** How European society experienced political, economic, and cultural transformations in an age of global intercommunication, 1450–1750.

TIME REQUIRED

45–60 minutes

MATERIALS

- Classroom set of Activity 18.1

- Classroom set of Activity 18.2

- Classroom set of Activity 18.3

- Classroom set of Activity 18.4

- Slides 18.1–18.6

PROCEDURE

1. Ask students to complete the following: "In 1492, Columbus sailed the _____ _____." Many will be able to complete the famous phrase with "ocean blue." Ask students how much they know about the famous explorer and his expedition.

   (Answers will vary.)

2. Tell students they will use a "think-pair-share" brainstorming activity to develop a class list of all they know about Columbus.

   - Think: Students write down as much as they know or have learned about Columbus on a sheet of paper (1 minute).

   - Pair: Students pair up with a neighbor and compare lists. Each student adds to his or her list (1 minute).

   - Share: Student teams now share their lists with the class. Teacher should list everything student teams suggest on the white board or overhead.

3. Discuss several of the items on the list. Show Slide 18.1. Students will likely have suggested proving the Earth was round, if not, focus on this last item in Slide 18.1.

4. Show Slide 18.2 (not showing the date of the map) and ask students to guess what the image is. *(It is a map of the world.)* Ask them to describe it. *(It depicts the Earth as round.)* Ask students to guess what year this map was produced. Reveal the answer: 1459. Repeat this sequence for the next two maps (Slides 18.3 and 18.4). Conclude by focusing students on the dates. Ask students to recall the year Columbus sailed "the ocean blue." *(1492)*

5. Discuss how these maps demonstrate that most educated people (including Columbus) did not believe the Earth was flat.

6. Ask students why, if most people believed the Earth was round, was Columbus' voyage really so different?

   (Accept any answer.)

   Tell students that today they will learn more about the real reasons for Columbus' expedition . . . the economic reasons!

7. Distribute Activity 18.1. Explain to students that this brief activity will give them an overview of several key economic concepts that can help explain Columbus' voyage. Have students answer the questions that follow the reading:

   a. What were some of the risks Columbus was willing to take?

      (The uncertainty of return, getting lost, starvation, success or failure, etc.)

   b. What is profit? What kind of share of the profits did Columbus expect?

(Profit is calculated by subtracting all of a business's explicit and implicit costs from its total revenues. Profit is understood by economists to be the net income received for entrepreneurial skills and risk-taking; Columbus expected to earn at least one-eighth of the total profits given his initial one-eighth investment in the voyage. Revenues would come from gold, spices, precious jewels, etc.)

   c. How was Queen Isabella and Spain's investment in Columbus like an investment by a venture capitalist today? What was new about Columbus' venture?

      (It was a new and untested technology—sailing west to China—and Queen Isabella was expecting great return on the investment: seven-eighths of the profits would go to Spain.)

8. Distribute copies of Activity 18.2. Assign students to the 16 roles in the script. (Circle their roles at the top of the script and hand out the 16 scripts to the actors.) Explain that the rest of the class will speak the lines assigned to "ALL" in the script. These lines represent different groups of people in different scenes.

9. Have the students read the play.

10. Distribute Activity 18.3. Review the reading about venture capitalists from Activity 18.1. Tell students they will use this information to compare Columbus to modern venture capitalists. Allow students to review the reader's theater script as they complete the charts. Review the examples students have used to complete the charts in Activity 18.3. See suggested answers below.

Was Queen Isabella a venture capitalist?

Characteristics of Venture Capitalists	Example from Columbus' Voyage?
Invest in new technologies	*Sailing west to reach India or China was an untested idea. Even though most people did not think the Earth was flat, this journey presented new challenges.*
Invest in risky ventures	*Many things could go wrong that would prevent Columbus from returning to Spain: getting lost, starving, shipwreck, illness and injury, etc. And Columbus—for all his passion—might have been wrong.*
Own a portion of the company	*Even after granting all Columbus' demands, Spain still retained seven-eighths of any returns from the first voyage, and seven-eighths of the returns from subsequent voyages.*

Was Columbus an entrepreneur?

Characteristics of Entrepreneurs	Example from Columbus' Voyage?
Start new businesses/ enterprises	*Sailing west to reach India or China was an untested idea. Even though most people did not think the Earth was flat, this journey presented new challenges, mainly because the distances involved were much longer than Columbus estimated.*
Bear all the risks of starting the business	*All Queen Isabella and Spain risked was investment capital. Columbus was risking his life. Many things could go wrong that would prevent Columbus from returning to Spain: getting lost, starving, shipwreck, injury and illness, etc. If the venture had failed, Columbus and his crew might be dead.*
Invest some of own resources in the business	*Columbus invested his time and resources. He also asked that he be allowed to invest an amount equal to one-eighth the cost of additional journeys in return for one-eighth of the profits.*

11. Review student responses using Slides 18.5–18.6.

12. Distribute Activity 18.4. Ask students to work in teams to use the T-chart to develop a cost/benefit analysis of Spain's investment in the voyage. Using the whiteboard or projector, list costs and benefits.

Costs of the Voyage	Benefits of the Voyage
• *3 small ships* • *Crew and supplies* • *10% of profits to Columbus* • *Titles conferred upon Columbus (e.g., Governor-General) and land ownership rights*	• *Vast riches (spices, gold, precious stones)* • *Glory of discovery (first to find a western route to China)* • *New territory* • *Spread of Christianity*

13. Ask students to ponder the question: "Given what you know, did Queen Isabella make a wise investment?"

(Answers will vary, but should focus on the relatively small investment for a very large potential return—both monetarily and otherwise. You may wish to point out that it is important to estimate the approximate odds of Columbus' success. The better the odds, the greater the possibility of return on the investment. To be wise, we need to consider how likely it was that Columbus was going to make it back with riches.)

CLOSURE

14. Ask the students why Christopher Columbus can be considered an entrepreneur?

(He took risks in order to earn profit.)

15. Ask the students how Queen Isabella can be considered a venture capitalist?

(She funded a new business started by Christopher Columbus in return for a share of the profits.)

ASSESSMENT

Multiple Choice

1. Queen Isabella and Spain did not fund Columbus when he asked initially in 1488. One reason Queen Isabella funded Columbus in 1492 was that

   a. new discoveries indicated the trip was likely to be successful.

   b. **Spain's war with the Moors was over, freeing up resources.**

   c. Portugal was attempting similar voyages.

   d. Columbus' brother made an earlier voyage.

2. Why didn't Portugal fund Columbus in 1484?

   a. King John and his royal advisers believed the Earth was flat.

   b. The Portuguese were not interested in spices.

   c. **Columbus miscalculated the distance to Cathay (China).**

   d. Portugal was engaged in a war with the Moors.

Constructed Response

1. Was Queen Isabella's investment in Columbus a wise decision? Explain your response using the results of our cost/benefit analysis.

   (Answers will vary, but should focus on the relatively small size of the investment for a very large potential return—both monetarily and otherwise. You may wish to point out that it is important to

estimate the odds of Columbus' success. The less likely the odds, the greater the possibility of return on the investment. To be wise, one would have had to consider how likely it was that Columbus was going to make it back with riches.)

2. If you were a venture capitalist and could travel back in time to invest in explorers, which of the following would you choose to fund and why: Vasco da Gama, Ferdinand Magellan, Henry Hudson, Juan Ponce de León.

(Answers will vary. Answers should include information about why the explorer would make a good profit and, therefore, be a good investment. The students will probably not choose Ponce de León based on his—historically debated—search for the fountain of youth.)

CONNECTIONS: VENTURE CAPITALISTS TODAY

Venture capitalists like Queen Isabella and Luis de Santangel exist today, as well. One of the most famous is John Doerr (http://en.wikipedia.org/wiki/John_Doerr). Doerr has famously provided venture capital to several well-known technology start-ups, including Google, Amazon, and Netscape. For his successful venture capital investing, Doerr has been named to *Fortune Magazine's* "Midas List" as one of the top technology investors.

ACTIVITY 18.1

The Economic Story Behind Columbus' Expedition[1]

In order to understand Christopher Columbus and his impact on history, you must first understand that Columbus was an **entrepreneur**. What is an entrepreneur? An entrepreneur is a person who has an idea for a business venture. An entrepreneur bears many of the **risks** of success and failure that are associated with starting the business. In return, entrepreneurs expect to earn profits. **Profit** is defined as income that remains after a business pays all its expenses. Entrepreneurs are important to economic growth. They help themselves and others identify new ways of doing things. They discover new resources. They innovate and advance beyond the current ways of doing things. Some economists classify entrepreneurship as one of four types of resources; natural resources, human resources, capital resources, and entrepreneurship. Columbus' "business" was his expedition, which was based on an exciting idea. He believed he could find a new trade route to the spice-rich Indies by sailing west from Europe. He was willing to accept many risks to make this journey, including the possibility of getting lost, the uncertainty of returning, starvation, etc. Before embarking, Columbus, as the entrepreneur, needed to find the resources necessary to take the trip. He needed to acquire *capital resources* such as ships and tools, and *human resources*—a crew.

In 1484, Columbus asked King John (Joao) II of Portugal to fund his venture. King John declined. Columbus then spent six years in Spain trying to convince King Ferdinand and Queen Isabella of Spain to invest in his venture. Finally, in 1492, King Ferdinand and Queen Isabella agreed to provide Columbus with three small ships, men, and supplies.

Why didn't Columbus succeed in securing private financing? Columbus needed a *royal* investor. He needed the power of the Spanish throne to defend any claims he made to the territory he discovered. Only a monarch could enforce these claims.

When entrepreneurs start new businesses, they often invest some of their own money. In Columbus' case, he invested his valuable time (nearly 10 years). Columbus asked the king and queen that he be allowed to finance one-eighth

[1] Drawn from *A Venture Capital Primer for Small Business, Financial Management Series* (Washington, DC: Small Business Administration. April 2009, http://www.sba.gov/idc/groups/public/documents/sba_homepage/pub_fm5.pdf) and *A Primer on Venture Capital* (downloaded from http://www.vnpartners.com/primer.htm on November 1, 2010).

ACTIVITY 18.1, CONTINUED

of the cost of future voyages. In return, he asked for a one-eighth share of the profits. He obviously expected to get back much more in profits than his one-eighth. Columbus also requested he be given the title Admiral of the Ocean and Governor-General, titles offering power and prestige.

VENTURE CAPITALISTS

Sometimes entrepreneurs cannot cover all of their expenses and start-up costs by themselves. Often entrepreneurs look to others for help. **Venture capitalists** provide financial resources to start-up companies that they believe have a high potential for success. Venture capitalists (VCs) make money by owning part of the companies they invest in. Many of these new businesses are selling a new technology in fields such as biotechnology or computer software. Because VCs invest in risky ventures, they do not expect that they will earn a positive profit every time. To compensate for the possibility of failure and the loss of their initial investments, VCs often expect a large share of the profits from the start-up company. Many VCs help manage such companies. When King Ferdinand and Queen Isabella agreed to fund Columbus, they fulfilled the role of venture capitalists. They were funding an untested technology: sailing west to China. They expected a great return on their investment: nearly 90 percent of the profits would go to Spain!

QUESTIONS:

1. What were some of the risks Columbus was willing to take?

2. What is profit? What kind of share of the profits did Columbus expect?

3. How was Queen Isabella and Spain's investment in Columbus like an investment by a venture capitalist today? What was new about Columbus' venture?

ACTIVITY 18.2

Columbus Looks for a Venture Capitalist, a Reader's Theater[1]

Characters	
Narrator	Father Diaz
Columbus	Hernando de Talavera, Father Confessor to Queen Isabella
King John of Portugal	Duke Medina-Sidonia
Bishop of Ceuta	Duke Medina-Celi
Royal Mapmaker	Herald
Prior of La Rabida Monastery	Grand Cardinal Mendoza
Servant	Marquesa de Deza (Queen Isabella's lady-in-waiting)
Father Marchena	Queen Isabella

Act 1, Scene 1 (Royal Palace in Lisbon, Portugal 1483)

Narrator: Christopher Columbus, Genoese captain and former weaver and wine merchant, who is now an experienced sea captain, has sent a proposal to King John II of Portugal. King John and his advisers grant Columbus an audience.

---

[1] This reader's theater was developed using the following sources:

Davidson, M. 1997. *Columbus: Then and Now*, Norman, OK: University of Oklahoma Press.

Flowers, B., Suiter, M., and McCorkle, S. 1992. *The Voyages of Columbus: An Economic Enterprise*. St. Louis, MO: Curators of University of Missouri.

Macneice, L. 1944. *Christopher Columbus: A Radio Play*. London: Faber and Faber.

Russell, J. 1991. *Inventing the Flat Earth*. New York: Praeger.

Taviani, P. 1991. *Columbus, The Great Adventure: His Life, His Times, His Voyage*. New York: Orion Books.

ACTIVITY 18.2, CONTINUED

Columbus:	Your Majesty, I have been reading maps and accounts of sailors who have sailed west past the Canary Islands. I believe that the world is not flat, but round. I think that by sailing west, I can reach Cathay for spices and also the Indies, the land of gold.
King John:	Of course you are aware of my late uncle, the great explorer Henry the Navigator. He knew, as do all of us, that the world is indeed round. In fact, we too have sent ships exploring westward. We would like to know how you propose to reach Cathay and what materials and supplies you would need.
Columbus:	Your Majesty, I need at least three ships, men to outfit them, and food and supplies for three months.
Bishop of Ceuta:	Three months? Is that all the time you believe the voyage will take?
Columbus:	Yes. My calculations are based on a letter and a map made by the great scholar Toscanelli, which lead me to believe the distance from Lisbon to Cipangu[2] is 700 leagues.
ALL (the Lestrados or king's advisers):	Seven hundred leagues? Why, this is lunacy!
Bishop of Ceuta:	Yes, senhor Columbus. Our mapmakers and scholars believe that the distance is at least 2,000 leagues.
Royal Mapmaker:	Senhor Columbus, we don't know where you get your information, but it is wrong. Our cosmologists[3] are very confident you have miscalculated, given their studies of location and distance between stars.
ALL (the Lestrados, *laughing*):	What does he know? He used to be a weaver!
King John:	Silence! Show our visitor some courtesy. I apologize, senhor Columbus. However, I agree. The distance you suggest is too short. The voyage is much longer and much more risky than you propose. Indeed, we are content to seek a route to the Indies around Africa.

[2] Modern Japan
[3] Scientists who studied the stars to determine their location and distance.

ACTIVITY 18.2, CONTINUED

ALL (the Lestrados):	Yes, Africa!
Bishop of Ceuta:	We have a number of captains who have been working their way down the coast of Africa, and once they round the tip, we believe it will be a short trip to Cathay and the Indies.
King John:	The risks are too high and the reward too low given our other investments. Captain Columbus, I'm afraid I cannot grant your request. Portugal declines to invest in your expedition. We wish you well. . . .
Columbus:	I will sail on, no matter how the winds might lash me.
ALL (the Lestrados):	Good luck, senhor Columbus!

Act 2, Scene 1

Narrator:	The year is 1484. Following Columbus' rejection by King John, Columbus' wife dies in Lisbon. Shortly thereafter, Columbus sets off for Spain. Upon landing, Columbus and his young son immediately travel to the local monastery, where he meets Father Marchena, a priest and an astronomer.
Prior of La Rabida Monastery (*looking out the front gate*):	Who is this traveler arriving?
Servant:	I'm not sure, Prior, but he looks weary from his journey.
Prior:	Go and bring him in. Let's give him food and rest.
Columbus:	Greetings, Prior, thank you for your generosity.
Prior:	It is our tradition. Tell me about yourself.
Columbus:	I am a sea captain who has come from Portugal to make a proposal to King Ferdinand and Queen Isabella.
Prior:	What sort of proposal?
Columbus:	I plan to sail west to the lands of Cipango and Cathay and to return with spices and riches beyond men's dreams.

ACTIVITY 18.2, CONTINUED

Prior:	Hmm. . . . You might like to talk with one of our priests, Father Marchena. He is an astronomer and a mapmaker, as well. *(To servant)* Go and get Father Marchena. Tell him to bring his maps.
Columbus *(quietly to himself)*:	The maps are all wrong, except for perhaps Toscanelli's. . . .
Servant:	Yes, Prior.

Scene 2 (Later that evening, at dinner)

Columbus:	So you admit the world is round.
Father Marchena:	Most learned men believe so.
ALL (monks in the diner):	The world is round? Heresy! The world is flat! You'll sail off the edge!
Columbus:	Father, the world is round, which is my first point. The second is that one can sail west to reach Cathay.
Father Marchena:	Have you ever thought that there may be other lands between here and Cathay?
Columbus:	Of course. Marco Polo wrote of Cipango and Seven Thousand Islands. I believe that God has granted me the gift of knowledge and revealed that it is feasible to sail to the Indies. I must carry out this journey!
Prior:	So you want to carry faith to the unknown parts of the world?
Columbus:	That is my mission, but so far no one has accepted my proposal.
Prior:	You have been rejected?
Columbus:	By the King of Portugal.
Father Marchena:	Spain, I fear, will give you the same answer.
Prior:	I'm not so sure, Father. Our Queen Isabella has great faith.

ACTIVITY 18.2, CONTINUED

Father Diaz *(overhearing the conversation)*:	Yes, she is full of faith, but Spain's treasury is empty! The war with the Moors rages on and on. Once the Spanish armies defeat the Moors, perhaps Spain can turn to a new world.
Prior:	If our King and Queen are to invest in your proposal, they must be very sure of the return on their investment.
Father Marchena:	I am convinced señor Columbus will be successful. How shall we first get him into an audience with the Queen?
Prior:	Did you know that, for many years, I was the Queen's Father Confessor?
Father Marchena:	I did not!
Prior:	The Queen's new Father Confessor is Hernando de Talavera, and he is currently in Cordoba. I will give you a letter of introduction, but be careful when you meet him—he is a very conservative man.
Columbus:	Thank you, Prior!
ALL (monks):	Good luck to señor Columbus! Good luck in Cordoba! You will need it . . .!

Scene 3

Narrator:	Columbus takes his letter of introduction to Father Hernando de Talavera . . . which begins a series of encounters.
Hernando de Talavera:	I cannot believe you are serious. A foreigner with no standing, wanting to see Queen Isabella, her Catholic Majesty! She is too busy with our war against the Moors to invest in such nonsense. However, the Prior says you are a very faithful man and so I will give you a letter of introduction to the Duke of Medina-Sidonia. . . .
Narrator:	Sometime later. . . .

ACTIVITY 18.2, CONTINUED

Medina-Sidonia:	Señor Columbus, while your project is most original and it stirs my blood, unfortunately my estates require my full attention. I can, however, introduce you to someone who has your spirit of adventure, Duke of Medini-Celi....
Narrator:	Sometime even later . . .
Medini-Celi:	If it were not for this blessed war with the Moors, I would support your mission . . . but, at this time, no one can do so without royal authority. However, when the time is right, I will give you a letter of introduction to the real power behind the crown.
Columbus:	The Grand Cardinal of Spain?
Medini-Celi:	Mendoza himself. . . . Until then, I am happy to provide our hospitality.

Act 3 (Several years later)

Narrator:	After several years, Columbus finally has his letter of introduction to the Grand Cardinal, and arrives for his meeting with Mendoza to great fanfare.
Herald:	His Excellency, the Cardinal Don Pedro de Mendoza!
Grand Cardinal Mendoza:	Señor Columbus, I have here a letter from the Duke of Medini-Celi, to whom you were sent by the Duke of Medina-Sidonia, to whom you were sent by Hernando de Talavera—Where is it you are heading, exactly?
Columbus:	I hope, your Eminence, to Queen Isabella.
Grand Cardinal Mendoza:	As I mentioned, I have a letter from Talavera, Queen Isabella's Father Confessor.
Columbus:	Supporting me?
Grand Cardinal:	No. He thinks you are insane!
ALL (Audience and advisers):	And we agree!
Grand Cardinal:	I, however, do believe in your plan, and I myself will arrange an audience with the queen.

ACTIVITY 18.2, CONTINUED

Columbus:	Thank you, Cardinal.
ALL (audience and advisors):	Good luck at court, Columbus. You will need it!

Act 4 (The Court at Castille)

Scene 1 (Queen's anteroom, just off the main court)

Narrator:	It is now 1489, five years after Columbus left Portugal. He is finally about to have an audience with Queen Isabella. The court is abuzz with expectation. . . .
Marquesa de Deza (Queen's Lady in Waiting):	Your Majesty, señor Columbus waits.
Queen Isabella:	Let him wait awhile longer.
Marquesa de Deza:	Your Majesty, what will you tell him?
Queen:	My Father Confessor thinks his scheme is nonsense.
Marquesa de Deza:	My husband thinks it's possible. If you support it, think of all you can do for Spain.
Queen:	I have already done much for Spain. I brought the country together and restored our universities. . . . Now, if only we could defeat the Moors.
Marquesa de Deza:	But what of Portugal? They have explored all along the coast of Africa and have established trading ports. Think of the possibilities!
Queen:	Such an investment must be made on much more than possibilities. Show señor Columbus in.

Scene 2

Columbus:	Your Majesty. . . .
Queen:	Señor Columbus, my Father Confessor tells me you're insane, but I'm intrigued by your plan. . . .
Columbus (interrupting):	Give me three ships with men and supplies. I will show you I'm not mad. . . . I can carry out this expedition. I alone have the knowledge required to successfully make this journey.

Activity 18.2, continued

Queen:	Watch your tone, señor. Address me in the appropriate manner! I cannot make such an investment on my own, I must consult the King and the authorities.
Columbus:	Authorities?
Queen:	A Royal Commission . . . headed by Father Talavera.
Columbus:	But Your Majesty. . . .
Queen:	Quiet! Listen!
ALL (townspeople):	Granada has fallen. The Moors have been defeated. Spain has triumphed. The Moors have been defeated!

Act 5 (Early spring 1492)

Scene 1

Narrator:	The Spanish have defeated the Moors at Granada. Spain no longer has to commit resources to fund the war. The Queen has called a royal commission to review Columbus' plan, headed by her Father Confessor Talavera.
Hernando de Talavera:	Señor Columbus, as President of the Royal Commission, it is I who will decide to authorize your voyage to the west, but only on certain terms.
Columbus:	I have terms of my own.
Hernando de Talavera:	And what are they?
Columbus:	In return for undertaking the voyage, I demand. . . .
ALL (members of the commission):	HE DEMANDS? The impertinence!
Columbus:	. . . the title Viceroy and Governor-General of all I discover for Spain.
ALL:	Viceroy, Governor-General! (Laughter)
Columbus:	. . . and I demand the title Admiral of the Western Ocean. . . .
ALL (members of the commission):	Admiral of the Western Ocean?

ACTIVITY 18.2, CONTINUED

Columbus:	. . . and one-eighth of all treasure, spices, gold and precious stones found on the islands I discover. . . .
ALL (members of the commission):	One eighth, he is mad!
Columbus:	. . . and I will own one eighth of all land discovered and the profits from these lands. . . .
Hernando de Talavera:	. . . That is quite enough, señor. . . .
Columbus:	. . . and, finally, I demand that by Royal Charter my family will have all rights and privileges.
Hernando de Talavera:	Is that all?
ALL (members of the commission, *sarcastically*):	Is that ALL?
Columbus:	Yes. . . .
ALL (members of the commission, *laughing*):	Oh, that is all?
Hernando de Talavera:	I insist you withdraw all of these demands or the commission cannot support your proposal.
Columbus:	No, I refuse to withdraw any of these demands.
Hernando de Talavera:	In that case, as President of the Royal Commission, I reject your proposal.
ALL (members of the commission):	Yes! Yes! The end of señor Columbus!
Columbus:	This is the second time the royal commission has rejected me. I will not return a third time.
ALL (members of the commission):	Thank goodness!
Columbus:	I will take my case directly to Her Majesty.

ACTIVITY 18.2, CONTINUED
Scene 2

Queen:	Marquesa, you have heard that Talavera and the commission have rejected him again.
Marquesa de Deza:	Yes, but Your Majesty, I have heard talk that Luis de Santangel might be willing to loan you the money to finance Columbus.
Queen:	Santangel? He loaned us money to fight the Moors.
Marquesa de Deza:	Indeed, Santangel is a very successful businessman. He believes Columbus' scheme may be worth millions.
Queen:	If Santangel supports it, then I agree . . . it is done.
Marquesa de Deza:	But his demands are high!
Queen:	Yes, they are extravagant, but what risk is in it for us? Surely Santangel sees that there is very little risk for us and a potentially great reward. Columbus has asked for so little—three ships, a crew, supplies, and a few titles. If he is successful, think of the reward for our treasury.
Marquesa de Deza:	And he is a man of faith. . . .
Queen:	Yes, indeed, he can spread the faith throughout this new world. My husband agrees! Send in Columbus.

[Columbus enters.]

Queen:	I have decided to fund your venture.
Columbus *(excitedly)*:	Thank you, Your Majesty. *(To himself as he departs)* It is done! My voyage will take place. They have invested in my plan, and they will not be disappointed. I set sail as soon as possible. To Cathay! To the Indies!
Queen *(to herself)*:	Good luck, señor Columbus!
ALL (the queen's court):	Good luck, señor Columbus!

ACTIVITY 18.3

Columbus as Entrepreneur;
Queen Isabella as Venture Capitalist

After completing the reader's theater, review your script to find examples of Columbus acting as an entrepreneur and Queen Isabella acting as a venture capitalist. Fill in the examples in the tables below.

Was Queen Isabella a venture capitalist?

Characteristics of Venture Capitalists	Example from Columbus' Voyage?
Invest in new technologies	
Invest in risky ventures	
Own a portion of the company	

Was Columbus an entrepreneur?

Characteristics of Entrepreneurs	Example from Columbus' Voyage?
Start new businesses/enterprises	
Bear all the risks of starting the business	
Invest some of own resources in the business	

ACTIVITY 18.4

Cost/Benefit Analysis of Spain's Investment

Use the reader's theater script to develop a list of all the costs (monetary and non-monetary) Spain had to bear to invest in Columbus' journey and all the benefits Spain expected to receive.

Costs of the Voyage	Benefits of the Voyage

SLIDE 18.1

In 1492 . . .

- Italian sailor
- Trying to find a faster route to China and India
- Hard time getting funded
- Spices, gold, precious stones
- 3 ships (Niña, Pinta, Santa Maria)
- Queen Isabella (Spain)
- The voyage took longer than first thought
- People thought the Earth was flat and he would sail off the edge of the world...

SLIDE 18.2

Map #1

Fra Mauo map (1459)

SLIDE 18.3

LESSON 18 – CHRISTOPHER COLUMBUS, ENTREPRENEUR? QUEEN ISABELLA, VENTURE
CAPITALIST?

Map #2

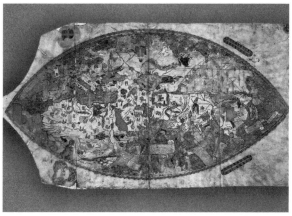

Genoese map (1457)

FOCUS MIDDLE SCHOOL WORLD HISTORY © COUNCIL FOR ECONOMIC EDUCATION, NEW YORK, NY

SLIDE 18.4

LESSON 18 – CHRISTOPHER COLUMBUS, ENTREPRENEUR? QUEEN ISABELLA, VENTURE
CAPITALIST?

Map #3

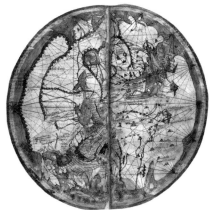

Pietro Vesconte's world map (1321)

FOCUS MIDDLE SCHOOL WORLD HISTORY © COUNCIL FOR ECONOMIC EDUCATION, NEW YORK, NY

SLIDE 18.5

LESSON 18 – CHRISTOPHER COLUMBUS, ENTREPRENEUR? QUEEN ISABELLA, VENTURE CAPITALIST?

King Ferdinand and Queen Isabella, Venture Capitalists?

Characteristics of Venture Capitalists	Example from Columbus' Voyage?
Invest in new technologies	*Sailing west to reach India or China was an untested idea. Even though most people did not think the Earth was flat, this journey presented new challenges.*
Invest in risky ventures	*Many things could go wrong that would prevent Columbus from returning to Spain: getting lost, starving, shipwreck, illness and injury, etc. And Columbus—for all his passion—might have been wrong.*
Own a portion of the company	*Even after granting all Columbus' demands, Spain still retained seven-eighths of any returns from the first voyage, and seven-eighths of the returns from subsequent voyages.*

SLIDE 18.6

LESSON 18 – CHRISTOPHER COLUMBUS, ENTREPRENEUR? QUEEN ISABELLA, VENTURE CAPITALIST?

Columbus as Entrepreneur?

Characteristics of Entrepreneurs	Example from Columbus' Voyage?
Start new businesses/ enterprises	*Sailing west to reach India or China was an untested idea. Even though most people did not think the Earth was flat, this journey presented new challenges, mainly because the distances involved were much longer than Columbus estimated.*
Bear all the risks of starting the business	*All Queen Isabella and Spain risked was investment capital. Columbus was risking his life. Many things could go wrong that would prevent Columbus from returning to Spain: getting lost, starving, shipwreck, injury and illness, etc. If the venture had failed, Columbus and his crew might be dead.*
Invest some of own resources in the business	*Columbus invested his time and resources. He also asked that he be allowed to invest an amount equal to one-eighth the cost of additional journeys in return for one-eighth of the profits.*

Lesson 19

What's the Big Deal About Spices?

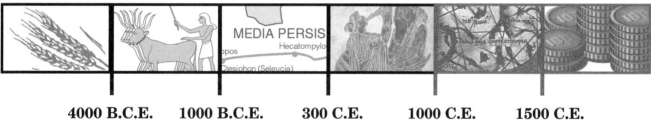

4000 B.C.E.   1000 B.C.E.   300 C.E.   1000 C.E.   1500 C.E.

INTRODUCTION

The index of almost any world history textbook has an entry for "spices" or "the spice trade." Why are spices so important in world history?[1] The short answer is that some spices—especially black pepper, cinnamon and cloves—were a highly sought-after commodity. At times, some spices were more valuable per pound than gold. Spices captured the imagination and taste (quite literally) of medieval European high society. Because spices were expensive and rare, Europeans used them lavishly on food to display their wealth. This very conspicuous consumption helped lead to the era of European exploration (approximately 1300–1600 C.E.), which in turn led to European conquest and colonization of much of the eastern hemisphere (India, Indonesia, etc.). It was European exploration in search of a water route to the Spice Islands—the only place in the world that spices were grown at the time—that led to this colonization. Historian Henry Hobhouse wrote that the "starting point for European Expansion . . . had nothing to do with the rise of religion or the rise of capitalism—but it had a great deal to do with pepper."[2]

Modern students may have trouble comprehending the fact that Europeans paid the modern equivalent of hundreds of dollars for one pound of cinnamon. Today, cinnamon is shaken liberally onto fresh local doughnuts in bakeries and black pepper is offered at every table in every restaurant. Why did these spices cost so much and lead to such a tremendous historical impact?

---

[1] This lesson draws heavily on the following sources:
Freedman, P. 2008. *Out of the East*. New Haven, CT: Yale University Press.
Choksy, J. and Dunn, R. (Eds.). 2006. "When Spice Ruled," *Calliope*, 16 (6).
Standage, T. 2009. *An Edible History of Humanity*. New York: Walker and Company.
[2] Hobhouse, H. 1986. *Seeds of Change: Six Plants That Changed the World*. New York: Harper and Row, p. *xiv*.

LESSON DESCRIPTION

Why were spices so highly prized? The spice trade offers an excellent example of how both buyers and sellers interact to determine prices in any market. In this lesson, students will (1) explore historical background for spices and the spice trade, including researching modern prices for three spices and comparing those prices to historical prices, (2) be briefly introduced to how supply and demand work to set prices in a market, (3) learn about factors that affect supply and demand in a market, and (4) apply that knowledge to scenarios that describe historical factors that impacted the price of spices.

CONCEPTS

Markets

Market price

Market demand

Market supply

Determinants of demand and supply

OBJECTIVES

Students will be able to:

- Explain why spices and the search for spices were such an important element of the Age of Exploration.

- Determine today's average price (per pound) of the three common spices cinnamon, cloves, and black pepper, and compare these prices to those from 1439.

- Determine the effect of several scenarios on the price of spices.

- State a hypothesis explaining today's relatively low price—compared to those of 1439—of cinnamon, black pepper, and cloves.

CONTENT STANDARDS

Voluntary Content Standards in Economics, 2nd edition

- **Standard 5:** Voluntary exchange occurs only when all participating parties

---

expect to gain. This is true for trade among individuals or organizations within a nation, and among individuals or organizations in different nations.

- **Standard 7:** A market exists when buyers and sellers interact. This interaction determines market prices and thereby allocates scarce goods and services.

World History Content Standards

Era 5: Intensified Hemispheric Interactions, 1000–1500 C.E.

- **Standard 1:** The maturing of an interregional system of communication, trade, and cultural exchange in an era of Chinese economic power and Islamic expansion.

- **Standard 7:** Major global trends from 1000–1500 C.E.

Era 6: The Emergence of the First Global Age, 1450–1770 C.E.

- **Standard 5:** Transformations in Asian societies in the era of European expansion.

TIME REQUIRED

90 minutes. Procedures 1–10, 45 minutes on the first day. Procedures 11 to lesson's end, 45 minutes on second day.

MATERIALS

- Activity 19.1, *Prices for Spices: Then and Now*, one copy for each student and the teacher

- Activity 19.2, *So What's Up with Spices?*, one copy for each student and the teacher

- Activity 19.3, *Determining the Market Price for Spices*, one copy for each student and the teacher

- Activity 19.4, *Why are Spices so Cheap Today?*, one copy for each student and the teacher

- Slides 19.1–19.16

- Internet access to www.netgrocer.com or similar site

PROCEDURE

Homework *before* Day 1:

1. Assign students Activity 19.1 as homework. Students can use the online grocery store Net Grocer (www.netgrocer. com). If they do not have Internet access at home, they can use the public library or visit the local grocery store with their parents or guardians. Explain that they must calculate the average price (per pound) for each spice so you can calculate a class average using their results. The three spices used in the activity are ground black pepper, ground cinnamon, and whole cloves. Students will find many brands and sizes, so assure students that they can use any brand or size.

Day 1:

2. Ask students to recall the last time they ate something with cinnamon in or on it. *(Answers will vary.)* Ask them to recall the last time they used black pepper at dinner. *(Answers will vary.)* Did they give these spices a second thought? *(Probably not.)* Tell the students that if they had been living about 575 years ago, using such spices would have been a very big deal.

3. Show Slide 19.1. Ask students what the author is claiming.

   (That spices were as important to world history as religion.)

4. Ask students to brainstorm everything they know from history about spices. After they have done so, show the partial list on Slide 19.2. Review any items on the list not discussed during the brainstorming activity.

5. Have students read Activity 19.2. In small groups, have the students answer the questions following the reading:

   1. How do spices differ from herbs?

      (Spices such as pepper and cinnamon are defined as the fruit, seeds, bark, or roots of a plant; herbs come from the leaves of the plant.)

Why were they difficult for Europeans to get?

(Spices could not be grown in Europe; they required warm, humid conditions such as those provided by the climates in India and modern Indonesia—both a long way from Europe.)

2. Why is the theory that Europeans used spices on rotten meat no longer believed?

(Historian Tom Standage says this would have been a "very odd thing to do, given (spices') expense." Standage argues that anyone who could have afforded spices could have afforded good meat because spices were the most expensive ingredient by far.)

3. Name three reasons spices were highly demanded.

(They were expensive imported goods that showed one's wealth, often used as medium of exchange, and important in medieval cooking to mask the saltiness of meat.)

6. Show Slides 19.3–19.5. Describe the three common spices imported by Europeans in the 1400s.

7. Tell students that they will now compare the prices for spices today with those 575 years ago. Ask students to get out their homework (Activity 19.1). Appoint a recorder to write down each student's results. (Note: this may be done best on a whiteboard or chalkboard). Ask the recorder to write down the average price per pound given by each student. After all the students have reported their results, have the recorder average the numbers using a calculator. Or, have students use the optional blank tables on the last page of Activity 19.1 to calculate the average price themselves.

8. Once class average prices for all three spices have been calculated, have students complete the first column in the table "Comparing Today's Prices with Prices in 1439" in Activity 19.1. Explain

to students that the average daily wage (pre-tax) for all workers in the United States was $170. Have them calculate the number of workdays the average U.S. worker had to work to buy one pound each of cinnamon, cloves, and black pepper.

(Note: This can be done by dividing the class average price per pound for each spice by $170; answers will vary, but at the time this lesson was written, it took an average worker in the U.S. about 0.09 workdays [about 43 minutes] to earn enough to buy a pound of cinnamon. A pound of whole cloves took about 0.62 workdays [about 279 minutes]. A pound of black pepper took about 0.13 workdays [about 62 minutes].)

9. Explain that historian John Munro calculated the average 1439 price (measured in nine-hour workdays[3]) for cinnamon, cloves, and black pepper. To compare prices from various eras, Munro had to use a common measure; therefore, he expressed the price of each spice as a portion of a workday, rather than in U.S. dollars or British pounds. Ask students to compare these average prices with those from 1439. Go over the answers to the questions.

(Spices were more expensive in 1439 than they are today. Based on the estimates in Procedure 8, cinnamon cost about 33 times more in 1439 than it costs today (.09 workdays now compared to 3 workdays in 1439); cloves cost seven times more; and black pepper cost 15 times more.)

10. Conclude the first day's activities by pointing out how much less of our income we spend on spices today. In 1439, the average worker had to work 27 hours (assuming a nine-hour workday) to earn enough to buy a pound of

---

[3] Historians have estimated that skilled workers such as masons worked nine hours a day. (Douglas Knoop and G.P. Jones, *The Medieval Mason.* New York: Barnes and Noble, 1967, p. 105).

cinnamon; today the average worker had to work only about 45 minutes to earn enough to buy a pound of cinnamon. Tell students that, in the next class, they will explore reasons why spices are relatively cheap today.

Day 2:

11. Briefly review the previous day's price comparisons—have students review the data chart from Activity 19.1. Have students answer the questions in Activity 19.1:

    1. In terms of the number of workdays it takes to buy spices, has the price of black pepper increased or decreased?

       (decreased)

    2. In terms of the number of workdays it takes to buy spices, has the price of whole cloves increased or decreased?

       (decreased)

    3. In terms of the number of workdays it takes to buy spices, has the price of cinnamon increased or decreased?

       (decreased)

    4. In 1439, which spice was cheapest?

       (black pepper)

    5. Today, which spice is cheapest?

       (Answers may vary, but black pepper is likely to be the least expensive of the three.)

12. Ask students to think about why these three spices might be so much less expensive today than they were in 1439. What factors may have led to the decrease in prices over time? *(Answers will vary.)*

13. State that market demand and market supply determine **market price**. Show Slide 19.6. Explain to students that you will use the cinnamon market as an example.

14. Define a **market** and **market demand**. Note that, as the price of cinnamon increases, less quantity is demanded and vice versa.

15. Show Slide 19.7. Ask students to follow along as you read the list of factors that lead to **changes in demand**. Note that that there are two additional factors, prices of related goods and expectations, that can affect market demand, but they will not be taught in this lesson. Note that increases in demand generally lead to increases in market price. Decreases in demand generally lead to decreases in market price.

16. Ask students to consider the cinnamon market and think of one example for each factor that shifts demand.

    (Answers may include consumer tastes, cinnamon's purported health benefits, the number of consumers due to immigration from countries that use cinnamon in cooking, and consumer income levels due to economic downturn.)

17. Show Slide 19.8. Define **market supply**. State that, generally, if the price of a good increases, more quantity will be supplied, and vice versa.

18. Show Slide 19.9. Ask students to follow along as you read factors that lead to a change in supply. State that generally, if a good costs more to produce, supply will decrease. If a good costs less to produce, supply will increase. Note that increases in supply generally lead to decreases in market price. Decreases in supply generally lead to increases in market price.

19. Ask students to consider the cinnamon market and think of one example for each factor that shifts supply.

    (Answers may include an increase in the number of producers, which increased supply; the cost of resources, e.g., a decrease in the price of raw cinnamon means companies can make more, increasing supply; changes in technology, e.g., invention of a better cinnamon grinder may result in more cinnamon being supplied; natural events, e.g., a tsunami wipes out many cinnamon tree farms, and supply decreases.)

20. Ask students how supply and demand explain the drop in prices of spices over the last 575 years.

    (Accept a wide variety of answers, but note that the next activity will help answer the question.)

21. Divide the class into groups of three to four and distribute copies of Activity 19.3. Assign each group a scenario. Have students read each scenario, determine whether supply or demand is affected, and decide the impact of the change on the price of spices. Have each group report their answers.

22. Show Slide 19.10 to review the answers. Be sure to emphasize the reason for the change in supply or demand.

    (Scenario 1: Consumer tastes, demand increases, price increases; Scenario 2: Improved technology, supply increases, price decreases; Scenario 3: Consumer tastes, demand increases, price increases; Scenario 4: Number of producers, supply increases, price decreases; Scenario 5: Consumer income, demand increases, price increases; Scenario 6: Cost of resources or number of producers, supply decreases, price increases; Scenario 7: Consumer tastes, demand decreases, price decreases.)

CLOSURE

23. Ask why the price for cinnamon (or other spices we've investigated) is so low today compared to 1439. What is the main reason?

    (Answers will vary, but students should list the following):

    1. *Improved technology and lower transport costs (supply)*

    2. *Changes in the way spices are used (demand)*

    3. *Changes in the "wow factor" associated with using spices (demand)*

OPTIONAL ACTIVITY: GRAPHICAL ANALYSIS

(Note: This is a more detailed activity introducing students to how market supply and market demand interact to determine prices. If you choose to use this activity with your students, you can do it before Step 20.)

A. Distribute copies of Activity 19.4. Have students read the introduction. Point out the relationship between price and quantity demanded and quantity supplied.

B. Have students use the *Demand Schedule for Cinnamon (1439)* in Section I of Activity 19.4 to plot quantity demanded on the blank graph *Market in Cinnamon*. Show Slide 19.11. Point out each price- and quantity-demanded combination. Have students plot each point, connect the points, and label the resulting line *Demand for cinnamon in 1439*. Show Slide 19.12 for review.

C. Repeat steps above for the supply schedule in Section II of Activity 19.4. Show Slide 19.13 and have the students plot each point. Show Slide 19.14 to review.

D. Bring students' attention to the point where the supply and demand curves intersect. Ask students to identify the price at this point.

    (24 pence)

    Inform students that this price is the *market price* for cinnamon, which is determined by both sellers and buyers.

E. Have students answer the questions in Section II of Activity 19.4:

    1. What is the price associated with the point where these two lines intersect?

        (24 pence)

    2. What do you notice about the quantity demanded and the quantity supplied at this price?

        (They are equal—10,000 pounds of cinnamon.)

F.	Have students read Section III of Activity 19.4. Show the new demand schedule on Slide 19.15. Have the students plot the new demand schedule, *Demand for Cinnamon (1440)*. Show Slide 19.16 to review.

G.	Have students answer the remaining questions in Section III of Activity 19.4. Tell students that the supply in 1440 is the same as in 1439.

1.	What has happened to the market price for cinnamon?

	(Increased)

2.	Why do you think this happened?

	(The medical benefit of cinnamon made it more desirable at all prices.)

3.	Generally speaking, what effect would an increase in market demand have on market price?

	(Increase)

4.	Generally speaking, what effect would a decrease in market demand have on market price?

	(Decrease)

5.	Predict what would happen to market price if the *supply* of cinnamon increased.

	(Price would decrease as cinnamon becomes more readily available. This is shown by the supply curve shifting to the right.)

ASSESSMENT
Multiple Choice

1.	Which of the following was NOT a reason spices were highly prized by Europeans in 1439?

	a.	Some people believed spices came from the Garden of Eden.

	b.	Spices were difficult to get and could not be grown in Europe.

	c.	**Advances in sailing cut the travel time to the Spice Islands.**

	d.	Many people used spices as medicines.

2.	Which of these would affect the supply of spices?

	a.	New methods of cooking use fewer spices.

	b.	**Advances in sailing cut the travel time to the Spice Islands.**

	c.	New methods of preserving meat require less salt.

	d.	New goods from America (e.g., tobacco) become very popular.

Constructed Response

1.	Briefly describe why the prices of spices were so much higher in 1439 than they are today.

	(Answers will vary, but should include discussion of the lower costs of transportation due to improved technology as well as the decreased enthusiasm for spices.)

CONNECTIONS: IN THE PAST AND TODAY

In the past: In the forward to his book *Seeds of Change: Six Plants that Transformed Mankind* (1986, New York: Harper and Roe), Henry Hobhouse makes the case that the discovery of America was due not to the search for gold or to convert heathens but, rather, due to black pepper. Hobhouse claims that the great Spanish, Portuguese, and Italian exploration movements were attempts to find new trade routes that circumvented the Silk Road, which was controlled by the Arabs and the Turks. "The Americas were discovered as a by-product in the search for pepper (p. xv)." Hobhouse goes on to state that historians have known this connection for years, but don't write about it because they didn't want children to know that their existence was "merely the outcome of an apparently casual affair." (p. xv)

Today: Although black pepper, cinnamon, and cloves are relatively cheap today, compared to 1439 prices, at least one spice remains extremely valuable—saffron. Saffron consists of the dried stigmas and part of the styles, tiny stem-like objects inside the bloom of the crocus flower. The expense comes not from the difficulty of growing crocuses, but from the intensive labor involved in harvesting it—80,000 flowers are needed to obtain one pound of saffron. Spain grows more saffron than any other nation, with India second in the saffron-producing market. Current prices for saffron range from $100 to over $500 dollars per ounce, depending on the quality. This means saffron costs as much as $8,000 a pound!

ACTIVITY 19.1
Prices for Spices: Then and Now

Before we can compare prices from long ago with prices today, we first need to determine how much spices cost today. For homework, you will complete the data retrieval chart below for three spices: cinnamon, cloves, and black pepper. You can find the data at your local grocery store or on the Internet at http://www.netgrocer.com/. If you use NetGrocer, type the name of each spice in the search tool. NetGrocer carries several different brands of each of these spices. Complete the chart using the first three brands returned by the search tool. A sample answer is shown for cinnamon.

Ground Cinnamon

Brand	Price	Ounces in container	Price per ounce	Price per pound (price/oz. x 16)
Spice Classics™ Ground Cinnamon	$1.29	3.37 oz.	$ 0.38	$ 6.08
Average (of price per pound)				

Whole Cloves

Brand	Price	Ounces in container	Price per ounce	Price per pound (price/oz. x 16)
Average (of price per pound)				

ACTIVITY 19.1, CONTINUED

Ground Black Pepper				
Brand	Price	Ounces in container	Price per ounce	Price per pound (price/ oz. x 16)
Average (of price per pound)				

To compare today's prices with those from the past, we need to use something other than today's dollars. A workman in England in 1439 did not use U.S. dollars to buy his cinnamon! One way to make such a comparison is to ask to find out how long the English workman would have had to work to pay for a pound of cinnamon. Historian John Munro has calculated wages for an average craftsman in England in 1439. He found that an average workman would have had to work two days to buy a pound of black pepper, three days to buy a pound of cinnamon, and 4.5 days to buy a pound of cloves. How many days would the average worker in the United States have to work to afford the same amounts of the same spices today? Assume that today's average daily wage is $170.[4]

Comparing Today's Prices with Prices in 1439			
	Avg. Price per pound (today)	Number of workdays needed to buy one pound today (Avg. price per pound ÷ $170)	Number of workdays need to buy one pound in 1439
Black pepper			2 days
Cinnamon			3 days
Cloves			4.5 days

[4] Updated values can be found at US Bureau of Labor Statistics: http://www.bls.gov/oes/current/oes_nat. htm#00-0000

ACTIVITY 19.1, CONTINUED

QUESTIONS:

1. In terms of the number of workdays it takes to buy spices, has the price of black pepper increased or decreased? _____

2. In terms of the number of workdays it takes to buy spices, has the price of whole cloves increased or decreased? _____

3. In terms of the number of workdays it takes to buy spices, has the price of cinnamon increased or decreased? _____

4. In 1439, which spice was cheapest? _____

5. Today, which spice is cheapest? _____

ACTIVITY 19.1, CONTINUED

Class results: Summary of student averages

Calculating Average Prices (Per Pound)

Cinnamon	Whole cloves	Black pepper
Total:	Total:	Total:
Average price (Total divided by number of students):	Average price (Total divided by number of students):	Average price (Total divided by number of students):

ACTIVITY 19.2

So What's Up with Spices?

Have you ever given much thought to the cinnamon on your toast in the morning? What about the black pepper on your family's dining room table? Next time you are in your favorite fast-food restaurant, ask for some black pepper. You will likely be given all you want in those little break-open pepper packets. Spices such as pepper and cinnamon are the fruit, seeds, bark, or roots of a plant. Herbs, such as oregano and rosemary, are the leaves of the plant. Spices such as cinnamon and black pepper are very common. But 500 or 600 years ago, spices were a lot "hotter" than they are today. In fact, at various times in history, spices were worth more than their weight in gold or silver. Spices were so valuable that people were willing to risk their lives on dangerous expeditions to find these valuable commodities.

At times, spices have been used like money. In the 5th century C.E., pepper was used as a medium of exchange and traded for other goods and services. In ancient Rome, merchants could pay their rent in peppercorns. The Romans had a great appetite for spices. In 408 C.E., Rome was about to be invaded by an army led by Alaric the Visigoth. To keep him from invading, Roman senators gave him 3,000 pounds of pepper! The Romans enjoyed cinnamon leaves (malabathrum) so much they were willing to pay six times the average Roman workers monthly salary for one pound! Pliny the Elder estimated that Rome's annual trade deficit with India and China (for spices alone) was equal to the value of 10 tons of gold. Egyptian Pharaohs were often buried with peppercorns in their noses to show their wealth to those in the afterlife.

Why were spices so valuable hundreds and thousands of years ago? Many believed that spices were valuable for masking the taste of rotten meat. The theory goes that it was difficult to preserve meat, so spices were used to make rotten meat edible. Historian Tom Standage believes this would have been a "very odd thing to do, given [spices'] expense." Standage argues that anyone who could have afforded spices could have afforded good meat—the spices were the most expensive ingredient by far. "With their richly spiced food," Standage writes, "the wealthy literally had expensive tastes." Standage believes about it is more likely that spices were valued to cover up meat's saltiness because salt curing was the primary method of preserving meat.

Spices were expensive imported goods. Spices such as cinnamon, cloves, and black pepper were native to the so-called Spice Islands (modern Indonesia and parts of New Guinea). Spices could only be grown in tropical climates with lots of rain, so they could not be grown in Europe. Travel to spice-growing regions required mostly land travel, which was very slow and often dangerous. The long travel made spices difficult for Europeans to get. Entrepreneurs found spices desirable to ship because they were both lightweight and extremely valuable. Many groups tried to control the spice trade: first, beginning in the 7th century C.E., spices were controlled by Muslim traders; later, the spice trade was controlled by Genoese descendants of Marco Polo; and then the Portuguese and the Dutch.

Europeans who could afford to buy and use spices were showing their neighbors how rich they were. Cookbooks from the 1400s show us that spices were used in more than three-quarters of all recipes and that some families in England spent as much on spices as on the meat they used them on.

Spices were also used in religious ceremonies. Frankincense and other spices were burned in medieval churches. Spices' aromas were thought to affect health and mood, creating a refined environment for those who burned them, which explains why they were frequently used in religious services and ceremonies.

QUESTIONS:

1. How do spices differ from herbs? Why were they difficult for Europeans to get?

2. Why is the theory that Europeans used spices on rotten meat no longer believed?

3. Name three reasons spices were highly demanded.

ACTIVITY 19.3

Determining the Market Price for Spices

Spices are much less expensive today than 500 years ago. Today, the average worker can earn enough money to buy a pound of cinnamon in 45 minutes. In 1439, the average worker needed three days of labor to earn enough to buy that same pound of cinnamon! Why has the price of spices such as cinnamon fallen so dramatically?

Both buyers and sellers are responsible for determining market prices. Market demand represents the desires of consumers. If the demand for cinnamon increases, the market price of cinnamon is pushed up in the market. If market demand decreases, the market price falls. But this is only half the story. Cinnamon suppliers (businesses) are responsible for the market supply. Market supply represents the willingness of producers to bring a good to market. If the supply of cinnamon increases, it pushes down the market price in the market. If supply decreases, the market price rises. Let's use the cinnamon market and prices from 1439 as an example to see how changes in demand and supply affect the price of cinnamon.

Use the following scenarios from history to complete the chart below. Consider each scenario that follows. Did the event described affect the supply of spices or the demand? According to the event described, was there an increase or decrease in supply or demand for cinnamon? Also indicate what affect this change (in supply or demand) will have on the market price for spices. Recall the factors that can shift market demand and market supply:

Supply Changes with	Demand Changes with
1. Number of producers	1. Consumer tastes
2. Cost of resources needed to make the good	2. Number of consumers
3. Improved technology	3. Increase in consumer income
4. Natural events	

ACTIVITY 19.3, CONTINUED

Scenario 1

One reason spices became so popular in medieval Europe was that buyers began to believe that they came directly from the Garden of Eden. Spices were referred to as "splinters of Paradise." Ancient authorities claimed that cinnamon and ginger were hauled from the Nile River in nets after washing down from the Garden of Eden. Legend had it that the Garden of Eden was perfumed with spices. Ordinary people tried to recreate a piece of the garden by using spices in their home.

Scenario 2

During the 1400s, improvements in sailing technology allowed European sailors to travel on longer and longer journeys. The fast and sturdy caravel (the type of ship Columbus used) was invented. Maps were improved using latitude and longitude, and new tools such as the astrolabe and better compasses improved navigation.

Scenario 3

Spices such as nutmeg and cloves were thought to cure disease. In particular, combinations of powdered cinnamon, cloves, and mace were thought to prevent the Black Death. In Italy, many people walked around carrying bottles of spices for smelling because people thought the plague was spread by bad air. Broth flavored with pepper, ginger, and cloves was believed to prevent disease.

Scenario 4

The Italian states of Genoa and Venice controlled the spice trade until the early 1500s. In 1501, Pedro Cabral from Portugal sailed around Africa to India and brought home many spices. In 1579, English explorer Sir Francis Drake sailed through the Spice Islands and brought back ship-loads of spices to England. In 1602, the Dutch East India Company took over the Spice Islands, including modern Indonesia, and began exporting spices to Europe.

ACTIVITY 19.3, CONTINUED

Scenario 5

Spices were a luxury good that demonstrated wealth. The more spices you used in food and as medicine, the richer you were. Spices were given as gifts, willed to family members after death, and even used as currency. Spices were used in perfumes and as incense in religious ceremonies.

Scenario 6

In 500 C.E., a Greek historian described the Arabs who were the first spice traders. These traders told outlandish stories about collecting cinnamon from caves guarded by winged, bat-like creatures. Arab traders claimed they had to wear full-body armor made from ox skins to protect themselves. Other stories claimed that cinnamon sticks were brought to Arabia by large birds that deposited them in their nests high on a mountain. Traders said that they cut up an ox, which the giant birds carried to their nests. The nests then fell to the ground with the weight of the meat, and then cinnamon sticks could be collected. These stories were told for two reasons: to hide the true location of the spices and to scare off competition.

Scenario 7

With the exploration of the New World (1500–1600), Europeans discovered new, exotic substances, including tobacco. Tobacco, (along with coffee, sugar and tea from other parts of the world) became status symbols because they were new. These soon overtook spices as status symbols. The use of spices for over-flavoring food fell out of fashion, and simpler foods became popular in Europe. By the 1620s, the Dutch controlled the spice trade. But by 1700, the portion of Dutch revenue from spices fell from 75 percent to just 23 percent. The golden age of spices was over.

ACTIVITY 19.3, CONTINUED

Scenario	Affects Supply or Demand?	Affects Market Price?
1		
2		
3		
4		
5		
6		
7		

ACTIVITY 19.4

Why Are Spices (Relatively) Cheap Today?

Spices are much less expensive today than 575 years ago. Today, the average worker can earn enough money to buy a pound of cinnamon spice in 45 minutes. In 1439, the average worker worked more than three days to earn enough to buy a pound of cinnamon. Why has the price of spices fallen so dramatically?

Prices of commodities are determined by the demand for them—the market. Both buyers and sellers are responsible for determining these prices. Market demand is the amount of a product—such as cinnamon—that consumers desire at different prices. The higher the price, the less cinnamon consumers desire. The lower the price, the more cinnamon consumers desire. But this is only half the story. Cinnamon suppliers (businesses) are responsible for the market supply. This is the amount of cinnamon they are willing to provide at different prices. The higher the price, the more cinnamon is supplied. The lower the price, the less cinnamon is supplied. Let's use the cinnamon market and prices from 1439 as an example. First, we'll draw a picture that represents the demand for cinnamon in 1439, and then we'll draw a picture that represents the supply of cinnamon.

First, let's review: Recall that an increase in market demand occurs when consumers are willing to buy more cinnamon at all prices. Several factors can shift market demand:

1. Consumer tastes: As we saw with the cinnamon market, if consumers' desire for a product increases, so will demand. The more fashionable a product (e.g., clothing) the greater the demand. This is often the case with electronics or other products. If desire decreases, so too does demand.

2. Number of consumers: The more buyers in a market, the higher the demand. If buyers leave a market, demand decreases.

3. Consumer income: As consumers earn more (overall), then they tend to spend more, increasing demand. If consumer income decreases, demand decreases as well.

Also recall that an increase in market supply occurs when producers are willing to supply more cinnamon at all prices. Several factors can shift market supply:

1. Number of producers. The more cinnamon suppliers, the greater the market supply of cinnamon. Fewer suppliers means less market supply of cinnamon.

ACTIVITY 19.4, CONTINUED

2. Cost of resources. The cost of resources (e.g., ships to transport cinnamon, wages paid to sailors, etc.) needed to produce cinnamon affects supply. If costs increase, less cinnamon can be supplied and market supply decreases. On the other hand, if these costs decrease, market supply will increase.

3. Changes in technology. Improved technology (the tools, machines, etc. needed to produce cinnamon) can mean an increase in market supply of cinnamon. For example, improved transportation (e.g., faster ships) would mean more cinnamon could be supplied leading to an increase in the market supply of cinnamon.

4. Natural events. Events that occur in nature such as floods, freezing weather, or hurricanes can disrupt supply. For example, a freeze in the orange groves of Florida will mean a lower supply of oranges.

I. DEMAND FOR CINNAMON IN 1439

The table below is called a demand schedule. It shows the relationship between price and how many pounds of cinnamon English consumers desired (what economists call the quantity demanded). Note how as the price increases, less quantity is demanded! Using the demand schedule, plot out each point on the blank graph below, and connect each point. Label the line *Demand for cinnamon in 1439*.

Demand Schedule for Cinnamon (1439)

Price (in pence, the English currency of 1439)	32	28	24	20	16
Quantity demanded (in pounds)	0	5,000	10,000	15,000	20,000

ACTIVITY 19.4, CONTINUED

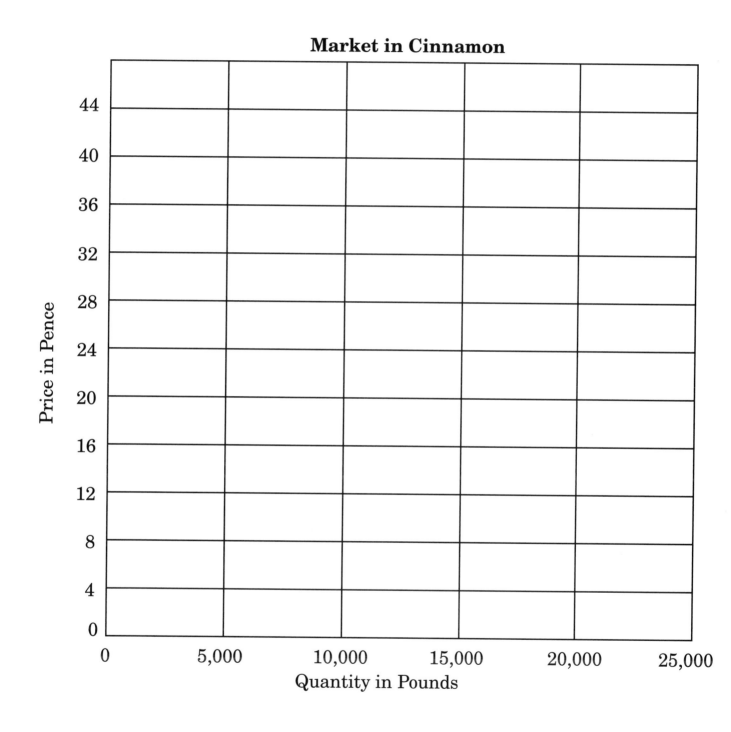

Market in Cinnamon

ACTIVITY 19.4, CONTINUED

II. SUPPLY FOR CINNAMON IN 1439

Next, we'll draw a picture of the supply of cinnamon in 1439. Plot out each point on *the Market in Cinnamon* graph and then draw a line to connect each point. Note how as the price increases, more quantity is supplied! Label the line *Supply of cinnamon in 1439*.

Supply Schedule for Cinnamon (1439)

Price (in pence, the English currency of 1439)	32	28	24	20	16
Quantity supplied (in pounds)	20,000	15,000	10,000	5,000	0

If you look closely at the *Market in Cinnamon* graph you have drawn, you will see that the *Demand for cinnamon* line and the *Supply of cinnamon* lines intersect.

1. What is the price associated with the point where these two lines intersect?

   _____

2. What do you notice about the quantity demanded and quantity supplied at this price? _____

This price is called **market price** for cinnamon. This is the price where the quantity of cinnamon consumers desire is equal to the amount of cinnamon that producers will provide.

ACTIVITY 19.4, CONTINUED

III. DEMAND FOR CINNAMON IN 1440

What happens to this market price if consumers suddenly change their minds and want more cinnamon at every price? For example, what if, in 1440, people begin to believe that cinnamon is the new "wonder drug"? We would say the demand for cinnamon has increased. Let's look at a new picture of the cinnamon market, if this were to happen.

Use the new demand schedule below and plot out each point on the *Market in Cinnamon* graph and then connect each point. Label the new line you create *Demand for cinnamon in 1440*.

Demand Schedule for Cinnamon (1440)

Price (in pence)	40	36	32	28	24
Quantity demanded (in pounds)	0	5,000	10,000	15,000	20,000

1. What has happened to the market price for cinnamon?

_____

2. Why do you think this happened?

_____

3. Generally speaking, what effect would an increase in market demand have on market price?

_____

4. Generally speaking, what effect would a decrease in market demand have on market price?

_____

5. Predict what would happen to market price if the *supply* of cinnamon increased.

_____

SLIDE 19.1

LESSON 19 – WHAT'S THE BIG DEAL ABOUT SPICES?

"The starting point for European expansion had nothing to do with religion or capitalism—but it had quite a great deal to do with pepper."

—Henry Hobson, *Seeds of Change: Five Plants That Transformed Mankind*

SLIDE 19.2

LESSON 19 – WHAT'S THE BIG DEAL ABOUT SPICES?

Why were spices so important?

- What do you know about spices in history?
  - Columbus was seeking the 'spice islands.'
  - Portugal, Spain, and Italy all wanted spices.
  - They were used to flavor foods.

SLIDE 19.3

Black Pepper

- Black pepper comes from the berry clusters called peppercorns that form on the pepper plant.
- Black pepper is one of the most popular spices in the world.
- Records show black pepper being traded from south Asia dating back to 4000 years.

SLIDE 19.4

Cinnamon

- Cinnamon has a long history both as a spice and as a medicine. It is the brown bark of the cinnamon tree, which is available in its dried tubular form or as ground powder. Chinese and Ceylon cinnamon are the most common varieties.
- Cinnamon is a perfect spice to use during the winter months.

SLIDE 19.5

Cloves

www.istockphoto.com/DomNichols

- Cloves are small nail-shaped flower buds that are dried.
- Sweet, somewhat penetrating flavor. Cloves can be bought whole or ground.
- Ground cloves are commonly used in baking. Cloves are native to Indonesia and are harvested mainly in Indonesia, Sri Lanka, and India.

SLIDE 19.6

Market in Cinnamon

- **Market:** Anytime buyers and sellers meet to exchange goods/services

- **Market Demand:** Amount of a good consumers desire at different prices
  - The higher the price of a good, the less of it consumers want.
  - The lower the price of a good, the more of it consumers want.

SLIDE 19.7

Changes in Demand

- A change in market demand for cinnamon occurs when consumers are willing to buy more (or less) cinnamon at all prices.
- Several factors can shift market demand:
  - **Consumer tastes**: As we saw with the cinnamon market, if consumers' desire for a product increases, so will demand. If desire decreases, so too does demand.
  - **Number of consumers**: The more buyers in a market, the higher the demand. If buyers leave a market, demand decreases.
  - **Consumer income**: As consumers earn more (overall), then they tend to spend more, increasing demand. If consumer income decreases, demand decreases as well.

SLIDE 19.8

Market in Cinnamon

- **Market Supply:** Amount of a good sellers want to provide at different prices
  - The higher the price of a good, the more of it sellers want to provide.
  - The lower the price of a good, the less of it sellers want to provide.

SLIDE 19.9

Changes in Supply

- A change in market supply of cinnamon occurs when sellers are willing to sell more (or less) cinnamon at all prices.
- Several factors can shift market supply:
  - **Number of producers:** The more cinnamon suppliers, the greater the market supply of cinnamon. Fewer suppliers means less market supply of cinnamon.
  - **Cost of resources:** If costs increase, less cinnamon can be supplied and market supply decreases. On the other hand, if these costs decrease, then market supply will increase.
  - **Changes in technology:** Improved technology (the tools, machines, etc. needed to produce cinnamon) can mean an increase in market supply of cinnamon.
  - **Natural events:** Events that occur in nature such as floods, freezing weather, or hurricanes can disrupt supply.

SLIDE 19.10

Determining the Market Price

Scenario	Affect Supply or Demand?	Affect Price?
1. "Splinters of Paradise"	Demand ↑	↑
2. Improvements in sailing technology	Supply ↑	↓
3. Nutmeg and cloves were thought to cure disease	Demand ↑	↑
4. Dutch East India Company took over the Spice Islands	Supply ↑	↓
5. Spices were a luxury good	Demand ↑	↑
6. Traders told outlandish stories	Supply ↓	↑
7. Tobacco, coffee, sugar, and tea became the new status symbols	Demand ↓	↓

SLIDE 19.11

Demand Schedule for Cinnamon (1439)

Price (in pence, the English currency of 1439)	32	28	24	20	16
Quantity demanded (in pounds)	0	5,000	10,000	15,000	20,000

SLIDE 19.12

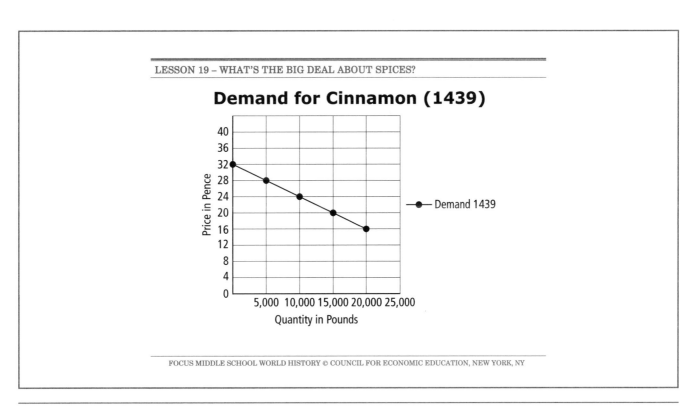

Demand for Cinnamon (1439)

SLIDE 19.13

Supply Schedule for Cinnamon (1439)

Price (in pence, the English currency of 1439)	32	28	24	20	16
Quantity supplied (in pounds)	20,000	15,000	10,000	5,000	0

SLIDE 19.14

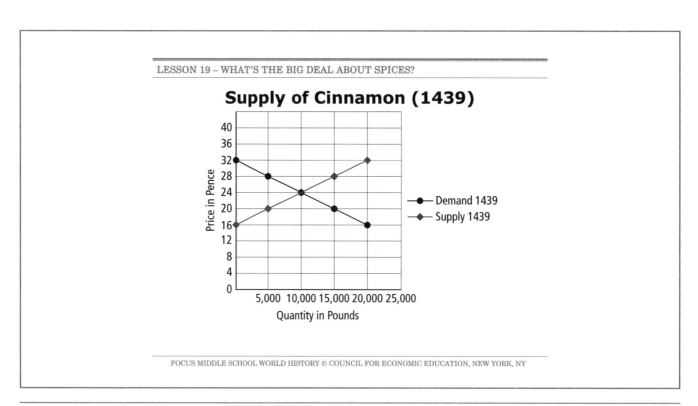

SLIDE 19.15

Demand Schedule for Cinnamon (1440)

Price (in pence)	40	36	32	28	24
Quantity demanded (in pounds)	0	5,000	10,000	15,000	20,000

SLIDE 19.16

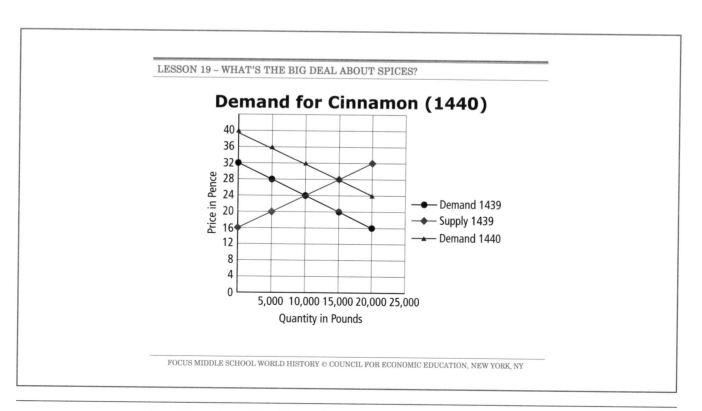

LESSON 20

THE COLUMBIAN EXCHANGE

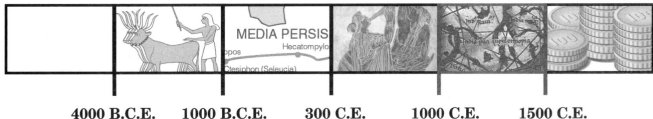

4000 B.C.E.   1000 B.C.E.   300 C.E.   1000 C.E.   1500 C.E.

LESSON 20
THE COLUMBIAN EXCHANGE

LESSON DESCRIPTION

In this lesson, students learn that the Columbian Exchange resulted in an enormous exchange of goods, resources, and institutions between the Old World and the New World and that the results of the Exchange were both positive and negative. The lesson begins with an activity in which students are divided into two groups: Old World consumers and New World consumers. Students are given food cards to keep or trade within each group, and later, among consumers from both groups. Although the expansion of trade provides students with more choices and has positive effects, some trades result in negative effects.

A second activity summarizes some of the positive and negative impacts of the Columbian Exchange, some of which students experience in the first activity. A final activity describes Tenochtitlan, the capital city of the Aztec civilization that had a relatively well-developed economy in the 15th century despite the lack of capital resources such as iron tools, wheels, and draft animals. The Aztecs adopted legal institutions that protected property rights and supported a market economy. The Spanish, who conquered the Aztecs in 1521, replaced these with institutions that restricted the ability of the native population of Mexico to produce and trade. Similar restrictions were imposed by European colonizers in other New World areas. Students learn that, in addition to the exchange of plants, animals, and culture, the exchange of institutions between the Old World and the New World had an important impact on the future economic growth of countries in the Western Hemisphere.

INTRODUCTION

Historian Alfred W. Crosby used the phrase "the Columbian Exchange" to describe the widespread exchange of plants, animals, culture, institutions, people, and disease between the world's Eastern and Western Hemispheres as a result of the voyages of discovery that began with Christopher Columbus in 1492. Crosby wrote that the Exchange "has created markets for Europe without which she would . . . be now a very different and a much poorer region. . . ." But Crosby also noted, "It is possible that [man] and the plants and animals he brings with him have caused the extinction of more species of life forms in the last four hundred years than the usual processes of evolution might kill off in a million."[1]

In addition to the profound effects it had in the areas of ecology, agriculture, and culture, the Columbian Exchange also had important economic impacts. The Columbian Exchange teaches us that economic growth is a product not just of resources—fertile land, minerals, machinery—but also of legal and political institutions.

CONCEPTS

Legal foundations of a market economy

Market economy

Productivity

Productive resources

Specialization

Standard of living

Trade

Voluntary exchange

OBJECTIVES

Students will be able to:

- List goods and resources that were brought to the New World from the Old World during the Columbian Exchange.

---

[1] Alfred W. Crosby, Jr. 1972. *The Columbian Exchange. Biological and Cultural Consequences of 1492.* Westport, CT: Greenwood Press, pp. 218–219.

- List goods and resources that were brought to the Old World from the New World during the Columbian Exchange.

- Identify the impacts of the Columbian Exchange as positive or negative.

- Describe the characteristics of the Aztec civilization that enabled it to achieve a relatively high standard of living in the 15th century.

CONTENT STANDARDS

Voluntary Content Standards in Economics, 2nd edition

- **Standard 3:** Different methods can be used to allocate goods and services. People acting individually or collectively must choose which methods to use to allocate different kinds of goods and services.

- **Standard 5:** Voluntary exchange occurs only when all participating parties expect to gain. This is true for trade among individuals or organizations within a nation, and among individuals or organizations in different nations.

World History Content Standards

World History Era 5. Intensified Hemispheric Interactions, 1000–1500 C.E.

- **Standard 6:** The expansion of states and civilizations in the Americas, 1000–1500

TIME REQUIRED

45 minutes, Procedures 1–9; 45 minutes, Procedures 10–17

MATERIALS

- Enough copies of New World Food Cards and Old World Food Cards from Activity 20.1 for each student to have two food cards (half of the students will have two New World Food Cards, the other half will have two Old World Food Cards)

- Copies for each student of Activities 20.2 and 20.3

- Slides 20.1–20.5

PROCEDURE

1. Before class, review Activity 20.1, which provides the teacher instructions for "Trading in The Old World–New World Market."

2. Begin the lesson by telling the students that before 1492 C.E., the New World was cut off from the rest of the world. The voyages of Christopher Columbus and other explorers introduced new animals, plants, culture, and institutions to the New World. The Old World received other plants, animals, etc., from the New World. Many of the exchanges between the New World and Old World had positive impacts, but there were also negative impacts.

3. Tell students that they will participate in a trading activity: "Trading in The Old World–New World Market." Show Slides 20.1 and 20.2. Review the rules of the activity. Allow trade.

4. After the first five-minute trading round is complete, ask students to report orally or by a show of hands whether they considered themselves better off as a result of their trades. Record the results on a chalkboard or whiteboard.

   (Some students may be satisfied with the cards they were given and prefer not to trade. Voluntary trade should allow students to be better off than they were before trade took place.)

5. Ask the students who among them were made better off by trade in the first round to explain why.

   (Answers will vary but students should conclude that people like different types of food. Voluntary trade gave students more choices and these choices allowed them to obtain the foods they valued most.)

6. Show Slide 20.3. Review the new rules of the activity (trade is allowed between New and Old World). Allow trade.

7. After the second five-minute trading round is complete, show Slide 20.4.

Note that some trade has resulted in unanticipated hardships for some.

8. Ask students to report orally or by a show of hands whether they consider themselves better off as a result of their trades. Allow New World consumers who have "perished" to report. Record these results on the board and compare them to the results from the first round. Ask the students who among them were made better off by trade in the second round to explain why.

(By expanding trade to all, students were given more choices and more opportunities for voluntary trade to make themselves better off.)

9. Ask students who were made worse off by their trades in the second round to explain why.

(The students who "perished" traded with incomplete information. They based their trades on benefits they expected to receive but did not realize they would become ill from the foods or animals they obtained or from the traders.)

10. Ask students why some New World consumers were negatively affected by their second-round trades but Old World consumers were not.

(The Old World consumers had developed immunity to diseases through previous exposure. New World consumers had little or no exposure to these diseases prior to their first contact with Old World traders.)

11. Distribute copies of Activity 20.2. The word "exchange" is often used to refer to **trade** (the voluntary exchange of goods and services for money or other goods and services). Those who engage in voluntary trade do so because they expect that they will be made better off. But many of the resources, goods, knowledge, diseases, and institutions that moved from the Old World to the New World and from the New World to the Old World were not the result of voluntary trades by buyers and sellers. Activity 20.2 identifies positive and negative impacts of the Columbian Exchange. Ask the students to read Activity 20.2, or read the activity aloud.

12. Tell students that exposure to smallpox and other diseases brought to the New World by European explorers caused the loss of life of millions of Native Americans. Ask students why Native Americans were so adversely affected by these diseases.

(As Europeans raised animals such as pigs, chickens, and cows, they were exposed to the diseases the animals carried. Europeans built up immunity to the diseases over many years. In contrast, there were almost no species of animals that were domesticated in America. Therefore, Native Americans were not immune to Old World diseases. Their first exposure to the diseases carried by the animals often led to serious illness and death.)

13. Summarize the class discussion by showing Slide 20.5, which depicts the movement of foodstuffs, resources, and diseases between the New World and the Old World that is known as the Columbian Exchange. Ask students why European governments were willing to provide financial support for voyages to the New World.

(They wanted valuable resources that were available in the New World, including silver and gold.)

14. Distribute copies of Activity 20.3. Tell students to read the activity.

15. Ask students why the Aztecs located their capital city in the middle of Lake Texcoco.

(This increased the difficulty that enemies of the Aztecs would face if they were to attack the city. They would have to enter Tenochtitlan in boats or along the city's causeways.)

16. Ask students what the term *standard of living* means.

*(Answers will vary. **Standard of living** refers to the level of subsistence of a*

nation, a social class, or an individual with reference to the adequacy of necessities and comforts of daily life.)

17. Tell students that even though the Aztecs did not use the wheel, iron tools, or draft animals to produce goods and services, they were able to achieve a standard of living that was higher than the standard of living in other areas of North and South America. Ask students to explain why.

*(The Aztec capital city prospered because the legal system and the institutions it established allowed trade to flourish. The Aztecs established the **legal foundations of a market economy**; that is, the laws and institutions that support a market economy, including protection of private property and enforcement of contracts. A **market economy** relies on a system of interdependent market prices to allocate goods, services, and productive resources and to coordinate the diverse plans of consumers and producers, all of them pursuing their own interests. **Productive resources** include natural resources, human resources, and capital resources used to make goods and services.)*

18. Tell students that, when people specialize in the production of one good, they must trade with other people to obtain the goods and services they do not produce. **Specialization** is a situation in which people produce a narrower range of goods and services than they consume. Specialization increases productivity; it also requires trade and increases interdependence. **Productivity** refers to the amount of output (goods and services) produced per unit of input (productive resources) used. Ask students why specialization and trade increase the standard of living for a nation or an individual.

(People will specialize in producing that which they have the skills for. Experience with producing one good or service over time improves worker productivity as people learn by doing.

People who specialize and trade are able to consume more goods and services than they would if they were self-sufficient.)

19. Conclude discussion of the reading by asking the following questions:

a. Would the Aztecs have increased their standard of living more by using iron tools, wheels, and draft animals?

(Students should agree that using these productive resources would have increased workers' productivity and raised the standard of living of the Aztecs.)

b. How were the Spanish conquistadors under the leadership of Hernán Cortés able to conquer the Aztecs?

(The Aztec population was decreased through exposure to infectious diseases, such as smallpox, and the Spanish were helped by tribes that the Aztecs had conquered. The Spanish had access to horses and steel weapons; the Aztecs did not.)

c. Why did some colonies thrive and others not thrive, according to the reading?

(Some colonies encouraged trade and private property—these colonies did well. Others colonies regulated trade and did not reward people for their efforts—these colonies did not prosper.)

CLOSURE

20. Conclude the lesson by reviewing the following points:

- The Columbian Exchange had important impacts in both the New World and the Old World, but not all of the impacts were positive.

- In addition to the exchange of resources, cultures, plants, animals, people, and disease between the Old and New Worlds after 1492, there was also an exchange of institutions that would have important effects on the economic growth of New World nations.

- Nations that adopted institutions that protected property rights and established legal systems that encourage trade had higher rates of growth than nations that did not establish these institutions.

ASSESSMENT

Multiple Choice

1. Usually, when two people make a voluntary trade they both benefit, but voluntary trade can make one person worse off if this person

   a. has less income than the other person.

   b. expects to receive greater benefits than the other person expects to receive.

   c. **has less information than the other person about the good or service that is traded.**

   d. is younger than the other person.

2. Which of the following factors was most responsible for the relatively high standard of living in Tenochtitlan in the late 15th century?

   a. The Aztecs used steam engines as sources of power for producing goods and services.

   b. **The Aztecs established institutions that protected rights to private property and encouraged trade.**

   c. Aztec workers had become very productive by being self-sufficient in production.

   d. The Aztecs allowed a small number of individuals to control their government and economy.

Constructed Response

1. The Columbian Exchange resulted in important positive as well as negative impacts. How can we determine whether the net, or total, impact of the Exchange was positive or negative?

   (Since the Exchange began, there has been a large increase in the world's population, and the standard of living in many countries, such as the United States, has risen. But millions of people died and millions more were enslaved because of the Exchange; these people only experienced negative effects. The comments by Alfred Crosby in the introduction to this lesson reflect the mixture of positive and negative impacts of the Exchange. Perhaps the best answer to this question is that the overall impact was positive, but the effects on some groups and individuals were not.)

CONNECTION: PRIVATE PROPERTY AND GROWTH

Since World War II, several small nations with meager supplies of natural resources have experienced high rates of economic growth. These nations include South Korea, Japan, Singapore, and, since it gained independence from the former Soviet Union, Estonia. An important reason for the high growth rates in these countries has been their adoption of legal systems that protect rights to private property. As was true with the Aztec civilization, the protection of private property rights and the enforcement of contracts have promoted trade and an efficient allocation of resources.

ACTIVITY 20.1
Trading in the Old World–New World Market

INTRODUCTION

Voluntary trade usually makes both buyers and sellers better off. But trade is based on the benefits buyers and sellers expect to receive. Occasionally, people regret trades that they have made because their expectations were not realized. For example, people use the word "lemon" to describe an automobile that needs frequent repairs and does not perform as well as the buyer thought it would. If a buyer knew an automobile was a "lemon" she or he would not buy it, but people sometimes make trades with incomplete information. This is why **voluntary exchange** is defined as trading goods and services with other people because both parties *expect* to benefit from the trade. This activity will teach students that some trades make people better off while other trades make people worse off because they have incomplete information.

In this activity, students trade New World food cards and Old World food cards. Each of the New World food cards has a number in the lower the right-hand corner (1 though 16). The main ingredients of New World foods were available only in the New World, or Western Hemisphere, prior to the Columbian Exchange. Each of the Old World food cards has a letter (A through P) in the lower right-hand corner. The primary ingredients of Old World foods were available only in the Old World, or Eastern Hemisphere, prior to the Columbian Exchange. Recipes for some foods (for example, baby-back ribs and eggplant parmesan) have multiple ingredients, some of which may have originated in the New World or the Old World. The classification of foods is based on the primary ingredient; for example, baby-back ribs are considered an Old World food because the primary ingredient, pork, is an Old World food.

INSTRUCTIONS

Step 1 — Half of the students will be New World consumers and the other half will be Old World consumers. Make enough copies of the cards so that each New World consumer receives two New World food cards and each Old World consumer receives two Old World food cards. You may choose to give some consumers two of the same card (for example, a New World consumer may be given two "Chocolate Syrup" cards).

Step 2 — On the backs of half of the Old World cards, write the letter X (big enough to be seen, but small enough not to attract attention). Leave the backs of the other Old World cards blank. Divide students into New World and Old World consumers and distribute the food cards.

Step 3 — Allow students five minutes to trade their food cards within their own groups, New World or Old World. Tell students that they may choose not to trade if they prefer the food cards they were given to the cards other students have. After trading ends, ask students to report orally or by a show of hands whether they considered themselves better off as a result of their trades. Record the results.

Step 4 — Conduct a second round of trading, allowing students to trade with all other students. After a second five-minute round, announce that some New World consumers have been exposed to diseases for which they have no immunity. To determine which consumers are affected, tell the students to look on the backs of their cards. Students who have an X on the back of one or more of their cards have been exposed to a disease. Old World consumers have been exposed to this disease previously and have developed immunity. New World consumers have no immunity; they become very ill and perish. Ask students whether they consider themselves better off as a result of their trades, including the New World consumers who have "perished." Record these results and compare them to results from the first round.

ACTIVITY 20.1, CONTINUED

New World Food Card

Pumpkin Pie 1	**Peanuts** 2
Nachos 3	**Potato Chips** 4
Pizza 5	**French Fries** 6
Pineapple 7	**Chocolate Syrup** 8

ACTIVITY 20.1, CONTINUED

New World Food Cards

Strawberries 9	**Beans** 10
Corn Flakes 11	**Potato Skins** 12
Potato Pancakes 13	**Tapioca Pudding** 14
Lima Beans 15	**Chocolate Bar** 16

ACTIVITY 20.1, CONTINUED

Old World Food Cards

Hamburger A	**Pulled Pork Sandwich** B
Milk Shake C	**Baby-Back Ribs** D
Cheese E	**Eggplant Parmesan** F
Rice G	**Ice Cream** H

ACTIVITY 20.1, CONTINUED

Old World Food Cards

Sugar I	**Chicken Quesadilla** J
Roast Beef Sandwich K	**Chicken Wings** L
Banana Split M	**Bacon** N
Cream O	**Eggs** P

ACTIVITY 20.2

The Columbian Exchange: Positive and Negative Impacts

Before 1492 C.E., the New World was cut off from the rest of the world. The voyages of Christopher Columbus and other explorers introduced new animals, plants, and institutions to the New World. The Old World received other plants and animals from the New World. Many of these exchanges had positive impacts, but the impact of some exchanges was negative.

POSITIVE IMPACTS

 From New World to Old World: **corn/maize**

Corn, or maize, is one of the most important foods the Old World received from the New World. Alfred Crosby wrote, "If maize were the only gift the American Indian ever presented to the world, he would deserve undying gratitude, for it has become one of the most important of all foods for men and their livestock."[1] Corn can be grown on land that can't easily grow rice or wheat. It has become an important food in Europe, Egypt, India, China, and other countries.

 From Old World to New World: **cows, oxen, horses, donkeys, pigs, sheep**

Cattle were brought to Mexico in 1521. They became an important source of food and can pull and lift heavy loads. Horses allowed hunters to travel great distances and increased the area over which natives could search for food. Donkeys were important pack animals. Pigs and sheep were used for food and clothing.

 From Old World to New World: **sugar cane**

The Spanish brought sugar to Mexico and Peru in the 16th century. It was soon grown in the Caribbean islands and other South American countries.

 From Old World to New World: **bananas**

Bananas were first grown in Southeast Asia and brought to the Caribbean islands (Cuba, Jamaica, Haiti, and other islands) in 1516. The climate of the islands allowed banana trees to grow rapidly.

 From New World to Old World: **potatoes**

At first, "Europeans looked upon the potato with fear and contempt."[2] But the climate and soil of northern Europe were well-suited to growing potatoes. Potatoes have become an important source of nutrition for many countries.

 From New World to Old World: **other foods**, including beans (lima, butter, kidney, and many others), peanuts, sweet potatoes, manioc (cassava or tapioca), squashes, pumpkins, papaya, guava, avocado, pineapple, tomatoes, chili peppers, strawberries, and cocoa beans

---

[1] Crosby, Alfred W., Jr. 1972. *The Columbian Exchange. Biological and Cultural Consequences of 1492.* Westport, CT: Greenwood Press, p. 171.
[2] *The Columbian Exchange*, p. 182.

ACTIVITY 20.2, CONTINUED

From Old World to New World: **other foods**, including wheat, coffee, beans, rice, and lettuce

NEGATIVE IMPACTS

From Old World to New World: **diseases that devastate humans**

Because they were separated from the rest of the world, Native Americans had no prior contact with smallpox and other deadly diseases. This made the diseases more dangerous than they were for Europeans. Between 1500 and 1650, large numbers of Native Americans died from measles, smallpox, influenza, and other diseases.[3]

From Old World to New World: **diseases that devastate animals**

European animals brought diseases with them that attacked llamas and alpacas.

From Old World to New World: **rat infestation**

Rats hitched rides on ships carrying English settlers in the 17th century. The rats infested the Bermuda islands and "set off one of the most spectacular . . . disasters of the age. . . . The rats spread to all the islands . . . and nearly ate the colonists out of house and home."[4]

From New World to Old World: **sand fleas**

Sand fleas, or chiggers, are insects that penetrate human skin. When they deposit eggs under the skin, they can cause dangerous infections.

From Old World to New World: **exploitation of workers and slavery**

Many explorers wanted to find gold and silver in the New World. They used any means available to them to bring these riches back to Europe. The loss of life from war and disease created a shortage of labor. Europeans turned to Africa to fill their needs for workers. Between 8 and 10.5 million slaves were forced to produce tobacco, rice, coffee, and sugar.[5]

Native Americans were employed through slavery and the Spanish system of "encomienda," which granted a person responsibility for a certain number of natives. Those who received the grant had to protect the natives and provide instruction in the Spanish language and the Catholic faith. Natives were forced to provide tribute in the form labor, gold, or other products.[6]

[3] For an example of how Native Americans in Florida may have been affected, see Mintz, S. 2007. "European Discovery of the New World." *Digital History*. Retrieved July 29, 2011 from http://www.digital-history.uh.edu (http://www.digitalhistory.uh.edu/historyonline/us1.cfm).
[4] *The Columbian Exchange*, p. 97.
[5] *The Columbian Exchange*, p. 213.
[6] Rodriguez, J.P. *Encyclopedia of Slave Resistance*, Vol. 1. 2007. Westport CT: Greenwood Press, p.184.

ACTIVITY 20.3

The Rise and Fall of Tenochtitlan[1]

THE AZTEC EMPIRE AND THE RISE OF TENOCHTITLAN

Mexico City was once called Tenochtitlan.[2] It was the capital of the empire of the Aztec people. In 1492, Tenochtitlan had a population of about 250,000. The city was on an island in Lake Texcoco. Canals and causeways[3] moved goods and people. Dikes controlled flood waters and aqueducts carried water to the city. The waterways also provided protection from attackers.

The Aztecs did not have iron tools, wheels or work animals to help grow food and make clothing and other goods. They increased their standard of living through specialization and trade. A worker would grow one crop, make one type of good, or provide one service. He would then trade some of what he produced for goods that others produced. Spanish explorers found a central market located near Tenochtitlan that was visited by 60,000 people a day. The market had separate trading areas for building materials, clothing, jewelry, and other goods.

The Aztecs developed a legal system that protected property rights. People were allowed to own and sell property. There were rules against dishonest trade. It was illegal to trade stolen goods. Judges settled disputes between traders. A large population made large-scale trade possible. The legal institutions allowed trade to grow.

However, the Aztec government also imposed heavy taxes on its subjects. In addition to paying taxes, people were required to provide the government with goods and labor services. Governments of tribes conquered by the Aztecs were also required to pay steep taxes. When Hernán Cortés, a Spanish conquistador,[4] led an expedition to conquer the Aztec empire in 1521, some of these tribes fought alongside Cortés. Exposure to diseases, such as smallpox, brought to the New World by the Spanish, caused sickness and death among the Aztecs. The Spanish had horses and steel weapons; the Aztecs did not. These factors helped Cortés to conquer the Aztecs.

---

[1] The information in this activity was taken from the following two sources: Daron Acemoglu, Daron, Simon Johnson, and James Robinson. "Understanding Poverty: Geography, Institutions and the Reversal of Fortune," http://team.univ-paris1.fr/teamperso/sponcet/SciencesPo/AJRreversal.pdf. Grennes, Thomas. "The Columbian Exchange and the Reversal of Fortune." *Cato Journal*, Vol. 27 No. 1 (Winter 2007).
[2] Tenochtitlan is pronounced "Tay-nōch-teet'-lan."
[3] A causeway is a road built above a body of water.
[4] Conquistador means "conqueror" in the Spanish language. This word refers to Spanish soldiers and explorers who conquered large parts of the New World for Spain between the 15th and 19th centuries following the discovery of the New World by Christopher Columbus in 1492.

ACTIVITY 20.3, CONTINUED

THE FALL OF TENOCHTITLAN

The Spanish conquistadores destroyed Tenochtitlan and filled in the lakes surrounding the city. Tenochtitlan was rebuilt and renamed Mexico City. Mexico City became a center of the Spanish colonial empire.

The conquistadores required all trade with Spanish settlements in the New World to pass through Seville. Seville is a city located in Spain, far from Mexico. The government gave control over foreign trade to the Mexico City merchant guild. The guild was a small number of people who benefited from their ties with the Spanish government. The guild favored workers born in Spain over workers born in Mexico. The Spanish allowed land to be owned by a small number of people. The landowners became wealthy by forcing workers to toil long hours for low wages. Limits were placed on the rights of Mexicans to own their own businesses.

In some colonies, Europeans created governments similar to the government of Mexico. They did not protect the property rights of citizens. These colonies were often located in areas where few Europeans settled. In these colonies, natives were forced to work for low wages. The natives had to pay taxes to the government of the home country.

In other colonies, different governments were established. There were many settlers from Europe, and their governments protected private property. These colonies included Canada and the United States. Over time, the standard of living of people in these colonies surpassed the standard of living of people in Mexico.

In addition to resources and goods, the Columbian Exchange led to an exchange of legal institutions between the Old World and New World. This exchange had an important impact on the future standard of living in the New World.

SLIDE 20.1

Trading in the Old World– New World Market

- Half of the students will be "New World Consumers" and the other half will be "Old World Consumers."
- Each New World Consumer will be given two New World food cards.
- Each Old World Consumer will be given two Old World Food Cards.
- Students will have five minutes to trade their cards.

FOCUS MIDDLE SCHOOL WORLD HISTORY © COUNCIL FOR ECONOMIC EDUCATION, NEW YORK, NY

SLIDE 20.2

Trading in the Old World– New World Market (Round 1)

- New World Consumers may only trade with other New World Consumers. Old World Consumers may only trade with other Old World Consumers.
- If you prefer the cards you were given, you don't have to trade.

FOCUS MIDDLE SCHOOL WORLD HISTORY © COUNCIL FOR ECONOMIC EDUCATION, NEW YORK, NY

SLIDE 20.3

LESSON 20 – THE COLUMBIAN EXCHANGE

Trading in the Old World– New World Market (Round 2)

- Students will have another five minutes to trade their cards.
- You can now trade with anyone in either the New World or Old World.
- If you prefer the cards you were given, you don't have to trade.

SLIDE 20.4

LESSON 20 – THE COLUMBIAN EXCHANGE

Trading in the Old World– New World Market (After Round 2)

- Those with a card that has an "X" on the back have been exposed to disease(s).
- Old World Consumers: You have immunity from the disease(s).
- New World Consumers: You have no immunity—you will perish!

SLIDE 20.5

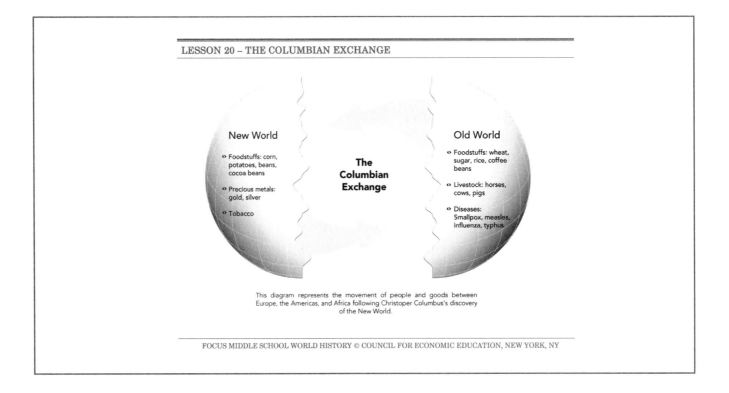

LESSON 20 – THE COLUMBIAN EXCHANGE

New World

- Foodstuffs: corn, potatoes, beans, cocoa beans
- Precious metals: gold, silver
- Tobacco

The Columbian Exchange

Old World

- Foodstuffs: wheat, sugar, rice, coffee beans
- Livestock: horses, cows, pigs
- Diseases: Smallpox, measles, influenza, typhus

This diagram represents the movement of people and goods between Europe, the Americas, and Africa following Christoper Columbus's discovery of the New World.

FOCUS MIDDLE SCHOOL WORLD HISTORY © COUNCIL FOR ECONOMIC EDUCATION, NEW YORK, NY

Lesson 21

Renaissance Banking

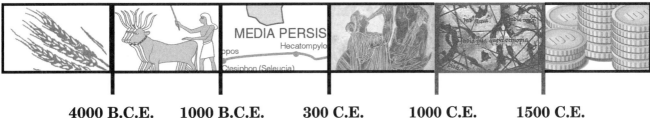

4000 B.C.E.   1000 B.C.E.   300 C.E.   1000 C.E.   1500 C.E.

LESSON 21
RENAISSANCE BANKING

LESSON DESCRIPTION

In this lesson, students learn about the important role that Italian bankers played during the Renaissance. They participate in a role-play activity in which they see how, using bills of exchange, Renaissance era bankers facilitated the transfer of funds over long distances. The students read about the successes and failures of bankers during the Renaissance. The students participate in a role-playing activity using playing cards. During the activity, students take deposits and make loans. The students learn how banks channel money from depositors to borrowers. The students also learn why banks charge higher interest rates for riskier loans.

INTRODUCTION

Throughout the Middle Ages and the Renaissance, the Italian city-states of Florence, Genoa, Pisa, and Venice were the strongest economic powers in Europe. Many traders from these powerful city-states were important traders of spices and other goods. Bankers, particularly those in Florence and Venice, became the most influential financial intermediaries in the western world. The bankers' biggest customer was the Roman Catholic Church, but they also provided banking services to royalty, nobles, and business people throughout Europe. The bankers made it possible for money to get from one place to another over long distances by establishing branches as far apart as England and Cyprus.

In the early 1300s, powerful companies developed in Florence, run by families such as the Bardi, the Peruzzi, and the Acciaiuoli. These large conglomerates participated both in trading and in banking. But just before the plague struck Europe, these companies went out of business. This was due, in part, to bad loans made to kings such as Edward III of England and Robert, King of Naples. These bankers were followed by bankers in the next century who further perfected banking practices.

In 1397, Giovanni di Bacci de'Medici moved to Florence and founded the Medici Bank. The Medici Bank would become the largest and most powerful bank of the 1400s. Members of the Medici family became some of the most influential people in Florence and throughout Europe. Members of the Medici family were important politicians and huge supporters of the arts. The money they made as bankers made it possible for them to become powerful politicians and to pay artists, writers, and builders to create some of the world's greatest art, literature, and buildings.

The Medici bank conducted money changing, deposit taking, dealings in bills of exchange, and foreign banking. Money changers, such as the Medici Bank, converted foreign money into local money and gold coins into silver coins for a fee. After nearly a century of significant successes, the Medici Bank went out of business because of poor management decisions, a significant number of bad loans, and bad conditions for doing business.

While the bankers of the Renaissance plied their trade over half a millennium ago, the basics of deposits, loans, and charges for banking services are similar to the practices of modern bankers. Like the bankers of the Renaissance, today's bankers channel funds from savers to borrowers. In so doing, they provide a valuable service that facilitates economic activity. Teaching students about the bankers of the Renaissance provides an opportunity to also teach students about the basics of how banks operate today.

CONCEPTS

Banking

Deposits

Interest

Loans

OBJECTIVES

Students will be able to:

- Explain why people save money in banks and why other people borrow money from banks.

- Describe the role that banks play in the economy.

- Understand why banks charge more interest on loans that are riskier.

- Explain how banks today differ from those of the Renaissance.

CONTENT STANDARDS

Voluntary National Content Standards in Economics, 2nd edition

- **Standard 10:** Institutions evolve and are created to help individuals and groups accomplish their goals. Banks, labor unions, markets, corporations, legal systems, and not-for-profit organizations are examples of important institutions. A different kind of institution, clearly defined and enforced property rights, is essential to a market economy.

- **Standard 12:** Interest rates, adjusted for inflation, rise and fall to balance the amount saved with the amount borrowed, which affects the allocation of scarce resources between present and future uses.

World History Content Standards

Era 5: Intensified Hemispheric Interactions, 1000–1500 C.E.

- **Standard 2:** The redefining of European society and culture, 1000–1300 C.E.

- **Standard 7:** Major global trends from 1000–1500 C.E.

TIME REQUIRED

60–75 minutes

MATERIALS

- One copy of Activity 21.1, printed on white card stock and cut apart

- One copy of Activities 21.2, 21.3, and 21.4 for each student

- One deck of 52 playing cards for each group of four students

- A pen or pencil for each student

- A calculator for each group of four students

PROCEDURE

1. Introduce the lesson by explaining to the students that they are going to learn about banking and the Renaissance. Ask the students the following:

    a. How would someone from Venice, Italy, pay someone hundreds of miles away in London, England, in the 15th century?

    (Answers will vary, but the students may say that the money would be sent via a courier on horseback or by ship.)

    b. What problems might arise from sending money over many miles via horseback or ship?

    (Answers will vary, but students may say that it's dangerous to transport money over a long distance or that it takes a long time. For example, bandits might attack a courier traveling on horseback and steal the money. A ship could be attacked by pirates or sink and the money could be lost. It might take months to transport gold and silver coins over a long distance.)

2. Tell students that they are going to participate in an activity that shows how banks long ago sent money from place to place over long distances.

3. Ask students to line up across the classroom from corner to corner. Choose two students to represent the two bankers. Choose one end of the line to represent Venice and place one of the bankers at that end of the line. Explain that the

other end of the line represents London and place the other banker at that end of the line. Choose one student to represent the payer and place him or her with the banker at the Venice end of the line. Choose another student to represent the person receiving payment, the payee, in England and place him or her at the London end of the line.

4. Give the 480 and 20 ducats cards from Activity 21.1 to the student playing the part of the payer in Venice. Explain to the students that the payer in Venice wants to pay the payee in London the equivalent of 480 ducats. Have the payer and the payee identify themselves to the class.

5. Explain that in order to facilitate this payment, the payer is going to make use of a banking system. Ask the Venice- and London-based bankers to identify themselves. Explain to students that, because London and Venice are a very long way apart, the Venice-based banker will charge a fee to cover the costs of the transaction. The fee is 20 ducats.

6. Instruct the paying student to present the 480 ducats card to the banker in Venice. Have the paying student instruct the banker to transmit the equivalent of 480 ducats to London for payment to the receiving student. Instruct the paying student to also present the 20 ducats card to the banker in Venice. Emphasize that this card is the 20 ducats fee charged by the banker in Venice to transmit the money to London.

7. Once the banker in Venice has received the 480 and 20 ducats cards, give the Venice banker the bill of exchange card from Activity 21.1 and a pen. Have the banker in Venice complete the bill of exchange with the names of the payer and the payee along with his or her signature. Explain to the class that the bill of exchange will tell the banker in London how much to pay the payee.

8. Once the bill of exchange has been filled in, ask the students how the bill

of exchange could get from Venice to London.

(Answers will vary, but the students will likely identify two methods: the bill of exchange could be passed from one student to another until it reached London or one student could take the bill of exchange all the way from Venice to London.)

9. Explain that the students are to pass the bill of exchange from one to another across the room as a relay until it reaches London. This process represents the way that the Medici passed bills of exchange between their branches across Europe. Invite the students to each take a look at the bill of exchange as it passes across the room. Instruct the banker in Venice to start the bill of exchange on its way to London by passing it to the first student in line on the Venice side of the classroom. Give students time to complete the transmission of the bill of exchange from Venice to London.

10. Once the bill of exchange has reached the last student in line before the London-based banker and the payee, stop the transmission and ask the students the following:

   a. The bill of exchange has reached London. Who should it be delivered to?

   (The banker in London.)

   b. What will the banker in London do with the bill of exchange?

   (Pay the payee the equivalent of 480 ducats in pounds sterling, which is 98 pounds based on the exchange rate implied on the bill of exchange.)

11. Complete the exchange by doing the following:

   • Give the 98 pounds sterling card from Activity 21.1 to the banker in London.

   • Instruct the last student in the line to deliver the bill of exchange to the banker in London.

- Instruct the banker in London to pay the payee using the 98 pound sterling card.

12. Ask the students the following:

    a. Did any money actually travel from Venice to London?

    (No)

    b. How will the two bankers be able to settle up now that the banker in Venice has received the money and the banker in London has paid out the money?

    (Answers will vary, but some students may identify the fact that another transaction from London to Venice may cancel out the one that just took place. In this way, using their record books, the two bankers, hundreds of miles apart, can transfer money between them.)

13. Explain to students that just as money today is not always coin or paper, but is sometimes just an electronic record in their bank account, during the 15th century bankers kept record books and could move money from one place to another using debits and credits in their books.

14. Ask students why it was safer to send the bill of exchange from Venice to London instead of actual money.

    (It was safer to send the bill of exchange from Venice to London because thieves are likely to want to steal money, but they are much less likely to want a bill of exchange.)

15. Have students return to their seats.

16. Distribute one copy of Activity 21.2 to each student. Give the students time to read the activity. Ask students the following:

    a. What services did the bankers of the Renaissance provide?

    (They provided loans to kings, nobles, and business people. Using their branches and a debit/credit system,

they made it possible to send money over long distances. They provided money-changing services.)

    b. Why did the banks of the 1300s go out of business?

    (They had made large loans, particularly to kings of England and Naples, that were not repaid.)

    c. What were the Medici known for in addition to being successful bankers?

    (The Medici became powerful politicians and important patrons of the arts.)

    d. Why were banks not allowed to charge interest?

    (The Roman Catholic Church had declared the charging of interest illegal.)

    e. To whom did pawnbrokers make most of their loans?

    (The poor people of the time)

17. Explain to students that they are now going to work in groups to simulate being bankers during the Renaissance. Divide the class into groups of four students. Instruct the groups to push four desks together to create a work surface, if possible. Distribute one deck of playing cards to each group. Instruct the groups to discard the jokers and divide the remaining 52 cards into two piles:

- Hearts and diamonds

- Spades and clubs

18. Explain the following:

- **Banks** are institutions where some people save money and earn interest, and other people borrow money and pay interest.

- Banks and other financial institutions channel funds from savers to borrowers and investors and make a profit in the process.

- While today's banks provide services to many individuals and businesses, during the Renaissance bankers' primary customers were royalty and nobles from across Europe as well as powerful business people. Ordinary people would not likely have used bankers; they would have used pawnbrokers and money changers.

- Banks today make their money by taking in deposits—money put into a bank account. They may or may not pay interest—money paid regularly, at a particular rate for the use of borrowed money—on those deposits. Unlike during the Renaissance, the charging and paying of interest is not illegal today.

- Banks also make loans—money given to someone on the promise to repay in the future—on which the banks charge interest. The interest banks charge on loans is higher than the interest it pays on deposits. The difference is revenue (profit) for banks.

19. Explain that each student in each group will be a banker. Ask students what each banker needs to do in order to start business.

    (Take in deposits)

20. Distribute one copy of Activity 21.3 to each student. Instruct the groups to shuffle their pile of spades and clubs and place the pile face down. Then, each student is to draw five cards from the top of the spades and clubs pile.

21. Instruct students to record the rank (number or face card or ace) of each of the cards they drew in the CARD DRAWN column of the "Deposits" table at the top of Activity 21.3. Each of the five cards in each student's hand should be recorded on a separate line in the table.

22. Explain to students that for each card they will multiply the rank (number or face) of the card times 10 to get the amount of the deposit represented by the card. Face cards and aces are 10.

(For example, a 7 of spades would be worth $7 \times 10 = 70$; an ace of clubs would be worth $10 \times 10 = 100$.)

23. Instruct the students to enter the value of each of their cards in the first blank of the equation shown in each line of the CALCULATE CARD VALUE column of the "Deposits" table.

24. Distribute one calculator to each group. Instruct the students to complete the multiplication on each line of the "Deposits" table to get the value of each card in ducats. When they have calculated the value of all five cards in their hand, instruct them to add the value of the five cards in order to get a total amount deposited in their bank and enter the value in the table. The students should enter this value on the second page of Activity 21.3.

25. Ask the students the following questions:

    a. Why do people today deposit money in a bank?

       (Answers will vary, but the students are likely to say for safekeeping, to save for the future, to earn interest, and to write checks on.)

    b. What are banks likely to do with the money that they receive in deposits?

       (Answers will vary, but the students are likely to say make loans.)

    c. Why do people today want to take out loans?

       (Answers will vary, but the students are likely to say to buy a house, to go to college, to buy a car, and to start a business. People take out loans to get something now and pay for it later.)

26. Distribute one copy of Activity 21.4 to each student. Explain the following:

    - Activity 21.4 provides details on each of the loans they can make. For each of the loans, the borrower, the loan description, the loan amount, and the loan amount plus interest that will be repaid to them (if all goes well) is listed.

- With any loan, whether made today or during the Renaissance, there is always the risk that the borrower will default—not repay the loan. Each of the loans in the list on the activity has a different risk of default.

- Each student will select between one and four loans to make. They must make at least one loan and cannot make more than four loans. Once they have made their loans, they will draw a card from the pile of hearts and diamonds to determine how the loan performed.

- The table in the middle of Activity 21.4 shows how the different loans, based on their riskiness and the card drawn, will perform.

- The riskier the loan, the greater the chance that the loan will not be repaid or that only the loan principle will be repaid.

- Higher risk loans, if fully repaid with interest, provide a higher return. The borrower is required to pay more interest to compensate for the fact that they are a riskier borrower.

- The student(s) with the most money after making loans and getting the loan results, will be the proclaimed the winner of the activity.

27. Ask students the following questions:

a. Do you have enough money in your bank to make four loans?

(Answers will vary. Some students will have enough; others will not.)

b. Why is knowing the riskiness of a loan important to a banker?

(More risky loans are less likely to be repaid. Less risky loans are more likely to be repaid.)

c. What will happen to the bank if it makes a loan and it doesn't get repaid?

(The bank will be out the money it loaned, but it will still owe the depositors.)

d. Should you loan out all of the money that you took in as deposits? *(No)* Why not? *(If you loan out all of the money that you took in as deposits, there will be no money left in the bank to pay out if one of the depositors comes in to take out money.)*

28. Instruct students to decide which loans they want to make. Emphasize that they cannot loan out more than the total amount of their deposits. They should keep in mind that not all of their loans may be repaid in full and their goal is to have made a profit by the end of the game. They should consider the amount of the loan, its risk, and the amount they are likely to be repaid when deciding which loans to make. Each student must make at least one loan.

29. Once students have decided which loans they are going to make, have them enter each loan on a separate line of the table at the bottom of Activity 21.3. For each loan, they should enter the loan number, the risk level (VL, L, H, or VH), and the loan amount. Have each student add up the value of all of the loans he or she made and enter the value in the blank following "2. Total Amount of Loans Made" on the second page of Activity 21.3.

30. Ask the students the following questions:

a. Did anyone make only one loan?

(Answers will vary.) **Why?** *(Answers will vary, but the students may say that they didn't have enough money in deposits to make more than one loan.)*

b. Did anyone make only very low risk loans? *(Answers will vary.)* **Why?** *(Answers will vary, but the students* *may say that they didn't want to take a chance on making the higher risk loans despite the possibility of a higher return on those loans if they draw a good result card.)*

c. Did anyone make all very high risk loans? *(Answers will vary.)* Why? *(Answers will vary, but the students may say that they were willing to take on the higher risk in hopes of getting a higher return than with lower risk loans.)*

31. Explain the following to the students:

- In real life, a number of factors would determine whether or not a loan would actually be repaid. These factors include the borrower's willingness and ability to repay the loan. If a borrower's income drops significantly after taking out a loan, they may not be able to repay it or may only repay part of it.

- In real life, the repayment of the each of the loans they have made would depend on the actual behavior of the borrower. In this activity, the repayment of the loans and the amount of interest earned will be determined by drawing cards from the pile of hearts and diamonds.

- Due to the usury laws at the time, the Medici and other Renaissance bankers would not have charged interest, but for the sake of this activity, we are going to use the modern practice of loans being repaid with interest.

32. Instruct the groups to shuffle their pile of hearts and diamonds and place the pile face down. Each student is to draw one card from the top of the hearts and diamonds pile and record the rank of this card in the RESULT CARD DRAWN column for the first loan in their table. Instruct the students to use the information shown in the middle table and the repayment information on Activity 21.4 to determine the result for the loan. Instruct them to record

the result (either 0, the amount of the loan, or the amount of the loan repaid plus any interest) in the OUTCOME column of the table. Instruct the students to continue to draw cards from the hearts and diamonds pile until they have gotten the results for each of their loans.

33. Instruct the students to add the amount of loans repaid and any interest and enter the amount after the statement "3. Total Amount of Loans Repaid Plus Interest" beneath the "Loans" table. Instruct the students to compare the amount of loans they made with the amount of loans repaid plus interest to determine whether they gained or lost as a result of making these loans. Have them circle either GAIN or LOSE after Question 4. Instruct students to determine the amount they gained or lost and enter it after the statement "5. By how much did you gain or lose?"

34. Ask the students the following questions:

a. How many of you gained by making loans?

   (Answers will vary.)

b. How many of you lost money by making loans?

   (Answers will vary.)

c. If you lost money and you continue to lose money in future periods, what will happen to your bank?

   (Answers will vary, but the students will likely identify that if a bank continues to make bad loans, it will eventually be forced out of business.)

d. If you lost money by making loans in this round, how might you change the way you make loan decisions going forward?

   (Answers will vary, but the students may say that they will try to make smaller or fewer loans or try to make less risky loans.)

e. Did some of your loans that were considered less risky not get repaid?

(Answers will vary.)

Why might that happen in real life?

(A borrower who appeared to be less risky when the loan was actually made might run into trouble with his business or personal life before the loan actually has to be repaid.)

f. What eventually happened to the banks during the Renaissance?

(They were forced to close.)

g. Why were the banks during the Renaissance forced to close?

(They made a lot of loans that weren't repaid. They did not maintain the best business practices.)

h. Were there any loans that seemed like bad deals for the bank?

(Loan 14 was a very high-risk loan, but it paid very little interest. This kind of loan would be a bad choice that could get banks in trouble.)

35. Emphasize to students that the banks were profitable over most of their lifetimes, but the profits were distributed to their owners (shareholders) as they were earned. Eventually, they ran into bad periods and went bankrupt.

36. Ask students what advice, based on their experiences during the deposit and loan activity, they would give the bankers of the Renaissance period.

(Answers will vary, but the students will likely say that the bankers should make sure that they don't loan out too much of their deposits and that the bankers should only make loans to people who they expect to repay their loans.)

CLOSURE

37. Review the important points taught in the lesson by discussing the following:

a. Why do people save money in banks?

(To earn interest and for safekeeping)

b. Why do people borrow money from banks?

(To buy a new house, to start a business, to go to college, to buy a car)

c. What is the most important role that banks play in the economy?

(Banks channel funds from savers to borrowers.)

d. How do banks today differ from those of the Renaissance?

(Banks today provide their services to all kinds of people, not just the rich and powerful. Banks today can pay interest and charge interest without interference from a powerful church. Banks today make extensive use of technology for record-keeping and to speed up transactions.)

ASSESSMENT

Multiple Choice

1. Which of the following is *NOT* an important function of banks?

   a. Accepting deposits

   b. **Printing money**

   c. Making loans

   d. Making it possible for one person to pay another over long distances

2. Which of the following statements about banks today and banks during the Renaissance is correct?

   a. Banks today accept deposits, but banks during the Renaissance only made loans.

   b. Banks today pay interest on deposits and charge interest on loans, but banks during the Renaissance paid interest on both deposits and loans.

   c. **Banks today pay interest on deposits and charge interest on loans, but banks during the Renaissance were not allowed** to pay interest on deposits or charge interest on loans.

d. Banks today make loans, take in deposits, and pay interest, but banks during the Renaissance only stored valuables for people until they could come back to pick them up.

3. A banker today is trying to decide whether to loan money to a business. The banker believes the business is risky and that the loan may not be repaid. What should the banker do?

a. Charge a low rate of interest to help the business succeed.

b. **Charge a high rate of interest to compensate for the higher risk.**

c. Refuse to make the loan under any circumstances because the loan is risky.

d. Make the loan, but do not charge interest since this would be usury in today's world.

Constructed Response

1. Ask students to write a letter to the Medici Bank. The letter will be sent through a time machine back to the Renaissance. In the letter, the students should explain how the Medici should conduct their business in order to make sure that their bank survives. The students should also explain how banks in the 21st century differ from those in the 15th century. *(Answers should warn the Medici about making bad loans as well as give an explanation about the 21st century banking system.)*

CONNECTIONS: BANKING IN AMERICAN HISTORY

From nearly the first days of the new nation, banks have played a pivotal role in commerce in the United States. The first Bank of the United States, founded in 1791 on Alexander Hamilton's recommendation, provides an excellent study in both early banking practice and civics. The Federal Reserve Bank of Philadelphia's essay "The First Bank of the United States: A Chapter in the History of Central Banking" provides an excellent overview of the debate between Hamilton and Jefferson over the founding of the bank, the bank's operations, and the vote in Congress to close the bank in 1811.[1]

The Great Depression was the most significantly economic challenge to the American people and the nation's banking system in the 20th century. The period resulted in significant changes in the supervision and regulation of banks as well as the way banks conducted their business. The Federal Reserve Bank of St. Louis has produced a set of active-learning lessons as well as online resources for teaching about the Great Depression.[2]

[1] Federal Reserve Bank of Philadelphia. 2009. "The First Bank of the United States: A Chapter in Central Banking History", http://www.philadelphiafed.org/publications/economic-education/first-bank.pdf. The essay is accompanied by an active-learning lesson, which is highly adaptable to the middle grades. See also Andrew Hill, "A Lesson to Accompany 'The First Bank of the United States: A Chapter in Central Banking History'" (Federal Reserve Bank of Philadelphia), http://www.philadelphiafed.org/education/teachers/lesson-plans/first-bank.pdf.

[2] Federal Reserve Bank of St. Louis. 2007. "The Great Depression Curriculum," http://stlouisfed.org/greatdepression/default.html

ACTIVITY 21.1

Venice to London Cards

480 Ducats	**20 Ducats**
98 Pounds Sterling	

TO: Bank Branch in London

Please pay _____ **the equivalent of 480**
        (Payee's Name Goes Here)

Ducats (98 Pounds Sterling) from _____.
                                            (Payer's Name Goes Here)

                            Signed: _____
                                    (Venice Banker Signs Here)
                                    Branch Manager in Venice

ACTIVITY 21.2

Banking in the Italian City-States

Throughout the Middle Ages and the Renaissance, the Italian city-states of Florence, Genoa, Pisa, and Venice were the strongest economic powers in Europe. Italy had not yet become one country. Instead, the area was made up of a number of separate countries centered around important cities. Many traders from these cities were important traders of spices, cloth, and other goods.

During this time, bankers in these city-states (in particular, Florence and Venice) were also very powerful. The bankers' biggest customer was the Roman Catholic Church. Banks also provided services to kings, nobles, and business people throughout Europe. The bankers made it possible for money to get from one place to another because they had branch banks located in countries as far as way as England and Cyprus.

In the early 1300s, a number of powerful companies developed in Florence. These partnerships centered on families with names like Bardi, Peruzzi, and Acciaiuoli and participated both in trading and in banking. They had many branches located throughout Europe. These companies went out of business just before the plague struck Europe. These companies were driven out of business primarily because they had made too many loans to kings, such as Edward III of England and Robert, King of Naples, that weren't repaid in full.

THE MEDICI BANK

In 1397, Giovanni di Bacci de'Medici moved to Florence and founded the Medici Bank. The Medici Bank became the largest and most powerful bank of the 1400s, and members of the Medici family became some of the most wealthy and influential people in Florence and throughout Europe. Members of the Medici family were important politicians and huge supporters of the arts. They paid artists, writers, and builders to create some of the world's greatest art, literature, and buildings.

The Medici bank conducted money changing, took in deposits, dealt in bills of exchange, and carried out foreign banking transactions. Money changers, such as the Medici Bank, converted foreign money into the local money and converted gold coins into silver coins for a fee.

ACTIVITY 21.2, CONTINUED

The Medici Bank went out of business because of bad management decisions during a period of bad business conditions in the general economy. In the second half of the 1400s, the Medici Bank struggled to coordinate the operations of its branches throughout Europe, and during a period of economic decline in the 1470s, it became increasingly difficult to do business. Throughout this period, many of its branches, including those in London and Bruges, went out of business. Back in Florence, members of the Medici family concentrated most of their attention on politics. Unfortunately, they were not careful enough in managing the operations of the bank. The bank made a lot of bad loans, which eventually caused the bank to go out of business in the 1490s.

INTEREST IN THE RENAISSANCE

The Roman Catholic Church forbade anyone from charging interest, which the church called usury. When people talk about usury today, they are talking about a very high interest rate. During the Renaissance, though, usury meant charging *any* interest at all. Since bankers were not able to charge interest, they had to find other ways to make a profit from lending. The primary way that Renaissance bankers such as the Medici got around the rules against charging interest was to use bills of exchange, like the one used at the beginning of the lesson. Built into the bill of exchange transaction would be a profit for the banker. These profits on transactions using bills of exchange were not considered usury.

Bankers such as the Medici were respected citizens, well regarded by the Roman Catholic Church. The Medici were not considered usurers. In contrast, pawnbrokers were business people who lent money to individuals in exchange for holding onto those individuals' belongings. Pawnbrokers were considered usurers, and they were not considered respectable citizens. The church banned pawnbrokers from communion, marrying in a church, and holding church funerals. Because bankers such as the Medici only made large loans to important and wealthy people such as kings, nobles, and business people, the pawnbrokers played a role in the Renaissance economy by allowing poor people to borrow money. Without pawnbrokers and some other money lenders that did business with the poor, the poor would not have been able to borrow money.

SOURCE

DeRoover, Raymond. 1963. *The Rise and Decline of the Medici Bank, 1397–1494.* Cambridge, MA: Harvard University Press.

ACTIVITY 21.3

Deposits and Loans Worksheet

Deposits

	CARD DRAWN (circle one)	CALCULATE CARD VALUE
#1	2 3 4 5 6 7 8 9 10 J Q K A	_____ × 10 = _____ ducats
#2	2 3 4 5 6 7 8 9 10 J Q K A	_____ × 10 = _____ ducats
#3	2 3 4 5 6 7 8 9 10 J Q K A	_____ × 10 = _____ ducats
#4	2 3 4 5 6 7 8 9 10 J Q K A	_____ × 10 = _____ ducats
#5	2 3 4 5 6 7 8 9 10 J Q K A	_____ × 10 = _____ ducats
	TOTAL DEPOSITS =	_____ ducats

Loans

Loans have different risks. The loans will pay according to the following table:

Risk Level	Loan pays NOTHING if card drawn is	ONLY the loan amount is repaid if card drawn is	Loan amount plus interest is repaid if card drawn is
Very Low	2	3	4 to A
Low	2, 3	4	5 to A
High	2, 3, 4	5	6 to A
Very High	2, 3, 4, 5	6	7 to A

Activity 21.3, continued

Loan # Chosen	RISK LEVEL	LOAN AMOUNT	RESULT CARD DRAWN (circle one)	OUTCOME
		_____ ducats	2 3 4 5 6 7 8 9 10 J Q K A	_____ ducats
		_____ ducats	2 3 4 5 6 7 8 9 10 J Q K A	_____ ducats
		_____ ducats	2 3 4 5 6 7 8 9 10 J Q K A	_____ ducats
		_____ ducats	2 3 4 5 6 7 8 9 10 J Q K A	_____ ducats

1. **Total amount of deposits:** _____ ducats

2. **Total amount of loans made:** _____ ducats

3. **Total amount of loans repaid plus interest:** _____ ducats

4. **Did you gain or lose as a result of making these loans?** (*circle one*)
Gain   Lose

5. **By how much did you gain or lose?** _____ ducats

ACTIVITY 21.4

Loan Specifics

LOAN #	BORROWER AND LOAN DESCRIPTION	LOAN AMOUNT	RISK OF DEFAULT	LOAN AMOUNT PLUS INTEREST
1	A Venetian merchant, to expand his very profitable textile business	140 ducats	Very Low Risk (VL)	182 ducats
2	A French bishop, to improve his cathedral's chapter house	190 ducats	Very Low Risk (VL)	247 ducats
3	The Pope, to finance a small mission to the eastern Mediterranean	270 ducats	Very Low Risk (VL)	351 ducats
4	The doge, for repairs to the wall coverings in the library of his palace	70 ducats	Very Low Risk (VL)	91 ducats
5	A French Duke, for the expansion of his manor house	300 ducats	Low Risk (L)	450 ducats
6	The Duke of Milan, for the equipping of new soldiers	220 ducats	Low Risk (L)	330 ducats
7	A Benedictine abbot, to expand his monastery's school in Sicily	110 ducats	Low Risk (L)	165 ducats
8	A successful Venetian printer, to purchase a new set of moveable type	94 ducats	Low Risk (L)	141 ducats
9	A Florentine shopkeeper, to double the size of his shop	125 ducats	High Risk (H)	225 ducats
10	An English earl interested in throwing an extravagant wedding for his son	275 ducats	High Risk (H)	495 ducats
11	A Hungarian feudal lord, to purchase farming tools for use in wheat production on his estate	60 ducats	High Risk (H)	108 ducats

Continued on next page.

ACTIVITY **21.4,** CONTINUED

LOAN #	BORROWER AND LOAN DESCRIPTION	LOAN AMOUNT	RISK OF DEFAULT	LOAN AMOUNT PLUS INTEREST
12	A Venetian spice merchant, to purchase a shipment of peppercorns and cinnamon from the Spice Islands	155 ducats	High Risk (H)	279 ducats
13	A Venetian merchant, to improve the decoration of the chapel in his palace	283 ducats	Very High Risk (VH)	622 ducats
14	A Sicilian sculptor, to create a new public statue in honor of a church martyr	58 ducats	Very High Risk (VH)	60 ducats
15	A Dutch sea captain, for personal supplies for a voyage to the Spice Islands	137 ducats	Very High Risk (VH)	301 ducats
16	A small-scale grape grower in Tuscany for the purchase of an adjoining plot of land	119 ducats	Very High Risk (VH)	262 ducats

GLOSSARY

abbot: The leader of a monastery.

chapter house: A building attached to or near a church where priests meet.

doge: The title given to the leaders of Venice and Genoa. Doges were elected for life by the city-states' aristocracies.

martyr: A person who chooses to die rather than go against his or her religious principles.

Spice Islands: A group of islands in modern eastern Indonesia rich in spices, such as peppercorns and cinnamon, and controlled by the Dutch from the 17th century onward.

LESSON 22

MERCANTILISTS AND THE MIDAS TOUCH

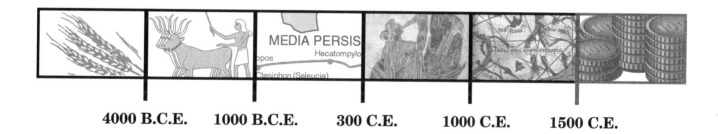

4000 B.C.E.   1000 B.C.E.   300 C.E.   1000 C.E.   1500 C.E.

LESSON 22
MERCANTILISTS AND THE MIDAS TOUCH

LESSON DESCRIPTION

The lesson begins with a reading, *Mercantilism—Show Me the Gold!,* which provides students with an understanding of the basic tenets of mercantilism. The impact of exports and imports on a nation's holdings of gold is discussed. A second reading, *The Golden Touch: Was King Midas a Mercantilist?,* tells the story of King Midas, who believed that being able to turn everything he touched into gold would make him the happiest man on earth. After he is granted his wish, he finds that the golden touch is a curse, rather than a blessing. The lesson asks students to compare the beliefs of the mercantilists with those of King Midas.

INTRODUCTION

Mercantilism was the dominant economic and political theory in Europe from the late 16th to the late 18th century. Mercantilism developed when isolated feudal states were replaced by centralized nation-states. As nations and urban centers grew, the volume of international **trade**[1] also grew rapidly. Mercantilist theory is based on the belief that the total volume of international trade is fixed and unchangeable; therefore, one nation's exports can only be at the expense of some other nation's exports. Another mercantilist belief is that a nation's wealth is measured by its holdings of precious metals—gold and silver—which were used as domestic and international money. Mercantilists believed a nation could increase its supply of precious metals and become wealthier by maintaining a positive **balance of trade**[2] with other nations (the

value of its **exports**[3] would exceed the value of its **imports**[4]) and establishing colonies that would be new sources of gold and silver. Mercantilist theory led to mercantilist trade policies: encouraging exports and discouraging imports. These policies led to trade wars and, in some cases, military conflicts because not all nations were able to maintain a positive trade balance at the same time.

CONCEPTS

Balance of trade

Exports

Imports

Scarcity

Trade

OBJECTIVES

Student will be able to:

- Identify the characteristics of mercantilism.

- Explain that mercantilist governments taxed foreign trade to raise the revenue they needed to build armies and navies and to buy other goods and services.

- Understand why mercantilists believed that exports of goods and services made their nations wealthier, while imports of goods and services made nations less wealthy.

- Know why economists believe that mercantilism's definition of the wealth of a nation and some of its beliefs concerning the value of international trade are false.

---

[1] Trade is the exchange of goods and services for money or other goods and services.
[2] The balance of trade is that part of a nation's balance of payments accounts that deals only with its imports and exports of goods and services. The balance of trade is divided into the balance on goods (merchandise) and the balance on services. If the value of a country's exports of goods and services is greater than its imports, it has a balance of trade

surplus. If the value of a country's imports of goods and services is greater than its exports, it has a balance of trade deficit.
[3] Exports are goods and services produced in one nation and sold in other nations.
[4] Imports are goods and services bought from sellers in another nation.

CONTENT STANDARDS

Voluntary Content Standards in Economics, 2nd edition

- **Standard 5:** Voluntary exchange occurs only when all participating parties expect to gain. This is true for trade among individuals or organizations within a nation, and among individuals or organizations in different nations.

- **Standard 16:** There is an economic role for government in a market economy whenever the benefits of a government policy outweigh its costs. Governments often provide for national defense, address environmental concerns, define and protect property rights, and attempt to make markets more competitive. Most government policies also have direct or indirect effects on people's incomes.

World History Content Standards

World History Era 6. The Emergence of the First Golden Age, 1450–1770.

- **Standard 2:** How European society experienced political, economic, and cultural transformations in an age of global intercommunication, 1450–1750.

TIME REQUIRED

90 minutes. Procedures 1–3, 45 minutes on the first day. Procedures 4–5, 45 minutes on the second day.

MATERIALS

- A copy for each student of Activities 22.1 and 22.2

- Slides 22.1–22.2

PROCEDURE

1. Begin the lesson by distributing a copy of Activity 22.1 to each student. The activity describes the basic tenets of mercantilism, a philosophy of government popular among leaders of the nations of Europe between 1500 and 1750 C.E. Tell the students to read Activity 22.1, and ask them the following questions:

a. During the Age of Mercantilism, between the 16th and 18th centuries, why did Europeans want gold?

(During this era many people believed that a strong government was needed for their society to advance. A powerful army and navy were considered necessary to protect the nation in time of war. Gold was used as domestic and international money and to pay for a strong military. Monarchs used gold to buy goods and services to support their lavish lifestyles.)

b. Why did European nations use taxes on international trade, rather than other taxes, to raise revenue?

(By 1500, international trade was growing rapidly. Taxing international trade raised revenue without the more visible negative effects of domestic taxes. European governments established companies that were given rights to trade with their overseas colonies. In exchange for these privileges, the companies were willing to pay taxes to their governments.)

c. How did nations increase the amount of gold they owned?

(Governments encouraged people to export goods and services to other countries and discouraged people from importing goods and services from other countries. Exports had to be paid for with gold. If the value of a nation's exports exceeded the value of its imports, its supply of gold would increase.)

d. What did mercantilist nations give up when they held on to their gold, rather than spend it?

(They gave up the opportunity to buy goods and services from other countries that could have been purchased at lower prices than those charged by domestic producers. Some of these goods could have been of better quality than similar goods produced by domestic producers.)

2. Ask students to define exports and imports.

   (Exports are goods and services produced in one nation and sold in other nations. Imports are goods and services bought from sellers in another nation.)

3. Show Slide 22.1, which uses arrows to show how the export of wheat (worth 400 gold coins) from Spain to England resulted in a payment of gold from England to Spain. Show Slide 22.2. Ask students to describe how arrows could be used to show how an import of cloth (worth 300 gold coins) from England by Spanish traders would result in a payment of gold from Spain to England.

   (Arrows would point counterclockwise from England to Spain in the top half of Slide 22.2. Arrows would point counterclockwise from Spain to England in the bottom half of Slide 22.2.)

4. Ask the students the following questions:

   a. After the two trades of wheat and cloth, which country exported more than it imported? By how much?

      (Spain. 100 gold coins worth, because Spain exported wheat worth 400 gold coins and imported cloth worth only 300 gold coins.)

   b. Which country had an inflow of gold?

      (Spain ends up with an inflow of 100 gold coins.)

5. Distribute copies of Activity 22.2 to each student, and tell the students to read the story of King Midas. Alternatively, you can read Activity 22.2 to the class. Note: The reading is excerpted from the story, which can also be found at http://www.ibiblio.org/eldritch/nh/wb2b.html or http://www.archive.org/stream/goldentouchtoldt00hawt#page/n35/mode/2up. The entire story is about 6,000 words at a 7th grade reading level, and may be assigned as homework before Activity 22.2.

6. Ask students for their opinion of King Midas before he is given "the golden touch."

   (Answers will vary. Students are likely to believe that Midas was greedy, lonely, foolish, etc., because of his obsession with gold.)

7. At the end of Activity 22.2, ask the following questions:

   a. Why did King Midas want gold?

      (Answers will vary. Midas was happy when he was counting his gold. He wanted more gold, but we don't know why. We know only that "The very tiptop of enjoyment would never be reached, unless the whole world were to become his treasure-room, and be filled with yellow metal which should be all his own. . . .")

   b. Why did King Midas want the golden touch?

      (Despite owning lots of gold, Midas was not satisfied. He says: "I am weary of collecting my treasures with so much trouble, and beholding the heap so diminutive, after I have done my best." The golden touch allowed Midas to increase the amount of gold he owned without having to work for it.)

   c. What did King Midas give up when he was given the golden touch?

      (Answers will vary. At first, Midas is pleased that he can turn objects into gold, but changes his mind after his touch turns food, water, flowers, and even his daughter into gold.)

   d. How were the mercantilists like King Midas?

      (Both mercantilists and King Midas believed that their wealth was equal to their holdings of gold. Only obtaining more gold would make them wealthier.)

   e. How were the mercantilists different from King Midas?

(Midas received pleasure from accumulating and counting the gold he had. Midas was happy when he was alone, counting his gold in "a dark and dreary apartment . . . at the basement of his palace." Midas wanted gold for its own sake rather than to buy goods and services with it. Mercantilists sought to increase their nations' supplies of gold in order to spend them. Mercantilist rulers used gold to build their military forces and spend lavishly on themselves and their courts.)

f. **Why did King Midas want to give up his golden touch?**

*(When Midas was able to turn everything he touched into gold, gold was no longer scarce. **Scarcity** is the condition that exists because human wants exceed the capacity of available resources to satisfy those wants. When gold was not scarce, Midas realized he didn't want any more and that he needed more than gold to live happily.)*

g. **Why do you suppose mercantilist ideas about gold were eventually given up?**

(Responses will vary. After several responses are given, tell the students that most economists now believe that mercantilist policies were based on a false assumption: The wealth of a nation is measured by its supply of precious metals. While accumulating gold may help pay for wars, gold becomes less important in a more peaceful world. Today, most economists believe that per capita income is a better measure of the standard of living, or well-being of a nation. Income is used by people to buy goods and services.

Also, economists today do not believe that the total amount of world trade is fixed, another assumption made by mercantilists. The competition for exports among nations contributed to a number

of wars that occurred during the Age of Mercantilism. Economists believe that international trade benefits those who import, as well as those who export, goods and services. Mercantilists believed that international trade only benefited nations when they exported. Despite these criticisms, mercantilist policies helped to create strong national governments in Europe that may have provided more political stability and economic prosperity than existed during the earlier period of feudalism.)

CLOSURE

8. Summarize the following points:

- Mercantilism refers to policies and laws that were adopted by many European nations between the 16th and 18th centuries.

- Mercantilists believed a strong government was necessary for their society to advance.

- Mercantilists believed that the wealth of a nation was measured by its holdings of precious metals, especially gold.

- Mercantilists believed that the total volume of international trade was fixed, and that exports made a nation wealthier while making its trading partners less wealthy because exports were paid for with gold.

- Mercantilist policies helped to create strong national governments in Europe that may have provided more political stability and economic prosperity than existed during the earlier period of feudalism. However, economists today believe that a nation's wealth is not measured by its holdings of precious metals. Economists also believe that international trade benefits those who import, as well as those who export, goods and services, and that the total volume of trade is not fixed.

ASSESSMENT

Multiple Choice

1. Which of the following taxes was commonly used to raise government revenue during the Age of Mercantilism?

   a. Taxes on the working class

   b. Taxes on land

   c. Income taxes

   d. **Taxes on international trade**

2. Today most economists believe that mercantilism was based on false assumptions. One of these false assumptions is that

   a. a country benefits from both exports and imports. Today economists believe that a country benefits from exports but not imports.

   b. **the wealth of a nation is measured by its supplies of gold and other precious metals.**

   c. the total amount of world trade is unlimited. Economists today believe that the total amount of world trade is fixed.

   d. gold should be used to buy goods and services from other countries.

Constructed Response

1. Explain how imports of goods and services provide benefits to consumers.

   (People import goods and services that have lower prices, or higher quality, than similar goods and services sold by domestic producers. People also buy imports of goods that are not produced domestically; for example, bananas and coffee in the U.S. Imports of services include payments related to tourism; for example, traveling to France or India results in the import of services.)

CONNECTION: MERCANTILISM TODAY

   The period of mercantilism ended around 1750, but today some people accept some mercantilist beliefs. For example, many people believe that a nation benefits when it exports goods and services but not when it imports goods and services. Imports are often seen to harm domestic workers and businesses that compete with imports. In fact, some domestic sales and jobs are lost when, for example, U.S. citizens buy imported goods made in China or India. But the firms that sell these imports receive dollars that they will use to buy other goods and services (or, in some cases, stocks and bonds) from the United States. These expenditures increase sales and employment in the United States, but the sales and jobs lost from imports are usually easier to identify than the sales and jobs gained from exports in other industries. It is true that, *on the whole,* a country is better off when it engages in international trade, although individuals in the country may be harmed.

ACTIVITY 22.1

Mercantilism – Show Me the Gold![1]

Mercantilism refers to policies and laws that were adopted by many nations of Europe between the 16th and 18th centuries.[2] Mercantilists were people who accepted mercantilism's policies and laws. They believed a strong government was necessary for their society to advance.

An important reason for a strong government was to build a strong army and navy. Wars between the nations of Europe had become more frequent. The monarchs of these nations expected their lifestyles to reflect the important role they played, so they spent lavishly on themselves and their courts.

The problem with wars and large courts is that both require large amounts of money—gold being a common means of payment. Before 1500, monarchs and their governments could tax working-class peasants to pay their bills. Peasants were not politically powerful and did little to resist. This changed in the 14th century when violent peasant revolts erupted in England, France, and other nations. Taxes on land were not popular among wealthy landowners either. A new source of tax revenue had to be found.

Luckily for the monarchs, a new source of revenue emerged. By 1500, international trade was growing rapidly. Trade would grow even more because of the exploration and colonization that followed the voyages of Christopher Columbus to the New World and Vasco da Gama to India. Duties (taxes) on foreign trade went directly to the monarch's treasury. Taxing overseas trade raised revenue without the more visible negative effects of domestic taxes. European governments established companies that were given rights to trade with overseas colonies. For these privileges the companies were willing to pay taxes to their governments.

Mercantilists believed that their governments should promote their own exports (goods and services produced in one nation and sold in other nations) but discourage imports (goods and services bought from sellers in another nation). If Spain exported wheat to England, England would pay for the wheat with some of its gold. Spain would try to hold onto the gold and not spend it on imported goods from England.

[1] Sources: John J. McCusker, "British Mercantilist Policies and the American Colonies," in *The Cambridge History of the United States: The Colonial Era*. Eds. Stanley L. Engerman and Robert E. Gallman. Cambridge University Press, 1996; Laura LaHaye, "Mercantilism," *The Concise Encyclopedia of Economics*. http://www.econlib.org/library/Enc/Mercantilism.html
[2] The period from about 1500 to 1750 C.E. is called the "Age of Mercantilism."

ACTIVITY 22.1, CONTINUED

In the mind of a mercantilist, the transaction provided a double benefit for Spain. Spain would have more gold to wage war or support its courts while England would have less. Mercantilists believed that the total amount of trade and gold in the world was fixed. For them, international trade always resulted in one nation gaining at the expense of another nation. During the Age of Mercantilism, the nations of Europe were always preparing for wars with other nations. Trading for another nation's gold would make the importing nation weaker while making the exporting nation stronger.

QUESTIONS:

1. During the Age of Mercantilism between the 16th and 18th centuries, why did European nations want gold?

2. Why did European nations use taxes on international trade, rather than other taxes, to raise revenue?

3. How did nations increase the amount of gold they owned?

4. What did mercantilist nations give up when they held on to their gold, rather than spend it?

ACTIVITY 22.2

The Golden Touch: Was King Midas a Mercantilist?

In 1851, American writer Nathaniel Hawthorne wrote a book of stories based on several classical myths. The result, *A Wonder-Book for Girls and Boys*, was published in 1852.[1] In retelling these stories, Hawthorne stressed the moral lessons they offered to young people. One of the stories was "The Golden Touch," which told the tale of King Midas, a man rich in gold, but not satisfied with the amount of gold he owned.

> *ONCE upon a time, there lived a very rich man, and a king besides, whose name was Midas. . . . This King Midas was fonder of gold than of anything else in the world. . . . If he loved anything better . . . it was the one little maiden who played so merrily around her father's footstool. But the more Midas loved his daughter, the more did he desire and seek for wealth. . . .*
>
> *Midas . . . made it his custom, therefore, to pass a large portion of every day in a dark and dreary apartment . . . at the basement of his palace. It was here that he kept his wealth. . . . Here, after carefully locking the door, he would take a bag of gold coins. . . . And then would he reckon over the coins in the bag . . . and whisper to himself, "O Midas, rich King Midas, what a happy man art thou!". . .*
>
> *Midas called himself a happy man, but felt that he was not yet quite so happy as he might be. The very tiptop of enjoyment would never be reached, unless the whole world were to become his treasure-room and be filled with yellow metal which should be all his own. . .*
>
> *Midas was . . . in his treasure-room one day . . . [when] what should he behold but the figure of a stranger. . . ."You are a wealthy man, friend Midas!" he observed. "I doubt whether any other four walls on earth, contain so much gold as you have contrived to pile up in this room."*
>
> *"I have done pretty well, pretty well," answered Midas, in a discontented tone. "But, after all, it is but a trifle, when you consider that it has taken me my whole life to get it together. . . .*
>
> *"What!" exclaimed the stranger. "Then you are not satisfied?"*
>
> *Midas shook his head.*

---

[1] Source: Nathaniel Hawthorne, "The Golden Touch" in *The Wonder-Book for Girls and Boys*. 1852. http://www.ibiblio.org/eldritch/nh/wb2b.html or another illustrated version at http://www.archive.org/stream/goldentouchtoldt00hawt#page/n35/mode/2up

ACTIVITY 22.2, CONTINUED

"And pray what would satisfy you?" asked the stranger.

"It is only this," replied Midas. "I am weary of collecting my treasures with so much trouble, and beholding the heap so diminutive, after I have done my best. I wish everything that I touch to be changed to gold!"

The stranger magically grants King Midas his wish; at first the king is thrilled to have "the golden touch." But he soon realizes that beautiful flowers, food, and even his young daughter are turned to gold with his touch. By the time the mysterious stranger returns, Midas believes the golden touch is a curse. Midas begs the stranger to free him from the golden touch. After his new wish is granted, the king's flowers, food, and his daughter are restored. King Midas has learned his lesson: He no longer believes that the best things in life are made of gold.

When we first meet King Midas, he believes that gold is the true source of wealth, just like mercantilists did. But in the end, Midas realizes that more gold does not make him happy. The "golden" ideas of mercantilists also faded as countries focused on trading for goods they desire as opposed to hoarding gold for war and lavish royal lifestyles.

QUESTIONS:

1. Why did King Midas want gold?

2. Why did King Midas want the golden touch?

3. What did King Midas give up when he was given the golden touch?

4. How were the mercantilists like King Midas?

5. How were the mercantilists different from King Midas?

6. Why did King Midas want to give up his golden touch?

7. Why do you suppose mercantilist ideas about gold were eventually given up?

SLIDE 22.1

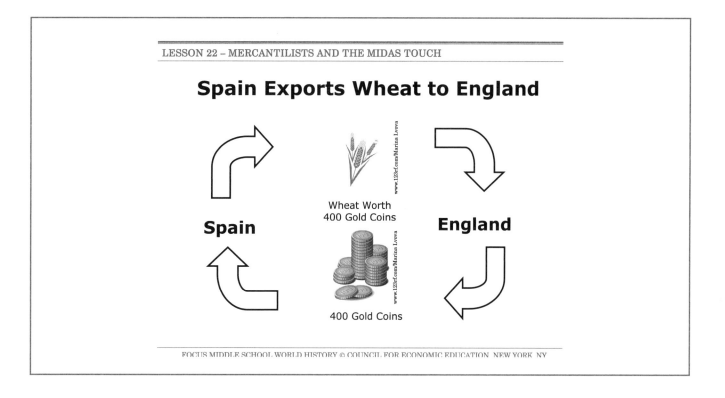

SLIDE 22.2

Focus: Middle School World History © Council for Economic Education, New York, NY

MORALITY IN MARKETS: THE TWO FACES OF ADAM SMITH

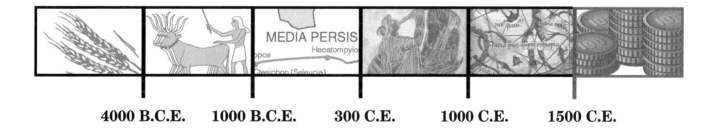

4000 B.C.E.   1000 B.C.E.   300 C.E.   1000 C.E.   1500 C.E.

LESSON 23
MORALITY IN MARKETS: THE TWO FACES OF ADAM SMITH

LESSON DESCRIPTION

This lesson introduces the student to the two sides of the work of Adam Smith. First, students participate in an active learning exercise that illustrates how free trade in markets can help individuals and nations accumulate wealth. This activity also highlights the benefits of competitive and free markets. Second, students participate in discussions that help them understand the importance of morality in markets, as explained by Smith and others.

Overall, this lesson addresses these important questions: How can free trade help individuals accumulate wealth? Are competitive individuals who pursue their own self-interests able to provide valuable services to others? Do you gain or lose when you trade with people who only care about themselves? What do you do if trading partners are dishonest and untrustworthy and do not reveal all of the pertinent information? Why is morality important to people who want to help themselves and others grow and develop in their communities, states, and nations through mutually advantageous exchanges?

INTRODUCTION

Adam Smith, the Father of Economics, is well known for his support of free trade. Contrary to popular beliefs of the time, he argued that nations did not build wealth through mercantilism—the building of a country's stock of gold and silver through exports and the closing of a nation to imports from other countries. According to Smith, overall prosperity required cooperation among individuals pursuing their self-interests. Sustainable wealth-building is possible only if individuals exchange goods and services of value under mutually agreeable and harmonious terms, as if guided by an invisible hand, not a government. Stealing, lying, cheating, reneging on agreements, using force to take possession of others' items, and engaging in selfish and greedy behaviors can consume resources and consequently stifle economic progress.

Adam Smith is given much credit for bringing discussions on the benefits of free trade to competition in markets to the forefront in *An Inquiry into the Nature and Causes of the Wealth of Nations* (1776). He contended that individuals had natural inclinations to think and express themselves freely. If given these freedoms, individuals would naturally act in their own best interests and cooperate with others so that they both would gain from mutually beneficial exchanges, especially in markets. Through the pursuit of self-interest, individuals could trade goods and services in cooperative and harmonious fashion, even when trading internationally. By helping others meet their wants, needs, and desires, individuals would accumulate wealth. At the same time, traders help the people with whom they interact build wealth, too. Minimal government intervention is needed. All that is required of government is to protect individual rights to life, liberty, and the pursuit of happiness. The government should supply only goods and services private individuals and businesses cannot easily provide, like national defense.

Adam Smith believed that markets made up of free-thinking individuals could work if individuals were able to pursue their advantages in markets with minimal government direction. Furthermore, nations would prosper in the process of doing so, if the majority of individuals made decisions within a solid moral framework. In *The Theory of Moral Sentiments* (1759), Smith stressed individual honesty, self-control, keeping promises, being prudent or thrifty, treating others as we want to be treated, and other virtuous behaviors. Smith claimed that order—not chaos—would emerge from people continuously interacting with each other in various settings and environments. Through cooperation, they would learn to examine their choices, consider the consequences of each, and make mutually beneficial decisions.

In Smith's world, a solid reserve of moral capital combined with market interactions worked far better than the government in helping people accumulate wealth.

CONCEPTS

Exchange

Free trade

Voluntary trade

Wealth

Mercantilism

OBJECTIVES

Students will be able to:

- Explain Adam Smith's views.

- Show how individuals are made better off if they trade.

- Explain that markets reward those individuals who treat others honestly, respectfully, kindly, and fairly.

- Understand why voluntary exchange and cooperation are important to economic prosperity.

CONTENT STANDARDS

Voluntary Content Standards in Economics, 2nd edition

- **Standard 6**: When individuals, regions, and nations specialize in what they can produce at the lowest cost and then trade with others, both production and consumption increase.

- **Standard 7**: A market exists when buyers and sellers interact. This interaction determines market prices and thereby allocates scarce goods and services.

World History Content Standards

World History Era 7. An Age of Revolutions, 1750–1914 C.E.

- **Standard 2:** The causes and consequences of the agricultural and industrial revolutions, 1700–1850.

- **Standard 3:** The transformation of Eurasian societies in an era of global trade and rising European power, 1750–1870.

TIME REQUIRED

Preparation prior to class is needed. One class, 60 minutes

MATERIALS

- Students bring in items from home to trade. One item is needed per student. Items should be in paper lunch bags when brought into class. (Alternatively, teachers may also purchase small items from a dollar store if they do not want students to bring in their own items. A large bag of mixed, wrapped, candies also works well. Another alternative is to write the names of goods on index cards and have the students pretend they are trading the actual item. The cards do not need to be put into paper bags. To add realism, you can tell the students that one person will actually get the good they have at the end of the game. This can be a single candy bar—obviously, do not announce which good is the one you will be giving at the end of the game.)

- One tube of lip balm and one can of cat food

- Two sealable envelopes

- Sides 23.1–23.5

- Copy of Activity 23.1 for each student

PROCEDURE

1. A few days before the lesson, tell students they will be participating in a trading activity called the "Trash to Treasure Game." Ask them to get permission from their parents or guardians to donate a gently used item or small items to be traded with classmates. Give the students examples such as a popular book that has been read, a T-shirt that is too small for its owner but is still in good shape, a video game that is no longer challenging or interesting, a once-popular DVD, an unopened granola bar, a small bag of chips, a pair of not-so-new earrings, an unused picture frame, or something of some value to the student or other middle-school students. Tell them to think about what

others may want when deciding what to bring to class.

2. Tell students that their donated item(s) will not be returned. Instruct them to place the item(s) in a paper bag, and to make the game more fun, keep the contents of their bags secret.

3. In preparation for the trading game, place the lip balm in a paper bag and the cat food in another paper bag.

4. In preparation for the trading game, get two envelopes. The envelopes will be used to illustrate to students that cheating matters. Label one envelope "Answers to An Upcoming Quiz." Do not place anything in the envelope. Write "Answers will not be accepted if seal is broken!" on the seal of the envelope. Place a note in the second that states: "Upon receipt, teacher will give student [extra credit points or some other classroom reward]." Label the envelope "Reward." Set the "Reward" envelope aside. Note: With the "Answers to An Upcoming Quiz" you are going to "cheat" a student out of the correct answers at some point in the game. Choose this student carefully to select a person with the ability to laugh and respectfully call you out on "cheating."

5. On the day of the "Trash to Treasure Game," ask students to place their bags of items on your desk. Add the bags that contain lip balm and cat food. (Note: If one or two students forget to bring an item, the two items you supply will ensure every student gets a bag.)

6. Start to distribute bags. Ask if there is someone who does not have a cat. With a smile and a wink, while not letting the student know what the bag contains, give the bag of canned cat food to a student who does not have a cat. While continuing to distribute bags, ask students for a show of hands by those who have cats. Draw attention to these students and let the students know that they may want to pay attention. Give the lip balm to a student you think may not want it.

7. After every student has a bag, ask if there is a student who would like the correct answers to an upcoming quiz. *(Students should be interested.)* Show the students the envelope marked "Answers to an Upcoming Quiz." Ask a student volunteer to explain the resources that were used to generate the answers. *(Examples: Brain power, or human resources, were used to generate the correct answers. A printer or capital was used to print the sheet with answers. Ink and the natural resources in it were used for printing.)* After looking around the room at the sea of paper bags in front of the interested students, say: "I don't *see* anything that I **want or value** more than the answers to an upcoming quiz. I need these answers to grade! So I will **voluntarily choose** not to trade at this time."

8. Conduct Round 1 of the "Trash to Treasure Game." (In this round, students do not trade.) Ask students to now look into their bags and place a personal value on the item they have without showing it to others. A "trash" value of 0 indicates no value to the student. A "treasure" value of 10 suggests that the student could not be happier with the item even if provided the opportunity to exchange it for something else. Tell students that they may not want to give a value of 10, because they do not know what may could be in others' bags.

9. Show Slide 23.1. In the column labeled "Classroom Wealth without Trade," record the individual numbers reported by students. Alternatively, you can write these on the board. When you ask students with the cat food and lip balm for their values, remark that those values seem to indicate that they got something not very useful to them.

10. Total the values and explain that the sum provides a measurement of the total wealth or "value" in today's classroom society.

(For example, the total individual values may be 35 points in Round 1, so the total wealth in the class is 35 satisfaction or happiness points across all students in today's classroom society.)

Explain to students that **wealth** can be anything people value. Wealth may or may not come in the form of money.

11. Ask if students are curious about what is in other people's bags. *(They should answer yes.)* Tell students information is important when trading. Information helps individuals make informed decisions and facilitates trade. Scarce resources must be used to gather information.

12. Prepare to conduct Round 2 of the trade game. Ask students to form six to eight groups of three to five students. (The exact number of students and groups is not important as long as you have about the same number of students in each group.) Tell students that each group represents a country. Tell the members of each country that they can share information about what is in each bag only with members of his or her country. Encourage them to show the contents of their bags to one another for a couple of minutes.

13. Approach a group that has a student likely to be able to handle your cheating him or her out of answers with humor and understanding. As you approach this student, loudly announce that you may be interested in trading the "Answers to an Upcoming Quiz" envelope. If the student wants to, trade the envelope for his or her bag. If the student elects not to trade, approach other students until you find someone willing to trade.

14. Announce the start of Round 2. Students can now trade items within their own countries, but not with others. Remind students that a trade should not take place unless it increases happiness or satisfaction. Remind students that they are not required to trade. After three minutes, stop the trading.

15. Show Slide 23.1 again. Ask students to assign a value to the good in their possession. Again total and show students how much their "wealth" increased from trade by pointing to the new total in the column "Classroom Wealth with Limited Trade."

(After trading takes place, total classroom wealth should increase as goods move from students who value the items least to students who value them most.)

16. Ask students how wealth could be increased even more.

(They should suggest that the classroom should be opened to trade across groups, or countries.)

17. Conduct Round 3. This is the round of **free trade**. Permit students to get up from their desks and trade openly and voluntarily with others throughout the classroom. After five minutes, bring the game to a close.

18. Show Slide 23.1. Ask students to place a value on the item(s) in their possession after free trade. Record each value, add them together, and place the total in the column "Classroom Wealth under Free Trade." Ask the student who had the cat food if she or he managed to trade it. *(The student may have traded it.)*

Ask the student how they knew who might have wanted it. *(The student should have noted who had cats when they were asked.)* Ask the student who had the lip balm if he or she traded the lip balm. *(The student may have traded it.)* Ask the student how they knew who might have wanted it. *(Answers will vary.)*

19. Compare the new total to the previous two. Ask the students why the total increased.

(Classroom wealth increased as a result of goods freely flowing to the students who valued the items the most from

the students who valued them least in a cooperative and agreeable environment. Exchanges were mutually beneficial. If they were not, trading should not have taken place. Therefore, everyone who trades wins in a free trading environment!)

20. Ask the students if they were forced to trade or given directions about with whom to trade.

(During the classroom game, no one was forced to trade. Everyone who traded did so out of a desire to be better off—to satisfy their own wants. Exchange partners cooperated. A third party, such as the government or a teacher, was not needed to supervise the trades. As if guided by an invisible hand, voluntary exchanges helped items move to those who valued them most and away from those who valued them least.)

21. Starting with Slide 23.2, show slides 23.2 through 23.5 to review why voluntary trade benefits everyone in a market. The review is in terms of producers and consumers in a market. Compare the steps to what was done in the trading activity. The students had goods they brought to the market to sell. They also purchased goods they viewed as more valuable.

22. Ask for the student holding the "Answers" envelope to raise his or her hand. Ask the student to open the envelope. Upon the student's discovery that it is empty, ask the student how he or she feels. *(Cheated.)* Ask students to consider past experiences when they felt cheated. Ask how these experiences affected their overall happiness or satisfaction. *(Such experiences diminish happiness.)* Ask how being cheated affects their willingness to trade, work, and interact with the person who cheated them in the future.

(Students should say that cheating upsets them and that it is unfair. They were promised one thing and it was not delivered. In the future, they will take

this into account when interacting with the cheater. People tend to avoid cheaters, especially those who cheat repeatedly. Some people will spend time and resources to take action against the cheater—go to the principal, get their guardians involved, etc.)

23. Explain to students that in the business world, people have to spend valuable resources that they had planned to use for production to hire lawyers to demand restitution and threaten legal action. So cheating and other types of immoral behaviors obstruct trading goods and services for the benefit of many. Simply put, people who steal, lie, cheat, fail to follow through on agreements, forcibly take others' property, and engage in other types of socially unacceptable conduct increase the costs of exchange.

24. Ask the cheated student if she or he would like to trade the empty envelope for the one labeled "Reward." If the student hesitates, ask why. *(The student may say you are trying to cheat him again.)* Reassure the student, but note that the point of the lesson is that, once cheated, people hesitate to deal with the person who cheated them. After trading with the student, have the student open the envelope so that the class's faith in teachers is restored!

25. Tell students you are going to introduce them to the "Father of Economics." Distribute Activity 23.1. One paragraph at a time, invite student volunteers to read it.

26. After the reading, ask students to pinpoint the two important sides of Adam Smith.

(Point 1: In Adam Smith's world, a nation of individuals builds wealth. Everyone is made better off by unrestricted trade when they bring resources, goods, services, and ideas of value to others and are permitted to freely exchange them. Individuals, not governments, are best at making trading decisions. They

know best what is in their self-interest and the interest of those with whom they interact. Individuals, as if guided by an invisible hand, incur the costs as well as reap the benefits of their exchanges. Point 2: Adam Smith argued that a solid moral foundation built on people's desires to cooperate and harmonize with others through respect, honesty, integrity, and other traits guaranteed the sustainability of wealth building through free trade.)

CLOSURE

27. Tell students that, prior to publication and acceptance of Adam Smith's *Wealth of Nations*, government intervention was widespread in markets and mercantilism was favored. Smith and other believers in a free market economy shifted the thinking on mercantilism and the role and functions of government. In a free market economy, individuals are free to move goods, services, resources, and ideas to the people who value them most, and, through the pursuit of their own advantages and interests, individuals will interact cooperatively and help themselves and others accumulate wealth. Government's role is to protect their rights to do so and to pursue life, liberty, and happiness without harming others.

28. Summarize the lesson in a short sentence: In Smith's world, morality and free trade matter. Ask the students why free trade is important. *(They should explain how people gain from trade.)* Ask the students why morality is important in markets. *(The students should explain how it is easier to trade with people who are not trying to cheat you, for example.)*

ASSESSMENT

Multiple Choice

1. Which of the following statements is correct? Voluntary trade

   a. **helps individuals build wealth through mutually beneficial exchanges.**

   b. takes things from the people who value them most and gives them to the people who value them least.

   c. requires that one person gain at the expense of another.

   d. requires government-sponsored programs.

2. A solid moral foundation helps individuals prosper by

   a. force.

   b. government.

   c. **making exchanges easier and less costly.**

   d. encouraging wildly erratic behavior in unfamiliar settings.

Constructed Response

1. Describe how the following behaviors will affect your willingness to work, play, or trade goods with someone showing the following traits.

   a. Trustworthy

   b. Irresponsible

   c. Hard-working

   d. Lazy

   (People are more likely to interact with those who are trustworthy and hard-working. This includes playing, working, or trading with people.)

RESOURCES FOR TEACHERS

Crain, Cynthia and Dwight Lee. 2010. *Adam Smith (Profiles in Economics)*. Greensboro, NC: *Morgan Reynolds Publishing.*

Wight, Jonathan. 2001. *Saving Adam Smith: A Tale of Wealth, Transformation, and Virtue.* Upper Saddle River, NJ: Financial Times Press. This book brings Adam Smith to life and considers how he may view the way his theories on free markets have been applied. Here, the reincarnated Smith argues that selfishness is not enough and explains and illustrates why.

CONNECTIONS: MORAL FOUNDATIONS IN TODAY'S WORLD

1. Ask students to describe a time when immoral behavior in one instance caused them to stop being friends with someone. What did the person have to do to regain their friendship? What would have happened if this person had not changed?

   (Accept a variety of answers.)

2. Ask students to apply this exercise to the world of business: What if you or your parents repeatedly got bad food and service at a local restaurant? What if many customers shared the same experience? What would happen to the profits of the restaurant owner? What does the restaurant owner need to do to stay in business?

   (Accept a variety of answers. Consumers have choices and can choose the competitors, especially when dissatisfied. Customers can choose to return to those businesses that delivered on their promises and whose prices accurately reflected value to consumers. In essence, bad service results in lower profits because consumers go elsewhere to do business. In the example, the struggling restaurant owner would have to deliver on promises and improve food services to get customers to return and boost profits. Profits measure how well businesses satisfy customers.)

ACTIVITY 23.1

The Two Faces of Adam Smith

In 1723, Adam Smith was born in a small village in Kirkcaldy, Scotland. His father was a customs agent. That is, Adam's dad inspected the different products, bags, and objects carried on the ships entering or leaving Kirkcaldy. Unfortunately, Adam's dad died before Adam was born, leaving his wife to raise Adam. Adam went on to learn about his dad's business. He often sat and watched ships enter the harbor with goods from other countries and leave port with exported goods from Scotland. Adam was fascinated with the work of the customs agents. He watched them carefully inspect the goods carried by the ships. The young Smith took special note of the ships leaving his country with goods produced in Scotland for people in other countries to consume.

Exported goods were considered good for the country. The people buying them paid in gold and silver, helping the country build wealth. By contrast, the goods imported into Scotland through Kirkcaldy were considered bad for the country because it was thought that they drained the mother country of its precious metals. This thinking was called **mercantilism**. This system based the wealth of Scotland and other countries like England on the amount of gold and silver held in each country's coffers. International trade was considered a positive to the exporting country but a negative to the importing one because the exporting country received gold and silver from the trade partner.

At 14, Adam entered college. Although his poor health had kept him from attending college when his classmates went at age 12, he was a good student and accepted a scholarship to the University of Glasgow. He later pursued graduate studies at Balliol College at Oxford. After that, he taught, researched, and traveled. Education benefited Adam greatly. It helped him broaden his world view and opened new opportunities to him.

In 1759, economics was not a subject unto itself. Adam Smith's first book, *The Theory of Moral Sentiments,* explained why and how people cooperate in a variety of settings. Smith believed people helped others by carefully managing their emotions, behaviors, actions, and interactions in ways that benefited them *and* others. Smith did not buy the notion that most people were selfish and greedy. Smith noticed that selfish and greedy people had a hard time getting others to cooperate, work with them, or help them in times of need. Why? People have a choice.

ACTIVITY 23.1, CONTINUED

People freely choose with whom to play, work, and do business, argued Smith. Selfish and greedy behaviors are not rewarded for long, even in the marketplace. People turn away from individuals who continuously lie, go back on their word, fail to do what they say they will, or cheat. People want to interact with honest, trustworthy, respectful, and honorable individuals.

Smith believed that a powerful authoritarian government was not needed to oversee business. Government's main role should be to protect the rights of individuals to pursue life, liberty, and happiness without harming others. Government was needed when individual rights were violated and justice was required.

In 1776, *The Wealth of Nations* was published. It showed how Smith's theories on morality applied to business. Today, many consider this book one of the first real economics books. Because of this book, Smith is sometimes called the "Father of Economics."

In *The Wealth of Nations*, Smith points out the weaknesses of mercantilism (government restricting imports to build up its purse of gold and silver). It focuses on how individuals' desires to cooperate and serve others lead to voluntary exchanges that make everyone better off—whether the trade is between individuals or countries. Contrary to popular belief at the time, Smith argued that wealth was not simply the amount of gold and silver piled up in a country's vaults. Wealth, Smith said, was increased by ordinary people being able to acquire the goods they valued through voluntary exchange.

Smith claimed that ordinary people benefit individually by pursuing their own interests. Individuals best serve their interests by helping and cooperating with others—even in markets. This voluntary exchange within a moral framework is how nations build wealth. Government control over production, consumption, or exchange is not required.

Individuals interacting in a free market choose what is best as they consider the different costs and rewards that their actions produce. As long as the benefits of an activity exceed its costs, people will continue doing it. They will stop when the costs exceed the benefits. As long as the additional benefits of an activity exceed the costs, wealth grows for everyone involved. Some wealth, like in the trading exercise, comes in the form of simply moving goods to those who value them most from those who value them least. Other types of wealth come from exchanges involving money, homes, buildings, education, computers, machines, stocks, bonds, and other assets.

SLIDE 23.1

Building Wealth through Expanded Trade "From Trash to Treasure: A Voluntary Trading Game"			
	List the Individual Values across Classroom Citizens	**Total Wealth in the Classroom Society**	**Change in Wealth**
	[0: no value, 1: a little value, … 10: highest value possible]		
Round 1: Classroom wealth without trade			----
Round 2: Classroom wealth under restricted trade			
Round 3: Classroom wealth under free trade			

SLIDE 23.2

Why Free Trade Benefits Everyone

1. Trade is voluntary. It does not take place unless everyone involved agrees.
2. Many types of markets for goods, services, and resources exist. Millions of people come together freely to exchange goods, services, and resources. They use prices and information to guide their decisions.

SLIDE 23.3

LESSON 23 – MORALITY IN MARKETS: THE TWO FACES OF ADAM SMITH

Why Free Trade Benefits Everyone

3. Consumers benefit from getting goods and services that they value.
   a. They value purchased goods more than the money they pay for the goods.
   b. If the price of something is too high, they simply do not buy it. They choose something else or save the money.
   c. Prices provide valuable information for consumers.

SLIDE 23.4

LESSON 23 – MORALITY IN MARKETS: THE TWO FACES OF ADAM SMITH

Why Free Trade Benefits Everyone

4. Producers benefit from the revenues the sale of consumed items generate.
   a. They either succeed or fail in producing what consumers want.
   b. They must use the revenues from sales to cover the costs of producing goods and providing services.
   c. If they do not benefit from a trade, they do not have to sell the product.
   d. Prices provide valuable information to them.

SLIDE 23.5

Why Free Trade Benefits Everyone

5. When consumers and producers agree on a price and then trade, both benefit from the exchange.

   a. Consumers get something valued more than the money used to buy the goods and services.

   b. Producers receive the revenues from their sales. These revenues are then used to cover the costs of production. What is left is used to reward producers for accepting the risks of doing business in rapidly changing markets.